GNOSIS OF THE
COSMIC CHRIST

ABOUT THE AUTHOR

Malachi Eben Ha-Elijah is a modern mystic. His journey on the spiritual path began when he was a young boy, when he encountered a tau of the Sophian Tradition of Gnostic Christianity, Tau Elijah Ben Miriam. He received the oral tradition of Sophian Gnosticism from Tau Elijah, and has been a student and practitioner of Gnostic Christianity for over thirty-four years. In 1983 he founded Sophia Fellowship as an expression of the Tradition, and has been teaching and initiating others into Christian Gnosticism, Rosicrucian philosophy, and the holy Kabbalah since that time. He is an initiate of Ordo Sanctus Gnosis and holds the recognition of an elder and tau of the Sophian Tradition.

Along with his studies in the Western Mystery Tradition, Tau Malachi has studied extensively in several Eastern Traditions, such as Vajrayana Buddhism and Vedanta, as well as studying and practicing a Middle Eastern Tradition of Sufism. While Gnostic Christianity has always been his heart-path and spiritual home, Malachi speaks of himself as a traveler and explorer of the spirit and truth, and his journey has taken him to many sacred places and into diverse Wisdom Traditions.

For many years Tau Malachi served as a hospice volunteer, a volunteer trainer, and for a period of time as a hospice chaplain. Although he worked with patients suffering from various forms of terminal illness, much of his work focused on individuals living with HIV and AIDS.

Today he lives in the Sierra foothills, in Nevada City, California.

GNOSIS OF THE
COSMIC CHRIST
A GNOSTIC CHRISTIAN KABBALAH

TAU MALACHI

Llewellyn Publications
Saint Paul, Minnesota

FIRST EDITION
First Printing, 2005

Cover design by Gavin Dayton Duffy
Cover painting "The Resurrection"
by Anton Laurids Johannes Dorph © SuperStock
Editing and interior design by Connie Hill

Scripture quotations contained herein are from the New Revised Standard Version Bible, copyright 1989 by the Division of Christian Education of the National Council of the Churches of Christ in the U.S.A., and are used by permission. All rights reserved.

Ten verses excerpted from the Thirty-Two Paths of Wisdom in *Sefer Yetzirah: The Book of Creation* by Aryeh Kaplan, used by permission of the publisher, Red Wheel/Weiser, York Beach, ME.

Library of Congress Cataloging-in-Publication Data
Malachi, Tau.
   Gnosis of the Cosmic Christ : a Gnostic Christian Kabbalah / Tau Malachi
— 1st ed.
      p.   cm.
   Includes bibliographical references (p.) and index.
   ISBN 0-7387-0591-8
   1. Cabala and Christianity. 2. Sefirot (Cabala). 3. Gnosticism. I. Title.

BM525.M27   2005
299'.932—dc22   2004058440

Llewellyn Publications
A Division of Llewellyn Worldwide, Ltd.
P.O. Box 64383, Dept. 0-7387-591-8
St. Paul, MN 55164-0383, U.S.A.
www.llewellyn.com

Printed in the United States of America

ALSO BY TAU MALACHI

The Gnostic Gospels of St. Thomas

and Forthcoming:

Living Gnosis
The Gnostic Legend of St. Mary Magdalene

AUTHOR'S NOTE

The Sophian Tradition of Gnostic Christianity is essentially an oral tradition passed mouth to ear from an elder or tau to their students. In writing this book I have followed this method, which only rarely directly references written text, such as in the case of Scriptural quotes. Thus, rather than referencing texts, teachings and stories are drawn from memory in the power of the moment, as is the way of oral traditions. For this reason one will find many quotes that do not have any source or reference listed, as what they represent are oral teachings received in the same way that they are recorded. This includes many ideas and stories that have evolved in the oral tradition of Sophian Gnosticism that are recorded in writing for the first time in this present book. Generally speaking, it is my intent to convey something of the experience of an oral tradition in my writing rather than conform to conventional wisdom established by modern academia; hence to communicate as a spiritual practitioner rather than an academic scholar. The bibliography provided is more for the sake of continued study and contemplation than a list of sources referenced during the writing of this book—an aid for those interested in taking their studies of Gnosticism and Kabbalah further (hence it serves as a suggested reading list).

CONTENTS

FIGURES

ACKNOWLEDGMENTS

I wish to thank those who have helped to make this book possible:

First and foremost, I wish to acknowledge my beloved teacher of blessed memory, Tau Elijah ben Miriam, and his circle of spiritual companions, who received me in the Path and taught and initiated me in the Tradition. Much of this book is a reflection of his teachings. Without him, it would never have been written.

Penelope, Christopher, Sunny, and Phillip, my spiritual companions, who gave practical support that made the project possible, acting as midwives.

Sophia Fellowship and all of my spiritual companions whose love, support, and encouragement is an inspiration to me and makes every aspect of the spiritual work possible.

My publisher, Llewellyn, who provides a vehicle for alternative spiritual voices and who brings my writing projects to fruition.

Sincerely,
Tau Malachi Eben Ha-Elijah

INTRODUCTION

According to legend, the holy Kabbalah was revealed by God to Adam, and from Adam, the Tradition has passed from one generation to another until the present day. In other words, its origin is shrouded in mystery and it appears to have emerged with the dawn of human history, reflecting the evolution of humankind from the animal kingdom. In classical Kabbalistic literature, the Kabbalah is said to be the revelation of the mysteries of creation and God, the mysteries of the human soul, and such things as prophecy and magic—in a word, mysticism or metaphysics. But as much as any of these things, the Kabbalah is a mirror in which is reflected the fiery intelligence that has caused humanity to rise beyond all other species of creatures on the earth—a fiery intelligence that makes us self-aware and empowers us with the capacity of a conscious evolution far beyond our present state.

Kabbalah basically means "something received and imparted." Thus, as much as a mirror of the fiery intelligence, it is the transmission of the fiery intelligence. The mere study and contemplation of the Kabbalah tends to kindle the spark of the fiery intelligence in us into a fire that blazes forth—an awakening of the greater power of our soul. Mystical experience, prophecy, and wonder-working are natural products of the power of the human soul imbued with the fiery intelligence, as is scientific discovery, art, philosophy, and every other expression of human intelligence.

This fiery intelligence is often spoken of in terms of divine genius because, when it is fully awakened, it appears as something more than ordinary human intelligence and the person in whom it awakens becomes something more than human in the ordinary sense of the word. When we speak of mystics and prophets, enlightened beings and magicians, we are really speaking of individuals who are emerging from the bestial state of humanity toward a new and divine state of humanity, something more than our present humanity—what one might call super humanity. As we look and see this, we realize that our present state is a transitional state of being, something in between what we have been and something else that we are in the process of becoming. The human being is a transitional being.

Within and behind all of the encrustation of religious dogma and creed that orthodox forms of Christianity have engendered, there is this message of a fiery intelligence and a conscious evolution toward a divine or super humanity. This fiery intelligence, the being-consciousness-force, from which creation emerges and that tends to generate increasingly higher and more refined life-forms of increasingly greater intelligence is, essentially, what the Kabbalah calls "God." One in whom this fiery intelligence is fully awakened would therefore rightly be called a son or daughter of God. While this term may be correctly applied to the person we have come to know as Jesus (Yeshua in Aramaic), according to Christian Gnosticism, it is not isolated to Yeshua but is equally true of anyone in whom the fiery intelligence awakens and, in this sense, is a term of our future self. Thus, the noble ideal of the Christian Kabbalah is not so much the worship of Yeshua Messiah (Jesus Christ) but rather a conscious evolution toward Christhood—a divine or super-humanity. In this regard, the Christian Kabbalah is quite different from the Jewish Kabbalah from which it evolved, and Gnostic Christianity is very different from any orthodox form of Christianity.

It has been said that mysticism begins where religion comes to its climax, as the peak of religion is the realization of God no longer conceived as something exclusively external to oneself but as internal to oneself. Hence, mysticism begins with the awareness of God, the fiery intelligence, within one's person. We may equally say that religion is the product of a misperception of the peak mystical attainment—the human beings who have realized this divine self, to one degree or another, who have given birth to all the world-wisdom traditions. Observing the proliferation of religions sparked by the dawn of this fiery intelligence in human individuals—"men and women of God"—one can't help but think of the scene in the movie 2001: *The Space Odyssey*, when apes were dancing around the great monolith with little, if any, comprehension of what it was! This is to say that pure Kabbalah and Gnosticism cannot be arbitrarily classified as a religion but are better defined as a path of spiritual evolution—a science and art of conscious evolution and, yes, as mysticism and metaphysics.

If terms used in Christian Gnosticism and the Christian Kabbalah seem to be religious at times, it is certainly not the intention or meaning of the Gnostic. Rather, it is the product of the proliferation of religious institutions for the masses and the use of similar terms in generating religious dogmas. Essentially, the true mystic will have a very different meaning in the terms and ideas he or she presents than would a religious person. The reason for this is simple. The religious person is, as yet, an outsider to the experience worshipped, while the mystic is an insider of the experience worshipped. This well defines the term Gnostic, which means "one who knows through direct experience" or "one who is a knower." Christian Gnosticism and Kabbalah, thus, are not theology, or "thinking about God," but are experiencing God and evolving toward God—hence, an endless journey of being in the process of becoming. Whether we recognize it yet or not, we are all in this journey of ever-becoming. This is the key message of Gnostic Christianity and the Christian Kabbalah, and of this book in your hands.

ONE

THE KABBALAH
OF GNOSTIC
CHRISTIANITY

Purpose and Nature of the Kabbalah

The Kabbalah is an archaic system of Jewish Mysticism that has its roots in the assembly of prophets of ancient Israel and the Merkavah Mysticism of Palestine during the time of Jesus (Yeshua in Aramaic). Considering that Yeshua was Jewish and his disciples were Jewish, and understanding him to be a mystic and prophet of his time, it is reasonable to assume that he taught a form of the mystical tradition that has come to be known as the Kabbalah.

For this reason, many mystical and gnostic currents of Christianity have arisen that take the Kabbalah as their foundation. This is certainly true of the Sophian Tradition, which is so interwoven with the teachings of the Kabbalah that it is impossible to separate out Gnosticism and Kabbalah in the Tradition. Essentially, one might call the Sophian Tradition a Christian Kabbalah or a form of Gnostic Christianity that draws heavily upon its Judaic roots. Therefore, to explore Gnostic Christianity, as expressed in the Sophian Tradition, we must explore some of the basic ideas of the Kabbalah from which the teachings and principles of our Gnostic Christianity are derived.

The principal teachings of the Kabbalah were designed to explore and find answers to some basic questions:

➢ The nature and attributes of God and the Godhead

➢ The development of a cosmology

➢ The mystery of the creation of angels and humankind

➢ The destiny of humankind and angels

➢ The nature of the human soul and its connection to the divine

➢ The nature of cosmic forces—angels, demons, elementals and such

➢ The inner meaning of the revealed law and Holy Gospel

➢ The transcendental symbolism of numbers and geometrical shapes

➢ The mysteries contained in the Hebrew letters

➢ The balance in the play of cosmic forces

➢ The mystery of divine revelation and prophetic states of consciousness

➢ The mystery of the divine incarnation and the divine plan on earth

Considering the vast height, depth, and breadth of these metaphysical questions, one can imagine the enormous amount of esoteric teachings, practices, and literature that has formed around the Kabbalah in the course of thousands of years. Although there are many modern truth-seekers who have read a book or two on the Kabbalah and mistakenly assumed they know the Kabbalah, the truth is that even a master of the Tradition, who has studied and practiced the Kabbalah all of his or her life and who actively embodies something of the enlightenment experience it represents, would not claim to know the Kabbalah. One could say that God knows the Kabbalah and that, for our part, we know what we have received of it in our own experience—which is a far cry from knowing the Kabbalah as God knows it.

Essentially, the teachings of the Kabbalah represent the accumulated knowledge, understanding, and wisdom of initiates, which have been gathered from their own direct spiritual experience of the metaphysical dimensions of creatures, creation, and God. The Kabbalah itself is the knowledge, understanding, and wisdom of the true nature of creatures, creation, and God—which is known in full only to God. If the whole of the Kabbalah is in a book, then it is the heavenly Book of Life of which the Holy Scriptures speak, and not any earthly book.

The teachings of the Kabbalah are founded upon the Bible, along with other books of Scripture that did not make their way into the canonized Bible. Thus, to study and understand the Kabbalah in its proper context is to study and understand the Scriptures also. Just as many mistakenly assume that they know the Kabbalah from reading a book or two, likewise many assume that they are knowledgeable in the Kabbalah without being well-studied in the Scriptures. Ultimately, however, one cannot study and understand the Kabbalah without also studying and gaining some understanding of the Holy Scriptures. To engage in the study and practice of the Kabbalah is to embark upon a mystical journey into hidden levels of the Scriptures and the secret wisdom they contain. In essence, the Scriptures and the Kabbalah are one and the same.

Three Branches of the Kabbalah

The teachings of the Kabbalah are divided into three principal forms: the theoretical or contemplative Kabbalah, the meditative Kabbalah, and the practical or magical Kabbalah. The theoretical or contemplative Kabbalah is an intellectual study and contemplation of the principles, doctrines, and correspondences of esoteric wisdom, including gematria, the associations of numbers and geometrical patterns, and so on. The meditative Kabbalah represents the teachings and practices of mystical prayer and prophetic meditation—methods through which one can enter a higher state of consciousness and experience unification with the divine. The practical or magical Kabbalah represents teachings of invocations, incantations, rituals, and such, through which one is able to shift states of consciousness at will and to consciously direct hidden spiritual forces. From this, one will understand that the Kabbalah is both a mystical and a magical Tradition. Here, we will be dealing primarily with the contemplative Kabbalah and to some extent the meditative Kabbalah. The magical Kabbalah will be referred to in passing at different points of this book; however, it is not the subject of this work.

The Ten Holy Sefirot and the Tree of Life

There are ten Sefirot (plural), which are generally referred to as Midot, meaning "measurements" or "dimensions" and, by extension, also meaning "attributes" or "qualities." The Sefirot are emanations of the divine presence and power of God, or the infinite light of God, and they are vessels receiving God's light and transmitting it to creation. They are gradations of the involution of the infinite light into finite creation, and thus are gradations of the evolution of creatures on the path of return—like rungs on a ladder of light. When we read of Jacob's vision of a ladder reaching up from the earth to the heavens, upon which he beheld angels ascending and descending, the Kabbalah would say that that Jacob had a vision of the constellation of the Sefirot that forms the Tree of Life.

The word Sefirah (singular) is related to the Hebrew word *saper*, meaning "to express" or "to communicate," and to the word *sapir*, meaning "sapphire," "brilliance," or "luminary." It is also related to the words *sefar*, meaning "boundary"; *sefer*, meaning "book"; and *safar*, meaning "number." All of these terms represent related concepts and indicate the two basic functions of the Sefirot: lights or emanations that act to reveal and express God's presence and power (Shekinah); and vessels that limit and delineate the infinite light of God, bringing it down into the finite realm of numeration and boundary.

Essentially, the Sefirot, and the various levels of their manifestation called Olamot or universes, represent the metaphysical structure of creation or the vehicle through which creature, creation, and God are connected and interact. In Genesis, ten utterances are listed through which God creates. These correspond with the ten Sefirot and suggest the idea of creature and creation as the revelation or expression of God and as the vessel receiving and imparting the divine presence—hence the body of God. Through the Sefirot, God reaches out to us and we are able to reach into God.

The most common way these Sefirot are represented is as a glyph called the Tree of Life (*Otz ha-Hayyim*). The Sefirot are depicted as ten circles that form three triads, one atop, one in the middle, and one below, with a single Sefirah set as a pendant below the lowest triad. In this same configuration they also appear as ten circles divided into three columns—

one to the right, one to the left, and one in the middle—which are called "pillars." These are two ways to view the same glyph (figure 1, below).

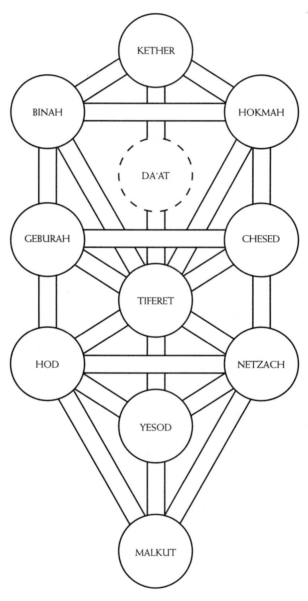

Figure 1. The Tree of Life.

In the view of the three triads of Sefirot and one Sefirah as a pendant, the top triad is called the supernal triad, the triad in the middle is called the moral triad, the triad below is called the action triad. The Sefirah that appears as a pendant is called Malkut (Kingdom). Malkut is the "fruit" of the Tree of Life, as well as the vessel receiving the influence of all the emanations above it. In the view of the Tree of Life as three pillars, the right and left pillars are composed of three Sefirot each, and the middle pillar is composed of four Sefirot. The pillar on the right is called the Pillar of Mercy and the pillar on the left is called the Pillar of Severity—the Pillars of Jachin and Boaz in the temple of King Solomon. One is positive and the other negative; one is male and the other is female; one is white, the other is black—so that these two pillars represent the eternal play of opposites in dynamic interaction. Evil is imbalanced force, out of place or out of harmony. Severity in imbalance is cruelty and oppression, and mercy in imbalance is weakness that allows and facilitates great evil. True compassion is a dynamic balance of severity and mercy.

The Middle Pillar is therefore the path of the ascension, representing the dynamic balance of all polarities or opposites, and the integration of everything that would otherwise be fragmented. The Kabbalah teaches the Middle Way, akin to what is found in forms of Hinduism and Buddhism in the Eastern schools. For this reason, whether the tree is viewed in terms of the triads or the three pillars, the Sefirah Tiferet (beauty), which is the Christ center on the tree, is in the middle.

As there are ten circles representing the Sefirot on the Tree of Life, so also are there twenty-two lines connecting the Sefirot, to which the Hebrew letters are attributed. Thus the tree is composed of thirty-two paths, which in the *Sefer Yetzirah* are called the "Thirty-Two Paths of Wisdom." Various correspondences are given to both the Sefirot and the Hebrew letters. Through the interrelationship of correspondences, initiates are able to look and see the mysteries contained in the Scriptures and are able to gain insight into the mysteries of creation and God. Yet more, they are able to receive the ongoing divine revelation in the same way as the prophets and apostles of God before them.

The Olamot-Universes

The ten Sefirot manifest through five different levels or dimensions, which are called Olamot, meaning "universes." These Olamot are known as the universe of Adam Kadmon (primordial human being), the universe of Atzilut (emanation or nearness), the universe of Beriyah (creation), the universe of Yetzirah (formation), and the universe of Asiyah (action or making). The Olamot extend from the supernal abode of the divine to the material plane of existence, the universe of Adam Kadmon being nearest to the light of the Infinite and Asiyah being the material plane of existence. The ten Sefirot manifest in each Olam, thus there are ten Sefirot of Adam Kadmon, ten Sefirot of Atzilut, ten Sefirot of Beriyah, ten Sefirot of Yetzirah, and ten Sefirot of Asiyah, for a total of fifty Sefirot, which are called the "Fifty Gates of Understanding."

These five Olamot correspond to the divine name of Yahweh (Yod-He-Vau-He), frequently called the "Tetragrammaton" because it is composed of four letters. Adam Kadmon is represented by the upper tip of the Yod (י), Atzilut by the body of the Yod, Beriyah by the first He (ה), Yetzirah by the Vau (ו), and Asiyah by the final He. This divine name is said to be contained in the universe of Adam Kadmon and it is said to contain all other divine names, the divine names being within it and yet being worn by it as "garments."

The divine name of Yeshua or Yeheshuah (Yod-He-Shin-Vau-He), which is the name of Yahweh with the addition of the letter Shin (ש), represents the embodiment of the divine presence and power of Yahweh and thus something of the spiritual energy of Adam Kadmon. The universe of Adam Kadmon and the Sefirot it contains, therefore, represent the Soul of the Messiah. This gives insight into the title "Son of Adam" (son of man), used for Yeshua in the Gospels.

To gain some insight into the nature of the Olamot, one might contemplate them in terms of the sun and its light and the moon that reflects the light. First, one must understand that, looking at the sun, one does not see the sun but rather sees the glory or radiance of the sun. Therefore, within and beyond what one sees is the sun itself. From the "sun within the sun," light is generated and that hidden place of the generation of light would correspond to Adam Kadmon. The glory or light of the sun one beholds would correspond to Atzilut. The light passing to the moon would correspond to Beriyah. The light of the moon itself would correspond to Yetzirah, and the light of the full moon shining upon the earth would correspond to Asiyah. In a similar way, the light of the Infinite passes through the Olamot from Adam Kadmon to Asiyah, and thus, the supernal light is progressively veiled and reduced in intensity.

Another way of gaining some understanding of the Olamot is to consider them at the level of human experience. The inmost will of a human being corresponds to the universe of Adam Kadmon. The level of pure awareness or preconceptual and undifferentiated mind corresponds to Atzilut. The process of thought itself corresponds to Beriyah. Speech or communication corresponds to Yetzirah, and action corresponds to Asiyah.

Adam Kadmon	=	Will
Atzilut	=	Mind
Beriyah	=	Thought
Yetzirah	=	Speech
Asiyah	=	Action

The best way to contemplate this is to consider the creative process of an architect who is designing a large building complex. First he or she decides what kind of buildings will fit the purposes for which they are being constructed. Then he or she draws up the corresponding plans and considers how each building will serve its function in relationship to the other structures. Finally, he or she gives orders to his or her workers and the actual construction begins.

In our analogy, the level of Adam Kadmon is represented by the desire and decision of the architect to build before there is any particular plan in mind. Atzilut would be represented by the process of designing a plan for the building on the most abstract level. Once there is a blueprint, everything still remains at an abstract level and thought must be given to figure out exactly how the plan will work or how it can actually be implemented. Up to this point, everything has taken place in the architect's office, but now seeking to practically apply the plan, the architect must go to the site.

Going to the site and thinking things through on a more practical level, bringing the idea down from the abstract symbolic form into something that can be implemented, would represent Beriyah. When the architect communicates the actual ideas and methods of construction to the workers, this would be akin to Yetzirah. The actual work of construction would correspond to Asiyah; the finished product itself would represent the final Sefirah of Asiyah (Malkut of Asiyah).

The analogy can be taken even further into all purposeful human activity. Any time a person decides to do something, he or she conceives a general plan. As he or she gets closer to enacting it, his or her thought processes almost spontaneously trigger nerve impulses, which then travel through the body. The person's muscles follow the commands of the brain and bring about the corresponding action.

We are experiencing something of the Olamot all of the time through our own process of translating will or desire into awareness, thought, speech, and action—a communication that happens at light-speed through our nervous system. From the most subtle and imperceptible levels to the actual manifestation, life comes forth, as though something from nothing. This is true throughout creation.

The Universe of Adam Kadmon

One of the most basic teachings of the Kabbalah is that God and Godhead is ultimately nameless and unknowable, and that, therefore, nothing can be said about God. We can talk about emanations and manifestations of God's presence and power, about attributes or qualities of God and how we encounter the presence of God in our experience, but not about God as God is. We can allude to or indicate something about God, but we cannot speak of God directly. For this reason, the most common reference to God in the Kabbalah is Ain Sof, which literally means the "One-Without-End." God has no beginning or end, but is the Infinite, and therefore cannot be characterized or defined.

At the level of Ain Sof, there is only the one being-consciousness-force, the Infinite and eternal, and nothing else exists. Even the distinction of God and Godhead does not exist at this level, and thus, from our point of view, Ain Sof is the unmanifest—completely inconceivable and incomprehensible. From this state of no-thingness (Ain), every idea or category of existence must be created, formed and made as though out of nothing; yet as everything comes from this no-thingness, it can also be called divine fullness. Although nothing exists in it, the unmanifest is pregnant with the divine potential of everything.

Will or desire (Ratzon) is the first expression of Ain Sof in the creative act, for in order to create and sustain creation, God must will or desire to create and sustain creation. The level of Adam Kadmon corresponds to the will or desire of God that is the underlying foundation for all the proceeding levels of existence—the initiating principle of creation. In essence, the first emanation of God's presence and power is the will or desire to create, which precedes creation itself, and that will or desire is what is called Logos and Sophia—the word and wisdom of God.

To say that God "created" this divine will or desire is a fundamental misconception according to the Christian Kabbalah, for this will or desire that is called Adam Kadmon is, in fact, inseparable from the light of Ain Sof (light of the infinite). It is an emanation of the bornless Spirit of God, which, although made distinct from Ain Sof, is completely inseparable from the infinite and eternal. Adam Kadmon always existed in Ain Sof, although as divine potential. At the outset of creation, this divine potential emerged as the first of all holy emanations and is the interface of the infinite with the finite creation.

Because Adam Kadmon is inseparable from Ain Sof, it is called Ain (no-thingness), and thus the Sefer Yetzirah speaks of the Sefirot of Adam Kadmon as "Sefirot of nothingness." The whole of creation comes forth, as it were, from the womb of Adam Kadmon, the womb of God's will; therefore, this idea of nothingness does not imply a lack of existence. It is an emanation of the divine fullness in the no-thingness, from which the whole of creation is brought forth.

Adam Kadmon alludes to the ultimate purpose or intention of God in creating. The term itself is an anthropomorphism that literally means "primordial human being." If the letters of the Tetragrammaton are placed on a vertical line, with Yod at the top and the remaining letters placed in their proper order in descent, the image of a human being is formed by them (see figure 2). Likewise, the configuration of the Sefirot is frequently depicted as the body parts of a human form, each Sefirah corresponding to a part of the human body. What is suggested by this is that the ultimate purpose of God creating was to create the human one—the image and likeness of God.

To understand more deeply what this means, one must consider what a human being is, or is meant to be. A human being is a creature of higher intelligence that is self-aware and therefore can be aware of the existence of God. Because of this intelligence and self-awareness, a human being is capable of conscious evolution toward higher states of awareness and more

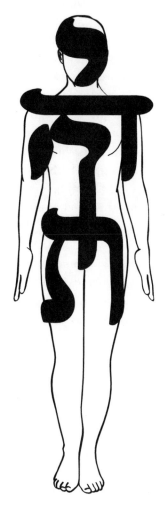

Figure 2. The Primordial Human Being.

refined and higher forms of life—specifically, an evolution toward unification with God. A human being has the capacity to consciously unite him- or herself with God and to embody something of God and the Godhead— the capacity to attain supernal consciousness or enlightenment.

To say that the ultimate purpose of creation is the human one is to say that God's ultimate purpose is to express or communicate him- or herself—to reveal him- or herself and make him- or herself known. The ultimate knowledge of God is unification with God and embodiment of God—Messianic consciousness or Christhood. It is as though God, who is the Being of the Becoming, seeks self-knowledge through the act of creation. God creates because it is God's nature to create—to express and know God. While one can know nothing of God at the ordinary level of consciousness, in a state of conscious unity with God, the presence of God within oneself knows God and Godhead beyond oneself.

This fruition of creation is prefigured in the person of Yeshua Messiah (Jesus Christ), who represents the first human one to emerge from within humanity, embodying something of the Soul of Messiah—one anointed with the supernal light of God. The universe of Adam Kadmon in the Christian Kabbalah represents this level of attainment and all of the mysteries associated with it. It is the universe of the Soul of the Messiah, the Olam of supernal light.

At the level of Atzilut, the divine names and the Sefirot are one and the same; the Sefirot are the divine names and the divine names are the Sefirot. Therefore, the level of Adam Kadmon corresponds to the holy letters from which the names are derived and, specifically, to the power of the word-wisdom of God of which the holy names of God serve as vehicles or channels.

The Universe of Atzilut

The word "Atzilut" is derived from the root *etzel*, which means "nearness." As the name implies, Atzilut is near to the infinite light, so near, in fact, that, like Adam Kadmon, Atzilut is also called Ain or no-thingness. Atzilut is the domain of the Sefirot proper, the holy vessels of Atzilut being filled with the infinite light via Adam Kadmon. If the existence of the primordial essence of the Sefirot at the level of the universe of Adam Kadmon were conceived of as the body of Adam Kadmon, the Sefirot at the level of Atzilut would be as garments of light.

The concept of Atzilut is not an easy one to describe. For all intents and purposes, one could say that it is truly alien to our perception of reality. One could characterize Atzilut as the level of reality that does not yet exist, or a level of reality beyond the space-time-consciousness continuum in which past, present, and future exist as a simultaneous reality—one ever-present reality. If this is not alien enough, at the level of Atzilut, not only are past, present, and future a simultaneous reality, but so also is every possible outcome, which is to say every possibility of the past, present, and future, not only of one single space-time continuum but of all possible space-time continuums!

Another characteristic of Atzilut is that knowledge, the knower, and the known exist in complete unity, so that there is no subject-object relationship and, in truth, no duality whatsoever. It is supernal or supramental. If one were to experience consciousness at the level of Atzilut, one would experience the knowledge and reality of everything within oneself—a state of pure radiant awareness. In the words of St. Paul, "One would know fully, even as one has been known."

With the coming into being of the Sefirot proper in Atzilut, along with God's will or desire, God's wisdom, understanding, love, power, lordship, dominion, splendor, righteousness and kingdom emerge, and through them the great name of God is revealed. At the level of Atzilut, the Sefirot exist in an archetypal state and in perfect unity and harmony with one another—without any differentiation or division between them. God is One and he and his name are One. Only at the point when the Sefirot are manifest in a lower universe can they be conceived of as separate forces.

The Universe of Beriyah

Adam Kadmon and Atzilut together form the realm of Yichud (Unity), but at the level of Beriyah, the realm of Perud (Separation) begins, which is to say, the appearance of independent existence and separation. According to the Kabbalah, creation occurs through a process of tzimtzum (constriction), in which God must withdraw his or her infinite light into him- or herself to make a primordial space in which creation can take place. The

effects of this tzimtzum begin to manifest and play themselves out at the
level of Beriyah.

The term "Beriyah" is derived from the Hebrew word *bara*, meaning "to
create" and the Aramaic word *bar*, meaning "outside" or "external." Therefore, Beriyah indicates the concept of creation brought from within God
and distinct from God—"outside" of God or "separate" from God to some
degree. Likewise, it suggests the creation of something new and distinct
or creation "ex nihilo." In Hebrew, this idea is represented in the phrase
Yesh Mi-Ani—"Something from nothing." In relationship to Atzilut,
which is near unto the divine, Beriyah is outside or apart from the divine—two dimensions removed from the divine.

While the Sefirot at the level of Atzilut are expressed by the divine
names, at the level of Beriyah they are expressed by the archangels—the
divine powers of creation. However, all cosmic or spiritual forces at the
level of Beriyah are not divine, for with the constriction of the infinite
light and separation, cosmic ignorance emerges and, with cosmic ignorance, forces of evil and darkness enter into creation. Therefore, along
with the divine powers, there are admixed powers and dark powers. All of
these together are the cosmic forces through which Beriyah, Yetzirah, and
Asiyah come into being—Beriyah being mostly divine and Asiyah being
mostly admixed and dark.

Beriyah corresponds to the first He of the Tetragrammaton, which is the
"window" through which the true nature of existence is revealed and the
mysteries made accessible. But in the process of this revelation, the cosmic
forces become distinct and individual entities, some oriented to the universe above and others oriented to the universe below—some in submission to divine will and others seeking their own dominion over creatures
and creation. Thus gods and goddesses, archdemons and demons, and all
manner of spiritual entities came into being with the holy archangels. In
Gnostic Christianity, Beriyah is therefore called the beginning of the dominion of the demiurgos and archons—the cosmic forces of ignorance.

In mentioning the reality of evil at the level of Beriyah, it must be said
that evil is not seen as having an independent existence apart from God, as
nothing whatsoever can exist in complete separation from God's presence
and power. In the Kabbalah, the cosmic forces of ignorance and the "Evil
One" are understood to be a secret operation of the Holy Spirit—so secret

that such entities do not even know that, ultimately, they are serving God's plan in creation. Cosmic ignorance and evil is what makes free will possible in creation and therefore is an integral part of the divine plan.

The Universe of Yetzirah

The word Yetzirah comes from the root *yetzar*, which means "to form." Yetzirah therefore denotes the formation of something from a preexistent substance, hence the Hebrew phrase *Yesh Mi-Yesh*, "something from something." This is illustrated in a verse from the prophet Isaiah in which God says, "I form (*yotzer*) the light and create (*boreh*) darkness" (Isaiah 45:7). The light exists before creation and comes from within God and therefore is "something from something," but darkness did not exist before creation, did not come from within God and the Godhead, and therefore was created "something from nothing." However, at the level of Yetzirah, both the light and the darkness are formed, for darkness was created at the level of Beriyah, as were all cosmic principles and cosmic forces. In Yetzirah, the principles and forces found in Beriyah are shaped into more distinct patterns of form—hence the universe of formation.

In this process, there is a further division or separation of things—a further involution of the one becoming many. This is represented by the manifestation of the Sefirot in Yetzirah as orders of angels. Whereas, at the level of Beriyah, the presence and power of the Sefirot manifests as a singular entity, namely an archangel, in Yetzirah, the Sefirot become hosts or choirs of angels, the one presence and power manifesting as the countless many. This further division or separation of things happens through the cosmic ignorance that was created in the process of the tzimtzum. Thus, along with the generation of hosts of holy angels in Yetzirah, there is also the generation of legions of impure and evil spirits—beings-forces of admixture and darkness. At this level of creation, the divine order and the dominion of the demiurge exist in a dynamic balance so that Yetzirah is equally of the light and of the darkness.

In comparison with the realm of Yichud formed by Adam Kadmon and Atzilut, the light of the infinite is extremely restricted and therefore distinctly veiled in Yetzirah. There is a great difference between manifestation at the level of Atzilut and at the level of Yetzirah, which is well reflected by the correspondence of pure awareness or undifferentiated mind to the former and speech to the latter. One need only consider the difficulty of conveying one's mind and one's thoughts through speech to another person and the gap of subjectivity between the speaker and the listener. One might speak quite clearly and yet be sorely misunderstood as the meaning of one's words can easily be taken out of context. The same is true of cosmic forces manifesting at this level. They are often distorted and certainly less than the divine glory of the higher Olamot.

Speech, being attributed to Yetzirah, represents the feeling or emotional level as well as actual words. Speech not only conveys thought but is also a translation of thought into feelings and emotions, which represents a lower gradation of the original *ratzon* (will or desire) underlying creation. Therefore, emotion is the motivating force at the level of Yetzirah—speech and emotion.

The universe of Yetzirah is often called the world of angels and, conversely, the world of demons. Asiyah is the material or physical universe. Therefore, speaking of Yetzirah as a world of spirits alludes to the play of spiritual forces within and behind everything that transpires in the material world. Essentially, as human beings, whatever we link ourselves with through our thoughts, emotions, speech, and actions, we bring *down* from Yetzirah into substantial being at the level of Asiyah, whether that be something angelic, admixed, or demonic. Contact with something angelic is a link to the divine, as angels are links between human beings and God. Contact with something admixed or impure is a distorted or imperfect link to the divine, while contact with something demonic is a removal of oneself from the divine presence. To commune with angelic beings and righteous spirits, one merely needs to align one's thoughts, feelings-emotions, words, and actions to those of the holy angels. Angelic beings are always seeking contact with humanity and contact is made any time we are willing. As the Kabbalah says, "Think of the holy angels and they will think of you and come to you."

The Universe of Asiyah

Asiyah is the universe of making, the word Asiyah being derived from the root *asab*, meaning "to make." Asiyah therefore connotes the final outcome or completion of the process of creation. At the level of Asiyah, the spiritual world and material world interpenetrate and interact, the material world being the most restricted or dense manifestation of spiritual energy. It is in Asiyah where potential is fully realized and actualized—the fulfillment of creation.

The supernal light of Atzilut is the secret center of every particle of matter, matter itself being crystallized light that has assumed the densest possible form—form representing force locked up into patterns of its own making. Thus, at the level of Asiyah, the light of the Infinite is most thickly veiled and hidden. In this sense, Asiyah is the dimension most removed from God's presence or the realm in which God's presence is most restricted, and yet the presence of God is everywhere within creation at the level of Asiyah—within everyone and everything.

Cosmic ignorance is the principle of constriction or restriction; therefore, cosmic ignorance tends to dominate the universe of Asiyah. Although this means that impure and evil forces have a great influence upon creatures and creation at this level, it also means that there is a full and complete freedom of will in Asiyah. Although restriction and bondage is the function of cosmic ignorance, its ultimate purpose is freedom or liberation.

Through cosmic ignorance, the light of the Infinite evolves into the material universe through gradations. Likewise, through gradations, creation is linked with the Infinite and is able to evolve toward the Infinite. Along with making free will possible, darkness also makes evolution possible, providing the resistance, tension, stress, and friction necessary for the development of higher and more refined life-forms and, thus, the development of higher and more refined states of consciousness-being. Therefore, Asiyah is designed for the awakening of souls—for the realization and actualization of divine potential.

This truth is given in the name of Yeshua, one of the esoteric meanings of which is "knowledge of the truth will set you free!" Only through a process of incarnations in Asiyah is a soul able to awaken and actualize the divine potential of the infinite light within it, and thus to evolve beyond the need for the dense forms of physical or material existence. Asiyah allows for individuation so that, returning to the realm of Yichud and uniting itself with the universal and primordial dimensions of divine being, the soul is able to maintain self-awareness while in unification with the divine. Hence, the individual is not simply reabsorbed into an unconscious union but is fulfilled and completed in a conscious unification. It is Asiyah that makes this possible.

The Kabbalah says that, at the level of Asiyah, the spiritual energy of the Sefirot manifests through the stars and planets. Because of this, astrology is often the primary method of divination into the purpose and meaning of the soul's incarnation, as the birth chart reflects the configuration of Sefirotic influence at the time of one's birth. There is also a teaching in the Kabbalah that proposes that the stars serve as the bodies of archangels in the physical universe, their cosmic rays and light being likened to angels. Gnostic Christianity often speaks of God's presence in Asiyah as our "earthly Mother," and of features of the land, creatures, and forces of nature as "angels of our earthly Mother."

While these ideas may fall upon many modern ears as superstition, or seem silly to a noninitiate, the meaning is quite simple: the material and spiritual worlds are intimately connected and are ultimately inseparable. The material universe comes forth from the spiritual universe and is the outermost manifestation of the universe of the Spirit. There is a vast metaphysical reality within and behind the material plane of the universe. In fact, there are countless inner dimensions that are as equally "real" and distinct as the physical or material dimension. When there is the appearance of a miracle, it is simply the operation of the cosmic law acting through the hidden dimensions upon the material dimension. It only appears as a miracle to one who is unaware of the metaphysical dimensions of reality and the play of spiritual forces within and behind what transpires in the material world.

TWO

AIN SOF
AND THE
SOUL OF LIGHT

The Great Unmanifest

There are no words to speak the mystery of God and Godhead; no concepts or definitions can be applied to the Great Unmanifest. It is unthinkable and unspeakable—the nameless and unknown. Yet it is the source and cause of everything that manifests; the inmost essence and nature of everything is this no-thingness.

Ain (no-thingness), Ain Sof (the one-without-end, or the infinite), and Ain Sof Or (endless light)—with these terms, Kabbalah indicates the reality of God and Godhead, the primordial ground and source of creation. To get some sense of what is meant by these terms, one must look into one's own consciousness and being—one's own mind—and find the source of one's thoughts and the nature of one's thoughts. If one looks to see the source of one's thoughts, following the stream of thoughts to its point of origin, one will discover that no source can be identified. Thoughts arise in the mind, abide in the mind, and disappear in the mind, but the source cannot be found. Because the source cannot be found, one cannot correctly say the source is something, but because something (thought) comes from this hidden source, one cannot correctly call it nothing either. One can only say that it is *no-thing*, which is to say neither something nor nothing.

Thoughts emerge from no-thingness of mind, abide in no-thingness, and return again to no-thingness when they disappear. If one looks closely, one will see that the thoughts themselves share in the substance and nature of no-thingness; therefore, although distinct individuations of the mind, they are nevertheless inseparable. The same is true of Ain, the Sefirot, and the inmost part of one's soul. They emerge from within Ain, abide in Ain, return to Ain, and share the same substance and nature as Ain.

Taking this observation of the mind further, one will notice that the mind spontaneously generates thoughts without end, that the mind has an endless capacity to generate thoughts and that it is the nature of mind to do so. The same is true of Ain Sof. God is the Infinite—an infinite potential of creation without beginning or end. Because of this infinite capacity to conceive and create, the no-thingness of God is also divine fullness.

Continuing to observe the mind one step further, one will recognize a third quality of the nature of mind—that the mind is self-aware. The process of observing the mind itself reveals this quality—the power to observe and be aware. This is akin to Ain Sof Or, which is the omniscience, omnipresence, and omnipotence of God and the Godhead—the life-power.

Thus, in the Kabbalah, there is a direct parallel to the concept of God in Hinduism as the one being-consciousness-force and to the concept of ultimate reality in Buddhism as the primordial nature of mind, which is called clear light bliss.

Ain is the nature of divine being, Ain Sof is the nature of divine consciousness, and Ain Sof Or is the nature of divine force. The Olamot and Sefirot share in this threefold divine nature, being the emanation of the divine presence and power of the one being-consciousness-force. Likewise, the soul of light also shares in this divine nature, the inmost part of the soul being a divine spark of Ain Sof Or. It is this shared divine nature that gives the soul the capacity to unite itself with the Sefirot and to ultimately experience unification with God and Godhead. Because the Sefirot are inseparable in their essence from God and Godhead, they serve as the vehicle of this unification for both the individual and the universal (creature and creation).

The Soul of Light

The soul of light is composed of five parts or aspects, that correspond to the five Olamot and to specific Sefirot of the Tree of Life. The inmost part of the soul is Yechidah (the holy or divine spark). The radiance or glory of Yechidah is the Hayyah (life-force or life-power), and the abode or image of Yechidah is Neshamah (divine nature, heavenly soul, supernal soul, or holy soul). Then below the level of the Neshamah are Ruach (spirit or intelligence) and Nefesh (bestial or earthly soul). These five parts of the soul are inseparable in their essence; however, until the soul-being evolves and awakens, all of these levels of the soul are not realized and actualized; so in effect, everyone does not necessarily have the fullness of their soul of light.

". . . then Yahweh Elohim formed the human one from the dust of the ground, and breathed into his-her nostrils the breath of life; and the Human One became a living being" (Genesis 2:7, modified translation). Each of the Hebrew terms for the soul connote "breath," "wind," or "air," and allude to the radiant holy breath of God, which is the life-power. The suggestion is that the soul and life are the breath of God—that life, creature, and creation is God breathing. You are the radiant holy breath of God!

In essence, the origin of the soul of light in a human being comes from the highest realms and from within God. Therefore, in our soul, we are intimately connected with the Olamot and Sefirot, as well as to Ain Sof. This relationship can be illustrated through a classical analogy:

> Imagine a glassblower, who decides to fashion an elegant vessel. The will or desire to do so, emanating from the inmost place within the glassblower, is the level of Yechidah. It corresponds to the tip of the Yod of the Tetragrammaton and to the universe of Adam Kadmon.
>
> The next level is represented by the glassblower himself, just before he begins to blow out and the breath remains in his lungs. This is the level of Hayyah, and it corresponds to Atzilut and the body of the Yod.
>
> The breath passing through the glassblower's lips represents Neshamah. It corresponds to the first He and the universe of

Beriyah. The pressurized air flowing through the tube represents
Ruach, the Vau of the great name, and the universe of Yetzirah.
This breath, as it expands to form the glass vessel, would repre-
sent Nefesh, the final He of Yahweh, and the universe of Asiyah.

In much the same way, our holy soul is a movement of God's spirit—a
direct expression of the one lifepower. From this, you will understand that
it is the soul of light, which is created in the image and likeness of God. Although emanating forth from God, the soul remains ever within God, just
as the word God spoke outwardly remains ever present within God.

As indicated above, the highest levels of the soul are not separate from
their divine source. Per the analogy, they are in the mind and lungs of the
glassblower. From the divine point of view, the highest aspects of the soul
are internal to God, while the lower aspects are external. From the human
point of view, the opposite is the case; Hayyah and Yechidah completely
transcend the ordinary person and are external, while the lower aspects
are internal. From either point of view, Neshamah is the threshold between what is internal and what is external.

In this teaching of the soul having five parts or aspects, the three lower
parts—Neshamah, Ruach, and Nefesh—are called *Penimi'im*, or internalizations, because we have the capacity to bring these aspects into our
earthly incarnation and embody them. The two highest levels, Yechidah
and Hayyah, on the other hand, are rarely embodied and, save in the case
of a perfect master like Yeshua Messiah, will only be internalized in the
world to come. Therefore, they are typically called Makifim (envelopments) or Atarot (crowns), because they transcend the ordinary individual
personality entirely. In this sense, it is said that one who draws down the
influence of Hayyah and Yechidah becomes more than human, and that
such holy masters are like unto archangels.

Nefesh

The lowest part of the soul is the basis of the personality, the life-display,
and is the matrix of vital energy within and behind the physical body. It is
through the Nefesh that the soul is interfaced with the physical body and
life in material form is sustained.

The Nefesh is not inherently spiritual, nor is it inherently connected to the Neshamah. The term "flesh" in the Scriptures is actually referring to the Nefesh in an unregenerated and unrefined state, which is called Nefesh Behamit (the bestial soul). On the level of Nefesh, a person can gain an awareness of the body, life, and personality as a vessel or vehicle of spiritual energy. However, this awareness can only come about when a person is able to turn inward and upward—Godward—and isolate him- or herself from all the internal and external stimuli that typically occupy his or her mind. Likewise, a person must engage in work on him- or herself, seeking to refine the personality and life-display so that it is brought into harmony with Neshamah and the divine.

A person who does this receives the higher level of his or her soul, the Ruach or divine intelligence, through which he or she may also receive the influence of his or her Neshamah. This link to the Neshamah through the agency of Ruach transforms Nefesh Behamit into Nefesh Elokit (the godly soul). When the Gnostic teachings speak of the *elect* or *chosen* person, it is an individual who has made the Nefesh an actual vehicle of the divine presence and power, and who has received something of the fiery intelligence (holy spirit) in so doing. Thus, we understand that it is not an arbitrary decision of God that makes a person elect or chosen by God. Rather, it is the person who has made a decision to make him or herself receptive to the divine and to draw near unto the divine. He or she is essentially cooperating with divine grace and making him or herself a partner with God in the great work.

Nefesh is the mortal part of us; it does not survive death. The only way Nefesh survives death is in the case of a holy person who fully embodies his or her Neshamah and who is able to draw down something of the Hayyah and Yechidah, which is to say when a person attains Messianic consciousness and fully embodies the supernal light-presence (state of enlightenment and liberation). Until that time, from one incarnation to another, a new Nefesh is generated for each new incarnation. At the level of Nefesh, there is no real connection between one incarnation and another, save for the karmic continuum. Only in the case of a person who embodies his or her Neshamah is there a direct link between diverse incarnations, for it is at the level of the Neshamah that all incarnations are interconnected.

Ruach

Ruach is our spirit or intelligence and, like the Nefesh, there are two distinct manifestations of Ruach. They are called the upper Ruach and the lower Ruach. The lower Ruach is the ordinary human intelligence, which is oriented on the Nefesh and the external world. It is the mind of the worldly or profane individual. The term "lower Ruach" thus indicates the unenlightened condition. The upper Ruach comes into being through the cultivation of a spiritual life and practice—an active seeking of enlightenment that leads to one degree or another of the enlightenment experience. It is this that is the Ruach proper, which is a divine intelligence or divine genius.

The upper Ruach is oriented to the Neshamah and to the divine. As a result, it is an awareness of the ocean of spirituality that surrounds us—awareness of the play of spiritual or cosmic forces, the metaphysical dimensions of reality, and God's holy Shekinah (presence and power) within and behind everything that transpires. At this level, we begin to get a sense of God's will for our soul—the mission of our soul. We are also able to receive the inspiration of the Holy Spirit, to receive communication from the divine powers, and to experience higher states of consciousness well beyond the ordinary level. Reaching the level of upper Ruach more and more, we find ourselves guided by the Spirit and moved by the Spirit. At the highest levels, we can experience unification with the Holy Spirit (Ruach Ha-Kodesh), which is a prophetic state of consciousness in which a person feels him- or herself completely elevated and transformed.

When the level of upper Ruach is present in a person, they are rightly called a spiritual or holy person, for more than a godly soul, he or she is a Spirit-filled soul.

Neshamah

At the level of Neshamah, one experiences the radiant holy breath of God. Neshamah is the vessel that holds the spiritual power that God wants to give us. One could say that Nefesh is like the hand open to receive and Neshamah is the hand opening to give. Thus, to the degree one is willing to become open and sensitive to the holy Shekinah, the influence of the Neshamah is able to enter into oneself—or, more truly, to be brought forth from within oneself.

Ruach is the intermediate link between Nefesh and Neshamah—the link through which they are connected and potentially united. In the spiritual dimension, there is no concept of space as we would typically think of it. Rather, closeness can only be defined as resemblance, similarity, or likeness. Conversely, distance is the product of difference, opposition, or dissimilarity. Therefore, spiritually, to be like unto something is to be close to it and to be unlike something is to be removed or distant from it. Thus, to draw near to our Neshamah, we must shape our thoughts, feelings-emotions, words, and actions in harmony with our divine nature. To the degree we are able to do this, we embody something of our Neshamah and bring the Neshamah into our experience.

Nefesh is the vessel for the reception of Ruach and Neshamah. In a similar way, Neshamah is the vessel for the reception of the Hayyah and Yechidah. Nefesh forms a material body, but the Neshamah forms a body of light or heavenly image (Zelem). This is an angelic image or glorified image of oneself—the image of one's Christ-self or future self. It is this divine image resembling a human being that the prophets behold in the peak of their divine visions—the heavenly image of the prophet him- or herself, which is called the glory or likeness of God.

The enlightenment experience begins at the level of Ruach, but enlightenment and liberation proper corresponds to the level of Neshamah when something of the Hayyah and Yechidah are drawn into it. It is at this level that a true Messianic consciousness dawns and the Christ-self is realized. While many initiates attain the level of Ruach, relatively few attain the level of the holy Neshamah. Those who do embody something of the Neshamah are called tau in the Gnostic Tradition.

Hayyah

The Hayyah is the most subtle life-force or living essence—so heavenly that it has little connection with the body and dwells mostly in other realms. It is the radiant holy breath of God that is experienced at the level of Neshamah. Yet at the level of Hayyah, the holy breath is completely within God and one who experiences this presence and power experiences a conscious unification with God.

Most individuals will only gain the awareness of Hayyah in altered states. In these rare moments of peak experience, it is as though one is light in an ocean of light—the world of supernal light being experienced within and all around oneself. Quite literally, one sees and experiences everything as this light-force. In this experience of supernal consciousness, individuality is not lost, but rather is fulfilled and made complete. Instead of the drop of light being poured back into the ocean of light, it is as though the whole ocean of light pours through the drop—the primordial and cosmic power flowing through the individual and manifesting as the individual.

While many initiates may experience something of Hayyah in peak mystical experience, the actual attainment of Hayyah is very rare. The power of the Hayyah is the power to resurrect the dead—very few masters have walked on earth with this divine power.

Hayyah is associated with the supernal Sefirah of Hokmah (wisdom) from which Binah (understanding) comes. Thus the attainment of Hayyah represents a state of non-dual Gnostic awareness—all understanding—which is a complete enlightenment and liberation.

Yechidah

There is an even higher level of the soul of light than Hayyah. It is called Yechidah—the holy or divine spark. It is a grade of unification beyond Hayyah of which nothing can really be said. One who attains this level is the light of all worlds and is the way, truth, and life. This is the essence of the spiritual sun, the Christos—Christ, the Logos (Word) and Christ, the Sophia (Wisdom).

Of this inmost part of the soul of light, it is said that it is so holy that only God and Godhead can enter it. Even the greatest among the angels of God cannot enter it. God and Godhead indwell us at this inmost level and we dwell in God and Godhead, and we are inseparable from the Holy One. Yechidah is our true self, our divine or Christ-self, which is at once no-thing and everything. It is the being of our becoming.

If Hayyah represents enlightenment proper and Yechidah is something beyond that holy attainment, then something subtle and profound is being said of enlightenment. What appears to us as a supreme or ultimate attainment is, in truth, but the beginning of a whole new level of evolution to which there is no end in sight!

The Transmigrations of the Soul—Gilgulim

Gilgul is the term for reincarnation in Kabbalah. The word implies swirling, cycling, rounds, or revolutions, as in the turning of a wheel— hence the cycles of life, death, and rebirth. According to the Tradition, the soul-being develops and evolves through a process of transmigration from one incarnation to another until the soul of light is fully embodied and, thus, actualized and realized.

From Hayyah, Nefeshim are generated and emanate through the matrix of Neshamah. With the formation of each Nefesh, the Ruach is drawn down from Yechidah, the Nefesh and Ruach below being a representation of the Hayyah and Yechidah above. There is an outer and an inner aspect of the Neshamah, the outer representing the soul-being that evolves and the inner representing something of the bornless being beyond the realm of becoming. It is this outer level of the Neshamah that is the karmic or causal matrix of the soul, so that, from one incarnation to another, there is a certain continuity that allows for either progress or regress in the evolutionary process of the soul-being. In this sense, Neshamah is both within and beyond the transmigrations of the soul, the inner aspect being transcendental.

The capacity of Hayyah to generate Nefeshim is potentially exhaustless. This is reflected in the capacity of the mind to generate thoughts without end and suggests the power of Ain Sof in Hayyah. This means that, without divine assistance—specifically the grace of the divine incarnation—and a conscious evolution toward Messianic consciousness or enlightenment, the soul-being could potentially be bound forever to endless transmigrations through life, death, and rebirth.

Gnostic Christianity does speak of a need for salvation, in the sense of an enlightenment and liberation from the endless rounds of gilgulim. However, there is no teaching of eternal damnation, for until the realization of supernal or Messianic consciousness, all states of existence are transitional, whether life or the afterlife, including the heavens, the earths, and the hells. One's experience in life, as well as the afterlife, reflects the karmic conditioning of the soul, which is the condition of the soul-being and the grade to which it has evolved.

Before incarnation as a human being, the soul-being evolves through subhuman life-forms. According to the Tradition, the human form—our present condition—is also transitional. Therefore, just as the soul-being has evolved through subhuman life-forms, so also shall it pass through superhuman forms akin to those of angelic beings, although superior to the orders of holy angels. The divine image of the Risen Christ represents the superhuman form which the human soul is destined to attain—the "omega point" of our present cycle of evolution, as Pierre Teilhard de Chardin put it.

It is at the level of Asiyah, in this life, that our soul-being is able to make progress in this evolutionary process and to ascend from one grade of the enlightenment experience to another. While, on one hand, the involution and incarnation of the soul represents a state of restriction or bondage, on the other hand, involution and incarnation is the only way the soul-being can awaken and evolve itself—that which binds or obstructs is at one and the same time the vehicle for liberation. Afterlife states reflect the progressions and regressions of the evolutionary process that have transpired in life; however, actual progress cannot transpire in the afterlife. Rather, the potential for progress exists only when the soul is incarnate in Asiyah or the material plane of the universe. Therefore, although the aim of the Gnostic Christian is an ascent to a higher plane of existence in which physical incarnation is no longer necessary, this ascent transpires through the descent of the Neshamah fully into incarnation—the embodiment of the supernal soul and Christ-self. Only in this way do we ultimately transcend Asiyah and accomplish the ascension or great transformation.

The study and practice of Christian Kabbalah or Christian Gnosticism are, essentially, a conscious evolution of the soul-being through the various levels of the soul to Christ consciousness. For this reason, Gnostic initiates often refer to the Tradition as the path of the ascension or way of the great transformation.

THREE

THE PRIMORDIAL CHRISTOS AND HOLY SEFIROT

A Prologue

In the beginning was the Word, and the Word was with God, and the Word was God. He was in the beginning with God. All things came into being through him, and without him not one thing came into being. What has come into being in him was life, and the life was the light of all people. The light shines in the darkness, and the darkness did not overcome it (Gospel of St. John 1:1–5).

The Timeless Primordial and the Beginning

At the outset of creation, there was Ain, Ain Sof, Ain Sof Or—there was only God, the one being-consciousness-force. Before all things were created, the light of the Infinite was simple. It pervaded the whole of existence. Endless space and endless light being one and the same, there was no empty space that could be space, emptiness, or void apart from the infinite. There was no beginning and no end. There was no boundary or limit whatsoever. All was one simple primordial light.

When it arose in God's simple will to create all of the Olamot, God constricted God's infinite light, creating a distance of primordial space to all sides around a primordial point, leaving a great void space in the midst of the infinite light. This was the original tzimtzum or constriction, and the primordial space created by it was spherical, for the light of the infinite was withdrawn evenly from around all sides

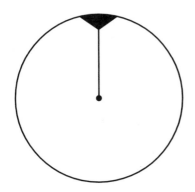

Figure 3: The line of light at the center of primordial space.

of the primordial center. Therefore the possibility of creation arose in God through God's simple will. Once this transpired, God constricted the infinite light into a point, which became a ray or line of light that penetrated to the center of primordial space (figure 3). This is the light of the primordial Christos, the word and wisdom of God, through which creation took place. "In the beginning was the light of Messiah, and the light of Messiah was with God, and the light of Messiah was God."

Mystery of the Sefirot and Divine Incarnation

God's ratzon to create is the first and most essential quality of God as creator and thus is the first primordial expression of God's word and wisdom, the light of the Messiah. It is through ratzon that the original tzimtzum takes place. It is called a "depth of good," because it is the pure desire to impart or to give. God creates in order to express and reveal Godself and to give of Godself to creation. Forming a desire to give, through the original tzimtzum, God also created the desire to receive, the creation of the great void, representing the most primitive form of the desire to receive, which makes it possible for God's desire to give to be fulfilled.

Ratzon is Keter (crown), the first of the holy Sefirot, which is the structure or measurement of the Olamot. Keter is the light of life or life-will, within which is the principle of life-force and life-form, the father and mother of creation, and all of the divine potential of creation. The life-force is a depth of beginning and the life-form is a depth of end, Hokmah and Binah, the second and third Sefirot, respectively. From these, Da'at (knowledge or gnosis) comes into being, which is the manifestation of Keter in creation, and this Da'at becomes the six Sefirot, which are the Son: Hesed (mercy or loving-kindness), Gevurah (strength or rigor), Tiferet (beauty, the son proper), Netzach (dominion or victory), Hod (empathy or splendor), and Yesod (foundation or righteousness). These six Sefirot are called a depth of south, a depth of north, a depth of east, a depth of above, a depth of below, and a depth of west, respectively. These six Sefirot are the space continuum of the Olamot. Hokmah and Binah, which are a depth of beginning and a depth of end, form the time continuum. Keter, the crown, implies Malkut, the kingdom, which is the final Sefirah of the ten, called a depth of evil. Therefore, Keter and Malkut form the moral dimension of the Olamot or the continuum of consciousness or soul.

All of this is contained in Keter, God's will or desire to create, the creative process being a progressive unfolding of this divine potential in Adam Kadmon. In the primordial state, the Sefirot of Adam Kadmon exist only as divine potential. They are "points of light within a point of light, existing in an undifferentiated primordial unity." That is to say, all of the Sefirot exist in God's ratzon, but as yet are not brought forth from the great unmanifest. At this level, the primordial human being, the prototype of humanity, which is God's ultimate intention in creation, exists in an unconscious unity with Ain Sof. In order for the creative process to continue and Adam Kadmon to awaken and enter into a conscious unity with God, this state of undifferentiated primordial unity must be broken. Thus the Sefirot of Adam Kadmon are shattered.

When this original primordial unity is broken, the primitive Sefirot had no connection or way to relate to one another and, therefore, existed in complete separation and anarchy. This primordial state is called the universe of Bohu Ve-Tohu (void and chaos). Kabbalah says that, in the process of the formation of the Sefirot of Atzilut, countless universes were created and destroyed, thus producing the substance through which the dark and hostile forces would later take shape.

What was only divine potential in the original state of Adam Kadmon becomes actualized and revealed at the level of Atzilut. The Sefirot appear as the divine names and Partzufim (divine personas), which mend or heal the Sefirot of Adam Kadmon, bringing them once again into a harmonious state of unity.

At the level of Atzilut, Keter becomes the Partzufim of Atik Yomin and Arik Anpin (ancient of days, the great face of God). Hokmah and Binah become the Partzufim of Abba and Aima (father and mother). The six become the Partzuf of Zer Anpin or Ben (lesser face of God, or son of God), and Malkut becomes the Partzuf of Nukva or Kallah (daughter or bride). All of the Partzufim in Atzilut are the reflection of the divine image of Adam Kadmon above, through which Adam Kadmon is actualized and realized in the Olamot below.

This process of the shattering of the Sefirot of Adam Kadmon and their mending or healing through the emanation of the Sefirot of Atzilut that prefigures the mystery of the divine incarnation of the Soul of the Messiah and the passion and death that open the way for the resurrection and ascension. Likewise, the Partzufim of Atzilut—particularly mother, son, and daughter or bride—prefigure the persons of the divine incarnation of the Soul of the Messiah in the Gospel: the Son in the person of Yeshua Messiah, the Mother in the person of Mother Mary, and the Daughter or Bride in the person of St. Mary Magdalene. The Holy Father, being Hokmah of Atzilut, is invisible and hidden and is revealed only in reflection through the Mother, Son, and Holy Bride. As the Partzufim are represented in the Gospel in this way, so are the Sefirot as the divine names represented in the Gospel as the power of the Holy Spirit, which is the "baptism" given by the Messiah.

This process of tzimtzum and the shattering of the vessels takes place at the level of all the Olamot, from Atzilut to Asiyah. Every time a new Olam is to be created at a lower level or gradation, the former order of the Sefirot must first be broken to be reformed through their manifestation at the next stage of creation. The revelation of the law in the Old Testament and the revelation of the Messiah in the New Testament represent the process of the shattering and the mending of the vessels in the universe of Asiyah—the completion and fulfillment of the process of creation according to the Christian Kabbalah.

The Sefirot of a given Olam are gradations of the infinite light or the holy Shekinah of God and, from one Olam to another, represent a further involution of the infinite light in creation. Hence, the Sefirot of the five Olamot are gradations that link Ain Sof with finite creatures and creation. These same gradations of involution are also gradations of evolution through which creature and creation are able to ascend to conscious unity with God and Godhead. Through the incarnation of the Soul of the Messiah, all these levels or gradations of being-consciousness-force are linked in us so that we are empowered through the persons of Yeshua Messiah, the Holy Mother and the Bride in a conscious evolution. The path of the great ascension is opened to us.

Creation and Revelation

"The Disciples said to Jesus, 'Tell us how our end will be.' Jesus said, 'Have you discovered, then, the beginning, that you look for the end? For where the beginning is, there will the end be. Blessed is he who will take his place in the beginning; he will know the end and will not experience death'" (Gospel of St. Thomas, saying 18).

Creation begins in the infinite and eternal. The beginning is engraved in the timeless primordial and pours out everywhere within space-time-consciousness, past, present, and future. Although we may think in terms of past, present, and future, from the eyes of eternity, creation and the divine revelation is one simultaneous event in space-time-consciousness. There is no past. There is no future. There is only now—always.

The masters of the Tradition say that creation-revelation is a river of light that continually pours forth from the Infinite. The Sefirot of the five Olamot are currents in the river of light and channels of the light through which creation-revelation transpires. The influx of the supernal light is constant—creature and creation are continually flowing out of God and Godhead. The reality-truth continuum of creator and creation is not fixed or static but is in constant flux, continually pouring out of the divine in what appears to be flow and ebb. Everyone and everything is an expression of God's word and wisdom—the light of Messiah. One could say that it is as though God is continually breathing out and breathing in creatures and creation, and that everything is the radiant holy breath of God—the holy and bornless Spirit.

Vessels are continually being created and shattered, and the process of their mending or healing (tikkune) is a continual process. If the Sefirot and Olamot are the macrocosm (the universe or creation) and we are microcosms (the universe or creation in miniature), then our soul is a vessel constantly being formed, shattered, and reformed at a new level in the

process of creative evolution. While creation speaks of a descent or involution, revelation speaks of an ascent or evolution.

Creature, creation, and the divine revelation are works in progress. The
divine revelation is the purpose of God in creation. Until creature and creation are redeemed—made perfect and complete—and God is made known
in creatures and creation, the process of shattering and tikkune (mending or
healing) will continue on the level of Beriyah, Yetzirah, and Asiyah.

We see this process in the Scriptures: the two stories of creation, the
fall of Adam and Eve, the tower of Babel, the fallen and the flood, the first
tablets of the law which are broken, the rise and fall of the first and second temples, the prophetic succession giving way to the apostolic succession, the crucifixion of Christ and rejection of the Holy Bride, and the
apocalypse. The vessel of a covenant-continuum is formed and then shattered, only to be reformed at a new level in an ascent of conscious evolution. In speaking of the mysteries of the Book of Genesis, the Kabbalah is
speaking of the mysteries of the Book of Revelation.

The Sefirot appear in the Scriptures as the Ten Utterances of Creation,
the Ten Plagues, the Ten Commandments, and the Ten Sayings that open
the Sermon on the Mount. The six days of creation and the holy Shabbat
represent the seven lower Sefirot, as do all things listed in the Book of
Revelation to which the number seven is attributed. The image of the
great angel of the Lord speaking the Book of Apocalypse, itself, is the
image of the Tree of Life.

In the same way that creation is an ever-present process, so also is the
apocalypse. Creation is not the past and the apocalypse is not the future.
Rather, creation and apocalypse are the present reality. Through knowledge of the Sefirot and Olamot, we become conscious co-creators with
God and conscious agents of the divine revelation. It is for this reason
that God has created and is creating the metaphysical structure depicted
in the Kabbalah, so that God might be in relationship with us and we
might be in relationship with God, and we might ultimately evolve to
consciously unite with God and embody God. It is in this light that the
Christian Kabbalah or Gnostic Christianity views the divine incarnation—a call to a conscious evolution toward Christhood (enlightenment
and liberation).

FOUR

KETER, THE HOLY CROWN WHICH IS THE ROOT

Attributes

Thirty-Two Paths of Wisdom: Mystical Consciousness (Sekhel Mufla). This is the Light that was originally conceived, and it is the First Glory; no creature can attain to its excellence

Keter: Holy Crown

Place on the Tree of Life: Head of the Pillar of Compassion in the supernal triad

Divine Name: Eheieh—I am or I shall be; Eheieh Asher Eheieh—I Am That I Am

Alternative Divine Names: El Elyon, God Most High; Atoh, You or Thou Art; Hua, He-She or the One; Ain, No-Thingness

Partzuf Above: Atik Yomin, Ancient of Days; Arik Anpin, Big Face or Long Face

Partzuf Below: Enoch

Divine Image: Ancient, bearded king, viewed in profile

Archangel: Metatron

Order of Angels: Hayyot Ha-Kodesh, Holy Living Creatures

Celestial Attribute: Reshit Ha-Gilgulim, Beginning of Cycles, First Motion; also the planet Pluto in modern astrology

Titles Given to Keter: The Concealed of the Concealed; the Hidden One; Holy One of Being; Ratzon; the Primordial Point; the Smooth Point; the Point within the Circle; Head-Which-Is-Not; the White Head; Bornless Spirit; Amen, So Be It; Depth of Good; Light of Adam Kadmon; Light of the Messiah; Transparent or Clear Light; Hidden Light; Supernal Light; Light Within; Bornless One; Supernal Being

Level of the Soul: Yechidah, Holy or Divine Spark, Unique Essence

Heavenly Abode: The World of Supernal Light

Spiritual Experience: Ascension or Unification with God and Godhead

Virtue: Supreme Attainment, Attainment of Supernal Being, Self-Made-Perfect, Enlightenment and Liberation, Christhood

Vice: None

Commandment: You shall have no other gods before me (Exodus 20:3)

Sermon on the Mount: You are the light of the world (Matthew 5:14–16)

Angel of the Apocalypse and the Churches: Source of the Light of the Great Angel (Revelation 1:12–16)

The Holy Crown

We must smile often, and even chuckle a bit, as we explore the Kabbalah, for often we are speaking of the unthinkable, which admittedly is rather funny. Theology means "thinking about God," which is something of an oxymoron, since we cannot actually think about God or Godhead. Theosophy means "God's wisdom," but who among us is wise as God is wise? Yet we are destined to turn our thoughts toward the source of our true being and to seek our holy and supernal root, to be and become that which is God's will or desire for us to be. Theology and theosophy is our doing exactly that, which in turn leads to prayer and meditation, sacred ritual and worship, and thus something of a direct spiritual or mystical experience. In the mystical experience, we go beyond theology and the theologian, and enter into the realm of theosophy—sharing in something of God's wisdom—although, indeed, that wisdom runs deep and is unfathomable.

Keter is God's will or desire from which God's word-wisdom emanates—the silent and supernal will, which is the life-will of all creatures and creation. The Thirty-Two Paths of Wisdom speaks of this Sefirah as the primordial light and calls it the "first glory," saying "no creature can attain its excellence." It is akin to the instant before the big bang from which our universe came into being—a primordial singularity that is inconceivable. When Keter is called the smooth point, what is meant is that it cannot be grasped or comprehended by the mental being at all. It is completely supernal or supramental.

This Sefirah is the first mystery, which is to say the ultimate mystery, that can never be grasped by finite creatures like ourselves. A truth-seeker may probe and explore only so far into the origin of the universe and the being of God. Beyond that threshold, one may go no further. This "ring-pass-not" or event horizon is Hokmah, and Keter is beyond it. Therefore, the Zohar calls Hokmah "Reshit," meaning the beginning, the point beyond which there is nothing knowable.

Within Keter, there is no-thingness to be found—no individuality or differentiation as we would typically understand it. Keter is infinite and eternal, inseparable from Ain Sof, the one-without-end, as the term "crown" implies, it is beyond the body of creation, and yet is within the body of creation as the secret Sefirah Da'at (which will be discussed in detail later). The key word for Keter is transcendent!

Free Will and the Principle of Uncertainty

Often in orthodox Christian theology, God's will is spoken of as something predetermined, as though, with God, everything is absolutely determined. In a certain sense, this is true. However, it is equally false. On the one hand, this represents a finite egoistic projection upon God or reality to make it like we wish it would be; on the other hand, it expresses the truth of eternity to which past, present, and future are one simultaneous event. As inconceivable as it may be to us, God is both a principle of certainty and, at the same time, a principle of uncertainty.

God has fashioned a creation that has free will inherently woven into its very fabric, and if we are to assume that creation is a reflection of the creator, then God must also have free will. Free will is only possible if there is a principle of uncertainty. This is reflected in the prophets and the prophecies. God communicates God's ratzon to the prophets—the prophecy—as a guide to humankind. Humanity can choose to act according to that Will or can choose not to act in harmony with it. Whatever is spoken in prophecy is not engraved in stone, as the saying goes, but rather is subject to change. In creation, humanity itself is a principle of uncertainty; humankind may or may not enact God's ratzon. Correspondingly, God responds according to the choices human beings make to guide humanity toward its divine destiny. While we can say that the ultimate fruition or destiny of creation is predetermined, how, when, and where it will arrive at that fruition is uncertain. Thus, there is a principle of uncertainty and a principle of certainty that interact in creation.

We can liken this relationship to a chess master playing a novice chess player. There are certain rules of the game that both players agree to follow—and thus there is a game. However, how both players will apply those rules is uncertain. Hence, it remains to be seen at the outset of the game. The master and the novice play by the same rules. Yet the chess master can manipulate the play of the novice, responding to each move of the novice to direct the game as he or she desires. In the case of a master playing a novice, the outcome of the game is pretty much certain. The master chess player will win, but exactly how the master player will win is uncertain; no one can predict what the moves of the novice will be. This is akin to God's relationship with creation via the law upon which creation is founded. The law is certain and the ultimate outcome is certain, but how everything will be played out is uncertain. This principle of uncertainty and principle of certainty is Keter-Da'at—the principle of uncertainty being Keter.

The Self That Is No-Self

Keter is the first and highest of the Sefirot, representing the source of all beginnings and the sovereignty and authority of God over all forces of creation. On the one hand, Keter is Ain Sof; on the other hand, as the first of the ten Sefirot, Keter is distinct from Ain Sof. Keter is completely concealed in Ain Sof; yet, although concealed, it is revealed through the

Sefirot that emanate from it. Therefore, it is called Ain, or nothingness, and Ani, or selfhood.

This can be understood in the following way. The most primary relationship of creator and creation is cause and effect. When something acts as a cause, it is called Ani, but when the same cause is viewed as the effect of a higher cause, it is Ain. Thus, Keter, as the emanation and vehicle of Ain Sof, is Ain-nothingness, being nullified in the sense that it does not have any independent existence. In relationship to the Sefirot, however, it is Ain-selfhood because it is the cause of which they are the effect. Keter is not known directly, but only through the effects of which it is the cause.

This is like the phenomenon of a black hole in space, which is *seen* only by its effects upon objects around it, namely, the forms of matter, energy, and light it devours. If Keter is like the big bang to the Sefirot and Olamot, perhaps it is akin to a black hole in relationship to Ain Sof. This description of Keter has become common among modern initiates of the Kabbalah.

There is a saying in the Kabbalah: "Keter is in Malkut and Malkut is in Keter." This suggests that the potential of Malkut, the last Sefirah, is contained in Keter, and the actualization of Keter is contained in Malkut. The most essential connection, though, is found in Ain-Ani, for Malkut is also called both Ain-nothingness and Ani-selfhood. Keter expresses God's sovereignty over creation, while Malkut is God's holy Shekinah within creation—God's causal relationship with creation. Therefore, Malkut is as the person of God immanent in creature and creation, thus being called Ani. But Malkut is the ultimate effect of the divine cause, an empty vessel whose existence is completely dependent upon the Sefirot above it, and so it is also called Ain.

This teaching holds an important truth regarding the human experience, for much the same may be said regarding our own true being or self. The Hebrew word for "I" is Ani, which is spelled with the same letters as the word Ain, which means "nothingness." There is, thus, the suggestion that the real I or me is the no-thingness within me.

We all have a sense of this truth, but never looking deeply into it, rather than something liberating, it serves as a source of frustration and bondage. The feeling of oneself as nothing leads to the play of insecurity and arrogance from which all other forms of negativity arise, but that is only because of our ignorance regarding the true nature of Ain within us. While it is a negative state in the sense of being receptive, it is a dynamic capacity for light or darkness, good or evil. This no-thingness is, in fact, our connectedness to God and to Keter. It is our capacity to unite ourselves with God and to act as channels or vehicles of something divine.

To gain insight into this, we can turn inward and go looking for the I or self. Everyone will agree that they experience a sense of self in much the same way as they experience thought. Descartes made this observation when he said, "I think, therefore I am." However, like the source of thought, if one goes looking for the self, one will not find the self. When one is not looking for the self, there is a sense of self. Yet the instant one turns inward to look at the self, the self vanishes. Thus, through meditation upon the self, we discover that the self is no-self, just as the source of thought is no-thingness. This real self and the source of our thoughts is Ani-Ain.

In the Gospels, Yeshua says, "I do nothing of myself, but I do what I see my Father doing." Likewise, he also says, "I and the Father are one" and "He who has seen me has seen the Father." All of these statements refer directly to Hokmah, which is Abba-Father; however, they also relate to Keter. The nature of Keter, which is Ani-Ain, is the nature of all the Sefirot and the nature of all creatures and creation. The I or me that Lord Yeshua is speaking about is Ani, which is Ain. This realization of Ani-Ain is the realization of the Christ-self, our true self, which is enlightenment and liberation as demonstrated in the life of Yeshua Messiah.

The teaching being addressed here, as with everything of Keter, is extremely subtle and sublime. In truth, it cannot be communicated outside of the experience of Christ consciousness. Apart from the actual experience, we can only allude to it. But this self-realization reflects the key secret of the magical Kabbalah and all of the "miracles" performed by Yeshua. We may approach this secret by saying that if the essence and nature of everything is no-thing then anything can be transformed into something else, because in its root it is neither "this" nor "that."

Consider the first magical act of Lord Yeshua recounted in the Gospel of St. John. Yeshua changes water into wine at the wedding feast of Cana. The Master can do this because the root essence and nature of water and wine are the same—Ain. Thus, dissolving the Ani of water into Ain, he brings forth the Ani of wine. Although other principles are also involved, depending on the nature of the spiritual work to be accomplished, this applies to every magical act that the Master performs,

In terms of self-realization, this is also an important key—for with this gnosis of Ani-Ain, one is not bound to one limited manifestation of self or personal history. One is free to personal growth and change of oneself—a conscious evolution toward one's Christ-self. At the very heart of the path of self-realization is the ability to dissolve one manifestation of Ani into Ain and thus to remanifest Ani at a higher level. Rather than a fixed or static state, the enlightenment of Christ consciousness is dynamic and active—a quickening of the pace of the evolution of the soul-being—so that, rather than arriving at some fixed point, one is actually in more rapid motion. One might say that a person enlightened by Messianic consciousness is evolving at the speed of light instead of the typical snail's pace of the ordinary earthbound soul.

Ultimately, this process of conscious evolution involves the drawing down of spiritual energies into the physical dimension and integrating the highest levels of consciousness into a person's life. A human being truly resembles Christ when, after transcending his or her own selfhood and recognizing his or her essence is somehow one with Christ and therefore God, he or she realizes life itself as an awesome gift of love and compassion that must be shared with others. In the same way God is immanent in creatures and creation, and constantly labors to bring the world to its ultimate perfection; the purpose of the human being is to labor for a new heaven and new earth. When the human being connects his or her will to God's will, his or her potential for transforming the world into a heavenly kingdom (Malkut) is unlimited (without end). This is what is called the great work, the nature of which is love and charity.

The Being of the Becoming

Keter at the level of Atzilut is the divine name Eheieh, which literally means "I am" or "I shall be." This divine name, which is the highest name of God, appears in the Torah in Moses' experience of the burning bush (Exodus 3:14). The prophet Moses asks God what name he should proclaim God by, and God responds, saying "Eheieh Asher Eheieh"—"I Shall Be That I Shall Be" or "I Am Who I Am."

Eheieh is Keter, Asher is Malkut, thus to say Eheieh Asher Eheieh is to speak of an involution that conceals the supernal light of Keter in Malkut and an evolution that ultimately reveals the supernal light. This God name is reflected in the incarnation of the Soul of Messiah and is the ultimate fruition of the divine incarnation in the resurrection and ascension of Yeshua Messiah.

Like the Tetragrammaton (Yahweh), in Hebrew, Eheieh is composed of four holy letters: Aleph (א)-He (ה)-Yod (י)-He (ה). Aleph is the first letter of the Hebrew alphabet and represents the Spirit and Light of God. It is the number one and, as a word, it means "ox" or "yoke"—the object that directs an ox while plowing the field. With this meaning in mind, we may recall the saying of the Anointed: "Come to me, all you who are weary and are carrying heavy burdens, and I will give you rest. Take my yoke upon you, and learn from me; for I am gentle and humble in heart, and you will find rest for your souls. For my yoke is easy and my burden is light" (Gospel of St. Matthew 11:28–30). This alludes to Aleph as the power of the Spirit of Messiah.

Aleph is also the first letter of the name Adam, hence Adam Kadmon, and the first letter in the word Atzilut. This suggests that Aleph is the very essence of the realm of Yichud. In the name Adam, the Aleph means spirit and Dalet (ד)-Mem (ם) means blood; thus the name Adam literally means spirit in the blood. To speak of the blood of Christ, which gives enlightenment and liberation, is thus to speak of the power of Aleph drawn down from Keter and the realm of Yichud.

Aleph also begins the words *achad* (unity) and *ahava* (love), which is the very essence of the Gospel of peace. The number of both these words is thirteen and therefore they are reflected in Yeshua Messiah and the twelve disciples. Aleph is the light or power of Messiah, which is Ain Sof Or.

Contemplating the shape of the letter Aleph, the masters of the Tradition say that it is composed of two Yods connected by a Vau, suggesting the realm of Yichud above and the realm of Perud below or the union of the spiritual world and the material world. This is the basic function of the divine incarnation of the Messiah and of all human beings.

The letter He appears twice in both Eheieh and the Tetragrammaton. It represents the divine matrix or divine feminine principle through which the divine potential is actualized and revealed. He is the number five and, as a word, it means "window"—something through which light and air (spirit) passes or enters. The first He is the upper world in which the light or Spirit of God is revealed; the second He is the lower world in which the light or Spirit of God is concealed.

Yod is the number ten and means "hand." Its shape looks like a seed. This is the seed of supernal light brought down via the incarnation and suggests the inmost part of the soul of light, Yechidah, which it is the purpose of the human being to realize and embody. Yod of the Tetragrammaton is Adam Kadmon and Atzilut; thus it is this supernal force that is being invoked and brought down through this holy name of God.

The Yod stands in between the two He in the same way that Yeshua Messiah stands in between the Holy Mother and Bride, or Tiferet stands in between Binah and Malkut. Thus as Eheieh is the essential name of Yahweh, it is also the essential name of Yeshua.

The Gospels are filled with "I am" sayings of the Master: "Before Abraham was, I am"; "I am the Way, and the Truth, and the Life"; "I am the gate." The Gospel of St. John places special emphasis on the connection between Lord Yeshua and Eheieh, giving more "I am" sayings than any other Gospel.

Eheieh actually says, "I am within creation, yet ever beyond creation"—hence the cosmic and primordial Christ, respectively. This truth is spoken in verse 77 of the Gospel of St. Thomas: "It is I who am the Light which is above them all. It is I who am the all. From me did all come forth, and unto me did the all extend. Split a piece of wood, and I am there. Lift up the stone, and you will find me."

Eheieh also says, "I am the being of the becoming, the one who is changeless and the one who is ever changing—the bornless Spirit." God is transcendental being, within yet ever beyond the becoming. There is that of God which is without change and there is that of God which is evolving in creation. This may be understood as follows: if everything is always changing, then the one thing that does not change is change itself. One may also understand it in terms of Ain and Ani. Ain-nothingness never changes, but Ani-selfhood is always changing. This is true both in

terms of the creator and of creation, which share the same essence and nature. Like the principles of certainty and uncertainty, the principle of
changelessness and change is integral to the Christian Kabbalah. The radical message is this: God, the creator, is ever-coming into substantial
being and evolving through creation!

To gain gnosis of Yeshua Messiah thus means to know the being of
one's becoming and to realize that supernal being within oneself. The
power of this self-realization in Messianic consciousness is Keter or
Eheieh—the Divine I Am.

In the context of the divine name of Eheieh, one may consider the
third commandment, which corresponds to Binah: "Do not make wrongful use of the name of the Lord your God." If we take the name Eheieh in
conjunction with this verse and consider Eheieh not only as the name of
God above, but also as the name of our true self, then we will realize that
we use this holy name every time we say "I am this" or "I am that." Wrongful use of the name would be any time we append the name "I am" to any
negation of ourselves or, equally, to any negation of another person by
saying "you are." The proper use of this divine name is only for affirmation—in phrases that affirm the spirit and truth and uphold the dignity of
the indwelling Christ.

We are constantly using this divine name, saying "I am this" or "I am
that." Any time it is used to negate, demean, or degrade oneself (or others
with "you are"), the Gnostic considers it a "sin"—a missing the mark of
truth. Any time a Gnostic initiate hears him- or herself speaking a negation, he or she corrects his or her error through affirmations. Affirmations
using "I am"—such as "I am part of the sacred unity God is and never am I
lacking" or "I am a child of light, the dark ones have no power over me,"
and so on—are a common spiritual practice in modern Gnosticism and the
New Age. When we speak in such a way so as to uplift ourselves and others, we are uplifted. It is a simple and basic truth—the power of Eheieh.

The Christ-Self and True Will

Tiferet is called the Christ center on the Tree of Life because it represents
the indwelling Christ within the individual, what may be called the inner
self. The Christ-self proper, however, is attributed to Keter, for it is in

Keter that Yechidah abides. This is the higher and transcendental self, the transpersonal Christ-presence, which is bornless being.

Christian Gnosticism teaches three principle aspects of the Christos: the primordial Christ, the cosmic Christ, and the indwelling Christ. The primordial Christ is the transcendental aspect of the Christos, corresponding to the universe of Adam Kadmon. The cosmic Christ is the immanent aspect of the Christos—Christ in all creatures and the whole of creation—corresponding to the universe of Beriyah. Thus the universe of Atzilut links the primordial and cosmic Christ. The indwelling Christ is the manifestation of the cosmic Christ within an individual soul-being. It is through the indwelling Christ that we are able to realize the cosmic Christ and to experience something of the primordial Christ. Although distinctly different levels of the Christos, these three are completely interconnected and inseparable. There is one Christos, one light-presence.

These three levels of the Christos are represented by the Sefirot of Tiferet (indwelling Christ), Da'at (cosmic Christ), and Keter (primordial Christ). Thus, in Ruach is the gnosis of the indwelling Christ, in Neshamah is the gnosis of the cosmic Christ, and in Yechidah is the Gnosis of the primordial Christ. The cosmic and indwelling Christ are reflections of the primordial Christos within space-time-consciousness, and more than the reflection of the Christ-self, they are the presence of the Christ-self in the realm of becoming.

When we speak of the Christ-self proper, or Yechidah, we are referring to the real or ultimate "I am" that cannot be known. It is the intangible source of one's will and desire energy that impels one in a conscious evolution. It is higher than thought, for it is clear that it is what tells the mind to think. Because this will-desire is on a level beyond thought and mental being, it is impossible to imagine it even though it is within and behind one's experience all of the time. This true self is our true will.

As previously said, one meaning of Yechidah is "uniqueness," which suggests true individuality. This uniqueness is reflected in our Neshamah as a true will or mission of the soul that spans all incarnations. Of this level of our true will, it is said that it is possible to fulfill it in any incarnation. Hence, it is possible to fulfill the soul's mission in this present life. Within the incarnate person or Nefesh, this true will is the Ruach and it represents the purpose or mission of the soul in the present life, which to some degree, more or less, reflects the overall true will or mission of our Neshamah throughout all lives. These two levels of true will are expressions of the Christ-self.

Often, we may hear teachings on God's will for us and think of God's will as something outside of us, b ut nothing could be further from the truth. God's will for us, which is our true will, is part of our innate being, woven into our individuality, so that, in being who and what we are, we naturally and spontaneously do God's will.

Unfortunately, very few people know themselves and therefore very few people are able to truly be themselves and to fully enact their true will. Often, we are trying to be somebody else or chasing after the things others desire, never actually considering who we are and what we truly desire. Likewise, when we are aware of something of our true will, we are often afraid to enact it because of concern for what others might think, or fear of failure, but as the saying goes, "Nothing ventured, nothing gained." As for what people might think, one's true will is not going to harm others; it will only serve to benefit and uplift others. It will not violate the divine law, but will be in harmony with the law and will fulfill the law. True will, which is the expression of Yechidah, is all-good.

Your true will is not something remote or hidden from you. It is revealed in your true heart's desire, your abilities and talents, and your inclinations surrounding these. We cannot say that enacting our true will might not entail hard work, but on the other hand, it will certainly be something that comes naturally to us in the sense that we will naturally shine when we are doing it. In the actual experience of *doing* our true will, it will ultimately be effortless, for we will find that the egoistic self is not the doer, but rather that Christ in us is the doer and all cosmic forces move with us in the action of our true will.

One's true will represents the manifestation of the Christos within oneself—how one will embody Christ. If the Kabbalistic term for this divine will is uniqueness, then how Christ manifests and appears through each and every one of us will be different because we are different and unique individuals. Far from taking upon oneself some dogmatic doctrine imposed on oneself from the outside, Gnosticism is a seeking of the divine will within oneself and living according to it; hence it is a path of self-realization.

The Face of Light

In Atzilut, the Sefirot are the divine names and divine personas—Partzufim. There are five primary Partzufim and the divine name of Elohim has five letters, Elohim being the primary name in the creative process. Masters of the Tradition thus say that the Partzufim each correspond to one of the letters of Elohim: Aleph (א), Arik Anpin; Lamed (ל), Abba; He (ה), Aima; Yod (י), Zer Anpin; and Mem (ם), Nukva or Kallah. The sixth or hidden Partzuf, Atik Yomin, would represent the divine name of Yahweh, which is the source and ground of Elohim.

Atik Yomin and Arik Anpin are the Partzufim of Keter. The image of an ancient, bearded king viewed in profile alludes to the attribute of two Partzufim, the side of the image that is unseen representing Atik Yomin and the side of the face that is seen representing Arik Anpin. Essentially, these two Partzufim represent two aspects of ratzon—will and desire.

Atik Yomin appears in the vision of the prophet Daniel that addresses the eventual conclusion of the Babylonian exile along with prophecies concerning the end of days. The image of the Ancient of Days is an assurance to Israel that God has a plan, even though oftentimes human beings cannot understand it, and that redemption is being worked out in secret at a higher level, which is hidden.

Kabbalah says God restrains Godself in order to reveal Godself. Even if God restrains Godself to reveal something of Godself and the divine will, nevertheless there is always an unknown will that transcends our understanding.

Thus we find that God has two aspects in relationship to us—one that is revealed and one that is hidden. On the one hand, we are not able to fathom God's will because it originates at a level that totally transcends our linear logic. This is the level of Atik Yomin—God's will that cannot be known or understood. On the other hand, there is a part of God's will that operates through linear logic, which involves God constricting God's will in order to make his or her will known to humankind. This will is revealed through prophecy and the divine incarnation, which transpires through the agency of the Sefirot. This is the level of Arik Anpin—the big face of mercy and compassion.

The Tradition teaches that God's will is emanated and that God's will is created. As an emanation of God, it serves as an interface between Ain Sof and creation. As something God has fashioned or created, it serves as the will-force that God uses in order to create. This means that Keter, God's ratzon, is both infinite and finite. The higher or infinite aspect of God's will as an emanation of God is Atik Yomin, the Ancient of Days, while the aspect that God uses to create is Arik Anpin, the Big Face.

Arik Anpin is called a face of light, for this face is composed of the ten Sefirot of Atzilut, which are lights. The same is true of Zer Anpin, the little face below. However, as much as being a face of light, Zer Anpin can also be a face of darkness—hence a countenance of mercy (peace) or a countenance of judgment (wrath). Life, as we experience it, is a dance of beauty and horror. To actually meditate upon reality as it is proves to be a terrifying but very powerful meditation—invoking awe and wonder. As difficult as it is for us to understand, God is that which is within everything that transpires—the beauty and the horror alike. Understanding this in his own prophetic meditation, Isaiah writes, "I form the light and create darkness, I make weal and create woe; I the Lord do all these things" (Isaiah 45:7).

The dance of beauty and horror is properly considered in the discussion of Tiferet and the moral triad, which are lower on the Tree of Life. However, it is relevant here in that Keter represents a level of awareness in which one understands this play of light and darkness as part of God's ultimate plan, and thus as a vehicle of God's ultimate will, which is Keter. At the level of Keter-Hokmah, one becomes aware that both the light and the darkness are the operation of the Holy Spirit and that, ultimately, everything serves to enlighten and liberate living souls—the universe or creation is not restrictive but liberative. It is only our limited view and the play of an illusion-power that makes it seem to us as something restrictive. The vision of Arik Anpin is a supernal or transcendental consciousness in which one is aware of a pure delight within the beauty and horror alike— one could say an awareness of the whole creation as orgasmic bliss.

How this is so will become clearer as our exploration of the Sefirot takes us down the Tree of Life into levels closer to our present experience. In an exploration of Keter and the supernals, one must bear in mind that we are speaking of levels of consciousness that completely transcend our ordinary consciousness. Much of what is said can only be bewildering, representing the supreme mystery. Obviously, only in an altered state of consciousness would we be able to look into the face of horror and see the face of beauty and, therefore, experience pure delight in the midst of great darkness. Nevertheless, at the level of Keter-Hokmah, that is exactly what our experience would be, for there is no duality at this level.

The Initiate and the Great Angel

In the stories of Enoch and the prophet Elijah, the mystery of the resurrection and ascension are prefigured in the Torah. It is Enoch's story that corresponds to Keter—a story in which more is concealed than is revealed in the Scriptures.

> *When Enoch had lived sixty-five years, he became the father of Methuselah.*
> *Enoch walked with God after the birth of Methuselah three hundred years,*
> *and had sons and daughters. Thus all the days of Enoch were three hundred*
> *sixty-five years. Enoch walked with God; then he was no more, because God*
> *took him."* (Genesis 5:21–24)

This is the whole story of Enoch as told in the Book of Genesis. Although brief, it has served to attract a great deal of attention because, while the death of all other characters is recorded in this section of the Torah, of Enoch it is said "God took him," as though to say that Enoch departed this world without tasting death. This is exactly the interpretation given to the phrase "God took him." Enoch did not die but was taken up in ascension. It is the story of Enoch from which the idea of divine rapture is derived. The attribute of Enoch to Keter means that supernal consciousness at the level of Keter and attainment of Yechidah result in the fruition of the ascension. Keter is the principle of divine rapture.

In the Tradition, there are stories within the stories given in the Scripture, as though encoded in the words themselves and in between the lines of what has been written. This is called *Midrash*, and the collection of these stories is called *Midrashim*. The midrash within the story of Enoch is as follows: Enoch walked in the presence of God and became transparent to God's holy Shekinah, so that his body shone with the supernal light of God and was transformed into an angelic image, the Zelem of his divine self. This Zelem is the great angel Metatron, who is set above all angels of God. Thus Enoch became more than human and something more than the angels of God. In the story of Enoch, we have a story of the divine destiny of the human being—the aim of the great work, which is a process of spiritual evolution into something more than human, something divine and supernal.

The word Enoch means "initiate." That he lived sixty-five years before fathering his first child is significant. It is the number of the name of Adonai, which is Malkut and the holy Shekinah below, and it is the number of the Hebrew word for chamber (*hekhal*). Thus this number of years says that the initiate makes him or herself a vessel or chamber for the holy Shekinah, like unto Malkut.

That Enoch lived another three hundred years is also significant. Three hundred is the number of the Hebrew letter Shin (שׁ), which is the letter representing the fiery intelligence (Holy Spirit) through which all initiation occurs. It is the letter inserted into the divine name of Yahweh to form the name of Yeshua (Yahweh delivers). Ruach Elohim also equals three hundred when the letter Mem is counted as forty. The total of three hundred sixty-five is significant as it is the number of days in the solar year and represents the complete journey of the earth around the sun and the sun's journey through all twelve signs of the zodiac, representing completion of the human experience. Therefore, in the story of Enoch in the Torah, we discover the Gospel of Christ in seed form, in the same way we find the whole Tree of Life in seed form at the level of Keter.

As Elijah represents the spirit of the prophets (Ruach Ha-Elijah), Enoch represents the spirit of the initiates (Ruach Ha-Enoch). These two together are the Spirit of the Messiah (Ruach Ha-Messiah). Metatron, which is Keter in Beriyah, represents the great angel of the Initiates, and Sandalfon, which is Malkut in Beriyah, represents the great angel of the prophets. According to an inner and secret teaching, these two great angels are in fact one holy angel—the archangel of Christ, which is called the great angel Hua. This is the holy angel of the apocalypse to which one of the many names of Metatron is given—Torahkiel Yahweh.

Although an archangel can assume a human form in dream and vision, or even generate a material body (body of emanation) and appear like a human being in the physical dimension, an archangel is a vast and inconceivable entity by human standards. A small archangel would be akin to an entity the size of an entire world or a star. One a bit larger might be the size of a constellation of stars. A very large archangel might represent the power of a whole galaxy. In the case of the archangel Metatron, it is said that his body and power would be akin to the entire universe coupled with the abode of supernal light—something completely unimaginable. Yet such a state of supernal being is our divine destiny—the image of Metatron representing a divine humanity. Thus there is a distinct connection between Adam Kadmon and Metatron, which in many Kabbalistic texts are used interchangeably.

One teaching attempting to give some sense to Metatron proposes that the image of Metatron is actually composed of all the divine images of all living souls that have been Christed, are Christed, or will be Christed in this present cosmic cycle—the composite of all enlightened beings.

Let us ground this in something that we can talk about—initiation. That the name of the character whom experiences the divine rapture is called Enoch, suggests that the path of ascension is a process of initiation. Keter is often called the Lord of Initiation. This title is also applied to Lord Yeshua and Lady Mary Magdalene in Christian Gnosticism—the Lord and Lady of Initiation. The idea of initiation in its basic form is quite simple. There is a transmission of spiritual energy passed person to person without which it is unlikely that an aspirant will be able to enter into the higher grades of Christ consciousness. Essentially, great souls of a very high level enter into incarnation to initiate currents of the light transmission. These are the great prophets and apostles of God, or great world teachers, who are said to come from the elder races. Once there is an incarnation of the light-presence, it is passed from one generation of initiates to another, from person to person—the adepts and masters of one generation imparting something of the light-presence to their disciples who form the next generation of initiates. In Gnostic Traditions, this process of initiation is seen as essential to any actual or authentic spiritual advancement, and, therefore, initiation plays a central role in Gnosticism.

Periodically, a new incarnation must appear to restore the light transmission, as over time the current dissipates and becomes diluted. Sometimes such masters restore a stream of the light transmission; other times they act to manifest a higher level of the light transmission. This process of the light-bearers entering into the world to facilitate the great work is one of the meanings of the term Reshit Ha-Gilgulim associated with Keter—the initiation of continuums of the light transmission.

Initiation essentially activates divine potential, which once recognized by an aspirant can then be realized. Some method of activation of latent psychic and spiritual potentials is necessary in the case of most ordinary individuals, as these potentials are largely obscured and unknown to the incarnate soul (Nefesh). We must be reminded of the divine light that is in us so that this inner light might no longer be eclipsed by our physical, vital, and mental being. The spiritual energy of the light-presence that an adept or master imparts to us awakens the light-presence in us. It is like a lighted candle touching another candle, igniting the potential that was latent in it. This is what is meant by initiation, and the methods through which this is done are called vehicles of initiation. Initiation itself corresponds to Keter, the vehicle of initiation corresponds to Malkut, and the self-realization that transpires corresponds to Tiferet.

The Middle Pillar or Pillar of Compassion, of which Keter is the summit, is the path of the great ascension. The apostolic succession is the light transmission through which the way of the ascension is opened to an aspirant in the Christian mysteries. What has been manifest of this divine revelation within space-time-consciousness is Da'at, and what is yet to be manifest is Keter. The apostolic succession continues upon the earth to this very day and the apostles of the light labor toward the second coming, which represents the fruition of the great ascension that is as yet hidden in Keter. The mysteries of this process are hidden in the story of Enoch-Metatron. Essentially, Keter represents the source from which comes the fiery intelligence that initiates. The practice of Gnostic Christianity is simply making oneself receptive to this divine gift of a fiery intelligence (the supernal light of Keter).

The Angels of Grace and the Divine Gift

Keter, at the level of Yetzirah, manifests as the Hayyot Ha-Kodesh (holy living creatures), which are the supreme order of holy angels on the Tree of Life, and are said to stand directly in the inner presence of God, continually worshipping the Lord in the supernal abode. They are otherworldly entities that, if one ever experiences them in an altered state of consciousness, can only be spoken of as something like a very alien presence—having an appearance like nothing the mortal imagination would typically conjure up. It is as though one is gazing upon the image of an entity that is constantly changing forms in an incredibly rapid succession, so that only here and there does one catch a glimpse of a stable image for the briefest instant. This shape-shifting produces the sound of vibration as though of the beating of countless millions of wings, which in turn produces harmonies composed of various frequencies of vibration that cannot be described. The sound is most terrible and most delightful at the same time. To actually describe these supernal beings in terms of linear and finite reason is impossible. It is as though they are the potential for all forms of life, specifically self-aware or intelligent life-forms.

If one experiences the presence of the Hayyot Ha-Kodesh, one has no doubt of life existing in other worlds of the universe or in the existence of higher intelligent life-forms, for one has glimpsed the infinite possibilities of the life-power. In their presence, one becomes aware, on the one hand, of an impulse of evolution within space-time-consciousness toward increasingly more refined and higher forms of life. On the other hand, one also becomes aware of an activity of divine grace beyond the continuum of space-time-consciousness that inspires evolution and imparts the gift of a fiery intelligence that is beyond the intelligence produced by the natural order—an intelligence of a divine order. This is knowledge of how races of intelligent beings appear in worlds.

First life-forms that have the capacity to receive and embody something of the fiery intelligence must evolve through the natural order in a world. These life-forms invoke an influx of the supernal light from the divine order above—the gift, as it were, of a fiery divine intelligence. The reception of this gift quickens the pace of evolution, generating a new race of beings that have the capacity to consciously evolve themselves or to consciously direct their evolution, whether for good or ill—hence the power of the upper Ruach. While this fiery intelligence may descend upon an entire race of beings, typically it descends upon individuals of a life-wave, forming a new race within the present race. This idea of a new and divine race within an intelligent race of the natural order is represented in the Scriptures by the chosen ones or the elect and directly reflects the principle of initiation and the light transmission.

Here, it must be made perfectly clear that the term "race" is not meant to be anything superficial, such as the color of a person's skin. What is meant is something deep within—a quickening of the soul-being. There is light within a child of the light that is of a divine order—and that holy child has a divine intelligence such as children of the natural order do not possess. This is something quite different than anything on the surface. It is seen in the eyes and the aura of a person, and in the direction of their thoughts and emotions, words and deeds.

This principle of a divine election is central to Gnosticism in all its forms. However, in the Sophian Tradition, the idea is not one of elitism but rather one of responsibility and a sacred trust. Not only does this light-presence come from *above*, it is passed from person to person here *below*, and those who receive it are responsible for imparting it to others— to anyone who desires to receive it. If anything, it means that one is an elder brother or sister who is responsible for the well-being of younger siblings—hence charity, which is the reflection of the pure grace of Keter.

Yeshua speaks of this gift of the fiery intelligence quite clearly. For example: "Very truly, I tell you, no one can see the kingdom of God without being born from above" (Gospel of St. John 3:3).

The Hayyot Ha-Kodesh, along with the higher classes of the order of Ashim at the level of Malkut, represents the holy order of angels that transmit this fiery intelligence. Understanding this, an aspirant who is seeking a quickening of the fiery intelligence will invoke the Hayyot Ha-Kodesh and labor to make him- or herself open and sensitive to divine grace.

The Beginning of Generation

Keter manifests in Asiyah as Reshit Ha-Gilgulim. The word "gilgulim" literally means "spinning," "swirling," "revolutions," or "rotations," as in the turning of a wheel. Thus, Reshit Ha-Gilgulim means the "beginning of revolutions" or "first swirling," denoting that Keter is the motivation within and behind the movement of all creatures and creation—the first cause of the universe. As a celestial attribute on the level of the physical universe, this term would apply to the big bang, which was the material genesis of our existence.

This term holds something far more subtle and sublime with regard to the beginning than the idea of a fixed or static starting point. Gilgulim is the word used for the transmigration of souls in the Kabbalah. On a higher level, there is the suggestion not only of the reincarnation of individual souls but of a cosmic reincarnation, as though the matter-energy-light of one universe transmigrates to form a different universe in another dimension—like the passing of the soul of the cosmos from one cosmic body to another.

What was once theory concerning the existence of black holes is now more than merely a theory. Their existence has been discovered. In a certain respect, they are like a cosmic funnel or drain through which matter-energy-light are drawn out of the material universe in which we exist. That being so, the question naturally arises, "Where does the matter-energy-light go?" One theory holds that, if a black hole becomes big enough, which is to say draws in sufficient matter-energy-light, that it becomes the big bang, generating a universe in another dimension. In effect, this represents the idea of the matter-energy-light of one universe pouring out into another universe in a succession of universes without end.

Once upon a time, we thought that our own planet was the center of the entire universe, and thought the heavens revolved around it. Today, we know that is not true. We continue to think of our universe as the center of all creation, but what if that is not true and, in fact, there are countless universes spanning countless dimensions? This is exactly what Kabbalah proposes to us. God is much bigger than we think, and so also is God's creation!

Metaphorically speaking, Keter essentially represents all big bangs and black holes of all universes as one primordial event—the very essence of the principle of black hole-big bangs. At the level of Asiyah, there is one black hole-big bang from which our universe has come into being—the cosmic Christ. At the level of Beriyah there are countless black hole-big bangs generating countless universes, yet at the level of Adam Kadmon and Atzilut, all of these cosmic events are a single primordial event—the primordial Christos.

Using the metaphor of Keter as the principle of the black hole-big bang gives some sense of what may actually be meant by the term Reshit Ha-Gilgulim, as well as some insight into the nature of Keter. For in the same way the singularity at the center of a black hole and at the center of the big bang are both outside of our physical space-time continuum, so is Keter transcendent of our metaphysical continuum of space-time-consciousness. This singularity, whether considered in terms of the physical or metaphysical universe, is the beginning and motivation of everything.

Contemplating the Sefirah Keter in this way, another truth emerges. In the same way that in looking for the self we discover no-self, as explained above, so also in looking for a beginning to creation we find no beginning. If creation spans countless universes pouring out of and into one another, without beginning or end, then whatever we might speak of as the beginning of our universe is merely a relative point of reference. In fact, it is no-beginning because, in the absolute sense, it is not the beginning of creation but only a relative reference point in a continuum of endless light. This is the truth of Reshit Ha-Gilgulim.

Non-Dual Gnostic Awareness

The spiritual attainments of Keter, Hokmah, and Binah are intimately interconnected, for though each of the supernal Sefirot represents a distinct manifestation of supernal being, they are completely inseparable from one another. In speaking about the supreme attainment associated with Keter, we must speak of the spiritual attainments of Hokmah and Binah also, as they are lower grades of the same attainment—supernal or Messianic consciousness.

The spiritual attainment of Binah is cosmic consciousness, which is the threshold of supernal consciousness. Essentially, cosmic consciousness is the peak or fruition of the mental being, the universal mind. All of the Sefirot below Binah, from Malkut to Da'at, represent gradations of the physical, vital, and mental being. The peak of the mental being, the universal mind, actually corresponds with Da'at and not Binah, for cosmic consciousness at the level of Binah is the shift toward supernal consciousness—a shift from the universal mind to the supramental. This distinction is extremely subtle. There is a level of cosmic consciousness that experiences the sacred unity underlying creation, and at that level one feels oneself united with the whole of creation. This is the universal mind of Da'at. However, at this level there is no sense of unification with God and no experience of supernal consciousness. Only at the level of cosmic consciousness associated with Binah is there a true sense of unity with the presence of God and a glimpse of supernal consciousness.

The spiritual attainment of Da'at is the peak of the experience of upper Ruach, with a strong influence of the Neshamah. The spiritual attainment of Binah, however, is the Neshamah itself, which is the first degree of supernal or supramental consciousness. This is a very lofty spiritual attainment, but it is not a complete unification of oneself with supernal consciousness nor is it a full and true unification of oneself with God. Unification with the supernal consciousness proper is the spiritual attainment of Hokmah, which is the second degree of supernal or supramental consciousness. Although unified with the supernal consciousness, however, there still remains a most subtle and sublime separation of oneself and God. The full unification of oneself with God is the supreme attainment associated with Keter. This is the third and final degree of supernal consciousness.

At the level of Binah, the initiate contacts the supernal force; at the level of Hokmah, the initiate merges with supernal consciousness; and at the level of Keter, the initiate is transformed into supernal being. This is all one supernal being-consciousness-force. Yet in the experience of the initiate, these stages are quite distinct and represent very different aspects of the great work. At the level of Binah, the work of the Gnostic initiate is to bring down the supernal force into all levels of consciousness, including the lower vital and physical consciousness, and to transform every level of consciousness with supernal light. Only when this divine labor is fully accomplished can the Gnostic merge him- or herself completely with the supernal consciousness. The work of the Gnostic then becomes one of light transmission on a higher level than at any previous stage of development and, through this light transmission, he or she experiences a conscious unity with God or supernal being. Exactly what this light transmission is, as compared to the labor of the light transmission of the lower grades of adepts and masters, is difficult to convey outside of the actual experience. It would be akin to the difference of being a channel of the light versus being the light-presence itself.

The supernal force has been likened unto a spiritual nuclear fire that transforms everything to be like unto itself. It is a divine power that the adept experiences as coming from above and beyond him- or herself, but ultimately realizes was always within him- or herself. Once this light-force is active in the initiate, he or she *sees* that it is within everyone and everything and that it is the secret center of every particle of matter in creation—hence an awareness of the hidden light. He or she experiences the world of supernal light within and all around him- or herself and, eventually, is able to unite him- or herself with the light-presence completely.

Supernal consciousness is completely beyond the level of mental being; therefore, it is often called a metamind state, or supramental consciousness. At the level of supernal consciousness, there is no thought or thinking, which is the function of the mental being; it is a state of pure radiant awareness. Because there is no conceptualization, there is no subject-object relationship or any other form of dualism in consciousness. It is a state of pure gnosis (knowing) or what is called non-dual Gnostic awareness in which everything is known inwardly and completely. St. Paul was speaking of this supramental consciousness when he wrote: "For now we see in a mirror, dimly, but then we will see face to face. Now I know only in part; then I will know fully, even as I have been fully known" (1 Corinthians 13:12).

In the teachings of Rosicrucian enlightenment, there is a term used for a master who attains self-realization in supernal being—the *Ipsissimus,* which means "one who is him or herself." This idea of supreme attainment is important. First, because it suggests that the attainment is a union with Eheieh or the Divine I Am. Second, because it clearly states that uniqueness or individuality is not lost in the ultimate self-realization or enlightenment but rather that the individual is fulfilled and made complete. Many would consider the peak of enlightenment as though the individual were a drop of saltwater drawn from the cosmic ocean, which in enlightenment is simply merged again with the ocean, individuality being lost in the process. However, that represents a lower or imperfect degree of the enlightenment experience and is not a mature self-realization at all. In a full and true self-realization, it is more like the ocean pouring through the drop of saltwater—God and Godhead becoming the individual. We see this in the person of Yeshua Messiah. Although attaining supernal being, his individuality was in no way compromised or lost but rather was actualized and fulfilled. The individual and the universal are completely interdependent, and neither the individual nor the universal are lost in union.

Likewise, the universalized individual is not lost in union with the supernal or primordial being.

The spiritual attainments of the supernals are the grades of the spiritual masters—the sacred tau—and only the masters can distinguish one grade of attainment from another at this level. Within these levels of attainment there are said to be many different levels. For example, the supreme attainment at the level of Keter is said to be composed of forty planes. Who can say what these planes are except for those who experience them? Even if a perfect master of such a high level of attainment were to speak of them, who among us would be able to comprehend what he or she was saying? Even the most general and superficial explanation given here can be difficult to understand, let alone anything more detailed and in depth. It is all "a finger pointing at the moon," as the saying goes!

It does not really matter whether or not we understand what is said of these higher levels of attainment. We need to hear it so that we can open our minds and hearts to the divine possibility, have faith in it, and consciously evolve ourselves toward it. We may not understand the mystery of the resurrection and ascension at the outset of our mystical journey. But because Master Yeshua revealed it to us through the drama of the incarnation, we know it is part of our divine destiny and we are able to actively aspire toward it through our faith. It is for this reason that we speak of the supernals and their spiritual attainments—in order to plant seeds of light in our consciousness that we might nurture to fruition. The attainment of supernal consciousness is our noble ideal or spiritual hope.

Spiritual Practices for the Holy Crown

Simple Being

Anywhere you like, sit down and just be. Let your body find its own natural rhythm of breath. Relax, yet remain alert. Gently set your mind upon your breath, focusing upon the exhalation and the space at the end of the exhalation, letting your mind enter into that gap. Do not close your eyes while you do this. Keep them at least partially open, so that while having perhaps a third of your attention upon the breath, two-thirds remains free, completely aware of where you are and everything that is transpiring. After you have followed your breath in this way for some time, let go of the breath and just be, aware of God's presence within and all around you. You are perfect as you are; everything is perfect as it is. It is enough, just being! Praise God!

The Power of Affirmation—Innate Goodness

There is an innate goodness/godliness in us. It is our soul of light. The divine name of Keter, Eheieh, reminds us of this goodness and of the power of affirmation when we use the phrase "I am" in conjunction with a positive phrase about ourselves. Through affirmations, we draw upon our innate goodness and invoke the blessings of the Holy One upon ourselves. Affirmations can be in all manner of forms, from purely spiritual or heavenly to practical or earthly—the two, in fact, being one and the same. Affirmations that we create for ourselves tend to be more powerful, as they are in our own language or way of speaking, and are an expression of the creative spirit that we are at the level of our inmost being. The following are examples of possible affirmations:

- ➤ I am the light of the world, the light of the Messiah is in me, and I will let the light shine from within me

- ➤ I am the holy vessel of the Christ-presence, and I am at-one with the Christ-presence; as I walk in the world, I bear forth the Light of Christ

- ➤ I am a holy person, the Holy Spirit works with, in, and through me to accomplish everything good—I am successful in all that I do

- ➤ I am good at my work; I can and I will be able to do every task given to me well—I will shine in my job

- ➤ I am healthy and happy; I am successful and prosperous

- ➤ I am empowered by the Holy Mother and illuminated by the Holy Bride—I am a child of light

- ➤ I am loving and will experience love

- ➤ I am an intelligent person and will understand whatever I choose to study

- ➤ I am always in the embrace of the beloved and always under divine protection

➢ I am never powerless, for the holy Shekinah is with me

➢ I am connected to all that lives—all creatures are my relations

➢ I am a creative person, creativity comes naturally to me

Any time you notice insecurity, fear, or any negativity surrounding something, it is good to actively respond with affirmations. Even when there is already a positive flow, it is good to support and encourage the positive flow with affirmations. The aim of the Gnostic initiate is to make a habit of affirmation rather than negation—to use the creative power wisely.

When you wish to engage in affirmation, first intone the divine name of Eheieh, pronouncing it *ee-high-yah*. Chant the divine name several times, remembering the truth of Keter and the inmost part of your holy soul, the Yechidah (divine spark or Christ-self). Then clearly and consciously repeat your affirmation ten times, preferably out loud. Using the divine name before repeating your affirmation invokes the corresponding divine power into it. When the divine name and affirmation are spoken with full concentration, what you speak will be: Amen. Have complete faith in the affirmations you speak and the power of the divine name, allowing no doubt to enter—have faith in your soul of light and the Christ-self.

In place of Eheieh, other divine names can also be used that correspond directly to the intention of your affirmation. For example, an affirmation of abundance corresponds to Hesed. Therefore, the divine name "El" could be used in place of Eheieh, drawing upon the divine power of Hesed, which directly relates to abundance in all its forms. In the case of another divine name, you would call to mind the truth of that Sefirah and the corresponding aspect of the Christ-self. As you become more familiar with the Sefirot, you can use the divine name that specifically relates to the intention of your affirmation-invocation.

FIVE

DA'AT,
THE SECRET
SEFIRAH

Attributes

Thirty-Two Paths of Wisdom: Nothing is said of the Hidden Sefirah in The Thirty-Two Paths of Wisdom; however, masters of the Gnostic Tradition have said this: "This is the Holy Sefirah of True Gnosis, which the Lord communicated to St. Lazarus; it is the secret knowledge of the One who descends and ascends, known only to the living ones who are no longer among the dead; it is the Holy Prism through which the Light passes to become the Rainbow Glory of the Lord"

Da'at: Gnosis or Knowledge

Place on the Tree of Life: Between Keter and Tiferet

Divine Name: Yahweh Elohim

Alternative Divine Names: Io Adonai; IAO

Partzuf Above: Crown of Zer Anpin

Partzuf Below: Seth; St. Lazarus

Divine Image: The Great Angel of the Apocalypse; the Holy Lamb with seven horns and seven eyes

Archangel: The Archangels of the Cardinal Directions—Raphael, Gabriel, Michael and Uriel; the Great Angel Hua, Angel of the Apocalypse; Abaddon, the Angel of the Pit

Celestial Attribute: Neptune; Sirius; Void Space

Titles Given to Da'at: The Secret or Hidden Sefirah; the Midnight Sun; Secret Star of Grace; the Empty Tomb; the Upper Room; Universal Mind; Fire of the Pentecost; Gate of the Abyss; the Pit; the Great Inane; the Great Void; the Abyss; the Gnosis of the Trapezoid; the Cosmic Illusion-Power; Dominion of the Demiurgos and Archons; Depth of Void

Level of the Soul: Peak of the Upper Ruach; Base of the Holy Neshamah

Heavenly Abode: All seven heavens and seven hells

Spiritual Experience: Vision of the Play of Cosmic Forces or Vision of the Apocalypse; Gnosis of the Cosmic Christ; Universal Mind or Cosmic Consciousness; Baptism of Pentecostal Fire

Virtue: Transpersonal Awareness; Detachment; Spiritual Hope; Integrity

Vice: Disillusionment; Doubt; Double-mindedness; Pride; Cowardice; Apathy

Symbols: Prism; Crystal ball; Prison cell; Empty room; Sacred Mountain; A grain of wheat; The complete absence of all symbols; The figure of the trapezoid with an inverted pentagram within it

Commandment: I am the Lord your God (Exodus 20:2)

Sermon on the Mount: Do not think that I have come to abolish the law or the prophets; I have not come to abolish but to fulfill (Matthew 5:17–18)

Angel of the Apocalypse and the Churches: Image of the Holy Angel

The Open Secret

Da'at follows after Hokmah and Binah on the Tree of Life, but it is properly spoken of following a discussion of Keter. It is intimately linked to the mystery of Keter and represents a secret connection between Arik

Anpin, the big face, and Zer Anpin, the little face—Keter and Tiferet, respectively. On the one hand, Da'at is the known or revealed aspect of Keter; on the other hand, it is a secret or concealed aspect of Tiferet.

Keter and Da'at are basically the internal and external manifestations of the same thing. In the previous chapter, we saw that Keter is akin to a person's essential will or volition. Keter is a person's inner selfhood and inmost volition. Da'at is the intelligence that a person shows outwardly to the world, composed of all the qualities through which the self or person is known.

In relationship with Hokmah and Binah, like its relationship with Keter, Da'at is also external. Hokmah and Binah are completely internal processes, the radiant awareness of the mind and the thoughts and understanding formed in the mind. Da'at is a person's ability to express or communicate his or her intelligence to others. Thus Da'at is the revelation of a person's intelligence, understanding, and wisdom, as well as all qualities that may arise from such knowledge or the lack of knowledge.

Da'at, in relationship to Tiferet, is hidden. For, in truth, Da'at is within and behind what is known of a person. It is the capacity and will to communicate, and it is the substance of what can be communicated—the intelligence of a person. However, there is always something of a person's intelligence that is hidden, and we do not really ever know the whole person. First, there are always aspects of a person that he or she does not choose to share or communicate. Second, it is impossible for a person to share or communicate the whole of his or her intelligence. Therefore, what is or can be communicated is limited and something is always hidden or concealed.

What is true of Da'at in terms of a human person is basically true in terms of the person of God and that is what the Sefirot represent—the impersonal God or consciousness-force that becomes personal in order to be linked to or in relationship with creatures and creation. However, in speaking of limitations upon God's ability to communicate or reveal Godself, it is not actually a limitation of God but rather the limitation of creatures to receive God's communication of Godself. God communicates Godself to the degree that creatures are able to receive God's communication. What is it that God desires to give or communicate to us? God wants to give us Godself. When we are completely open and sensitive to God's presence,

God reveals Godself in full. This is the perfection and completion of creation.

The Torah and the Gospel—Da'at

In the previous chapter, we spoke of the principle of uncertainty and the principle of certainty in relationship to Keter-Da'at. Da'at is the principle of certainty in creation, being God's knowledge, which is absolute and deterministic. The psalmist speaks of this principle when he writes, "The Lord has sworn and will not change his mind, you are a priest forever according to the order of Melchizedek" (Psalm 110:4).

The Torah and Gospel, and all the Scriptures of the world wisdom traditions correspond to Da'at. Creation is founded upon the Torah or cosmic law, behind which is the principle of sacred unity represented by the supernals. The purpose or aim of creation, however, is the Gospel, which is the fulfillment of the law and the prophets—the revelation of God to creatures and creation and, yet more, within creatures and creation.

When it is said that creation is founded upon the Torah, it is akin to the idea of a game, which is founded upon certain rules. The rules of a game make the game itself. Without the rules, there is no game. The same is true of the cosmic law upon which creation and the existence of creatures are founded. Without it, the heavens and earth would not exist because they are made by the law.

Within and behind all world wisdom traditions, there is a primordial Tradition from which they are all derived. If we were to speak of this primordial Tradition as a light transmission, Da'at would be the holy prism through which the light passes, becoming the rainbow rays of the different light transmissions that form the world wisdom traditions. All are expressions of the same supernal light, but each is a distinct and unique manifestation of the light—a current in the great river of the divine revelation. Da'at is the Gnosis of primordial Tradition, and it is the gnosis of each individual world wisdom tradition. When speaking of the Torah as the foundation of all creation, we are actually speaking about the primordial Tradition within and behind the Scriptures, which is within and behind the Scriptures of other wisdom traditions as well.

The spiritual realization of an adept who attains the level of Da'at is the awareness that things manifest as he or she expects them to manifest and, likewise, it is the awareness that things appear corresponding to one's angle of view. He or she realizes the cosmic illusion-power or principle of relativity spiritually. Thus, Da'at is going to appear according to the way or tradition of the aspirant who approaches it. To the Gnostic Christian, this Gnosis or knowledge (Da'at) appears in the form of the Torah and Gospel and the secret wisdom of the Kabbalah contained in these Scriptures. To the adept of another wisdom tradition, Da'at will assume the form of his or her own Scriptures and the esoteric wisdom they contain. It is the same truth and light, but the appearance is relative to the observer at this level. Essentially, a tradition is a vehicle of attainment and a spiritual language through which the attainment is communicated. What is actually attained and communicated transcends any single tradition.

The inmost secret essence of the Scriptures is the primordial Tradition, of which the written and oral Torah and Gospel are an outward expression. It is this inmost secret essence—the primordial law and Tradition—that is being spoken of when masters of wisdom say "the Torah is the foundation of creation and the Gospel is the fulfillment of creation."

There is a secret contained in the verse of Psalm 110 quoted above. In the Scriptures of our Western Tradition, the order of Melchizedek is a code word for the primordial Tradition, which is the source of all wisdom traditions. A holy priest-king of the order of Melchizedek is an adept who realizes the primordial Tradition within and behind his or her own wisdom tradition and therefore becomes an initiate of the primordial Tradition.

The first degree of this holy order corresponds to the spiritual attainment of Binah, which is called Magister Templi in Rosicrucian teachings and, as previously discussed, is a direct contact with the supernal light-force. It is through this attainment that an adept becomes a master of his or her tradition.

According to the anonymous author of the Letter to the Hebrews, the incarnation of the Soul of Messiah in the person of Lord Yeshua is to be understood as the incarnation of the high priest of the order of Melchizedek—hence the incarnation of the soul of the great world-teacher or primordial Christos. The Gnosis of Yeshua Messiah is therefore the Gnosis of the order of Melchizedek—the primordial light transmission.

The inmost secret level of initiation in Christian Gnosticism is called the Melchizedek teachings. According to the introduction given to the

Melchizedek teachings, the Soul of the Messiah entered into twenty-six worlds before the incarnation on planet earth, and thus the light transmission passed through many worlds before entering into this world. The last world through which it passed before the incarnation in our world was a world orbiting the star Sirius. For this reason, Sirius is one of the celestial attributes of the hidden Sefirah. Because the light transmission passed through other worlds, and thus other races, Da'at is also said to be the point of contact with initiates of the elder race—initiates of the order of Melchizedek or what some have called *ascended masters*. This would include initiates who attained in our own world and those who attained in other worlds. According to legend, the Soul of Yeshua previously attained supernal consciousness in the star system of Sirius. Then through a series of incarnations in our race, the Soul of Yeshua brought the supernal light into our life-wave, until finally embodying the Soul of Messiah or supernal being here on earth in the person of Yeshua Messiah. This legend suggests that souls who attain Christ consciousness on earth may eventually become the incarnation or light-bearer to other worlds.

As fantastic as these ideas sound, whether taken literally or metaphorically, they express something of the reality and experience of adepts contacting Da'at. In the experience of Da'at, one may well find the actual experience far more fantastic than anything that can be said of it.

The Foundation of Knowledge

When Keter turns toward Ain Sof, Da'at appears on the Tree of Life; when Keter turns toward the Sefirot below, Da'at vanishes from the Tree of Life. As the *Sepher Yetzirah* says, there are always ten Sefirot appearing on the Tree of Life, not nine or eleven, but always ten. The appearance of Da'at maintains the balance of ten Sefirot when Keter merges with Ain Sof. But where does Da'at go when it disappears? The answer to this is that Da'at exists in a different dimension than the other Sefirot. In the rapid oscillation of Keter disappearing and reappearing, Da'at is *here* and *there* simultaneously. Essentially, Da'at is the Yesod-foundation of the universe beyond this present universe of our experience. Thus, Da'at of Asiyah is Yesod of Yetzirah. For the Olamot are not really separate from one another, but rather are interconnected and interpenetrate one another—one figure of the Tree of Life overlapping another.

If you look at the Tree of Life glyph (see figure 4, below), you will see that there are two great triangles on the glyph, an upper one and a lower one. The upper triangle is formed by Hokmah, Binah, and Tiferet; the lower triangle is formed by Netzach, Hod, and Malkut. It is at this place

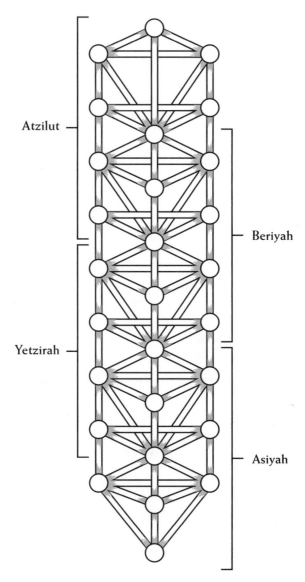

Figure 4. The Composite Tree of Life.

on the Tree of Life that the trees of different universes overlap, one Tree of Life glyph locking together with another to form the great Tree of Life. Thus the Hokmah, Binah, and Tiferet of a lower universe are the Netzach, Hod, and Malkut of the universe just above it. Likewise, Da'at of the lower universe is the Yesod of the higher universe—actually having its existence in another dimension.

Keter of a lower universe is the Tiferet of a higher universe, except in the universe of Adam Kadmon; and Malkut of a higher universe is the Tiferet of a lower universe, except in the universe of Asiyah. Yesod is the holy Sefirah that links Tiferet and Malkut; therefore, Da'at is a secret link between Keter and Tiferet in Atzilut, Beriyah, and Yetzirah. Yesod is the foundation of Da'at knowledge.

From the discussion of the primordial Tradition that is the source of the world wisdom traditions in the last section, the primordial Tradition itself would be the Yesod of Adam Kadmon, which is the Da'at of Atzilut. The refraction of the light would take place at Yesod of Atzilut, which is the Da'at of Beriyah, where distinctly different wisdom traditions appear. This is an example of insights into the mysteries that can be gained through contemplation of the great Tree of Life. However, in this present book, we are concerned primarily with a discussion of one single Tree of Life glyph, as is proper to the most basic level of Kabbalistic instruction. The great Tree of Life is only mentioned here as it relates our exploration of Da'at, which cannot really be understood apart from an awareness of the interlocking of one Tree of Life glyph with another through which the great tree is formed. When we discuss the Sefirah Yesod in another chapter of this book, with an awareness of the great Tree of Life, it will undoubtedly shed more light upon the mystery of Da'at.

The Great Enigma

Da'at is, perhaps, the most mysterious and enigmatic of all the Sefirot—the revealed aspect of Keter, the concealed aspect of Tiferet, Yesod in another dimension. It is as though Da'at is everything other than itself. At the level of Atzilut, it is the perfect thunder mind—the Gnosis mind of Christ—and in Beriyah, it is the root of all world wisdom Traditions. Yet, at the level of Beriyah, Da'at assumes a dual nature, having a light and a dark side. This is suggested by the association of Da'at and Yesod, the moon being the celestial attribute of Yesod, which has both a light and dark side.

In a most subtle and sublime way, the dual nature of Da'at is alluded to by the association of the divine name of Yahweh Elohim with both Da'at and Binah. Binah is often the name Elohim; however, it is also the name Yahweh Elohim. This leads to the question of exactly what is different between the expression of Binah as Yahweh Elohim and Da'at as Yahweh Elohim. One way to answer this is that Yahweh Elohim suggests the Divine Mother who is pregnant, for Yahweh indicates the heavenly Father and Elohim the Holy Mother—a union through which the conception of creation occurs. Thus, there is the suggestion of Da'at, and all the Sefirot that follow Binah, as a child in the mother's womb. When the child emerges, it is Yahweh Elohim, the image of the Father-Mother. Da'at is the crown of the child, hence the crown of Zer Anpin (little face). But there is also a more subtle suggestion, for at the level of Binah, Yahweh Elohim is *pure*. It is the supernal light that is the root essence of all cosmic forces in the supernal or archetypal world. At the level of Da'at, this light is refracted into the rainbow splendor of the cosmic forces, and in this process of the actualization of cosmic forces, the light is divided from the darkness—thus a light and dark side of Yahweh appears.

Yahweh is the one consciousness-force; Elohim is the one consciousness-force becoming many cosmic forces in creation. In Binah, all cosmic forces are united in the one force, but through Da'at, they are separated into distinct individual forms of the force. While the bright side of Da'at is the intelligence of Christ—the pattern-that-connects—the dark side of Da'at is cosmic ignorance, which may also be called the cosmic illusion-power. The cause of this duality exists in Binah, but it is actualized in Da'at. Therefore, from the point of Da'at on the Tree of Life, the Tree of Knowledge of Good and Evil comes into being, which is to say that a dark side of the Tree of Life comes into being, which is called the Tree of Death. The nature of the Tree of Death is ignorance or falsehood, for the word "death" in Hebrew is *Met* and the word for "truth" is *Amet*. When Aleph, the spirit of truth, is removed, ignorance comes into being, and the result of ignorance is death. Da'at linked to the supernals is the Christ-Spirit, but when the connection of Da'at to the supernals is severed and it is linked to the spirit of ignorance, it is the antichrist-spirit.

The traditional Gnostic term for the dark side of the tree is the dominion of the demiurgos and archons. Demiurgos is the false god or false creator and specifically refers to cosmic ignorance. The archons are cosmic rulers or authorities and specifically are cosmic forces of ignorance. The dominion of the demiurgos and archons represents two manifestations of cosmic forces. One manifestation is titanic forces, which are neither divine nor evil, but rather are admixed forces. These beings-forces do not directly oppose the divine plan in creation, but neither do they necessarily facilitate the divine plan. In essence, they have their own interests and agenda, which sometimes are in harmony with the divine plan and sometimes are not. These forces of an admixed nature are strongly reflected in unenlightened humanity, which also tends to have its own ambitions apart from the divine plan. The second manifestation is what would typically be called evil and can be considered dark forces. These are dark and hostile forces that directly oppose the divine plan in creation and are demonic in nature.

In the Kabbalah, the dominion of the demiurgos and archons is called the realm of impure emanations or the klippot (plural). Klippah (singular) literally means "husk" or "shell," as in a husk on a grain of wheat or a shell protecting a nut. This sheds light on the saying of Lord Yeshua: "Very truly, I tell you, unless a grain of wheat falls into the earth and dies, it remains just a single grain of wheat; but if it dies, it bears much fruit" (Gospel of St. John 12:24). Likewise, light is shed on the saying of John the Baptist concerning the Messiah: "His winnowing fork is in his hand, to clear the threshing floor and to gather wheat into his granary; but the chaff he will burn with unquenchable fire" (Gospel of St. Luke 3:17). The message is that the klippot are what must be first shed, then they must be transformed and integrated. Yet, the term "klippot" for unclean and evil spirits or titanic and demonic beings suggests that they are a necessary part of creative evolution—for the husk protects the fruit until the fruit is ripe and mature. Likewise, in order for an actual evolution in creation, there must be tension, stress, pressure, and resistance, if what evolves is to be strong, good, and true. The titanic and demonic beings-forces provide the necessary resistance and put every development in evolution to the test to see if it is ripe and mature.

As unfathomable as it may seem to us, darkness and evil have an integral role to play in creation. Perhaps we may consider the role of darkness and evil purely in terms of characters in a story. Unless there is a villain in a story, neither will there be a heroic person—the greater the villain, the greater the hero or heroine.

The struggle between Jacob and the angel of Esau (Genesis 32) represents the necessity of the spiritual aspirant to struggle with and overcome klippotic influence in the mystical journey. The kings of Edom, which are the descendants of Esau, of which eight are listed (Genesis 36) are taken by Kabbalists as an allusion to the klippot that span from Da'at to Malkut. There is a secret connection between the kings of Edom and the kings that Abram defeats to liberate Lot from bondage. Only after Abram struggles with these kings and overcomes them does he encounter Melchizedek, who celebrates the Holy Eucharist with Abram and initiates Abram in the name El Elyon (God most high, a name of Keter). Thus, as aspirants, we must be willing to face the ordeals of initiation—the challenge of klippotic forces—and work to transform and integrate these forces. In essence, in the Gnostic Christian view, even demons are in need of enlightenment and liberation.

Da'at may appear as a depth of good or as a depth of evil and therefore is called a depth of void—being neither good nor evil in and of itself. Per its association with Yesod, it has a mirror-like nature—the nature of mind—and assumes an appearance relative to the soul that approaches it. One who has overcome klippotic influences (selfishness, pride, arrogance, jealousy, greed, fear, hatred, and the like) will experience Da'at as the Gnosis mind of Christ that leads to supernal consciousness. Conversely, one who has not shed the influence of the klippot will find Da'at a gate to the dark side and a pit of destruction. Da'at is akin to a mirror in which one will see oneself. If one is like unto the divine, then it will be a vision of the divine; if one is not like unto the divine, then it will be a vision of something dark and demonic. One could correctly say that Da'at is the radiant nature of one's own mind or soul and that its appearance reflects the state of one's mind or soul.

The Demon of the Abyss—The Angel of the Abyss

Da'at is often called the great abyss because it represents the illusion of separation from God in our experience before cosmic ignorance is dispelled. As indicated above, Da'at appears according to the state of mind of one who approaches it. Thus, at the level of Beriyah, it can appear as a great angel or a great demon.

The name of the demon of the abyss is Samael, or Satan. Samael means the "poison of God," and Satan means the "opponent" or "adversary." If God is knowledge, understanding, and wisdom, then the devil is ignorance and falsehood. Angels, thus, represent beings-forces of enlightenment, and demons represent beings-forces of ignorance. The demon of the abyss is, therefore, the reflection of the unenlightened individual approaching Da'at, while the angel of abyss, which is the great angel of the apocalypse, is the reflection of the enlightened individual.

The attribute of Abaddon, the wrathful angel of destruction, to Da'at directly relates to the dual nature of the Shekinah encountered in Da'at. Abaddon, the angel of the bottomless pit, is not a demon. Rather, it is a wrathful or fierce angel of God, the mission of which is to shatter klippot and liberate the holy sparks trapped in them. This reveals the difference between a demon and an angel of wrath: by demon is meant something that carries one further away from enlightenment or God; by angel is meant something that ultimately brings one closer to the divine. Although an extremely dark and fierce presence, Abaddon is a holy angel, for this "destruction" or "shattering" liberates from the dominion of the klippot. In the Tradition, Abaddon is considered the dark face of the great angel of the apocalypse, which assumes the appearance of the great angel when its mission is complete.

This is reflected in a secret teaching concerning the four great archangels attributed to Da'at: Raphael, Gabriel, Michael, and Uriel. According to this teaching, the four crowned princes of hell—Lucifer, Leviathan, Satan, and Beliel—are the same consciousness-force as the corresponding archangel. Thus, these arch-demons are the dark side of the cosmic forces the archangels personify—archangels and arch-demons are opposite expressions of the same cosmic forces. The difference between angels and demons lies in their intention and the result that follows.

Teachings on the demon of the abyss and the angel of the abyss reflect that, at some point in the process of self-realization, we must confront and transform our fears and the darkness that is in us. This is the key lesson of Da'at.

The Play of Cosmic Forces

Although most ordinary individuals are unaware of it, we exist in a constant play of cosmic forces. Creation is founded upon this play of cosmic forces. At the level of Da'at, one becomes aware of this play and is able to consciously participate in the play of spiritual forces—thus the vision of the play of cosmic forces attributed to Da'at.

Metaphysically speaking, every move we make, every situation, circumstance, or event in our lives, as well as in the world—every thought, imagination, feeling-emotion, word and deed—is supported by a corresponding cosmic or spiritual force (hence angels, titans, or demons). Not only are angels, titans, or demons involved in everything we do, but according to the masters of the Tradition, everything we do also serves to create angels or demons.

When human beings are unconscious of the play of spiritual forces, then they are unconsciously compelled by spiritual forces, typically admixed or dark forces—the dominion of the demiurgos and archons. Because most ordinary individuals are unaware of the play of cosmic or spiritual forces, unenlightened human society and world events are more a product of the compulsion of cosmic ignorance than the impulse of the Christ-presence within us. The horror of the Book of Revelation essentially depicts in a symbolic form the fate of an intelligent race that continues to remain unconsciously driven by the dark side of the cosmic forces instead of seeking and following the impulse of the Christ-spirit.

Here, we understand the terms "children of darkness" and "children of light" commonly used in Gnosticism—the former meaning individuals who are unaware of the play of spiritual forces; the latter meaning those individuals who are aware. However, to be a son or daughter of light means something more. It means not only to be aware of the play of cosmic forces, but to consciously participate in the play of spiritual forces as a cocreator with God. This is the place of the wonder-working or magical

Kabbalah in the Tradition—for the magical Kabbalah represents the knowledge and power to consciously manipulate and direct psychic and spiritual forces. In the case of the Gnostic Christian, the intention is to direct the hidden forces in harmony with the divine will for the sake of the manifestation of the divine kingdom on earth. Magic of this form is properly called divine magic, which is reflected in the stories of the miracles performed by Yeshua Messiah and the holy apostles—they were magical workings.

The most fundamental level of divine magic begins with the most ordinary things—one's own thoughts, feeling-emotions, imaginations, words, and deeds. As mentioned above, the realization of an adept at the level of Da'at is that things manifest as one expects them to. Therefore, one's thoughts, feelings-emotions, and imagination play an important role. Affirmation, as discussed in the previous chapter, is a basic level of divine magic, along with the ability to control and direct one's thoughts and emotions, and the skill of creative visualization—hence the ability to consciously direct one's mind, heart, and life. Before engaging in any advanced methods of the magical Kabbalah, an aspirant must first learn to cut off or transform negativity whenever negativity arises in the mind and heart, and to keep the mind and heart positively focused and directed toward the divine. The ability to maintain positive thought, feeling-emotion, and visualization-imagination is what is meant by spiritual hope.

Faith must be joined to spiritual hope, for doubt cannot be allowed to enter into the mind and heart in a magical act. St. James speaks of this when he writes: "If any of you are lacking in wisdom (or anything), ask God, who gives to all generously and ungrudgingly, and it will be given to you. But ask in faith, never doubting, for the one who doubts is like a wave of the sea, driven and tossed by the wind; for the doubter, being double-minded and unstable in every way, must not expect to receive anything from the Lord" (James 1:5–8). Speaking of faith, the author of Hebrews writes: "Now faith is the assurance of things hoped for, the conviction of things not seen" (Hebrews 11:1). Faith, as understood in Christian Gnosticism, is a belief in the real power of the mind and specifically the power of the indwelling Christ; so that as much as faith in God and the incarnation in the person of Yeshua Messiah, it is faith also in oneself and one's inmost being. Seeing the miracles performed by Yeshua

Messiah and understanding him as both mystic and magician, faith is also a belief in the magic power in us that can produce radical changes in our consciousness and lives.

Everything first forms and comes into being on the inner planes of consciousness—in more subtle dimensions of reality. If, through positive thought, positive feeling-emotion, and creative visualization, we are able to make a change in these more subtle dimensions (Beriyah and Yetzirah), then a corresponding change will occur at the level of the physical plane (Asiyah).

This corresponds directly to the play of cosmic forces, for it is through our thoughts, feelings-emotions, imaginations, words, and deeds that we link ourselves with spiritual forces, whether of a divine, admixed, or demonic nature. In essence, positive thoughts, feelings-emotions and imaginations are inner angels; conversely, doubting and negative thoughts, feeling-emotions, and imaginations are inner demons. Through these inner angels or inner demons, we attract and connect ourselves with corresponding spiritual forces beyond us, and we become the agents of those spiritual forces in the material plane, whether for good or for ill. According to the magical Kabbalah, human beings are embodying or channeling spiritual forces all of the time, as well as generating spiritual forces all of the time—the very nature of a human being is as a receiver-transmitter and generator of spiritual force (Yahweh).

The True Knowledge of the Apocalypse—Revelation

Orthodox forms of Christianity have produced great misconceptions concerning the apocalypse and the Book of Revelation. These misconceptions all stem from the idea of a singular event in the past producing a fixed or static creation, which in turn leads to the idea of a singular event of an apocalypse in the future, which is also static or fixed. However, according to the Kabbalah of Gnostic Christianity, the creative act (Genesis) and divine revelation (apocalypse) is an ongoing event, not a singular event of the past or the future, and therefore is not static or fixed at all. Thus, creation is occurring now, and so also is the apocalypse in all of its great beauty and great horror.

First, with regard to the Book of Revelation, St. John's vision was a prophecy concerning Rome taking over Christianity and the development of orthodoxy that would attempt to destroy the living spirit of Christian Gnosis. Thus, the primary prophecy of the Book of Revelation has already occurred, to the extent that the esoteric wisdom of a Gnostic Christianity is almost completely lost in the West. In this sense, we can say that the spirit of the antichrist and great beast have performed their mission very well. However, a prophetic book is about far more than the outward situations, circumstances, and events it predicts, and prophecy itself is not engraved in stone. Because, as much as revealing potential events that may come to pass, prophecy also reveals the cosmic principles and play of spiritual forces within and behind events that transpire in the world. Thus, a prophetic book has relevance beyond the actual events it depicts, as all similar events that transpire in the world have the same universal principles and spiritual forces at play within and behind them. The Book of Genesis depicts the process of the creative act as an involution. The Book of Revelation depicts the creative act as an evolution. This involution and evolution, at the level of Da'at, is understood as one and the same movement.

You will recall our previous discussion concerning the shattering of vessels of a higher universe that is necessary for the creation of the next lower universe in the process of creation. The same is true of the destruction depicted in the Book of Revelation; except, in the apocalypse, it is the lower universe that is shattered for the sake of its unification with the higher universe. The messages to the seven churches represent a shattering in Asiyah for unification with Yetzirah. The first wave of destruction preceding one thousand years of peace on earth represents a shattering in Yetzirah for unification with Beriyah. The final conflict after the one thousand years of peace represents the shattering in Beriyah for unification with Atzilut, at which point the action of redemption-creation is fulfilled and complete. The Book of Revelation is a book of Christian Kabbalah.

This process of shattering on a lower level in order to bring about a unification and revelation on a higher level is directly reflected in the mystery of the crucifixion and resurrection. The breaking of the body-vessel at the levels of Asiyah, Yetzirah, and Beriyah allows for the revelation of the body of supernal light. In so doing, the supernal light is brought down in the Pentecost, opening the way for the full shattering of the klippot and restoration to sacred unity. The first coming is this advent in the individual—the second coming, depicted by the Book of Revelation, is the same advent in the collective of humanity (many).

The process of a development and evolution of the soul-being, specifically the human soul, toward supernal or Messianic consciousness that we witness of the person (Partzuf) of Yeshua Messiah is a process underway within each and every one of us—an evolution from vital and mental being to supramental or supernal being.

From nature, we may gain some insight into this evolutionary process; for a new species of being always comes from within a former species of being, and the development of a new species always transpires inwardly and in secret before being outwardly revealed. The same is true of the supramental being emerging from within our present state. It is a growth and transformation happening inwardly and in secret. This development, however, is very different than the evolution of new species in nature, for all previous developments occurred by way of an unconscious evolution, in which the species of being was not a conscious participant at all; rather, nature worked everything out on an unconscious level. The development of supramental being, however, cannot occur by way of an unconscious evolution. It can only happen by way of a conscious evolution on the part of the mental being—the present human being. This is the difference between a human being and all other creatures on earth. The human being has the capacity to consciously develop and evolve him- or herself into a new species of being. This new species is prefigured in Yeshua Messiah and the enlightened ones who have appeared among us.

The development and evolution from mental to supramental being is a critical stage in the evolution of life in worlds of sentient existence. One might say that it is the point of "make it or break it" as far as the evolution to the highest of life is concerned. Because it must be a conscious evolution, it is the race of intelligent beings themselves that determines the outcome of evolution in their world. Intervention from the divine order through tzaddikim and maggidim (adepts-masters and holy angels) can certainly provide divine assistance. However, a race of intelligent beings must exercise their free will and accept the divine assistance and consciously follow the Christ impulse to struggle toward a new level of being-consciousness. Essentially, members of the race or the race itself must choose to exercise their divine intelligence.

Today, perhaps more than at any other time in human history, we may understand how an intelligent race of beings will self-destruct if it is unable or unwilling to function from a higher level of consciousness. This inherently self-destructive principle is personified by the demon of the abyss. In the Book of Revelation, this backward pull or karmic drag is called the "great beast," and the active self-destructive tendency is the "Antichrist." With increasing access to greater material, psychic, and spiritual powers, overcoming this self-destructive tendency or evil inclination is critical to human survival and evolution to higher forms of life. It is this struggle between a backward pull and self-destructive tendency versus the Christ impulse that is depicted in the Book of Revelation.

The final conflict, which is called Armageddon, represents the struggle within ourselves against the violent or evil inclination of our bestial nature, the collective bestial nature being called the great beast. It becomes an external conflict only when we do not resolve the conflict inwardly. Selfishness, greed, and fear-hatred are the primary manifestations of the evil inclination, which lead us to exploit, oppress, and commit all manner of violence against one another and which lead to the great violence of wars. Rather than one single event, Armageddon is a progressively more intense and radical outbreak of this internal conflict externalized in the world. It unfolds at increasingly shorter intervals and continues to escalate until we either take the leap to live from our heart and the indwelling Christ, or end in complete self-destruction. Thus, the judgment does not come from outside of us but rather comes from within us—whether we choose life or death.

In terms of the Tree of Life, it is a question of whether or not we can rise to the level of Tiferet, or remain bound to the lower Sefirot, cut off from the presence of Christ within our hearts.

Here, a word must be said regarding our own expectations in the face of potentially dark times. Aware of the spiritual realization of Da'at—things manifest as we expect them to—you will understand the danger of large numbers of people holding on to a belief in a fated or predetermined global holocaust. This sort of expectation is rooted in doubt and fear, represents gross negativity, and is a grievous mistake. The horror of the apocalypse comes from our resistance to the dawn of Christ consciousness—our failure to overcome selfishness, greed, and fear through the cultivation of faith, hope, and love. Thus, in the face of potentially dark times, it is a vision of hope that the elect must focus upon, not only for oneself but for the whole of humanity.

This leads to an understanding of the second coming in the Gnostic view, which is a dawn of Messianic consciousness in larger collectives of human individuals. The second coming is not envisioned as a return of the person of Lord Yeshua, but rather as Messianic consciousness dawning in many individuals. In relationship to oneself, Yeshua is the first coming of Christ on earth. When Messianic consciousness dawns in oneself, it is the second coming. This also being true for others leads to the awareness of the second coming as the emergence of supernal or Messianic consciousness in a larger collective of humanity. In this light, you will understand that what each individual does in an effort of conscious evolution matters a great deal.

The Upper Room and Bridal Chamber

Da'at is often called the bridal chamber because it is the place of union of the Father (Hokmah) and Mother (Binah), and the union of the Bridegroom (Tiferet) and Bride (Malkut). From what was said previously regarding Da'at as the "child" of Hokmah and Binah, one will understand how Da'at is the union of the Father-Mother. In terms of the union of the Bridegroom and Bride, one need only remember that Da'at is Yesod in a universe beyond the one in which it appears and that it is Yesod that unites Tiferet and Malkut on the Tree of Life—hence, the union of the Bridegroom and Bride.

In Christian Gnosticism, the Father represents the transcendental aspect of God and the Mother represents the immanent aspect of God— hence, being and becoming, which are inseparable. This is reflected in the Bridegroom and Bride, who are the revealed image of the Father and Mother, respectively. Essentially, the Father is revealed via the Mother through the birth of the Son, and the Mother is fulfilled in the Daughter, when, as the Bridegroom and Bride, the Son and Daughter are united and become as Father and Mother.

This mystery is at the heart of the Gnostic Gospel, in which the incarnation of the Christos occurs through the person of Lord Yeshua and Mary of Magdal—the Bridegroom and Holy Bride. According to the Gnostic Gospel, Lord Yeshua embodies Christ, the Logos-Word, and Lady Mary embodies Christ, the Sophia-Wisdom. The two together represent the image of the Holy Father and Holy Mother in true manhood and true womanhood, respectively. Da'at in the Christian Kabbalah represents their mystical union and the light transmission that flows from it.

Yeshua is the light-presence, akin to the supernals beyond Da'at; Lady Mary is the prism of light, through which the light flows and becomes many rays of rainbow glory. He is the Master who embodies the light-presence; she is the First Apostle and the Apostle of the apostles, through whom the light transmission flows to others. In the Gnostic Gospel, it is on account of their mystical union that the light transmission occurs, in the same way that Da'at facilitates the flow of supernal light to the seven Sefirot below it.

Da'at is also called the upper room, which is the sacred space through which three key rites of initiation transpire: the Holy Eucharist or wedding feast, the transmission of the Holy Spirit via the radiant holy breath, and the reception of the fiery light of supernal being on the day of Pentecost. All three of these events are said to transpire through the union of the Bridegroom and Bride, and the secret knowledge (Da'at) associated with these initiations is said to be the foundation of the true apostolic succession in Gnosticism.

It is this light transmission that flows from the Risen Christ through the Holy Bride which initiates the apocalypse—the revelation of the light continuum. Thus, there are two images of the Bridegroom attributed to Da'at: the image of the great angel of the apocalypse and the image of the Lamb of God with seven horns and seven eyes. Likewise, there are two images of the Holy Bride: the image of the twenty-four elders and the image of New Jerusalem.

According to the masters of the Tradition, all of this occurs through the transmission in the upper room, which is to say this divine gnosis is acquired by the adept who is able to enter into Da'at and pass through it into the supernal abode. Symbolized by the upper room, one gets the sense that, rather than the supernal light itself, Da'at is the channel or vehicle of the light—hence, Da'at's frequent title as the "Non-Sefirah."

This alludes to the true purpose and meaning of a human being, which is a creature specifically associated with Da'at knowledge—that we are meant to be vehicles of the light-presence. Essentially, we experience the light-presence in us and acquire gnosis—spiritual knowledge—any time we are open and sensitive to it. To pass through Da'at or to "cross the abyss," we need only become transparent to the light that shines from within us and recognize and realize ourselves inseparable from the light continuum. In this state, there is no judgment, only the pure joy of divine rapture.

The Secret Saint and the Secret Sefirah

As he was setting out on a journey, a man ran up to him, and asked him, "Good teacher, what must I do to inherit eternal life?" Jesus said to him, "Why do you call me good? No one is good but God alone. You know the commandments: 'You shall not murder; You shall not commit adultery; You shall not steal; You shall not bear false witness; You shall not defraud; You shall honor your father and mother.'" He said to him, "Teacher, I have kept all these since my youth." Jesus, looking at him, loved him and said, "You lack one thing; go, sell what you own, and give to the poor, and you will have treasure in heaven; then, come, follow me." When he heard this, he was shocked and went away grieving, for he had many possessions. (Gospel of St. Mark 10:17–22)

According to Gnostic teachings, this was the first meeting of St. Lazarus and Master Yeshua. St. Lazarus becomes the most beloved disciple and is the only disciple, with the exception of St. Mary Magdalene, to whom Yeshua imparts the inmost secret teachings and initiation of Resurrection. Essentially, the Master says to his secret disciple: "Prepare for death." The experience of the afterlife state and the experience of Da'at are fundamentally one and the same. It is a direct reflection of the state of mind or the soul at the time of the crossing. In terms of the afterlife states, if one passes through the gate of death disturbed, grasping at negativity or clinging to the body and things of the world, then the transition will be difficult. Likewise, one cannot pass through Da'at while clinging to name and form, to things of the world, or to anything in the mind whatsoever, whether visions of heavens or visions of hells. One must cleave unto the Spirit of the Lord, the bornless nature of the soul, and nothing else; hence, one must be in a state of complete spiritual detachment, lest one fall into the dark side of Da'at.

St. Lazarus followed the instructions of the perfect master and was thus able to receive the inmost secret teachings and the initiation of the resurrection. He became the inmost disciple of the Lord and the secret apostle. According to one legend, St. Lazarus ascended with Lord Yeshua. According to another legend, St. Lazarus is the beloved disciple who will not die, but who remains living upon the earth until the time of the second coming. Essentially, St. Lazarus is the first disciple to realize the Divine fullness of the Soul of the Messiah in himself; thus, he is attributed to Da'at as the Partzuf below of this attainment.

Spiritual Practices for Divine Knowledge

The Kabbalistic Cross

> ➢ Invoke the light of the true cross; take up your holy cross and follow in the way of the Christ-presence.

> ➢ Standing or sitting, envision a sphere of light above your head, as though the light of many stars is gathered there, and abide in the awareness of the sacred unity of yourself, creation, and God.

> ➢ Reach up with your hand and touch the sphere of light above your head, and intone "Atoh," drawing the light down as you touch your forehead.

> ➢ Then bring your hand straight down to your throat, seeing the light descend there, and intone "Io Adonai."

> ➢ Bring your hand down the middle of your body, seeing the light descend down through you into the earth below, and with your hand pointing at your feet, intone "Malkut."

> ➢ Then bring your hand back up the middle of your body to your heart and extend the light to your right shoulder, and touching your right shoulder, intone "Ve-Gevurah."

> ➢ Then extend the light to your left shoulder, and touching your left shoulder, intone "Ve-Gedulah."

➤ Clasping your hands in front of your heart, as in prayer, envisioning the light of the cross within you, intone "Le-Olam, Amen."

This is the practice of the Kabbalistic Cross as given in the Sophian Tradition. Atoh means "you" and indicates Keter. Io Adonai means the "Anointed One" Bride and Bridegroom. Malkut means the "kingdom," indicating the last Sefirah of the Middle Pillar. Ve-Gevurah means the "power" and indicates the Sefirah Gevurah and the Pillar of Severity. Ve-Gedulah means the "glory" and indicates the Sefirah Hesed and the Pillar of Mercy. Le-Olam means "forever" and indicates the continuum of the light transmission. Amen means "so be it" or "so it is" and is the holy seal of truth. Thus, in tracing the cross of light in your body, you are saying, "You, Bride and Bridegroom, are the kingdom, and the power, and the glory, forever, Amen." It is an affirmation of your innate Spirit-connectedness and the truth of your inmost being as the Christ-self, and a simple method of invoking the light-presence. The Kabbalistic Cross can be used before and after any spiritual activity—spiritual study and contemplation, prayer, meditation, or sacred ritual—as an opening invocation and closing dedication. It can also be used any time one feels the need to center oneself or to invoke a blessing of the light-presence on oneself.

The Upper Room Meditation

➤ Sit in a place where you will not be disturbed. Bring your attention gently upon your breath, allowing your body to find its own natural rhythm of breath. As you breathe, relax, yet remain completely alert, letting go of all tension, stress, or negativity to just be present in the moment.

➤ When your body is relaxed and your mind is calm, envision the spiritual sun within behind your heart and envision your whole body becoming light.

➤ Then imagine that there is an upper room above you—a room filled with light, as though there is a luminous assembly of holy prophets and apostles, sages and saints, in sacred discourse. Feel yourself becoming lighter and lighter, and envision that you ascend into this upper room in a body of light, to sit among the holy ones gathered there. The upper room appears as a vast chamber. The Lord and

Holy Bride are in the center. Above the image of the Lord and Bride is a presence of white brilliance—a light-presence of diamond-like light. Around the presence of the anointed is the sacred circle of the twenty-four holy elders. Around the sacred circle of elders are circles upon circles of apostles and prophets, saints and sages, and even holy angels of God. The Lord is silent and the Holy Bride is giving teachings on the holy mysteries. Envision yourself among them. Open your mind and heart to the divine presence and power in the upper room—look and see, listen and hear, and see what knowledge you receive from the luminous assembly.

➤ When you feel it is time to leave the luminous assembly, envision yourself descending as you ascended, seeing yourself once again in the body below with the spiritual sun shining in your heart. Let the energy settle and allow yourself to ground fully before departing the place of the meditation, contemplating your experience of the upper room. Close the meditation with prayer, giving thanks to the divine for your experience and what you have received—give praise and thanksgiving to God.

This meditation can be used whenever one has a question, and in this case, one takes one's question into the upper room, but it can also be used without having any specific question, when one simply seeks the inspiration or revelation that divine grace would have one receive. It is a way to contact the luminous assembly of saints and angels and to receive secret teachings directly from the divine presence and power.

It is said that all of the prophets and apostles, or ascended masters, have Mystery Schools upon the inner planes. Gnostic initiates modify this practice to come into contact with the Mystery School of specific prophets or apostles by placing the image of the prophet or apostle in the center, in place of the Lord and Holy Bride, and envisioning a corresponding circle of disciples and holy angels gathered about that holy prophet or apostle of God. For example, an initiate might wish to connect the Mystery School of the prophet John the Baptist. He or she will consider how the heavenly image of John the Baptist would appear and envision that divine image in the center of the upper room. Likewise, the initiate would consider what the companions of John the Baptist would look like and what angels might be present, and envision the luminous assembly accordingly. This very process of developing a visualization can prove to be a product of divine instruction. Therefore, in many methods of the Tradition, a specific visualization is not given, but the creative spirit within the initiate is called upon to provide the images. Like an affirmation that one creates for oneself, oftentimes an image one creates for oneself will prove more powerful and effective than one imposed upon oneself from outside. There is a place for images generated by the adepts and masters of the Tradition, but there is equally a place for images one creates for oneself. The upper-room meditation is a method designed for one to generate one's own images—ideally under the inspiration of the Holy Spirit, which is a creative spirit.

SIX

HOKMAH, THE WISDOM OF CREATION

Attributes

Thirty-Two Paths of Wisdom: Radiant Consciousness (Sekhel Maz'hir); this is the Crown of creation and homogeneous unity that "exalts itself above all as the head"; the masters of Kabbalah call it the Second Glory

Hokmah: Sophia or Wisdom

Place on the Tree of Life: Head of the Pillar of Mercy

Divine Name: Yah; Yahweh

Alternative Divine Names: Hayyah Olam, Eternal Life; Yesh, "There Is"

Partzuf Above: Abba, Father

Partzuf Below: None

Divine Image: A bearded male image; the One-Who-Sits on the Throne

Archangel: Ratziel

Order of Angels: Ofanim

Celestial Attribute: Mazlot, the Wheel of the Zodiac

Titles Given to Hokmah: Reshit, the Point of the Beginning; Power of the Holy Angels; Splendor of Unity; Yod of the Tetragrammaton; The Tetragrammaton; Ab, Virgin Father; Abba, the Heavenly Father; The One-Who-Is-Not-Seen; Transcendental Awareness; Eternal Life; Master of the Worlds; Glorious One; The Beginning and End; the Depth of Beginning

Level of the Soul: Hayyah, the Life-Essence or Life-Force

Heavenly Abode: The World of Supernal Light

Spiritual Experience: The attainment of Supernal Consciousness; the Vision of Adam Kadmon; The Vision of God Face to Face

Virtue: Perfect Devotion, Devekut

Vice: None

Symbols: The Inner Robe of Glory; the Holy Staff; The Phallus or Lingam; The Standing-Stone; The Crystal Sphere; Yod

Commandment: You shall not make for yourself an idol (Exodus 20:4–6)

Sermon on the Mount: You are the salt of the earth (Matthew 5:13)

Angel of the Apocalypse and the Churches: The Light of the Great Angel

The Supernal Generator

Hokmah-Wisdom is essentially as incomprehensible as Keter. Using the analogy for Keter as the singularity from which the big bang comes, Hokmah would be the event horizon, which from our perspective is as inconceivable as the singularity itself. Hokmah is the instant of the big bang. As the instant of the big bang, one could say that this event horizon is outside and inside our metaphysical universe at one and the same time, so that exactly what it is can only be a complete mystery at the level of our ordinary consciousness. The instant before the big bang, if such a thing can be said, there is nothing knowable; from the instant of the big bang, everything knowable begins. In this sense, the masters of the Tradition have said that Hokmah is Reshit—the point of the beginning, beyond which there is nothing knowable.

Yod, the first letter of the Tetragrammaton, contains a contemplation of this mystery in geometrical terms. Yod, spelled out, is Yod (׳)-Vau (ו)-

Dalet (ד). Yod resembles a point, which represents Keter. A point has position but no dimension. Vau resembles a line. If from a point a line is traced, there is one dimension. Dalet resembles an angle, or two lines sharing an intersection. If two lines are drawn from the point, giving width and breadth, then there are two dimensions, which form a plane or a two-dimensional space. The shift from Keter to Hokmah is akin to this contemplation of Yod spelled out.

Yah, the divine name of Hokmah, spelled Yod (י)-Hey (ה), suggests the generation of a three-dimensional, space-time continuum, the He being the divine potential of Binah within Hokmah, which is actualized when the seven lower Sefirot emerge from within Binah-Da'at. At the level of Hokmah, however, space-time as we understand it is a potential. It is the instant within a moment of time, which is the touch of eternity everywhere within time and yet is ever beyond time, being timeless eternity—hence the divine name Hayyah Olam (eternal life) associated with Hokmah. Hokmah is timeless-eternity and Binah is time-eternity, which is to say Hokmah is eternity and Binah is forever. Forever is a vast duration of time that is inconceivable to us, as in the life span of the universe. Eternity, in essence, has nothing to do with time. While the true meaning of these words is meaningless to our ordinary consciousness, nevertheless, they give us some sense of the reality of Hokmah-wisdom.

This idea of eternity beyond space-time, and eternity penetrating everywhere within space-time suggests how Hokmah is united to Keter and yet is a distinct gradation of the supernal light on a lower level moving toward manifestation. It also directly reflects the idea of an event horizon or threshold that is simultaneously outside and inside our metaphysical universe.

The contemplation of a point that becomes a line alludes to the nature of Hokmah as the channel or flow of supernal energy that pours forth from Keter. One could say that Hokmah is Keter set in motion or that Hokmah is the activation of the potential of Keter. In relationship to Binah-Da'at, Hokmah is the supernal generator and the great stimulator of all life—the generator of all life-power. In a word, Hokmah is the *force;* hence the term "radiant consciousness" or "radiant force." Consciousness is force and force is consciousness (energy-intelligence).

The Play of Force and Form—Transformation

Hokmah and Binah are the head of the Pillar of Mercy and Pillar of Severity, respectively, which are represented in the temple of King Solomon as the Pillars of Jachin and Boaz. Keter-Da'at is the head of the Pillar of Compassion or Middle Pillar, which is represented by the mercy seat or ark of the covenant in the holy of holies in the temple. In essence, the Pillars of the Tree of Life represent the principles of force and form, and the dynamic balance of force and form. At the head of the Pillar of Mercy, Hokmah is pure force; at the head of the Pillar of Severity, Binah is pure form in an archetypal sense.

Keter-crown is the principle of being; Malkut-kingdom is the principle of becoming—hence the Middle Pillar is the principle of coming into substantial being. The nature of this coming into substantial being is a dynamic play of force and form that is rooted in Ain (no-thingness) and therefore is a constant continuum of transformation. In the process of transformation, force or energy is organized into forms and is manifest in form until the form eventually evolves and the force or energy is released back into the cosmic river of force (light) to become manifest in yet other forms. In this process, the force or energy is never changed in its essence or being and nothing of the force or energy is ever lost. It remains ever the same forever and for all eternity.

Hokmah and the Pillar of Mercy is the dynamism within and behind the continuum of transformation, which is creation. However, Hokmah is not the organizing agent; rather, Binah is the organizing agent—hence the principle of form on an archetypal level. Although, at the level of the supernals, there is no real distinction between the force in formlessness or in form, and thus there is no such thing as birth and death, the play of force and form at the archetypal level appears as the dance of life and death in the lower Olamot of the Tree. Thus birth, life, death, and the transmigration of the soul are a way of contemplating the play of Force and form in our own experience.

The soul is the force or energy of life—an individuation of the one life-power, which is called Hayyah. The archetypal or heavenly form of the soul, which is realized and actualized through the process of transmi-gration-transformation, is the Neshamah. That which is actualized and realized of the Neshamah is the Ruach. The names and forms, or the incarnations, are the Nefeshim. In the Zohar, the Nefesh is attributed to Hokmah because Hayyah is an exhaustless potential of countless Nefeshim in the same way that Hokmah is an exhaustless flow of the force or life-power from Keter.

Birth is the manifestation of the soul in the body or the personality and life-display of an incarnation. Life is the duration of that individual Nefesh or life-form. Death is the dissolution of the Nefesh and release of the soul-energy to another form. In this process of transmigration-transformation, the essence of the soul-energy or Hayyah never changes nor is anything of the soul-energy ever lost. This directly reflects the play of Hokmah and Binah or force and form, upon which the universe or creation is founded, and the idea of Hokmah as a "crown" that is "exalted above every head."

The Heavenly Father

Keter is the Partzuf of Arik Anpin, the big face, the face of the Holy One that shines upon the Sefirot, which no one has ever seen at any time. This face is Hu (He) and it is Hua (She), in the sense of containing the divine potential of maleness and femaleness, yet Keter or Arik Anpin is neither male nor female. Hokmah and Binah are male and female, respectively, and are the Partzufim of Abba (father) and Aima (mother).

Male and female in the Kabbalah represent positive and negative, as in the poles of a battery that allows the flow of the current of energy. Male means the principle of force and principle of imparting, while female means the principle of form and principle of receiving. All of the Sefirot are both male and female in their relationship to one another, depending on whether they are imparting or receiving. For example, Keter is called Hu (He) in relationship to all of the other Sefirot, because Keter is the all-giver to the Sefirot. In relationship to Ain Sof, however, Keter is called Hua (She), because Keter is the all-receiver to Ain Sof. Likewise, Malkut is all-female to the Sefirot, because Malkut is the vessel that "has no light of her own" but receives her light from above. Yet, receiving this light into herself, the Bride becomes the Mother, and as the Mother who gives birth to a child, Malkut gives something more back, thus becoming male in Kabbalistic terms. In the Kabbalah, the play of the terms of gender is filled with esoteric meaning.

The Kabbalistic meaning of male and female resolves what otherwise would be an endless paradox concerning Hokmah-Wisdom. For Hokmah-wisdom in the Kabbalah is Abba-Father, yet throughout the Scriptures Hokmah-wisdom is called Hua-She. In the Scriptures, Hokmah is, thus, always being spoken of in relationship with Keter and specifically with Ain Sof, to which Hokmah is female. On the Tree of Life, however, and in relationship to us, Hokmah is all-male—hence Abba, the Father.

The Partzuf of Abba denotes the relationship of Hokmah to all of the Sefirot below and to our soul of light (Neshamah-Ruach-Nefesh). We already have indicated Hokmah-Yahweh as the *force*, which is the generative principle or the Father. In the Gospel, Lord Yeshua continually makes reference to God as Abba-Father and thus is speaking specifically of Hokmah as the source of his inspiration and the attainment to which his message points. Thus, in effect, Yeshua Messiah comes in the *name of the force*—the light-force of the supernal father.

In the same way that we can contemplate Hokmah-Binah in terms of birth and death, we can also gain insight into Hokmah-Binah through the contemplation of maleness and femaleness, or the Father and the Mother. Conception of a child occurs through the union of the Father and the Mother. In terms of Hokmah-Binah, this child is creation and the Soul of the Messiah. The Father inseminates the Mother, fertilizing her, and she thus conceives. As far as the process of gestation and giving birth, while the Father may give support to the Mother and provide nourishment to the Mother, his actual role in the development of the child in the Mother's womb ends with the impregnation. The Mother is the matrix or environment in which the child is conceived and through which the child grows and develops in a continual process of transformation toward birth. The Father is thus transcendental to the child in the womb, but the Mother is immanent.

Hokmah, which is God the Father, is transcendental—ever beyond creature and creation, thus "exalted above every head." Binah, which is God the Mother, is immanent—within creature and creation. Essentially, Binah can be conceived of as the womb of God, and Hokmah can be conceived of as the phallus of God. The womb is the matrix of creation and the phallus is the dynamism of the force that sets the matrix in motion. In this sense, the Father is within us and the Mother is all around us, although that which is within us is, in truth, ever beyond us.

The birth of the child in this analogy is the enlightenment-liberation of the soul-being. Until the dawn of a complete self-realization in supernal or Christ-consciousness, which is the grade of attainment corresponding to Hokmah, the Heavenly Father is hidden and unknown. For this reason, there is no Partzuf below for Hokmah. In the Gospel, although Joseph is the earthly father of Yeshua, he is barely mentioned, because Abba-Father is completely invisible and transcendental, save through the image of the Son. On the other hand, the Holy Mother (Mother Mary) plays a significant role in the mystery drama of the Gospel, being the Partzuf below embodying and reflecting something of the Partzuf of Aima, which is Binah. The myth of the virgin birth is a metaphor of this relationship of the heavenly Father and Mother. To the Gnostic Christian, it forms the basis of a meditation on Hokmah and Binah.

The Great Name of God

Yah and Yahweh, the Tetragrammaton, is Hokmah at the level of Atzilut. Yah is composed of the letters Yod (י) and He (ה). The tip of the Yod, as said previously, is Keter and the universe of Adam Kadmon; the body of the Yod is Hokmah and the universe of Atzilut. The letter He is Binah and the universe of Beriyah. Thus, Yah is the power of the supernals and expresses the truth of Hokmah as the power generator on the Tree of Life. The supernal force passing through the Sefirot of Beriyah sustains the universe of Yetzirah, and thus Yah indicates Hokmah as the power behind the world of the angels, which is Yetzirah.

Yod and He are the supernal Father and Mother before conceiving and giving birth. Joined to Vau and He finally in the Tetragrammaton, Yod and He are Abba and Aima proper, which is to say the divine parent has given birth to the Son and Daughter. All five great Partzufim are, thus, represented by the great name of God—the name Yahweh (Yod-He-Vau-He). As previously explained, the name of Yahweh forms the pattern of a human being when the letters are placed one on top of the other vertically, indicating that Yahweh is the channel of the holy Shekinah of Adam Kadmon to the lower universes and that the five great Partzufim are the expression of what is contained within Adam Kadmon—the primordial human being.

The divine name of Eheieh is the highest name of God, and yet it is the Tetragrammaton that is called the great name of God. This, of course, invokes the question, "Why is Yahweh the great name instead of Eheieh, which is the highest divine name?" This directly parallels the use of the second letter of the Hebrew alphabet (Bet) as the initial letter of creation instead of the first letter (Aleph). Aleph is the first letter in the highest name of God and is the letter representing God's spirit or essence, which although within creation, is ever beyond creation. Therefore, creation begins with the letter Bet instead of Aleph because of the transcendental nature of the creator. Bet means "house" or "structure"—hence the matrix of creation. Aleph is the Spirit of God that pours through it; yet as much as within it, the Spirit of God is also surrounding it and beyond it. This idea also depicts the relationship of Eheieh to Yahweh, which is akin to the relationship of the soul to the body—in this case, a body of light or pure energy.

Eheieh is like the root of the Tree of Life—the root is the life of the holy tree. Therefore, it is the essential or highest name of God. Yahweh is like the trunk of the Tree of Life. The holy root is hidden in the secret depths of Ain Sof, but the trunk is the visible part of the holy tree emerging from the depths of the Infinite, which itself is Infinite. All other divine names are like branches of the holy tree that are all joined together by the trunk (Yahweh), and through the agency of Yahweh, all are sustained by Eheieh. Therefore, although Eheieh is the essential name of God, Yahweh is the great name, which contains all other divine names and to which all other names are as ornaments, each bearing its own specific fruit (Sefirah). Thus, Yahweh is the glory of Eheieh (second glory), and all other names are the glory of the glory (third glory—Elohim or Binah).

Eheieh is within Yahweh as a soul in a body of light, and Yahweh is in Eheieh as a body within an aura of brilliant light—through Yahweh, Eheieh is revealed. Yahweh literally means "That Which Was, and Is and Forever Shall Be," and Eheieh literally means "I Am" or "I Shall Be." Therefore, Yahweh indicates the outpouring of Eheieh, the activity or revelation of Eheieh, which while going out from Eheieh is at one and the same time a going into Eheieh.

Hokmah-Yahweh is the channel of the supernal being-consciousness-force or the supernal light. In the Kabbalah, this supernal light is called the ruhaniyut, which is said to breathe and shine from within the Sefirot, and also to breathe and shine around them. Ruhaniyut implies the idea of a spirit or soul of the divine names or Sefirot. Accordingly, there is an inner and an outer ruhaniyut, as it is said to breathe and shine from within the Sefirot like a soul, and to breathe and shine around them like an aura or garment.

The name of Yahweh is the inner ruhaniyut, and all of the other names are the outer ruhaniyut. Eheieh, which is concealed within Yahweh and yet revealed by Yahweh, is the inmost secret ruhaniyut, being the true essence of the inner and outer ruhaniyut. This ruhaniyut (supernal light of Ain Sof) is the life-force of the Names-Sefirot-Partzufim, their soul and spirit and aura. Ruhaniyut, like the word Ruach, implies breath and radiance—thus the radiant holy breath of God. Ruhaniyut is actually a plural term, suggesting various forms of the light-breath of God, all of which are the manifestation of one holy radiant breath.

In Genesis, it is written that God breathes into the nostrils of the human one, and the human one becomes a living soul. This is Adam Kadmon and it is Adam Ha-Rishon (first human being)—hence, the supernal ideal of humanity. The souls of the righteous ones (tzaddikim)—of all authentic human beings—are said to be drawn from the soul of Adam Kadmon. Thus, this ruhaniyut or radiant holy breath of God is within every human being. Through this ruhaniyut in us, we are linked to the Sefirot-Names-Partzufim, and we are able to bind our soul to the Sefirot and to bind the Sefirot to our soul—thus embodying something of the holy Shekinah.

Yahweh is the name of names, the unified power of the ruhaniyut of all the names of God. The name of Yeshua is the same divine name with the letter Shin (שׁ) inserted in the middle, suggesting a human being who has realized the ruhaniyut (radiant holy breath) within him- or herself and thus unified him- or herself with the Sefirot-Names-Partzufim. The name of Yeshua is not simply the name of one human person; it is the name of any Christed or enlightened human being.

This explains the esoteric meaning of the saying that "all spiritual forces are subject to the name of Yeshua" and that "before the name of

Yeshua Messiah every knee shall bend and every head shall bow." Indeed, the whole metaphysical universe (heaven and earth) and all cosmic forces in the universe move with one who has "put on this holy name."

The key to this self-realization is alluded to in the Kabbalistic terms for the soul and the term ruhaniyut itself—it is the breath of life. Within and behind the ordinary breath, there is a more subtle spiritual breath or spiritual force—a radiant and holy breath, which is the manifestation of Hayyah (the life-essence) attributed to Hokmah. Discovering this inner and secret breath and using the divine names as taught by the masters of wisdom, the initiate in the Christian mysteries has the power of the blessed name of Yeshua—the Gnosis of Yeshua Messiah (which is the perfect Gnosis of the great name of God).

Here, we come to a deeper understanding of the initiation of the upper room, when Lord Yeshua breathes upon the disciples, saying, "Receive the Holy Spirit," and when the fire of the Pentecost descends upon them in the presence of the Bride. For the supernal light-force is a fiery light, and the breath is the vehicle of this fiery light, so that one who knows how to breathe and how to vibrate the divine names is able to transmit this Holy Spirit to others and, thus, is able to awaken the Holy Spirit in them. This is the foundation of all Gnostic Christian initiation.

A Proverbial Secret

Yahweh by Hokmah-wisdom founded the earth; by Binah-Understanding he established the heavens; by his Da'at-knowledge the deeps broke open and the Arabot clouds drop down the dew (Proverbs 3:19–20).

Arabot, which means "clouds" or "plains," is the name of the seventh or highest heaven, and the mention of Hokmah-Binah-Da'at indicates the world of supernal light, which is beyond the highest heaven. The dew is the shefa or everflow that fills the Sefirot and pours forth from the Sefirot. This shefa is the nourishment of all living souls and all worlds, and its essence is in Hokmah. Just as through the divine names we are able to join the ruhaniyut in us to the ruhaniyut of the Sefirot, so through the names we are able to draw upon the shefa everflow. To intone the names is to invoke/evoke the corresponding manifestation of the everflow or divine power.

One may understand the relationship between ruhaniyut and shefa in the following way. ruhaniyut is like the soul of the tree; shefa is like the sap of the tree. Both the soul and the sap of the tree are called the life of the tree. Essentially, they are two manifestations of the same thing—the life-power of the holy tree. Ruhaniyut is the essence, and shefa is the presence. Ruhaniyut and shefa are what are conveyed by the wine and bread of the Holy Eucharist, respectively. In the initiation of the upper room, the Bridegroom conveys the ruhaniyut and the Bride conveys the shefa. This is the secret alluded to by the Holy Eucharist or wedding feast performed in the remembrance of the one anointed with the supernal light of God.

At the level of Hokmah of Atzilut, the ruhaniyut and shefa are one, in the same way that the Lord and his name are one. This supreme mystery is said to contain the secret of eternal life and it is said to be the meditation of the perfect tzaddikim—the great masters of the Tradition.

Radiant Breath, Word, and Wisdom

According to the Tradition, creation is founded upon Hokmah and Binah. Specifically, creation is founded upon ten utterances—sayings or axioms—which are found in the first chapter of Genesis. Thus, in a spiritual sense, Hokmah constitutes the ten utterances which would define creation, while Binah is the logical system of archetypal patterns connecting them. All laws of nature and creation are essentially wisdom sayings of God, even the simplest of which contains many levels of meaning or manifestation. Each Sefirah represents the various levels and aspects of one of these ten utterances. Thus each Sefirah, with all of its attributes or correspondences, is an expression of one saying or axiom of God, the essence of which is found in Hokmah and the principle of which plays out through Binah. For example, the first holy utterance of creation—"Let there be Light"—is Keter-Da'at with all of its correspondences manifesting at the level of Adam Kadmon, Atzilut, Beriyah, Yetzirah, and Asiyah. Everything Keter-Da'at was, is, or will be on every level is contained in this saying, and the essence of this saying is in Hokmah.

At the level of Hokmah of Atzilut, the word and wisdom of God are one and the same, just as the ruhaniyut and shefa are one and the Lord and his name are one. The word is brought forth from within wisdom as distinct individual sayings at the level of Beriyah. The word is the expression of God's wisdom which actualizes God's wisdom, and the vehicle of this expression-actualization is the radiant holy breath or Spirit of God. Breath, word, and wisdom are three in one and one in three—hence the secret mystery of the Holy Trinity of the Father, the Son, and the Holy Spirit, the Holy Spirit being the divine feminine principle represented by the Holy Mother and Bride (Binah-Malkut). Binah of Atzilut is the holy womb in which the saying-word is conceived and Malkut of Atzilut is the divine oracle (mouth) speaking the saying-word. This, in turn, leads to the playing out of the breath, word, and wisdom at the level of Beriyah, Yetzirah, and Asiyah.

As indicated above, something of this creative power is within the human one, and, in fact, the soul of the human one is this creative power. This is alluded to in the idea of God breathing into the nostrils of Adam, and Adam becoming a living soul in the image and likeness of God (Elohim). It is also alluded to by Adam being given the divine power to name creatures in creation. Esoterically, to know the name of a spirit or creature is to have the power to subject that spirit or creature to oneself or to "rule over it" and thus to consciously direct that being-force. The power to name a spirit or creature is the power to conceive a spirit or creature and to bring a new spirit or creature into being. This is the basis for the power of prayer in the mystical Kabbalah and incantations or spell-speaking using the divine names, and permutations of the divine names, in the magical Kabbalah—the secret mystery behind all of the miracles performed by the men and women of God in the Holy Scriptures.

Although the actual use of this creative power is the magical Kabbalah, the key of the secret mystery of this divine power is discovered through the mystical or meditative Kabbalah, for to actually engage in the magical Kabbalah, one must first recognize and realize the power of the radiant holy breath—the power of the soul—and learn to join one's soul to the Sefirot, thus drawing upon the ruhaniyut and shefa through which divine magic becomes possible. Therefore, daily prayer and meditation are integral to any real practice of divine magic, because that is how the initiate is able to access the divine knowledge and power.

The Divine Ideal of Magic

One may experience something of cosmic consciousness—the unity of all life—and yet remain ignorant of God, returning to the way of life one lived before the experience. In altered states of consciousness, cosmic consciousness is common. The sense of the vastness and unity of life is felt in nature herself when we encounter her wonders—the ocean, a great mountain, the glories of springtime or autumn. In moments of awe and wonder, we draw near to this level of awareness of the sacred unity—although cosmic consciousness proper is the experience of oneself completely and inseparably united with all that lives and the universe. Some mistake this mystical experience for the ultimate attainment, yet to be one with all creatures and creation is quite different from the experience of unification with the divine. Likewise, the experience of this lower level of cosmic consciousness is quite different from being able to draw upon the force of the universe or the ability to consciously direct cosmic or spiritual forces as can be done by a perfect tzaddik or master. The lower level of cosmic consciousness in Da'at is common, but the higher levels of cosmic consciousness in Binah, which lead to the various levels of supernal consciousness, are far less common.

Divine magic is not merely the ability to shift to higher states of consciousness at will. It is the ability to consciously direct the cosmic and spiritual forces while in a higher state of consciousness—specifically to direct them according to the divine will and kingdom. It is certainly possible to perform divine magic to various degrees prior to the attainment of the supernal grades. However, it is in Binah that mastery of divine magic is attained and it is in Hokmah that the perfection of divine magic is realized. The science of divine magic is attributed to Hod, which is the base of the Pillar of Severity, but the perfection of divine magic is attributed to Hokmah, which is the head of the Pillar of Mercy. Thus, in Rosicrucian teachings, the attainer of Hokmah is known as the magus—the master magician.

This secret relationship between Hod and Hokmah reveals the true nature and purpose of the magical Kabbalah, which is so often misrepresented by occultists writing on the subject. The nature and purpose of divine magic is not personal power for egoistic gratification, but rather has the aim of self-realization in a supernal or Christ consciousness. The actual practice of divine magic itself is to realize and actualize the divine power of the soul of light and to be empowered to render invisible spiritual assistance to others—to help others in their own process of enlightenment and liberation. Therefore, true divine magic is an active expression of spiritual love and compassion.

In Gnosticism, spiritual assistance is given to both visible living souls and invisible spirits. Thus, as much as seeking the help of spiritual beings-forces in a magical working, the Gnostic initiate seeks to enlighten and liberate the beings-forces involved in the magical working. In the same way spiritual assistance is given to visible living souls and invisible beings-forces, so also is assistance given to the spirits of the dead—all with the aim of a conscious evolution to supernal or Christ consciousness. In effect, the Gnostic seeks to serve as a conscious agent of the divine will and as a conscious cocreator with God, whether in mundane matters or spiritual matters. As the aim of divine magic is to enlighten and liberate, the highest expression of divine magic is the ability to initiate others into the stream of the light transmission or to convey something of the spiritual energy or power of one's own self-realization—hence the divine labor of the tzaddikim who serve as spiritual guides and impart the secret teachings and initiations.

Prophetic Consciousness

As indicated above, prayer and meditation are integral to the practice of real divine magic because it is through spiritual-mystical practices that an aspirant is able to realize and actualize the divine power of the radiant holy breath of God. Methods of mystical prayer and meditation are important to divine magic for another reason; they are how an initiate is able to enter into states of prophetic consciousness and receive divine guidance in the practice of his or her magic. Unless one is aware of the divine will, one cannot direct one's magical workings to serve the divine will and kingdom. Before any magical working, the initiate must first know the divine will in the matter, lest one could easily be engaging in a magical act contrary to the divine will. According to the Tradition, any magical working that is apart from the divine will and one's true will is defined as sorcery or black magic.

There are two grades of prophecy, and there are various degrees of prophecy within these two grades. Hod at the base of the Pillar of Severity and Netzach at the base of the Pillar of Mercy are called the hazy mirror of prophecy and clear mirror of prophecy, respectively. However, this attribute of prophetic states to Hod and Netzach can be deceiving if one is not aware of the great Tree of Life and the interpenetration of the Olamot with one another. Like Da'at, which is the expression of Yesod of a higher universe, Hokmah and Binah of a lower universe are the expression of Netzach and Hod of a higher universe. Thus it is at the level of Binah and Hokmah that prophetic consciousness occurs, the communication of the prophecy being Da'at. The levels of prophecy thus span the universes of Atzilut, Beriyah, and Yetzirah, and are enacted in Asiyah by the prophet or apostle—hence the speaking of a prophecy or a magical working founded upon the divine guidance he or she has received.

The terms "hazy mirror of prophecy" and "clear mirror of prophecy" denote the quality of the prophetic experience and the two grades of prophecy—the lesser prophet and the greater prophet. The lesser prophet is one who is able to look into the divine law and see what is going to happen and thus aligns him- or herself accordingly. What the prophet has seen at this level may or may not transpire, and he or she may or may not be able to effect a change in the course of events. The knowledge and understanding of the lesser prophet is, by nature, something partial and incomplete—"hazy."

The greater prophet, however, is at-one with the divine law, and therefore is able to perceive exactly what will come to pass and has the knowledge, understanding, and power to affect the flow of events, more or less. Because the greater prophet is united with the divine law, whatever he or she speaks will come to pass—it transpires as the greater prophet speaks it. Thus, prophecy from the level of Binah is always somewhat partial or hazy; while from the level of Hokmah, it is always complete and clear. This is true whether at the level Binah-Hokmah of Yetzirah or of Beriyah.

In terms of the levels of prophecy corresponding to the Olamot, while Binah and Hokmah speak of the clarity of the prophetic experience, the universes speak to the degree of directness in the experience itself—the directness of knowledge, understanding, and wisdom. At the level of Atzilut, there are no symbols or images; prophecy is a direct knowing or understanding in the mind of the prophet. He or she knows and understands without need of any dream or vision. At the level of Beriyah, the prophet has a direct experience of the presence and power of the Lord—the holy Shekinah. God speaks directly to the prophet. At the level of Atzilut, the holy Shekinah and the prophet are united in the prophetic experience—there is only the Holy One. At the level of Beriyah, there is the prophet and the Holy One, and although very near to the Holy One, the prophet experiences God distinct from him- or herself. The level of Yetzirah is a prophecy communicated in reflection through symbols and through the agency of the holy angels of God. Thus, whether the prophecy is a partial knowledge or complete knowledge, and the degree of directness through which the knowledge comes, determines the level of prophetic consciousness. Dreams and visions filled with symbolism and angelic visitations is the lowest degree of prophetic consciousness; the experience of a direct knowledge and understanding within oneself is the highest degree—between these two poles there are many gradations.

To enter into prophetic consciousness, one must turn one's consciousness inward and upward—Godward—through prayer and meditation. Through living according to the truth and light revealed in one's experience and magical ritual, one then enacts the divine will or knowledge of the kingdom. This is what it means to be a prophet or apostle of God. As Lord Yeshua said, "I do what I see my Father doing."

Gradations of Divine Magic

Just as there are various gradations of prophetic consciousness, there are also gradations of divine magic. At the level of Hokmah, the divine magic of the perfect master transpires through pure thought or silent will. The perfect Tzaddik does not need to do anything outwardly or say anything outwardly in order to bring about a change in consciousness or the flow of events. Whatever he or she might do outwardly is for the sake of others, so that others might understand what is being done and experience a link with the spirit of truth. The highest form of divine magic, therefore, has little or nothing to do with anything outward, such as ritual, talismans, magical weapons, and the like, but is purely a shift within consciousness itself, through which a corresponding change takes place outwardly. Consciousness-force is completely one and the same in supernal or Christ consciousness. Thus the forces move with a shift in consciousness according to the will of the perfect tzaddik, which is God's will.

The lowest form of divine magic, like the lowest form of prophetic consciousness, is heavily dependent upon symbolism and mediation of angelic and other spiritual beings-forces. At this level, the initiate must rely upon a sacred ritual outwardly performed and thus makes use of magical weapons, sigils and talismans, incantations, and the like. Between these two poles of divine magic are the adepts who perform their art purely on the inner planes through the projection of consciousness in a subtle or spiritual body. The divine magic of pure thought corresponds to Hokmah, the divine magic accomplished through the subtle or spiritual body on the inner planes corresponds to Tiferet-Da'at, and the divine magic of sacred ritual corresponds to Hod.

The virtue of the divine magic that initiates learn in the study and practice of the magical Kabbalah is that, at every level, whether sacred ritual or inner plane work in a spiritual body, all methods reflect the pure magic of supernal or Christ consciousness and have their source of inspiration from divine wisdom (Hokmah). This is not true of all systems of ceremonial magic, however, as many systems put forth by occultists of the twentieth century are not the product of the inspiration of divine wisdom or enlightenment, but rather are derived from klippotic influences. A fine example is the so-called "Enochian magic," which, its origin shows, was not received in a state of purity or holiness, nor by individuals seeking enlightenment and liberation. The spiritual beings-forces called in always reflect the consciousness of those who link with them. If the consciousness is impure and imperfect, so also will be the spiritual beings-forces invoked. In terms of systems of magic, we are wise to follow the advice of the Master Yeshua: "Beware of false prophets, who come to you in sheep's clothing but inwardly are ravenous wolves. You will know them by their fruits. Are grapes gathered from thorns, or figs from thistles? In the same way, every good tree bears good fruit, but the bad tree bears bad fruit. A good tree cannot bear bad fruit, nor can a bad tree bear good fruit. Every tree that does not bear good fruit is cut down and thrown into the fire. Thus you will know them by their fruits" (Gospel of Matthew 7:15–20).

As much as a mystic, Master Yeshua was also a magician. Divine magic is part of the Gnostic Christian Tradition; however, one must be discerning as to what forms of magic one practices and know how to put the spirits to the test, to ensure that the magic one practices is, in fact, inspired by the divine. The thought that one can attain more power through less than divine forms of magic, or attain power more swiftly, is not true. Have you ever met a magician who could wield more power than Yeshua, or through whom more acts of magic naturally flowed forth, or who was able to raise the dead? Given the deeds of Master Yeshua, it would seem obvious that the divine magic he practiced was the highest and most powerful form possible—divine magic as reflected in the teachings of all incarnations of the great world-teacher.

Radiant Wisdom in Creation

Few initiates can reach into Atzilut to glean knowledge of divine magic or to gain prophetic insight, let alone attain Hokmah of Atzilut, which is the divine fullness of supernal or Messianic consciousness. Therefore, more often than not, it is through the agency of the archangel Ratziel that most initiates and adepts come into contact with Hokmah—Ratziel being the personification of Hokmah at the level of Beriyah.

Ratziel means the "secret of God," "mystery of God," or "wisdom of God." Thus, Ratziel is said to hold the knowledge of the highest mysteries, specifically mysteries concerning prophecy and the magical Kabbalah. These mysteries are said to have been written down in a heavenly book by the archangel—the Book of Ratziel. Like so many other legendary holy books of the Kabbalah, the Book of Ratziel is read in a higher state of consciousness, most often in dreams or visionary states during deep meditation. Although at least one earthly book has been written bearing the title *The Book of Ratziel,* and undoubtedly many other books on the magical Kabbalah have been inspired from the heavenly book, the Book of Ratziel cannot be contained in a single earthly volume or any number of earthly volumes, for it is a book of God's infinite wisdom in creation, containing all mysteries of creation, with the exception of the mystery of the creation of Adam (the human one).

As much as a book of divine magic, the Book of Ratziel is a heavenly book of supernal prophecy. For all scientific or artistic discovery that will ever be made, and everything that will result from these discoveries, is in this holy book. From the perspective of Ratziel or Hokmah of Beriyah, all revelation and therefore all discovery has already happened. One might say that what is called magic today will be called science in the future, and what is called prophecy will become the creative outpouring of tomorrow's art. In a certain respect, one could call Ratziel the supernal muse.

The Book of Ratziel is actually a metaphor for the mind of the supernal angel, and the content of the holy book is the knowledge and understanding conveyed by contact with this manifestation of the holy Shekinah. Constantly, the Kabbalah is speaking in human and anthropomorphic terms of heavenly or spiritual things, and one must bear this in mind to gain a true understanding of what is actually being taught in the Kabbalah. If one wishes to read the Book of Ratziel, he or she must come into contact with Ratziel, or he or she must shift to the higher consciousness personified as Ratziel.

The traditional image through which Gnostic initiates envision Ratziel in meditation is both beautiful and powerful. Ratziel is envisioned in a gray hooded robe, formed from clouds. The face of Ratziel shines from within the hood as though the sun shining through the clouds, and the robe itself is inwardly illuminated as if the orb of the sun were in it. The effect produces rainbows streaming out from the image in all directions. The background to the visualization is deep, crystal-clear sky-blue, so that it is as though the archangel has gathered clouds to form a visible image. In his left hand, Ratziel holds a holy staff, the top of which is carved as the head of a great dragon, and the letters of the divine name Yahweh are engraved on the staff, ablaze like fire. In his right hand is a crystal sphere. With the chant of the divine names: Yahweh and Ya Ra-Tziel, the most basic form of meditation seeking contact with Ratziel is performed. It is quite possible that a meditation on this divine image could convey deeper insights into the reality of Hokmah than all the words written in this chapter. As the saying goes, "a picture is worth a thousand words." This is especially true of the divine images of visualization created by adepts and masters of the Tradition, which reflect and transmit something of the actual enlightenment experience they depict.

According to the Tradition, Ratziel was the holy guardian angel of supernal Adam in the Garden of Eden, and thus is said to be the great guardian and guide of the elect. Although Gabriel is considered the keeper of the holy grail and Michael has been called the guardian of the grail, Ratziel is said to know the inmost secret mystery of the holy grail, for Ratziel is the great angel of the Bride Sophia in Gnostic Tradition.

To speak of Ratziel in this way is to say that the holy ones—the elect—are guided and inspired in their divine labor by the wisdom of creation and seek to act in complete harmony with divine wisdom.

Wheels within Wheels

Merkavah Mysticism, which was the earliest form of the Kabbalah, was founded upon the first two chapters of Ezekiel in which the prophet describes his vision of a divine chariot (merkavah). Until the Book of Revelation, recording the vision of St. John, the vision of the divine chariot in the Book of Ezekiel was among the most detailed and complex descriptions of prophetic vision ever recorded. It was also unique in that typically, according to Jewish Tradition, prophecy did not occur outside of the holy land of Israel. However, that was not the case for Ezekiel. He experienced his prophetic vision during the Babylonian exile by the river Chebar, outside of the holy land. St. John's vision also occurred outside of the holy land, while he was in exile under Roman authority on the Isle of Patmos. Thus, the visions of these two prophets are also linked together in this way—both occurring outside of the holy land and apart from the temple in Jerusalem.

Essentially, these two prophetic visions happen under the same circumstances and are both prophetic visions of the same level—the clear mirror of prophecy at the level of Yetzirah. By sharing the imagery of the vision in great detail, both prophets not only share their prophecy, they provide us with insight into the divine continuum within and behind the material dimension, as well as instructions on how we might contact or enter into the divine continuum. Thus, along with other brief moments in the Scriptures in which the prophets speak of the opening of divine vision, these two holy books form a manual of instruction on prophetic meditation.

Prophecy cannot be invoked. Unlike the holy angels of God and other spiritual beings-forces, one cannot invoke/evoke the Spirit of God. One can create the conditions in which the Holy Spirit can move with, in, and through oneself, one can invite her and one can welcome her. But whether or not the Holy Spirit comes is a matter of divine will, not one's own will or one's mental or vital demand. One who seeks prophetic vision must learn how to wait upon the Spirit of Yahweh—how to become open and sensitive to divine grace.

We can invoke the archangel Ratziel and, in so doing, we can experience contact with the divine continuum through Ratziel and the Ofanim. The same is true of the other archangels and their hosts on the Tree of Life. Such a contact is a drawing down to us something of the influence of the divine continuum. However, to actually enter into the higher state of consciousness personified by the archangels and their hosts, we must be elevated by Ruach Ha-Kodesh (the holy spirit). Thus, through prayer, meditation, or sacred ritual, we can contact the continuum via the holy angels, but only through meditation can we wait upon the Spirit of Yahweh and fully enter into the divine continuum and prophetic consciousness.

In Gnostic Christianity, the divine continuum is a term for the spiritual world or metaphysical universe the initiate experiences within and behind the material dimension; specifically, by continuum is meant the force and matrix of the supernals as they manifest through the four Olamot. The archangels and the orders of angels that form their hosts serve as an interface between the divine continuum and creation, linking together the spiritual and material dimensions of creation. In relationship to God and humanity, they act as mediating agents bringing down the divine light to human beings and helping humanity in its ascent to the world of supernal light.

Archangels join Beriyah and Yetzirah, and the orders of holy angels that form their hosts serve to join Yetzirah and Asiyah. The dominion of an archangel plays out on a lower level through the order of angels under its charge. Thus, if Ratziel serves as a guide and guardian of human evolution, then so also does the order of the Ofanim under his charge.

The Ofanim appear in Ezekiel's vision and are described as having the appearance of wheels within wheels, with eyes on the rims of the wheels. Their color is said to be "gleaming beryl," which is typically associated with

aquamarine. According to Ezekiel, the Ofanim have a very close connection with the Hayyot Ha-Kodesh, so that the Ofanim move with the Hayyot and, when the Hayyot stop their movement, the Ofanim also stop their
motion. Ofan, literally "wheel," suggests the idea of continuum, cycles, and
movement. In terms of wheels on a chariot (Merkavah), they are the interaction of the chariot with the ground that serves to reduce friction or resistance and allow for movement. A chariot without wheels would not move
very well and the road beneath it would not last very long; without the
wheels, both the chariot and the earth would be torn up. Thus the Ofanim
represent the interaction of the spiritual dimension with the physical dimension, and as with the wheel of a chariot that allows the chariot to move
over the earth without tearing it up, the Ofanim serve to remove friction or
resistance between humanity and the influx of divine or spiritual energy.

The essential relationship of the Ofanim to humanity is reflected by
the wheel of the zodiac (Mazlot), which is the manifestation of Hokmah
at the level of Asiyah and represents the twelve archetypes of human per-
sonalities. It is also expressed through two archangels that the masters of
the Tradition identify as great Ofanim—Metatron and Sandalfon. You will
remember our previous exploration of Metatron as the image of the
human one in association with the story of Enoch. Sandalfon (Malkut in
Beriyah) is said to be the other face or other side of Metatron, as though
two sides of one Ofan. Sandalfon is the archangel that uplifts the prayers
of the faithful and elect before God and who transmits the blessings of
God in the assembly of believers. Her name literally means the "Shoe-
Angel," and like the wheel on the chariot, a shoe serves as the interface
between a foot and the ground. Metatron represents the divine ideal of
human evolution and Sandalfon, associated with prayer, meditation, and
sacred ritual, represents the way of that evolution.

Because of this function of serving as a direct interaction between the
spiritual and physical world, the Ofanim are often called the angels of
Asiyah and, as with the wheel of the zodiac, are often associated with the
movement of the moon, planets, and stars. In truth, the Ofanim are the
force in motion, through ebbs and flows, in every form within creation.
Thus, as much as the movement of the force in celestial bodies, they are
the movement of life-waves through world systems and all forms of continuums or cycles in creation.

The intimate connection between the Hayyot and the Ofanim given by Ezekiel alludes to the Hayyot as the agents of the divine will or divine plan at the level of Yetzirah and the Ofanim as the agents of the interface of that divine plan with the physical universe. Therefore, as the Ofanim are often called the angels of Asiyah, the Hayyot are often called the angels of Yetzirah.

These two orders of angels are linked together in the vision of Ezekiel in terms of movement, but they are also linked together through the faces ascribed to the Hayyot—the face of a human, the face of an ox, the face of a lion, and the face of an eagle. These correspond to the fixed signs of the zodiac—Aquarius, Taurus, Leo, and Scorpio, respectively—the Ofan of the zodiac.

Hayyot are the expression of the divine will and, thus, the intention of God within and behind every movement of the force. The Ofanim are the movements of God's Spirit according to God's intention.

Prophecy is the revelation of interactions of the holy Shekinah with the physical world and, specifically, with humanity. Thus, prophecy is an expression of the function of the Ofanim, and a given prophecy could be considered an Ofan. Likewise, divine magic is the result of a change in the relationship of the divine and the material world, which causes a corresponding change in the flow of the force and, therefore, a change in what actually transpires in the material dimension—specifically, a change through a human agent. This, too, is an expression of the function of the Ofanim, and a true magical act in harmony with the divine will could also be considered an Ofan.

If one contemplates the vision of Ezekiel and the vision of St. John, one will find that the former corresponds to Sandalfon (Malkut) and the latter corresponds to Metatron (Keter), as though one Great Ofan of the light continuum. This is true of all the prophets. However, as explained above, it is especially true of the visions of Ezekiel and St. John. In effect, the vision of St. John is contained in Ezekiel's vision of the divine merkavah, so that St. John's vision is the unfolding of the vision of Ezekiel and of all of the prophets to its completion and fulfillment—the fruition of the light continuum in the human life-wave.

Spiritual Practices for Hokmah

Giving and Receiving Meditation

The following practice is common to both Gnostic Christianity and Mahayana Buddhism. It corresponds to both Hokmah and Tiferet on the Tree of Life—to Hokmah as the awareness of sacred unity and realization of the radiant holy breath; to Tiferet as the awareness of the indwelling Christ, the development of spiritual compassion and the mystery of the crucifixion.

To fully acquire the power of the divine names, one must be aware of the sacred unity and have an awareness of oneself as part of the sacred unity. Likewise, one needs to become aware of the light-presence (Christos) within oneself and the light-force within one's breath. One also needs to develop spiritual love and compassion, which comes from the awareness of sacred unity, the light-presence and radiant holy breath of God that we share with all that lives.

In the Gnostic Christian Tradition, spiritual or mystical attainment is primary and such things as prophetic consciousness and magic powers are secondary. The truth is that, without a significant degree of spiritual development and self-discipline, we are deluding ourselves in chasing after the prophetic experience and magical powers. Giving and receiving meditation represents one of the preliminary practices for the spiritual development necessary for more advanced practices of prophetic meditation and divine magic.

That giving and receiving is given as a preliminary practice should not lead one to think that it is in any way less powerful than the more advanced practices. Preliminary practices are always the foundation of advanced forms of practice, and when practiced by adepts and masters of the Tradition, these basic practices have magical results. With this practice, an advanced initiate can uplift and heal others on physical, psychic, and spiritual levels. Likewise, he or she can banish negative forces from an environment or person. A master could conceivably use this practice to liberate a person from their karmic bondage. However, before such things are possible, one must learn to uplift and heal oneself—to enlighten and liberate oneself. Thus, such practices begin, in their basic form, as a work on oneself and are preliminary in this sense.

The Base of the Practice

The base of the practice is fundamentally the same for all forms of giving and receiving meditation. In fact, it is common to the vast majority of meditation practices in Gnostic Christianity. The base of the practice is as follows:

> ➤ Sit down and allow yourself to relax, yet remain completely alert. Let your body find its own natural rhythm of breath, and gently place your awareness on your breath—just being present with your breath and the moment.

> ➤ Then envision the light-presence (the indwelling Christ) as a spiritual sun within and behind your heart. Imagine your breath linked to this spiritual sun, as though the spiritual sun were breathing through you. Feel the warmth of the spiritual sun in the center of your being—the light, love, and healing power of Christ in you. Feel the depth of knowledge, understanding, and wisdom of the light-presence; the depth of forgiveness and compassion. Feel the sacred heart of Christ open in yourself and the acceptance of yourself, just as you are, by the Christ-presence. As you breathe, imagine that your whole body-mind is pervaded with the light—filled with the light and love of Christ. This is the base of the practice, which itself is the very essence of the practice.

Giving and Receiving with the Environment

> ➤ Begin with the base practice, establishing the spiritual sun within you and linking your breath to the spiritual sun. Feel the texture of your mind and heart—the mood and general atmosphere of your consciousness. If you feel uneasy, anxious, unclear, if you notice any form of mental or emotional negativity, if you feel resistance to the spirit of truth in any way, or if you feel anything that is dark and cloudy, then as you breathe in, breathe the negativity into the spiritual sun. When you breathe out, breathe out light in its place. Breathe in everything that is negative and unwholesome, and breathe out everything that is good and true. The spiritual sun transforms everything into the likeness of itself, so that you breathe out light in the place of darkness. Breathe peace, joy, light, love, clarity, hope, understanding, faith, and all good things into the atmosphere of your consciousness.

> ➤ Filled with the light-presence in this way, you can do the same
> thing with the environment around you. You can breathe in any-
> thing that is negative or dark, and as you breathe out, you can envi-
> sion the environment being filled with light. You need not worry or
> fear that anything can harm you that you breathe in, because the
> spiritual sun of Christ in you cannot be harmed by anything. Such
> is the real power of the Christ-self (the solar self).

Adepts and masters of the Tradition often use this method to uplift and
bless others in their environment, or to transmit substantial and helpful
spiritual energy.

Giving and Receiving with Oneself

> ➤ When you are comfortable with the above method, you can then
> progress to giving and receiving with oneself. In this method you
> visualize two selves, as it were, a light self and a dark elf. In the
> meditation, you are the light self and the dark self stands in front
> of you, perhaps five feet away.

> ➤ This dark self holds all the self-negativity of your consciousness—
> all the feelings of insecurity, fear, self-loathing; feelings of being
> abandoned, rejected, and judged; feelings of guilt, regret, or remorse;
> all the sorrow and suffering of your experience; all the pain and
> grief; every possible form of negativity, including bitterness, re-
> sentment, anger, and hatred, and all imaginable vices (selfishness,
> greed, and so on).

> ➤ Holding the image of the dark self before you, establish yourself in
> the light-presence, and open your mind and heart to this aspect of
> yourself completely. Feel the light-presence in you responding with
> love and compassion to this darkness—yearning to embrace and
> heal this dark and fragmented self. Open yourself to this dark self
> and let the Christ-self in you take on the sorrow and suffering of
> this lost soul completely. Breathe the breath of light. As you breathe
> in, envision the negativity of this dark self as a sooty, reddish-brown
> or black smoke, and see that smoke dissolved and transformed in
> the light of the spiritual sun. As you breathe out, breathe light into
> the dark self. In this way, continue to exchange your light and good
> for all the negative energies of the dark self, seeing yourself and
> this dark self progressively becoming brighter and brighter, until

both images are completely filled with the light. Then see yourself exchanging light with yourself, the whole environment becoming radiant with light—light upon light. Completing the meditation, envision these two selves merging into one light-presence and know yourself whole and complete, just as you are.

Giving and Receiving in Real Life

➤ Perform the base practice, and with the awareness and courage of the Christ-presence, imagine as vividly as possible any actual situation in which you have acted badly—a situation about which you feel guilty or have remorse or profound regret, and that is actually painful to even think about. Let yourself feel this whole thing deeply and consider the harm done by your actions.

➤ Then, as you breathe in, take total responsibility for your actions in that particular situation, but without any self-judgment or any attempt to justify your behavior. Acknowledge exactly what you have done wrong and with your whole heart ask for forgiveness. Now, as you breathe out, breathe out forgiveness, reconciliation, clarity, understanding, peace, healing, and love. So, in effect, you breathe in blame and breathe out undoing harm; you breathe in responsibility and breathe out forgiveness. As you accept responsibility, also let yourself accept forgiveness from the inner self or Christ-self, knowing that, in assuming responsibility and letting go of guilt, you are forgiven by God. God has already forgiven you, but you must forgive yourself. When you complete this process, know that there is peace between you and God.

➤ Oftentimes, initiates may complete this practice by actually seeking out the person or persons that they have harmed and asking them for their forgiveness. If that is not possible, instead they will seek out a spiritual brother or sister and ask him or her to listen to their confession of responsibility. Sometimes, such action is necessary for us to accept self-forgiveness and to actually experience full healing. Being responsible for one's actions is essential to authentic spirituality. In the end result, whatever we do to others, we have done to ourselves. This is the truth we discover in higher states of consciousness.

Giving and Receiving for Others

➤ Perform the base practice; then imagine someone to whom you feel very close magically appearing in the space before you—a friend or loved one you know to be suffering or having a difficult time in life. Follow the same steps as in giving and receiving with oneself, until the image of your friend or loved one is completely filled with the light-presence. When the process is complete, imagine that they are healed and fulfilled totally, with no doubt in your mind. Instead of merging with the image of the person, see them departing in joy, going their own way.

➤ Once you can do this well with friends and loved ones, practice doing it for strangers. At the point you can do this practice with deep feeling for strangers, you are ready to perform this practice upon those you would consider enemies or whom you do not like. The ultimate aim of this practice is to be able to perform it just as well for a friend, stranger or enemy. Such is the nature of true spiritual love and compassion or the sacred heart of Christ.

SEVEN

BINAH, THE DEPTH OF UNDERSTANDING, THE DIVINE INTELLIGENCE

Attributes

Thirty-Two Paths of Wisdom: Sanctified Consciousness (Sek-hel MeKudash); this is the foundation of Original Wisdom, and it is called "Faithful Faith"; its roots are in AMeN. It is the father of faith, and from its power faith emerges

Binah: Understanding

Place on the Tree of Life: Head of the Pillar of Severity

Divine Name: Elohim or Yahweh Elohim

Alternative Divine Names: Elohim Hayyim, Living God; Shekinah Aila, Upper Shekinah; Tzedek Elyon, Highest Justice

Partzuf Above: Aima, Mother

Partzuf Below: The Holy Mother, Mother Mary; the Matriarchs; Prophet Miriam in the Torah

Divine Image: A mature woman; the image of Mother Mary; Mother Mary enthroned with the Apocalyptic Lamb seated upon the Book of Seven Seals in her lap; the image of the Woman of Light in the Apocalypse

Archangel: Tzafkiel or Shabbatiel

Order of Angels: Aralim

Celestial Attribute: Shabbatai, Saturn

Titles Given to Binah: Mother Sophia or Mother Wisdom; Depth of End;
   The Holy Womb; the Matrix of Creation; the Matrix of Light;
   Khorsia, the Throne; Marah, the Bitter Sea or Great Sea; Pearl of
   Grace; Queen of Heaven; Star of Grace; Sophia Stellarum, Starry
   Wisdom; Mother of Faith; Holy Birther; the Crone or Old Hag;
   Woman of Light; Mother Israel; Throne of Glory; Divine Grace;
   Divine Fullness; God the Mother; The Matriarch; the Way; Cave
   of the Ancestors; The Eternal Sabbath; Bridal Chamber

Level of the Soul: Neshamah, Divine Nature or Heavenly Soul

Heavenly Abode: The World of Supernal Light

Spiritual Experience: The Radiant Holy Breath of God; the Anointing
   with the Supernal Light; the Vision of Pure Delight; the Vision
   of Sorrow

Virtues: Self-discipline; responsibility; silence; divine authority;
   discipleship

Vices: Lack of organization; greed; lack of self-discipline; betrayal;
   cupidity

Symbols: The Cave; The Vesica Piscis; the Kteis or Yoni; the cup, chal-
   ice or grail; the Outer Robe of Concealment; the letter He; The
   Chair of the Elder

Commandment: You shall not make wrongful use of the name of the Lord
   your God (Exodus 20:7)

Sermon on the Mount: Blessed are those who are persecuted for righteousness sake, for theirs is the kingdom of heaven (Matthew 5:10–12)

Angel of the Apocalypse and Churches: The Presence of the Holy Angel
   (Revelation 2:1–7)

The Radiant Darkness

Hokmah is the radiant fullness of all divine potential and Binah is the
emptiness or radiant darkness through which all divine potential is realized. In Keter, this divine fullness and primordial emptiness are one and

the same divine being. At the outset of the creative act, the divine being reveals itself in Hokmah-wisdom, its pure radiant awareness, to itself, its own infinite receptivity—Binah, its understanding or intelligence. On the one hand, Binah resides in THE luminous abundance of Hokmah like the emptiness or radiant darkness of a mirror, and emerges from within Hokmah and envelopes the divine radiance, becoming its super-intelligible plane of self-reflection. On the other hand, Binah emerges directly from within Keter as a simultaneous emanation with Hokmah, the dark and light aspect of the primordial divine essence—pure awareness and perfect receptivity.

Like a supernal circuit from which no cosmic energy escapes, Keter-Hokmah-Binah of Atzilut is a sacred unity—one and the same being-consciousness-force. Hokmah is the outpouring of the infinite possibility of Keter into the midst of Binah in a single and undifferentiated Emanation. The infinite radiation of Arik Anpin enters into the great void of his-her boundless receptivity. In that mirror-like nature, the great face of God is reflected and the Atik Yomin (the Ancient of Days) knows him-herself. Thus God receives Godself back into Godself, as it were, and it is this self-knowledge from which creation is born. Keter is the Gnostic or knowing being, Hokmah is the Gnosis or knowledge itself and Binah is that which is known. Every creature and the whole of creation are in Binah (God's understanding or intelligence) as in a womb.

To understand this, one must bear in mind that God's knowledge is not like our typical human knowledge, which is knowledge of things seemingly separate and apart from us. In our human knowledge, there is a division between the knower (subject) and that which is known (object), but in divine Gnosis there is no division between the knower and the known—God knows all things within Godself as Godself. Thus, knowing him-herself and perceiving him-herself, God knows and understands all things in Godself.

We have spoken previously of Keter appearing and disappearing from within Ain Sof—that is, when Keter turns toward Ain Sof, it merges with Ain Sof and disappears, but when Keter turns away from Ain Sof toward the Sefirot below, it appears. This is directly reflected in Binah. For when Binah is turned toward Keter, she and Hokmah merge and are the fullness of Arik Anpin—the big face of God. When she turns downward, giving birth to the seven Sefirot of construction below, she appears as Aima, the supernal Mother, and Hokmah appears as Abba, the supernal Father.

Binah, as the self-knowledge of God from which all of creation comes into being, is the "foundation of original or primordial wisdom," Her ability to unite herself with Hokmah in Keter is her "faithful faith" and the truth of her "roots being in Amen," a title of Keter. Binah is sanctified in her unity with the infinite.

The Archetypal World—The World of Supernal Light

As expressed in the last chapter, Hokmah represents the sayings or axioms upon which creation is founded—hence the wisdom of Creation. Binah is the underlying pattern or structure that gives order to these sayings so that their power might be actualized and their meaning understood. The sayings themselves are the force of Hokmah, and the pattern or structure that connects them creates the forms they assume—not the gross forms of actual manifestation, but rather the supernal or archetypal forms that are the patterns upon which all actual forms are founded. The force of Hokmah becomes the archetypal forms or heavenly images of creation in Binah—the meaning of the divine name Yahweh Elohim as the expression of Binah at the level of Atzilut. Yahweh is the one consciousness-force and Elohim is the archetypes through which the one consciousness-force manifests. What actually becomes manifest is Da'at and the seven Sefirot below the great abyss.

This is reflected in the story of the construction of the tabernacle, which was built based upon the pattern of the supernal world. Betzalel was chosen by divine election as the builder of the tabernacle, and it is said that Yahweh filled Betzalel with the spirit of wisdom, understanding, and knowledge (Exodus 31:3). Thus, the tabernacle was to be built with the same principles as the Olamot. Based upon our own experience, this may be explained in the following way. Hokmah is akin to the knowledge one receives from others, which has evolved through previous life experience. It represents the capacity to receive and integrate fundamental means or axioms into one's own mental being. Binah indicates the capacity to draw out additional information from what one has received, and

Da'at represents one's capacity to carry out actual work based upon one's acquired knowledge and understanding. In terms of the divine, this creative capacity of wisdom, understanding, and knowledge is infinite. In relationship to the ideal form of a tabernacle—the heavenly tabernacle—the actual forms of tabernacles or temples that can be generated to reflect the ideal form are potentially endless.

Essentially, Binah represents the idea of God as the ideal form and all archetypes as variations of that supreme ideal. These archetypes all exist in the sacred unity of the ideal form. Thus, the archetypes of all things are equal, although they are archetypes of unequal things—for in the ideal form that God is, they are all united and equal. The highest supernal angel, the soul of a human being, and the existence of the smallest creature have one single archetype in God—God's own divine being in which all ideal forms are identical. God imparts Godself to all things equally to the degree that they are from God and founded upon God. The holy angels, all humankind, and all creatures are equal as they first emerge from God. If one sees things at their source, in the very essence of their being, one sees that they are all equally great and wonderful—equal in every way. If one perceives this equality in space-time-consciousness, one can only wonder at the nature of equality to be found in eternity. For the smallest creature is far greater in the divine being than the highest supernal angel is in itself. In God, all things are perfectly equal and all are equally in God. Such a perception is a vision of delight, but it is also a vision of sorrow when one sees cosmic ignorance preventing this self-realization in so many good creatures of God.

The Pleroma—Divine Fullness

In the Jewish Kabbalah, the divine name for Binah is "Yahweh pronounced as Elohim." As we explored in the chapter on Da'at, which shares the divine name Yahweh Elohim with Binah, Yahweh Elohim alludes to the idea of the one force or life-power that assumes many forms. As we saw above, the pleroma or divine fullness proper is Hokmah, while Binah is the primordial emptiness or receptivity through which the divine fullness is actualized. The phrase "Yahweh pronounced as Elohim" suggests the principle of emptiness inherent in Elohim.

One way to understand this is in terms of the Partzuf of Binah, Aima, and the idea of the Mother's womb. Until activated by the reception of the Father's seed-force, the Mother's womb is a profound emptiness, but once the Mother receives the issuance of the Father, she becomes divine fullness. Until the seed-force passes into the Mother, the force of the Father is only potential, and likewise, the power of the Mother to matrix the force and manifest it in form is only potential. Thus, through their union, the Father and Mother actualize one another.

The analogy of the male and female in union is alluded to in the name of Elohim itself, which is a feminine noun with a masculine plural, suggesting the idea of the womb of the pregnant mother. It is a name suggesting an absolute unity in infinite multiplicity. Some occultists have ascribed the meaning of Elohim as a plethora of gods and goddesses, as the idea of the pagan faiths; however, such an association misses the subtlety of the divine name completely. First, one must understand that the idea of the Father and the Mother is not two but rather is one—the principle of force and form are one in the supernal world. Second, one must understand that the idea behind a feminine noun with a masculine plural does not suggest a multiplicity of goddesses and gods, but rather one divine parent who can infinitely generate and give birth—the endless generation of creation. Third, the plurality associated with the divine being is one of qualities, attributes, or apparent functions, akin to qualities, attributes, and functions that might be associated with a person. For example, a woman can be a specialist at work, like a lawyer, and as a lawyer she may have many different qualities. She may also be a daughter, sister, wife, mother, and a leader in a community service, among other things. Whatever qualities, attributes, or functions might be ascribed to her, they are all the expression of one person—one woman—and she is the unity behind all qualities, attributes, or functions that might be ascribed to her and she is more than all these qualities, attributes, and functions (she is herself). It is similar with the relationship of God to God's qualities, attributes, and functions in creation. Elohim as a name of God does not mean the plurality of many different gods and goddesses, but rather one supreme being that manifests him- or herself through countless qualities or attributes and functions, which form the matrix of creation.

This gives insight into the nature of the Olamot and Sefirot. They are Elohim, the many qualities or attributes and operations of God in creation. The Sefirot exist in the sacred unity that God is and cannot be seen in any way separate and apart from God or separate and apart from one another. They are "like the flame to the coal," as the Kabbalah says.

Elohim is composed of the letters Aleph (א)-Lamed (ל)-He (ה)-Yod (י)-Mem (ם). Aleph, as we have seen, is the letter of God's spirit. Lamed, which as a word means "ox goad," suggests a driving or directing force. He, which means a "window" or "opening," suggests the idea of a channel through which light and spirit pass. Yod, which means "hand," suggests the hand of God or power of God and specifically the seed-force of Hokmah. Mem is considered a "Mother Letter," associated with the primordial element of water. It literally means "seas" or "waters," and denotes the medium or substance of creation—consciousness. All of these ideas directly suggest the Mother, the womb or matrix—the living God (Elohim Hayyim).

The womb brings the spirit into form, and the pangs of giving birth are, indeed, an irresistible driving force. The womb is the channel of all-life, the passage through which all life comes into being. The nature of that life is the one force, and the one force is consciousness. Everything is the one consciousness-force, and this consciousness-force is inseparable from being. This is the meaning of Elohim.

Elohim is the divine name used throughout the story of creation. The name of Elohim appears thirty-two times in the story of creation, reflecting the ten sefirot and twenty-two letters, which form the circles and lines of the Tree of Life glyph and represents the diverse manifestations of the one consciousness-force in the creative act. Elohim means the divine presence and power of creation.

The Supernal Mother and Shekinah

The Partzuf of Binah is Aima, the supernal Mother, which is alluded to by the divine name of Elohim, as we have seen. All of the Partzufim of the Sefirot come into being through the Partzuf Aima, for it is through the supernal Mother that the transcendental and impersonal dimension of God becomes personal and immanent. Without the divine Mother, the heavenly Father is not the Father, and the Son and Daughter do not come into being. The Father-Mother is the great face of God (Arik Anpin), and thus, without the Mother, the face of God does not form and appear. As the divine matrix, the supernal Mother is the primordial space in which everything comes into being and she is the relationship or interconnectedness of everything, including the connectedness of the God and creation.

It is a great mystery exactly how the Godhead, the transcendental and impersonal, becomes translated into the personal and immanent God—how, on the one hand, we can experience God as completely impersonal and yet, on the other hand, experience God in a completely personal way. These two modes of experiencing the divine would seem to contradict one another. However, the nature of divine being is energy and intelligence, and the aspect of intelligence is self-awareness. Therefore intelligence, the Mother, tends to generate the phenomena of person.

The Mother is the power of God to limit or constrict Godself—the power of the tzimtzum. She is the Sefirot, the divine names, and Partzufim, and through her the archangels, orders of angels, and the worlds coming into being, which allow human beings to experience a connection with God and to consciously unite with God. A traditional saying in the Kabbalah is that "He and His Name are One." She is the holy name; uniting oneself with the name, one is united with the Holy One of Being.

The divine Mother is, thus, the divine power of Yichud-Unification and the Yichudim (plural), through which the Sefirot and Olamot are joined together in unity and harmony, and through which the soul is joined to the Sefirot and the Sefirot are joined to the soul.

The Mother is the Shekinah—the divine presence and power of God—in all of its forms. Binah is the upper Shekinah, the Queen of Heaven, and Malkut is the lower Shekinah, the earthly Mother. The Upper Shekinah (Mother) and the lower Shekinah (Daughter) are intimately linked together—the Daughter (Malkut kingdom) being the image of the Holy Mother below. In the soul of the tzaddik (righteous person or enlightened human), the unity of the Holy Mother and Daughter becomes fully conscious, which is to say fully realized and actualized—hence the divine power that moves with the prophets and apostles of God.

The Shekinah is synonymous with the Holy Spirit. Thus, the Holy Trinity of the Father, Son, and Holy Spirit is actually the Father, Son, and Mother-Spirit. The Holy Spirit is the divine Mother who, in union with the heavenly Father, gives birth to the Messiah, and She is the Daughter who is the Holy Bride of the Messiah. Thus, within and behind the Holy Trinity is the Holy Tetrad of the Father and the Mother, and the Son and the Daughter—the sacred unity of the Tetrad being represented by the sign of the cross (see Figure 5).

The hexagram or Star of David represents the union of the upper and lower Shekinah, and thus the unity of God the Mother with the elect (Israel).

Figure 5: The Sign of the Cross.

Specifically, the hexagram is the symbol of the macrocosm (God) and the pentagram or five-pointed star is the symbol of the Christed microcosm (human being). The hexagram is, therefore, the activity of the Shekinah above and the pentagram is the activity of the Shekinah below—the hexagram itself representing the unity of the Mother and Daughter because the power of the Daughter is the Holy Mother (Elohim).

The upper Shekinah is the Shekinah in the world of supernal light, and the lower Shekinah is the Shekinah in creation and the material world. The world of supernal light is the direct emanation of the divine presence and power of God and the Godhead. Therefore, in the Christian Kabbalah, the upper Shekinah is called Mother Sophia or uncreated wisdom, while the lower Shekinah is called Daughter Sophia or created wisdom. In essence, the upper and lower Shekinah are one presence and power and there is no division between them, so that everything that is said of the upper Shekinah is true of the lower Shekinah. For the lower Shekinah is simply the presence and power of God manifest at a lower grade, closer to our ordinary level of consciousness and experience.

The face of the Father is One, depicted by the great name of Yahweh, but the faces of the Mother are many, depicted by the name of Elohim. The face of the Father-Abba is not seen, save through the agency of the Mother-Aima. When the face of God appears to change from one face to another face, such as from mercy to judgment, the face of the Father has not changed; rather, we are beholding a different face of the divine Mother. The Mother is the all in all.

The Faces of the Shekinah—Our Divine Mother

In relationship to God and the Godhead, the Shekinah is Bride and Companion, and she is the Mother of God, giving birth to the God in creation. Everything we behold of God and experience of God is the Shekinah—God the Mother.

The Shekinah, as the supernal Mother at the level of Atzilut, is inseparable from God the Father and the Godhead. They abide together in perfect unity continually, never separating from one another. Yet, as the cosmic Mother at the level of Beriyah, the Shekinah enters into union and departs from union with the Holy One. She either is united with the holy one or acts independently of the Holy One, all according to the activity of creatures in creation, specifically humanity in whom there is the divine power to either effect unification or division. This divine power to unify or divide is the Shekinah herself, who is the divine presence and power within creature and creation and thus within the human soul. When human beings pray, meditate, perform sacred ceremony, and bring their souls into union with God, they join the Shekinah that indwells them to God. Conversely, when human beings give no thought of God and do not act to unite themselves with God, the Shekinah indwelling, in effect, is separated from God. Significantly, according to the Kabbalah, when a man and woman join together in love and there is an awareness of the divine in their union, their unification below brings about a spiritual union of God and the Shekinah above—and thus the union of the man and woman is blessed. Therefore, the covenant of marriage is most holy in the eyes of the Kabbalah, for it is one of the central ways through which a unification is brought about both above and below.

The relationship of the Shekinah and God is often viewed in sexual terms. On one level, the Song of Solomon in the Scriptures is interpreted as the love affair between God and the Shekinah; although, on other levels, it is contemplated as the love-play of the Bridegroom (Tiferet) and Holy Bride (Malkut) or as the relationship of the Christ-presence to the assembly of the elect. As the love affair of God and the Shekinah, the Song of Solomon indicates bliss or delight as the foundation of creation—for creation comes into being and is sustained through the love-play of God and the Shekinah. We saw in our exploration of Keter that ratzon is the very nature of the creative impulse—desire being the primary expression of the force or energy of creation. Therefore, one could rightly say that the ground of creation is a cosmic orgasmic bliss—the most essential experience of the divine power being one of divine joy. According to the masters of the Tradition, the love of the Shekinah for the Lord is passionate, and one who experiences that love is filled with unimaginable divine bliss.

The passion of the Shekinah does not only extend to God but also to the faithful and elect who are lovers of God, to whom she is also a companion. She cleaves to the Lord and she cleaves to those who unite themselves with her in her love of the Lord, and thus joins together lovers with their beloved.

The lower Shekinah is the Holy Shabbat (Sabbath) and the upper Shekinah is the queen of the Shabbat. When the faithful and elect remember and keep the Shabbat, withdrawing from mundane activity and focusing upon the supramundane activity of spiritual study and discourse, prayer, meditation, and sacred ritual, they join themselves to the lower Shekinah. Through their invocations, the upper and lower Shekinah are united, and the Shekinah and God are drawn into mystical embrace, so that blessings of grace pour out upon the assembly and the Shekinah is manifest in the world. The daily continuum of spiritual living and spiritual practice throughout the week is akin to the foreplay of love, and the Shabbat is akin to the climax of love-play in mystical union.

Immediately following Binah on the Tree of Life are the Sefirot of Hesed (mercy) and Gevurah (judgment), which are balanced by the Christ-center, the Sefirah Tiferet (beauty or compassion). This alludes to the two faces of the Shekinah or the Mother of enlightenment—the bright Mother and the dark Mother or Sophia Stellarum (starry wisdom) and Sophia Nigrans (dark wisdom). At the level of Atzilut, as indicated above, the bright Mother and the dark Mother is one and the same: She is the divine presence and power of the supernal light—hence the Mother of enlightenment. But at the levels of Beriyah, Yetzirah, and Asiyah, she is both the bright Mother and the dark Mother. She manifests as the mercy of God and the judgment of God, peaceful emanations and wrathful emanations.

This is reflected in the eightfold initiation into Christ consciousness, one version of which is as follows: Birth, Baptism, Transfiguration, Crucifixion, and Resurrection, which leads to the Ascension and the outpouring of the holy fire of Pentecost. In birth, the bright and dark Mother are one and the same; for in giving life, the Mother also brings the sorrow and suffering of death. Birth, itself, is a traumatic experience for both the mother and the child. Baptism is an initiation of rebirth in the Holy Spirit—a mystical death that leads to the temptation. The baptism is the bright Mother giving birth to Christ in us, and the temptation is the dark Mother manifesting as the ordeal of initiation. The transfiguration is the outpouring of the blessings of the bright Mother in divine revelation, which is followed by the manifestation of the dark Mother, once again, in the passion and crucifixion of the Christ-bearer. Through this dark night, the bright Mother shines forth in full glory as the redemption of the resurrection and the unification of the ascension—the supreme revelation of the mystery of Messianic consciousness. In this process of initiation into supernal or Messianic consciousness, both the bright Mother and the dark Mother act toward the same end—the enlightenment and liberation of the soul. She is the same divine Mother, whether manifest in mercy or judgment, peaceful or wrathful emanation. Within and behind the appearance of peaceful or wrathful emanation, she is the blissful emanation of mystical union—supernal or Messianic consciousness. To experience this divine bliss, the aspirant must enter into the embrace of the dark Mother (Sophia Nigrans), for only through the dark Mother is the full power and glory of the bright Mother (Sophia Stellarum) realized.

At the level of Beriyah, the divine Mother, the Shekinah, is both the light and the darkness. She is the Mother of enlightenment or the Messiah and the Mother of ignorance or the cosmic illusion-power. She is the consciousness-force within all creatures, whether enlightened or unenlightened. At the level of Yetzirah, the Shekinah is, thus, the queen of heaven, Mother of the holy angels of God, and she is the queen of demons, giving birth to the klippot. In Asiyah, she is the life-power in the saint and sinner alike, and she gives to both the righteous and the wicked according to their desire to receive. The Shekinah is the light of the kingdom of heaven, but she is also the purifying fire of Gehenna (the dominion of hell). Nothing exists apart from God; therefore, all things are the manifestation of the divine presence and power of God.

Thus, the Shekinah is called both a virgin and a harlot. In her essence and nature, the Shekinah is ever the same—pure and completely unchanged. She is like a mirror that reflects images of good and evil, light and darkness, beauty and horror, yet regardless of what forms she assumes or what images appear in her, neither trace nor taint, nor stain nor mark, is left upon her. Yet, because she consorts with good and evil, angel and demon, saint and sinner alike, refusing no one her embrace, she is called a harlot. Such is the nature of the divine Mother.

This explains the mystery of what the masters of the Tradition mean when they say the Partzuf of Mother-Aima below is both the Virgin Mary (Mother Miriam) and the Whore of Babylon. On the side of the holy emanations (Sefirot), the Virgin Mary is the divine incarnation of Mother-Aima or Partzuf of Binah below. However, on the side of the impure emanations (klippot), Binah appears as the Whore of Babylon, the mother of abominations. The Whore of Babylon essentially represents the view of life from the perspective of cosmic ignorance—selfishness, lust-greed and fear-anger. The Holy Virgin, thus, represents the view of life from the perspective of enlightenment.

From the most brilliant light and great beauty to the most unimaginable darkness and horror, from the heights of supernal consciousness to the depths of cosmic ignorance, and the whole spectrum of consciousness-force in between, all are the faces of the Divine Mother, the manifestation of the Shekinah—blissful, peaceful, and wrathful. Essentially, encountering the Holy Spirit, one encounters oneself, the state of one's own consciousness or soul, and the appearance of the Divine Mother is the radiant nature of one's own mind.

The Image of the Divine Mother—
Crown, Throne, and Kingdom

Until the divine vision of St. John, no book of prophecy that appears in the canonized Scriptures gave a specific image of Mother-Aima (The Woman of Light [Revelation, Chapter 12]), yet Mother-Aima appears at the heart of the experience of the prophets in the vision of the one-who-sits-upon-the-throne. The image of the one-who-sits-upon-the-throne is said to be "the appearance of the likeness of the glory of Yahweh," which appears "like a human form." The human being, according to Genesis, is created in the image of Elohim, and you will recall the traditional phrase from the Jewish Kabbalah for the divine name of Binah—"Yahweh pronounced Elohim." The description of the one-who-sits-upon-the-throne is a visual image of Yahweh pronounced Elohim and alludes to Mother-matrix of the divine vision.

From one prophetic vision to another in the Scriptures, the image of the one-who-sits-upon-the-throne is different, reflecting the grade of the prophecy or degree of the enlightenment experience of the prophet, as well as the nature of the interaction and interrelationship of the spiritual and material world at the time of the prophecy. Sometimes the divine image on the throne is a Partzuf proper, as in the vision of Daniel who beholds the image of Atik Yomin—the Ancient of Days (Daniel 7:9). Sometimes the image on the throne is an archangel, such as Metatron, Michael, or Gabriel. Esoterically, whether a Partzuf or an archangel, the one-who-sits-upon-the-throne is called Hua, which is intended to mean "he-she." However, in Hebrew, Hu means "he" and Hua means "she"; therefore, the term Hua suggests Aima-Elohim.

According to the masters of the Tradition, when the phrase "the angel of Yahweh appeared unto . . ." occurs in the Scriptures, it connotes the Shekinah, who is the great angel of Yahweh. In Exodus, two images of the great angel of Yahweh are given, the image of the Pillar of Cloud and the image of the Pillar of Fire, which are said to be Metatron and Sandalfon, respectively, the archangels of crown and kingdom. They are images of hua-she, the Shekinah. As the throne unites the crown and the kingdom, Aima-Binah is implied.

The appearance of the Mother-Shekinah as the angel of Yahweh is Binah at the level of Yetzirah. The appearance of the Mother-Shekinah as a Partzuf proper is Binah at the level of Beriyah. If an adept has a direct experience of supernal or Messianic consciousness—direct knowledge, understanding, and wisdom—then he or she has touched upon Binah of Atzilut.

In the vision of the one-who-sits-upon-the-throne, the holy Mother is the crown, throne, and kingdom. The throne itself is Mother-Aima, the crown is the upper Shekinah, and the kingdom is the lower Shekinah. These three symbols represent the threefold manifestation of the Holy Spirit. As the crown, the Holy Spirit is Ruach Ha-Enoch, the spirit of the initiates. As the kingdom, the Holy Spirit is Ruach Ha-Elijah, the Spirit of the prophets. As the throne, the Holy Spirit is Ruach Ha-Messiah, the spirit of the anointed one—supernal or Messianic consciousness.

Ruach Ha-Elijah represents the power of mystical attainment and Ruach Ha-Enoch represents the power of magical attainment. Mystical attainment is the ability to ascend into higher levels of consciousness; magical attainment is the ability to embody something of the higher levels of consciousness-force or to bring down spiritual power into the astral and material planes. Ruach Ha-Messiah represents the union of mystical and magical attainment, for the attainment of supernal or Messianic consciousness is both mystical and magical, as we see with Master Yeshua. The symbol of the throne representing supernal or Messianic consciousness identifies the Mother-Aima as the supernal consciousness.

The crown, throne, and kingdom all connote divine authority. It is the divine Mother or Shekinah that grants divine authority to the Tzaddik, and a true Tzaddik will only act according to the divine authority granted to him or her, always using the holy Shekinah by divine permission. This is the essential distinction between a wonder-working man or woman of God and a sorcerer or black magician, for the holy ones act for the sake of the divine will and divine kingdom and do not practice divine magic to serve their own self-will or self-interests. The aim of the true initiate, like the Shekinah herself, is always *to heal*—to enlighten and liberate.

These symbols of the holy Mother-Aima allude to the noble ideal of the holy priest-king Melchizedek and the primordial Tradition. The primordial Tradition—the order of Melchizedek—is the Mother of all wisdom, and Mother Wisdom is the Mother of all the enlightened ones.

The Holy Virgin—Mother Mary

The Partzuf of Aima, God the Mother, becomes incarnate in the Mother Mary. According to the stories and legends of the Tradition, Mary was something of a spiritual prodigy, experiencing dreams, visions, and visitation of saints and holy angels from her earliest youth. There was a mystical circle in the hills of Galilee, founded upon the way of the prophetic assembly, and she was recognized as a soul of a higher grade by the elders of the circle and was received as a disciple. Among the elders was an old

woman who was a prophet. This old woman saw that Mary was the reincarnation of the soul of the prophet Miriam and in a vision she saw that
Mary rediscovered the miracle of Miriam's Well, which was said to be hidden on the shores of the sea of Galilee.

Joseph was also part of the mystical circle and married Mary. Shortly
after their marriage, Mary had a dream that she was to give birth to a
great Soul of Light who would be able to become the Messiah. Joseph believed in Mary's dreams and they sought to conceive a child together
using special practices involving the sexual mysteries (Arayot), which
they learned from elders of the circle. Through these spiritual practices,
they were able to draw in a great Soul of Light, the Soul of Yeshua.

When the great Soul of Light entered into Mary's womb, the Shekinah
descended upon her, indwelt her, and joined her soul to the Partzuf of
Aima, so that she became God the Mother, for only the matrix of creation
could give birth to such a great Soul of Light and be the Mother of the
Messiah. As the child grew in her womb, Mary became filled with divine
illumination and the spirits of the prophets, the patriarchs and matriarchs,
and holy angels of God were constantly coming and going from her presence. Everyone who entertained her company felt the presence of Yahweh with her. When she gave birth, she gave birth to light and she
became Miriam's Well, for living waters came forth from her heart-song.
These waters mingled with the waters of the baptism in the Jordan, so
that on the day the soul of the Messiah descended upon her Son, she became the Mother of God.

According to the Gospel of St. John, like a great mother eagle, Mother
Mary gently pushed the fledgling Messiah out of her nest, initiating the
wonder-working ministry of the Son at the wedding feast of Cana. As the
Son grew in power, in knowledge, understanding, and wisdom, and embodied the fullness of divine love, the Mother grew in glory, and grace
upon grace poured forth from her through the Son and the Daughter, his
Holy Bride. The Mother and the Son are inseparable, for through the Son
of God, she is the Mother of God, and through God the Mother, he is
God the Son. The Son of Adam, Sun of God, is the advent of the supernal
light in the world, and the Mother is the space or environment in which
the advent transpires—the channel of divine grace. Everything transpires
in the holy Mother.

The incarnation of the holy Mother is different than the incarnation of the Son and the Daughter—for Mother Sophia, the uncreated Sophia, is infinite and eternal, and completely transcendental. She is Incarnate to the Son (Christ the Logos) and to the Daughter (Christ the Sophia) and to those who receive the divine fullness of Christ in themselves. Yet she remains transcendent and transparent to all others until she is fully glorified in the Son and she herself is taken up into heaven through ascension. Christ the Logos pervaded the Nefesh of Lord Yeshua, and Christ the Sophia (created Sophia) pervaded the Nefesh of St. Mary Magdalene, but uncreated Sophia—Mother Sophia—merged with the Neshamah of Mother Mary, being too glorious to fully dwell in the earthly form of a mortal being. Thus, only when Mother Mary shed the earthly form, assuming her heavenly image, did she become the Mother of creation—the Mother of all. What could be completely embodied of Sophia was in the Bride, and what was transcendental came in through the Mother. The Mother becomes immanent through the Son, her divine grace passing through the Son to the Daughter-Sophia, his Bride. For this reason, little is spoken of Mother Mary in the divine life of the Holy Gospel until after the assumption. It is then that the fullness of Mother-Aima is revealed in her.

Light came down to the children of Israel at Mount Sinai, and wisdom spoke in the prophets of Israel, but the presence of light was rejected. Therefore, light came down as the Mother, the Son, and the Daughter, so that through the Partzufim below, the grace of the Partzufim above might be in the world and the world might be joined to the world of supernal light. The Mother is the world of supernal light. The Bride is the supernal light within and all around us. The Son is the light transmission, the pattern-that-connects the world of supernal light and the material world. In the holy Mother, a new heaven and new earth has come into being, and a new humanity—a supernal or divine humanity. The faith of the Gnostic is in the great Mother, our spiritual hope is in the Holy Bride, and our love is the divine love of Yeshua Messiah—the sacred heart of Christ. The Mother is the all in all. One who calls her the "great goddess" has not misspoken, if by goddess they mean also the One God—Yahweh pronounced Elohim.

The image of the woman of light, Mother Israel, is the heavenly image of the Mother after the assumption, but there are other images of the

Holy Mother nearer to us. These, too, appear in meditations on Binah-Aima, as do various chants of the Mother. It is Binah that Christian Kabbalists contemplate in the image of the holy Mother.

Pistis Sophia—Faith Wisdom

Binah is called the "parent of faith" because faith is the influence of Neshamah, which resides in Binah. It is also attributed to Binah because faith is a manifestation of divine grace, and Mother-Aima is the channel of grace.

In Gnostic Christianity, faith is often called *Pistis Sophia*, which is Greek, meaning "faith wisdom." One cannot help but see the correspondence of Pistis Sophia to the name Yahweh Elohim, which links Binah and Hokmah—the parent of faith and wisdom on the Tree of Life. While orthodox forms of Christianity believe in salvation through faith in Jesus as the literal "only begotten Son of God," Gnostic Christianity teaches self-realization or enlightenment through direct spiritual experience—Gnosis. Thus, among Gnostics, faith assumes a different place and meaning.

Christian Gnosticism speaks of the gift of the fiery intelligence that awakens one to the divine life and leads one in the path of conscious evolution. This gift is the influence of one's Neshamah and is the power of the Holy Spirit. The first manifestation of the gift is Pistis Sophia, which is to say, the dawn of faith. This is something more than mere mental belief or vital sentimentality, for it comes from the depths of one's being. Gnostics speak of faith as "a sense of the great mystery," which impels one in a spiritual quest to gain Gnosis of the mystery. Likewise, it is said to be "an intuition of an experience not yet had," which becomes the invocation of the mystical experience through an opening of oneself to it.

Faith cannot be quantified, yet it is a real and dynamic power of the soul. It is both what leads us into spiritual practice and spiritual living, and it is the cornerstone of magic-power. Lord Yeshua said of faith, ". . . For truly I tell you, if you have faith the size of a mustard seed, you will say to this mountain, 'Move from here to there,' and it will move; and nothing will be impossible for you" (Gospel of St. Matthew 17:20).

Although Gnostic Christianity teaches self-realization through gnosis, nevertheless faith certainly plays a distinct role. For without faith in the possibility of enlightenment and liberation and awareness of our bondage to cosmic ignorance, we would not engage in spiritual practice and spiritual living through which Gnosis or enlightenment is acquired. Essentially, faith is like a seed and gnosis is like the fruit. Faith leads to the generation of gnosis, and gnosis leads to new levels of faith. They are like two wings that lift the soul in an ascent of consciousness. This is a gift that the Holy Mother gives—hence Binah, the parent of faith.

The Great Angel of Divine Intelligence— The Remembrance of God

There is a base level of cosmic consciousness that retains the patterns or impressions of everything that transpires in creation. It is the foundation of the continuum of evolution that serves as the cosmic memory, without which evolution would not be possible. Unless something of previous cycles of development and evolution are retained, new and higher forms of life could not come into being because the continuum of creation would have nothing upon which to build—no ground or foundation from which to evolve. In terms of evolution within space-time-consciousness, the future is rooted in the past and its progress is determined by what happens in the present. The events of the past are like the womb birthing the present, and the present is like the womb birthing the future.

Whether we are conscious or not, this base level of consciousness exists within each and every one of us and, in effect, records everything we see, hear, smell, touch, and taste of life, and every thought, feeling-emotion, word, and deed. When the Scriptures speak of a Book of Life in which the righteousness or wickedness of living souls is recorded, or the idea of the righteousness or sins of a person being forever present before the eyes of God, it is this base level of consciousness that is meant.

This principle of cosmic memory both facilitates and impedes the continuum of evolution. For while the principle of cosmic memory serves to retain all positive developments in evolution, it also serves to retain all the negative developments. Hence, it is the karmic matrix, which can either liberate or bind living souls.

The archangel Tzafkiel is the manifestation of Binah at the level of Beriyah and is the keeper of the Book of Life—the great angel of the cosmic memory. Ratziel and Tzafkiel represent the idea of the bright and dark angels that accompany the soul, which has been passed down in conventional wisdom as the accusing angel and merciful angel that seek to influence the soul in life and that, in the afterlife, plead the case of the soul in the judgment. However, in truth, these influences are actually divine principles, which ignorance depicts as good and evil. Essentially, the bright angel is the divine destiny of the soul, and the dark angel is the accumulation of the soul's karma. How the "dark angel" appears to the soul-being is dependent upon the previous developments in the evolution of the soul—the karma of the soul. To a soul immersed in extremely negative karma, Tzafkiel would appear as an angel of wrath and the judgment; yet to the soul founded in positive karma—a righteous soul—Tzafkiel would appear as an angel of mercy. Needless to say, not everyone would necessarily want to invoke the archangel Tzafkiel; to the wicked person or evil-doer, Tzafkiel would come as judgment founded upon the law of perfect justice.

Tzafkiel is far more than an angel of judgment, however. Through Tzafkiel, the initiate is able to gain knowledge of the tikkune (mending, healing, or work on the soul) that he or she has entered into incarnation to accomplish, along with an understanding of how to accomplish it. Likewise, through Tzafkiel, an initiate can gain knowledge of past lives of the soul and the greater mission of the soul that spans many lives. Thus, the archangel Tzafkiel serves as an angel of enlightenment. The Rosicrucian grade of magister templi, associated with Binah, reflects this aspect of Tzafkiel. Among the powers of the masters of the temple is a knowledge and understanding of their soul's divine mission and insight into the previous lives and the tikkune of other souls, and therefore an ability to guide and help others accomplish their tikkune.

Ratziel is said to preside over the "cosmic rays," which are represented by the twelve signs of the zodiac and the ten celestial bodies of our solar system. Tzafkiel is said to have dominion over the cosmic planes—the supernal, spiritual, causal, higher vital, mental, astral, and material planes of existence. Therefore, initiates who seek greater knowledge and understanding of the inner planes will seek to make contact with Tzafkiel.

The archangel Tzafkiel is also the great angel of the supernal temple and, according to the masters of the Tradition, is the influence behind the formation of all mystical circles and esoteric orders that emanate from the divine order. When something of a wisdom tradition is lost in the passage of space-time, through the inspiration of Tzafkiel, an adept or master can "remember" and restore it, if it is the divine will for it to be restored. When a revival of a wisdom tradition or stream of the light transmission is necessary, it is through the influence of Tzafkiel that a spiritual revival is sparked. In the same way the archangel Tzafkiel holds the knowledge of the tikkune and mission of individual souls, Tzafkiel holds the knowledge of the mission of groups of souls that are destined to a divine labor together, as well as knowledge of the overall great work to fulfill God's plan in creation.

This gnosis of the great work held by Tzafkiel is founded upon Tzafkiel's knowledge of the continuum of space-time. This is reflected by the attribute of Tzafkiel as the archangel of Shabbatai (Saturn), which represents the dominion of space-time and its affects/effects. Legend has it that Tzafkiel has granted certain great adepts and masters knowledge of how to create portals in the space-time through which they can magically travel through space and time. On a lower level, Tzafkiel is also said to grant initiates the ability to see at remote points in space-time—specifically, past and present—as though they were there.

The image of Tzafkiel used in meditation is akin to that of the archangel Ratziel, but rather than the day sky, Tzafkiel is robed in the night sky. Tzafkiel appears as a presence of radiant darkness robed in the starry night sky—as though the great angel takes the starry sky and forms a hooded robe about her. All around the image of Tzafkiel is a black void of endless and starless space, while her image appears as a robe of the Milky Way. From within the hood of the robe shines a brilliant white light, tinged with electric blue, and she holds the Book of Life in her hands, like a great scroll. Using this visualization, with the name Yahweh Elohim and the chant YoMa Tzafkiel, the great angel of remembrance is invoked by initiates of the Tradition.

Holy Thrones and Dominions

Aral means "throne," Aralim (plural) "thrones." Succession to the throne of a kingdom grants the heir the authority and power of a king or queen and the reign of the dominion or kingdom. Thus, the order of the Aralim, which is Binah at the level of Yetzirah, are holy angels that grant divine authority and power. Because a throne implies a dominion, the Aralim are also called dominions, or are said to move with the order of dominions.

In the vision of St. John, there are twenty-four crowned elders seated on thrones (Aralim) encircling the supernal throne of glory. These are great men and women of God who represent the male (Logos) and female (Sophia) attainment of Messianic consciousness corresponding to the twelve archetypal forms of humanity. The masters of the Tradition say, "Their crowns are in their heads, for the knowledge, understanding and wisdom of God is the holy crown of the sacred tau (elders)—the Gnosis of Yeshua Messiah." The elders being seated upon Aralim means that each elder is given the divine authority and power of a specific dominion of the divine kingdom. A study of the zodiacal signs according to esoteric astrology will reveal the nature of these twelve dominions of the divine kingdom.

The term "merkavah" actually implies a throne-chariot. Thus, in merkavah mysticism, to "ride the chariot" means to acquire the divine authority and power corresponding to the grade to which an initiate is able to ascend. Binah or the Shekinah, as we have seen, conveys divine authority and power, and it is through her that the vehicle of the ascension is formed.

The Aralim hold all spiritual gifts and dispense spiritual powers according to the will of the Holy One. Spiritual gifts are granted to the faithful and elect according to the capacity of each individual to receive and manage them and according to the mission God has given to them. Occasionally, once a spiritual gift or power is granted, it remains with a person throughout their whole life, and sometimes through many lives, but this is not always the case. Often a spiritual gift or power is granted only for a short period of time in order for a specific task to be fulfilled, or to uplift and empower a person in faith, or to prepare the way for other spiritual gifts or powers to be granted. Spiritual gifts may be permanent or temporary, all depending on the need of the soul and the needs of others around oneself.

Lusting after spiritual gifts for personal ambition, self-aggrandizement, or merely to have spiritual power for the sake of having power, apart from any noble or righteous intention, is certainly a dangerous pitfall and potentially a great obstruction to attainment. Nevertheless, seeking empowerment to be able to assist in the enlightenment and liberation of other living souls and spirits is part of the great work. Thus, the Gnostic initiate is encouraged to pray and meditate to acquire spiritual gifts that will empower him or her as a conscious agent of the great work. In seeking to receive spiritual gifts in harmony with one's true will, the order of the Aralim is often invoked by initiates in conjunction with their prayers and meditations.

The Holy Masters and the Temple of Light

The Zohar says that the tabernacle and the holy temple in Jerusalem were built upon the pattern of the supernal temple, so that what was above was reflected below. The temple was composed of the outer court, inner sanctuary, and holy of holies and was set in the center of Jerusalem, the City of God. The holy of holies represented the universe of Atzilut and was the place where the Shekinah dwelt. The inner sanctuary represented the universe of Beriyah and was the primary place of prayer, meditation, and worship conducted by the priesthood. The outer court represented the universe of Yetzirah and was the place of purification and holy sacrifice. The city of Jerusalem and the Holy Land surrounding it represented the universe of Asiyah manifest according to the holy law.

As mentioned above, the grade corresponding to Binah is that of the magister templi—the master of the temple. If we understand the holy temple as the Sefirot of the four Olamot, then we have some hint as to the nature of this attainment. The magister templi is a holy apostle of the supernal light—one who is anointed with the supernal light and who embodies something of his or her Neshamah. There are many different levels of the magister templi, corresponding to the degree to which the Neshamah is incarnate in the master and the degree to which the supernal light-presence of the Shekinah indwells the master. While in the grades of the Adepti, corresponding to the Sefirot of Hesed, Gevurah, and Tiferet, the initiate experiences the Shekinah coming and going, more or less, according to the grade of attainment, the Shekinah remains constant in the experience of the magister templi.

From the view of initiates of the lower grades, it would be very difficult to tell the difference between a magister templi established in Binah and an elect adept established in Hesed. However, the experience of the two grades of enlightenment are radically different. For although the elect adept may experience glimpses into cosmic consciousness at the level of Binah, he or she does not experience the womb of nirvana and the supernal consciousness that dawns in it. This is the dominion of the magister templi—the ability to enter into supernal consciousness more or less at will. Unlike the magus, however, the magister templi has not completely united him- or herself with the supernal consciousness and, thus, does not perpetually abide in Messianic consciousness. Likewise, although at times the magister templi experiences him- or herself inseparable from the supernal Shekinah, he or she often experiences the Shekinah as a presence and power distinct from him- or herself.

This level of the enlightenment experience gives the magister templi a mastery of the play of cosmic forces, more or less, according to the degree of attainment of this first supernal grade. He or she is Baal Shem, master of the name, established in the Gnosis of Yeshua Messiah, and he or she is a master of inner plane work, having communion in the Holy Spirit with the tzaddikim and maggidim (inner plane adepts and masters and holy angels). To the degree that the magister templi is able to integrate the Neshamah and the Shekinah into his or her personality and life-display, the master becomes a living temple of God.

Masters of the grade of magus and ipsissimus (corresponding to Hokmah and Keter) are very rare in this world, as there are very few human beings on earth who can directly receive the light transmission they embody. Most incarnate masters are of the magister templi or the elect adepti, and it is the magister templi and the adepti who primarily conduct the great work on planet earth.

According to the Tradition, when the supernal Shekinah descended upon Lord Yeshua in the Baptism, his body shone with visible light for a while, specifically his face. The light was all around him. In the transfiguration, his whole body shone with light and the light was within him and all around him, so that he was the supernal light. This shift in the light-presence from the Baptism to the transfiguration represents the ascent through the various degrees of magister templi to attainment of the magus.

The grades of initiation from the neophyte to the greater adept are most often conveyed via an incarnate human agent, although in some cases, they are conveyed by inner plane adepts and masters (as in the case of St. Paul). The grade of the elect adept and the supernal grades, however, are not conveyed by way of any human agency. They are granted by divine grace or directly through the Holy Spirit.

The magus serves to initiate continuums of the light transmission or to bring in new levels of attainment; the magister templi, along with the adepti, serve to tend the flame of the continuum in which they labor. Because of their divine gnosis, the masters of the temple are able to uplift and restore streams of the light transmission, to retrieve knowledge, understanding, and wisdom that has become lost over time, and to unfold new knowledge and understanding of the light transmission.

The most essential task of the magister templi is to maintain balance in the play of cosmic forces in creation, to guard the light transmission, and to serve as a vehicle of the light transmission. As members of the order of Melchizedek, they serve as laborers in the fields of sentient existence for the harvest of souls.

Spiritual Practices for Binah

It is good to pray to God the Mother and to meditate upon her, for she is near to us, as near as our body and this good earth, our soul, and very life. Yet, she is the heavens and the world of supernal light. She is the light and she is the darkness. She is the consciousness-force above and below. She is the all in all.

Because the Holy Mother is the queen of heaven and earth, all creatures and the whole of creation are in her. We are in the womb of God, our Mother, and she is continually giving birth to us, in life and in our dreams. When we die, we are born again from her holy womb, whether to continue our journey in the worlds or to our repose in the world of supernal light. All blessing and grace come through her; for she, herself, is grace and blessing power, the Shekinah.

The Mother is swift to answer the prayers of the faithful, and she is ever-present with the elect. Whether encumbered by great darkness or established in the light, just the same, she will come to those who invoke her, and she will give to those who ask of her as her child. Mother-Aima will refuse no one who seeks her, nor will she ever withhold her blessings from those who ask. The Lord has said, "Knock and the door will be opened unto you." The divine Mother is the holy sanctuary.

Sitting upon the Lap of the Holy Mother— The Throne of Glory

> ➤ Sit upon a chair, as upon a holy throne, and imagine yourself as a child of light sitting upon the lap of the great Mother. Feel your breath and the beat of your heart—the life that is in you and all around you—the presence of God the Mother. Breathing out, let go, and breathe yourself into her, letting yourself merge into her. At one with her, abide in her. In her, whole and complete, perfect as you are, you are she and she is you. This is the delight of perfect meditation!

Light-Womb Meditation

> ➤ Sit down and imagine that you are in the womb of the Holy Mother. Envision your body formed of light, with the spiritual sun shining in your heart, and a great sea of light all around you. Listen to the beat of your heart, and within behind the beat of your heart, hear the beat of the Mother's heart; listen to the thoughts in your mind, and within behind your thoughts, hear the thought of the Mother's mind. Speak with your divine Mother and hear her speaking in you. When you have communed with the Mother in this way, take up the chant Ama-Aima. As you chant, merge yourself completely with the light-presence of the Mother. In the silence following the sacred chant, abide as the light.

The Woman of Light, Mother Israel Meditation

> ➤ Envision the spiritual sun within your heart and gather yourself into it. Letting go of the surface and all movements on the surface, go deep within, as though into the womb of the self. Then, imagine you are seated on top of a mountain under the starry night sky,

with the moon rising in the east. As the moon rises above the horizon, as if by magic, the image of Mother Israel appears, standing on the moon.

➤ She wears a crown of twelve great stars and is clothed with the sun, and she is pregnant with child—full of the grace and glory of God. The moon disk shines under her feet. Heavenly hosts—holy angels—surround her and all of creation sings praise to her. Within behind the songs of praise, there is the celestial harmony of the stars. Feel the presence of the woman of light, the peace and joy of Mother Israel, and let the holy Shekinah pervade you to your core.

➤ If you seek liberation from darkness and klippot, pray for liberation; if you seek healing, pray to the Mother for healing; if you seek spiritual gifts, pray for spiritual gifts; if you seek illumination, pray to the Mother for divine illumination. Whatever you seek, ask the holy Mother, and abide in perfect faith that it is granted to you—and so it shall be.

➤ When you have prayed to the Mother, take up her chant, and hear the whole of creation and the heavenly hosts take up her chant with you:

> *Ha Isha Ha Elyona, Aima Israel*
> (The Woman of Light, Mother Israel)

➤ As you chant, imagine that you become pure light and that you, as the light, pour into the image of the woman of light, so that at the end of the sacred chant you dissolve into her. Abide in silent unity with the divine Mother as long as you can, whether it be but an instant or a longer duration—entertain this perfect peace and joy.

➤ When thoughts arise in the mind, and consciousness is set in motion again, then chant in worship of the divine Mother:

> *Aima Elohim*
> (Mother God)

➤ At the end of this chant abide in the knowledge of yourself blessed by the holy Mother, her divine presence within and all around you, and sit still for a while absorbing and grounding the spiritual energy of the Mother's blessing.

➢ You live, move, and have your being in her. All that appears is as her divine body; all sounds are as her heavenly voice; all thoughts and feelings are the radiance of her wisdom mind. Practice this holy awareness in your daily living—this is Mother Messianic consciousness, the Mother of enlightenment! Amen.

EIGHT

HESED, THE MERCY
AND BRIGHT
BLESSINGS OF GOD

Attributes

Thirty-Two Paths of Wisdom: Settled Consciousness (Sekhel Kavua). It is called this because the Spiritual Powers emanate from it as the [most] ethereal emanations; one emanates from the other by the power of the Original Emanator, may He be blessed

Hesed: Mercy or Loving-Kindness; also Gedulah, Glory

Place on the Tree of Life: The center of the Pillar of Mercy

Divine Name: El

Alternative Divine Names: Rav Hesed, Master of Compassion; Eheieh Zaken, I will be Old; Rachum Ve-Chanum El, Merciful and Pardoning God; Erech Apayim El, Long-Forbearing God; Gedulah El, Great God or Glorious God

Partzuf above: Zer Anpin, as the Holy Priest-King enthroned

Partzuf below: Yeshua Messiah forgiving sin and imparting blessings; Abraham and Sarah

Divine Image: The Holy Priest-King upon his throne; the Celestial Court; the Ascension of the Messiah

Archangel: Tzadkiel

Order of Angels: Hashmalim

Celestial Attribute: Tzedek, Jupiter

Titles Given to Hesed: Priest-King of Righteousness; Judge of Truth; The Elder (Zaken) or the Beloved Elder (Zakenu); Merciful One; Forgiving One; Divine Love; Lord of Peace; Sphere of the Tzaddikim; Divine Justice; Grace of God; Mercy of God; Blessings of God; Depth of South; White Father Seed; Righteousness of God; The Right; Life Abundant; Perfection of the Adepti; the First Day of Creation

Level of the Soul: Ruach, Human Spirit or Divine Intelligence (Specifically the Upper Ruach

Heavenly Abode: Arabot, the Seventh Heaven—Clouds, Plains, Desert, or Holy Place

Spiritual Experience: The dawn of True Spiritual Love or the Sacred Heart of Christ; Spiritual Abundance; the Blessing Power

Virtues: Charity; holy obedience; generosity; devotion; justice; loving-kindness; true friendship; hospitality

Vices: Miserliness; gluttony; tyranny; rebellion; hypocrisy; self-righteousness; injustice; complacency; unfaithfulness

Symbols: Equal-armed cross; the orb; the scepter; tetrahedron; pyramid; square; the crown of a prince; the wand; the shepherd's staff

Commandment: Remember the Shabbat Day, and keep it holy (Exodus 20:8–11)

Sermon on the Mount: Blessed are the peacemakers, for they will be called children of God (Matthew 5:9).

Angel of the Apocalypse and the Churches: The First Star, the First Lampstand, and the message to the angel of the church in Ephesus (Revelation 2:1–7)

The Supreme Mystery and Revelation of the Mystery

Previously, we spoke of the analogy of the Tree of Life as a great river of light. This river is formed of the endless light of God (Ain Sof Aur) and Keter is the hidden source of the river. Da'at is the secret place where the river emerges from the unknowable source, Hokmah is the river of light itself, and Binah is the great channel of the river. The seven lower Sefirot represent flows or currents within the river of light, which, although distinct, are inseparable from the river. The Sefirot of the moral triad (Hesed-Gevurah-Tiferet) represent currents in the depths of the river; the Sefirot of the action triad are currents closer to the surface. Malkut represents how the river appears to us—the ebbs and flows visible on the surface. Through this analogy, we may understand the sacred unity of the Sefirot and their true meaning, for according to the Kabbalah, creation is literally a continual outpouring of the supernal light of God, and the Sefirot are gradations of that light-force. Even the substance of matter itself is this light-force, the nature of which is Ain.

Da'at and the great abyss stand in between the supernals above and the seven lower Sefirot below on the Tree of Life. Essentially, the supernals are by nature transcendental. They are the realm of the archetypal or ideal. One could say that they are the realm of the exhaustless divine potential, which only becomes revealed and actualized at the level of the seven lower Sefirot. The moral triad is the revelation of the divine presence and power of the supernals. The action triad is the actualization of the holy Shekinah, Malkut being the actual realization and manifestation of the living presence and power in the material dimension. Thus, the seven lower Sefirot are often called the Sefirot of Construction, for they are the divine powers through which creation actually comes into being and through which the whole of creation is sustained—the real links between the infinite and the finite.

Descending below the great abyss in our exploration of the Tree of Life, we are coming into the realm of the holy Shekinah more directly in our present experience. The further we descend on the tree, the more we are coming down to earth to things we can actually think about, speak about, and, therefore, can know and understand as mental beings. While the supernals are lofty, abstract, and transcendental, the seven lower Sefirot are more concrete, accessible, and immanent. In essence, the supernals remain ever a supreme mystery and the seven lower Sefirot are the never-ending revelation of that mystery.

The Face of God that Appears

We may gain some insight into the relationship of the supernals and the seven Sefirot of construction through consideration of the Partzufim. As previously indicated, Arik Anpin is formed by the union of Abba and Aima. Thus, Arik Anpin is the supernal triad. When the big face of the transcendental turns toward the possibility of creation, it clothes itself in the sevenfold veil of the Sefirot of construction, becoming Zer Anpin, the small face, or the principle of the immanent divine presence and power.

Unlike the big face of God, the features of the small face are not inaccessible, but rather are gradations of the supernal light within the reach of human souls as the immediate principles of created things. This is the reason the small face is called *Eleh*, which means "these"—indicating things that are intelligible—while the big face is called *Mi*, which means the question "who?"—indicating that which is supra-intelligible and inexpressible. In truth, the two faces are but one face of God, Arik Anpin being the face of God unveiled to Godself and Zer Anpin being the face of God veiled when appearing to God's creatures. One might say that Arik Anpin is the actual appearance of the soul of the Sefirot, while Zer Anpin is the appearance of the soul clothed in the body of the Sefirot, which is a body of lights.

The unity of the big and small face of God is Atik Yomin, the ancient one. The small face depends on the ancient one completely and is within the ancient one, insofar as Arik Anpin includes within itself Abba and Aima, which give birth to Zer Anpin and Nukva (the daughter). The big face and the small face of God together represent the causal unity of all the ideal forms of the Sefirot, the force of which is in Hokmah and the forms of which are in Binah. As we saw in the previous chapter, the diversity of archetypes in sacred unity is expressed by the name of Binah, Elohim, which is essentially the union of the words Eleh and Mi. The prophet Isaiah, who beheld the image of the ancient one in his vision, indicates this holy mystery when he instructs us, saying: "Lift up your eyes on high and see: Who created these? He who brings out their hosts and numbers them, calling them by name; because he is great in strength, mighty in power, not one is missing" (Isaiah 40:26).

The Overwhelming Grace of God

Hesed means mercy or loving-kindness. Hesed is the first emanation proceeding from Binah via Da'at, the first feature or aspect of the small face, which is also called the bridegroom. As the first of the seven lower Sefirot, Hesed receives the influx of spiritual energy of the supernals and imparts it to all the Sefirot below the abyss. You will recall our discussion of Da'at as the holy prism through which the supernal light passes to become the many rays of rainbow glory. Hesed is the first ray of glory, which contains all the other rays of glory of the Sefirot that follow.

Gevurah, Tiferet, Netzach, Hod, Yesod, and Malkut all have their root and essence in Hesed, which has its root and essence in the supernals. Hesed is God's love or mercy; therefore, the foundation and purpose of all of the seven Sefirot of construction is God's love or mercy. Creation itself and all that God does in creation is the expression of God's love, which in Hesed is completely boundless and unconditional.

Essentially, Hesed is the all-giver in relationship to the lower Sefirot, and as the all-giver, Hesed represents the activity of Hokmah below the abyss. In relationship to the supernals, Hesed is the all-receiver and thus represents the activity of Binah below the abyss, specifically the face of the bright Mother.

In Hesed proper, there is no judgment, no restraint, restriction, limit, boundary, or condition placed upon grace. Hesed is unconditional love, boundless mercy, infinite light—in a word, pure grace. It is an unrestricted flow of divine blessing without end. The nature of the blessings God bestows through Hesed is the gift of Godself. Whatever the blessings that might be received, whether spiritual, psychic, or material, including life itself, all are the manifestation of the holy Shekinah—God imparting something of him- or herself.

There must be a dynamic balance between Hesed and its counterpart on the Pillar of Severity, Gevurah, which is judgment or severity. Without some degree of restraint, restriction, or limitation, Hesed would swiftly overwhelm creation. Gevurah acts as a regulator of Hesed. Previously, we spoke of the primordial beginning, which took place through tzimtzum-constriction followed by measured emanation. First, God had to withdraw Godself into him- or herself to make space for creation outside of Godself. Then, God emanated Godself in measured gradations, from the level of Ain Sof (the infinite) to the most dense and restricted level of finite creation, the physical or material universe (Asiyah). Gevurah is the principle of tzimtzum-constriction and Hesed is the principle of expansion or emanation. It is the dynamic interaction and balance of Gevurah and Hesed together that allows for measured gradations of the supernal light and thus the existence of creation. The two operating together make the gradations of the supernal light that are accessible to the manifest spirit, the dynamic balance of the two being Tiferet-beauty.

The traditional way this dynamic balance is expressed is in the following manner: Creation is sustained by God's presence and power. Completely dependent upon God, if God withdrew Godself completely, creation would instantly cease to exist. However, God being the Infinite and eternal, and creation being finite and temporal, were God to not restrain Godself and withdraw him-herself to some degree, creation would be completely overwhelmed and destroyed. For the present, creation cannot endure the direct influx of the divine fullness.

This reveals a popular misconception among aspiring Kabbalists that are inexperienced and unschooled who suggest that, in ascending the Tree of Life from one grade to another, one actually goes into the Sefirot of the Pillars of Mercy and Severity. While, indeed, in the process of ascending grade to grade, something of the soul is bound to each of the Sefirot, it is always from the Middle Pillar that the soul contacts the Sefirot of the right and left, never directly. The reality-truth-continuum is the Middle Pillar; the Pillar of Mercy and the Pillar of Severity represent the extremes in between which reality or creation actually exists. One could no more endure a direct entrance into God's absolute mercy than an entrance into absolute severity, for either extreme would be completely overwhelming. An initiate may draw ruhaniyut and shefa from the right or the left, and he or she may join the corresponding aspect of his or her soul to the Sefirot of the right or the left while cleaving to the Middle Pillar, but he or she cannot actually enter into the Pillar of Mercy nor the Pillar of Severity. For this reason, in the first ceremony of initiation into the mysteries of the Kabbalah, the neophyte is told: "Do not venture to the right or to the left, where certain destruction awaits, but stay in between and sojourn the middle way, cleaving neither to the right nor to the left, to heaven nor to hell. Wide is the way that leads to perdition, but straight and narrow is the path that leads to salvation. Through moderation true attainment is accomplished."

The Thirteen Attributes of Hesed-El

The Sefirah Hesed, at the level of Atzilut, is the divine name El. El is to Elohim as Yah is to Yahweh, so that all potential of Elohim is in the name of El in the same way all potential of Yahweh is in Yah. As we saw with the name Elohim, Aleph (א) is the Spirit of God, the radiant breath of God, which grants a living soul of intelligence to the human one. Lamed (ל), meaning "ox-goad," connotes a driving and directing force, specifically in the form of an impulse from within. This is the nature of God's love and mercy—the grace of God. It is God's Holy Spirit and it is the motivating factor of God's creation.

Moses proclaims thirteen attributes of mercy in connection with the name El (Exodus 34:6–7): God (1) merciful (2) and gracious (3), slow (4) to anger (5), and abundant in love (6), and truth (7). Keeping mercy (8) to the thousandth generation (9), forgiving sin (10), rebellion (11), and error (12), and cleansing (13).

These are all blessings associated with Hesed or El that an initiate draws to him- or herself through binding his or her soul to the name El. The ultimate blessing of joining one's soul to the name El is the experience of a conscious unification with God. The highest manifestation of grace is God giving Godself fully to oneself, pouring him- or herself into one's soul and awakening the soul in Godself (the Christ-self).

God is merciful in that God has placed an evolutionary impulse in the soul so that, in the depth of our soul, there is a desire to draw near to God and unite ourselves with God. To the degree that we draw ourselves nearer to God, God draws us into Godself. God is gracious in that God pours out blessings upon us when we cleave unto our Neshamah and unto God's presence. The nature of the blessings God bestows is Godself.

When it is said God is slow, God has fashioned into creation the principle of stability and a pause between cause and effect. When we miss the mark ("sin" actually means "missing the mark") or engender negative karma, the result or full affect/effect or the consequence is not immediate. There is time for us to change our minds and hearts, to adjust our aim and to mend whatever damage we have caused. Anger is also mercy and connotes chastisement, correction, or discipline, which mitigates negative karma, leads to healing and a higher quality of life, and enlightens and liberates the soul from bondage.

Abundant in love means that judgment and discipline is never an end in itself and does not last forever. The ultimate aim is redemption and healing, hence unification. There is no such thing as eternal damnation. Even hell does not last forever, however great the evil committed. As indicated in the previous chapter, the light of heaven and the fires of hell are the manifestation of the Holy Spirit, which aims to educate and therefore enlighten and liberate the soul. God loves the righteous and the unrighteous equally, and blesses one and all alike. Truth is the aim of creative evolution, and it is God's aim in creation that truth should endure and truth should be revealed, that nothing should be hidden or concealed forever. The ultimate truth is the sacred unity God is, in which we live, move, and have our being; that in our inmost being we are ever at one with God and the whole of creation.

Keeping mercy, God preserves and sustains all life. In the ultimate sense, death has never existed. What is called death is merely a transition from one state of existence to another. The Neshamah has never been born and therefore never dies, but abides perpetually in the one life-power. To the thousandth generation are the countless incarnations God grants to the soul so that it might develop and evolve to the highest of life and come to fruition in Christ consciousness. The idea that one lives a single life and either earns the reward of eternal heaven or the punishment of eternal damnation is obscene and contradicts God's purpose in creation, which is love and mercy. All souls will eventually be fulfilled in God.

Forgiving sin, God has given the human being the ability to repent and to mend all damage the soul might incur in the process of its development and evolution. Forgiving rebellion, God gives every soul the opportunity to work out all negative karma, even the greatest evil-doing performed with full conscious intention. Forgiving error, God grants us the opportunity to correct every mistake and to learn from our mistakes.

Cleansing or purification is the intention of any judgment or wrathful manifestation of the holy Shekinah. Unlike the injustice of what human beings call justice, God's justice is not founded upon punishment or vengeance but rather aims always at rehabilitation and redemption. God is truly just. That in all activities God aims to cleanse or purify alludes to the truth that the inmost nature and being of all creatures is God's Word and wisdom—that in our inmost being we are innately good.

All of these attributes of Hesed-mercy are the power of El and are in El. Aleph is the Spirit of God enacting mercy according to these attributes, and Lamed is the activity itself. Lamed is the Hebrew letter of justice and indicates that God's ultimate aim is justice or righteousness. The righteousness God seeks is the enlightenment and liberation of all living souls; hence God is a compassionate God, for the enlightenment and liberation of all is the Sacred Heart of Christ (compassion).

The Nature of Righteousness

To every Sefirah of construction, a man and a woman of God are attributed. In the case of Hesed, Gevurah, Tiferet, and Yesod, they are the patriarchs and matriarchs of the Torah. The masters of the Tradition have said that the patriarch of a Sefirah is a chariot or vehicle of the spiritual energy of the corresponding Sefirah and that the matriarch is the Shekinah-emanation of the Sefirah. Thus, the life story of the man and woman of God corresponding to a Sefirah reveals the mysteries of the Sefirah and is a way to contemplate and meditate upon the Sefirah. Hesed is represented by the story of Abraham and Sarah.

The story of Abraham and Sarah begins with God calling them out of their homeland and the security of their mundane life in unenlightened society to a sacred quest into an unknown wilderness, in which the Spirit of God will be their guide. Abraham and Sarah obey God and immediately depart, following the call of the Spirit. Obedience is a quality of Hesed, not so much obedience to anything imposed from outside of oneself, but rather obedience of the spiritual impulse or the inner guide within oneself.

Abraham and Sarah are noted for their compassion, generosity, and hospitality. They would provide for anyone in need, and rather than being

motivated by profit, they were motivated by justice. When strangers
would approach Abraham's camp he would run out to greet them and invite them to stay and share a meal. Sarah would prepare the best possible
meals, and Abraham and Sarah would attend to their guests, providing for
all of their guests' needs. Abraham and Sarah did not judge their guests.
They were hospitable to the righteous and the wicked alike, showing
grace to the righteous and mercy to the wicked. So great was their wel-
coming power that even holy angels of God appeared as their guests, and
holy angels were constantly coming and going from their tents.

These qualities of Abraham and Sarah, which are principles of Hesed,
are at the very heart of the teaching of Yeshua in the Gospel. In speaking
of the judgment, Lord Yeshua directly refers to the qualities of Hesed that
we see in Abraham and Sarah when he says:

> *Then the king will say to those at his right hand, "Come, you that are*
> *blessed by my Father, inherit the kingdom prepared for you from the founda-*
> *tion of the world; for I was hungry and you gave me food, I was thirsty and*
> *you gave me something to drink, I was a stranger and you welcomed me, I*
> *was naked and you gave me clothing, I was sick and you took care of me, I*
> *was in prison and you visited me." And then the righteous will answer him,*
> *"Lord, when was it that we saw you hungry and gave you food, or thirsty*
> *and gave you something to drink? And when was it that we saw you a*
> *stranger and welcomed you, or naked and gave you clothing? And when*
> *was it that we saw you sick or in prison and visited you?" And the king will*
> *answer, "Truly I tell you, just as you did it to one of the least of these who*
> *are members of my family, you did it to me."* (Gospel of St. Matthew
> 25:34–40)

Tending to the sick and visitation of the prisoner are a further extension of the Hesed qualities, which, in a word, is charity. Through active
love and compassion we establish the cause of prosperity and long life.

When God announced his intention to bring judgment upon Sodom,
out of love and compassion Abraham pleaded the case of Sodom with
God. At first, the number of tzaddikim needed to preserve the city was
fifty, reflecting the number of ten Sefirot of the five Olamot; however, the
final number of tzaddikim settled upon was ten, the essential number nec-

essary for the preservation and continuation of life on earth, reflecting the quality of Hesed as that which preserves and sustains creation. Acting in a way that preserves and sustains the life of others, we invoke the flow of grace from Hesed.

The final and ultimate action of Abraham and Sarah was their willingness to give to God their most precious possession of all, their only child. This prefigures the sacrifice of the first incarnation of the Soul of Messiah, the son of Joseph, through whom all negative karma is dispelled and the world is given a way to become consciously unified with God. The mercy and love of God embodied in Yeshua Messiah is Hesed, as is the love of God in Abraham and Sarah who were willing to give everything good to God. The request of God for the sacrifice of Isaac was not seeking the life of Isaac, but rather the perfection of holy obedience through which the ultimate unification with God becomes possible—one who obeys the presence of God within him or herself embodies something of the divine.

Significantly, God provides Abraham and Isaac with a ram for sacrifice. It is the function of Hesed that, when we have done all that we can do to follow the Holy Spirit, exhausting all our own efforts and capacity, the Holy Spirit will step in and fulfill our mission. When we completely surrender ourselves to divine grace, grace will accomplish the great work in us and bring us to fruition in Christ consciousness. This is the promise of God in Hesed.

Tzaddikim—Adepts and Masters of the Tradition

Tzaddikim literally means "righteous ones." On the one hand, tzaddikim is a term applied to all of the faithful and elect. On the other hand, tzaddikim is a term specifically used to indicate realized individuals—the adepts and masters of the Tradition.

In Gnostic Christianity, the grades of initiation actually correspond to various degrees of the enlightenment experience. Therefore, the grades corresponding to the adepts and masters of the Tradition indicate states of self-realization that qualify an initiate to serve as a spiritual teacher and guide to others. Tzaddikim, as the term is used in Christian Gnosticism, indicates both incarnate and disincarnate adepts and masters; thus, it includes the idea of inner plane masters and adepts. Hesed is said to be the "sphere of the tzaddikim" because it is through the tzaddikim that all wisdom teachings and initiations are imparted and spiritual assistance and empowerment on the path to self-realization are received.

In the Gnostic Tradition, a threefold divine order is spoken of—outer, inner, and secret. Previously, we spoke of the secret order, the order of Melchizedek, which represents the primordial Tradition from which all wisdom traditions are derived. In every wisdom tradition that manifests in the world, there is an inner and outer dimension—the spiritual or mystical dimension and the outer forms it assumes. In Gnostic Christianity, the inner order is called the "true and invisible Rosicrucian order," and the outer order is represented by Gnostic circles that serve as vehicles of the teachings and initiations—the light transmission—in the material world.

Essentially, the order of Melchizedek is a great luminous assembly of enlightened beings, who labor to bring the light transmission into worlds of sentient existence for the sake of the enlightenment and liberation of souls. To do so, they initiate various streams of the light transmission in a world—hence the diverse wisdom traditions that appear. An inner order represents a lineage of adepts and masters who impart the teachings and initiations of a specific stream of the light transmission—the Tzaddikim of a specific wisdom tradition. Basically, an inner order is a branch of the order of Melchizedek dedicated to a distinct form of the light transmission.

Authentic wisdom traditions are typically founded upon discipleship and initiation, which is to say an actual light transmission imparted by a tzaddik to his or her students and disciples, as we see in the Gospels. Most often, this transpires through incarnate tzaddikim who represent a lineage of adepts and masters imparting the teachings and initiations from one generation to another. However, it is not isolated to incarnate tzaddikim, as there are also disincarnate adepts and masters who serve to impart the light transmission of the tradition. Generally speaking, however, it is through incarnate tzaddikim that outer orders or Gnostic circles are formed, and it is through association with an incarnate tzaddik and an outer order that we receive the light transmission.

On the Tree of Life, the order of Melchizedek, the secret order, corresponds to the supernals. The Rosicrucian order of Gnostic Christianity corresponds to Tiferet. The outer order, in whatever form it assumes, corresponds to the triad of action and specifically to Malkut. Hesed represents the point on the Tree of Life where a specific stream of the light-transmission emerges from the primordial Tradition. The extension of the light continuum into the world via incarnate and disincarnate Tzaddikim is considered a manifestation of God's love and mercy; therefore, it is spoken about in conjunction with Hesed.

The Tzaddik and the Disciple

Many people in the West turn to Eastern Traditions because they are unaware of the spiritual depths of the Kabbalah within Western Tradition. Likewise, most are unaware that there are adepts and masters incarnate in the West who embody a degree of self-realization, just as there are in the East. Yet, although for thousands of years there have been Tzaddikim in Western Traditions, our Western societies neither recognize nor make a place for them as in the East.

In several Gnostic traditions founded upon a Christian Kabbalah, adepts and masters continue to exist and to teach and initiate others into a Western Tradition of enlightenment. Unlike gurus and lamas of Eastern Traditions, the Western adept or master is not part of a large institution; they typically teach and initiate in a relatively small circle, quietly and behind the scenes of the unenlightened society. The way of the Tzaddikim is quite different in the West, as are the methods for self-realization they teach. Tzaddikim of Western Traditions do not tend to make such a great show of themselves in the way they dress and are rarely as withdrawn from typical daily living as Eastern tzaddikim. The methods they use and teach do not require us to withdraw from mundane life; rather, we learn to transform daily living into a vehicle of self-realization. Essentially, one could well have a job, family, and enjoy the fullness of life and, at the same time, experience various degrees of self-realization. Western tzaddikim do not tend to conform to stereotypical images of enlightened masters. They teach by way of crazy wisdom, and do whatever it takes to help others progress in the path to enlightenment.

Although the term "discipleship" may put some folks off, basically what it means is a close spiritual friendship. In many Gnostic Traditions, discipleship is the foundation of the path, for it is through this sacred friendship that we receive secret teachings and experience the light transmission.

Essentially, a tzaddik is a person who embodies a higher consciousness—specifically, embodies something of the light-presence (Christos)—and is therefore a qualified teacher and guide. Through our spiritual friendship with a tzaddik, he or she is able to transmit this consciousness-force, thus serving to awaken it within us. It is akin to a candle that is lit and one that is unlit. When the two are drawn close together, the flame passes between them and both are illuminated. This is the basis of true initiation.

It is a great blessing to meet an incarnate tzaddik and a greater blessing to become a close spiritual friend to a tzaddik. Not everyone will be able to meet an incarnate tzaddik, let alone become a student or disciple of the tzaddik. However, the light transmission can transpire through contact with inner plane adepts or masters. The experience of St. Paul in the Book of Acts reflects this. Receiving initiation in this way, he referred to himself as the least of the apostles of light. Although it is the least stable mode of the light transmission, many have received such an initiation. One need only have an open heart and mind and a true desire for enlightenment and liberation.

The Tzaddik and the Threefold Body of Melchizedek

Within and behind the physical body, there is a subtle body of consciousness, which is a body of energy. When the teachings speak of the evolution of the soul-being, they are speaking of the development and evolution of this subtle body. Early in the development of the soul-being, this subtle body tends to be very dim and weak and is barely self-luminous—more akin to moonlight than sunlight. Advancing through grades of initiation and receiving the light transmission, more and more the subtle body becomes self-radiant and shines with a brighter light. Essentially, the subtle body is progressively transformed into a body of light in the path, what is called the solar body.

The generation of the body of light represents the development of consciousness beyond the body and, thus, represents an evolution beyond the need for material incarnation. It is through this spiritual body that the soul experiences the resurrection and ascension—specifically, an ascent into the supernal world of light.

In the Sophian Tradition, this body of light is called the threefold body of Melchizedek, the full generation of which constitutes initiation into the order of Melchizedek—hence, it is Messianic consciousness. In the teachings, it is spoken of as "three bodies," although it is understood to be one holy body, the true mystical body of Christ. The three aspects of this divine body are called the truth body, the body of glory, and the body of emanation, corresponding to Keter, Tiferet, and Malkut, respectively.

We may gain some understanding into the threefold body in the following way: The truth body is the Christos, specifically supernal or Christ consciousness. This dimension of the divine body is formed of transparent light or pure radiant awareness—the very essence of consciousness. Thus, the truth body is completely hidden and invisible, save to the tzaddikim who attain Messianic consciousness. It corresponds to Ain and to Yod of the Tetragrammaton.

Remaining purely in the body of truth, the tzaddikim would have no connection with unenlightened souls and the world; they would be completely transcendent and hidden. Therefore, in love and compassion, the Tzaddik generates a body of glory that allows the tzaddik to appear and manifest in the inner dimensions. This allows the tzaddik to contact individuals whose inner senses are opened and who are able to see in the subtle dimensions or to appear in the dreams and visions of people the tzaddik seeks to contact. This body of glory is akin to the divine images envisioned by initiates of the Tradition during prayer, meditation, and ritual. It is a body of translucent light, like unto the celestial bodies of luminous spirits and angels. Through this aspect of the threefold body, the tzaddikim are able to appear to souls of higher grades. It corresponds to Ain Sof and to the first He of the Tetragrammaton.

Although souls of higher grades can receive transmissions from the tzaddikim by way of the body of glory, amidst the masses of humanity such souls are relatively few. Therefore, the tzaddik will generate an emanation body that appears like the physical body and is visible to everyone. This may be a pure body of emanation, which is a temporary visible form, or it may be an actual body of incarnation that lasts the duration of a natural lifetime. What is distinct about an emanation body versus an ordinary physical body is that it is more energetic and able to serve as a conduit of vast spiritual energies, including the supernal light-force. Basically, such a

holy body is filled with the ruhaniyot and shefa of the Sefirot, and there
are fields of divine energy-intelligence around it. The body of emanation
corresponds to Ain Sof Or and to the Vau of the Tetragrammaton.

The appearance of Yeshua during his life and earthly ministry corresponds to the emanation body. His appearance in the transfiguration and
after the crucifixion corresponds to the body of glory. The ascension in
which he seemingly disappears into the light-continuum corresponds to
the body of truth. The process of the emanation of the threefold body
from truth body to body of emanation directly reflects the emanation of
the Sefirot from Atzilut to Asiyah. In the process of self-realization and
reception of the light transmission, this divine body is coming into being
with every truth-seeker. There are many teachings in the Sophian Tradition on the threefold body; however, time and space will not allow them
to be written here.

The Great Angel of Rainbow Glory—
Giver of All Blessings

Hesed at the level of Beriyah manifests as the archangel Tzadkiel, which
literally means the "righteousness of God" or "justice of God." The Kabbalah says that Tzadkiel grants blessings upon souls continually, according to their desire and capacity to receive. As the Kabbalah teaches, the
desire to receive for oneself alone is the most limited form of the desire to
receive, while the desire to receive for the sake of sharing and giving is
the greatest form of the desire to receive, creating an endless flow of
blessings and grace through oneself. This is the true secret to prosperity
and abundance in any form. The desire to share and give always creates a
greater flow and tends to make one more attractive and receptive of the
blessing power of God. The one who gives more, receives more, because
he or she does not block the flow of abundant life.

Hesed represents the exhaustless repository of energy, resource, opportunity, and ability to which we are intimately connected in the cosmos,
both physically and metaphysically. Essentially, dualistic consciousness,
produced by cosmic ignorance, creates an illusion of lack, and, thus, fear of
our not having enough, not being good enough, and a state of poverty-con-
sciousness arises. Fear prevents us from really living life to the fullest and

fear prevents us from true charity. God intends us to experience abundance and everything good; yet our own self-grasping, greed, and fear prevent us from receiving the greater blessings that God intends for us. While Tzadkiel is the archangel who will grant us all blessings—material, psychic, and spiritual—Tzadkiel is also the archangel that will help us see through the illusion of lack and realize the abundant life we already possess.

When it is said that Lord Yeshua favored one disciple above the other or that Yeshua loved certain disciples more than he loved others, the question naturally arises, "How can that be? Lord Yeshua is the embodiment of Hesed, specifically the pure and unconditional love of God. How could he then love one disciple more than another?" It is true. Our Lord loves all equally, friend, stranger, and enemy alike. Whether angel, titan, or demon, the Lord loves all living spirits and souls the same. However, not all are equally receptive to God's love, and therefore not all are equally able to receive. It is self-limitation in creatures that limits God's love.

In the same way that Tzadkiel helps the aspirant realize life abundant in the Christos, so, too, Tzadkiel helps the aspirant realize God's love. Of course, the secret of experiencing the love of God is the same as experiencing the flow of abundant life. When we, ourselves, are loving and love God and others, in the act of loving we experience the endless love of God.

Tzadkiel is invoked by Gnostic initiates seeking every possible kind of blessing one can imagine, from spiritual gifts and powers to all manner of psychic blessings, and even very mundane and material blessings, too—for all things necessary to perform the great work. The greatest blessing Tzadkiel can give, however, is the awareness of the sacred unity, spiritual love, and Gnosis of life abundant in Christ. Such is the very nature of Tzadkiel.

Listening and hearing the teachings concerning the archangel Tzadkiel, it might at first seem as though it is easy to approach and enter into this great angel's presence; however, that is often not the case. So great is the power of God—the love of God—that radiates from this holy angel that it can easily burn. It can be quite difficult to endure; for just as we see the great glory of El in the presence of Tzadkiel, we also see how far short of the great glory we fall. Thus, one cannot enter into the presence of Tzadkiel with extreme self-grasping and self-judgment. One must let go to God and let be.

The image of Tzadkiel appears like a human being, formed of brilliant translucent rainbow light—an angelic being that is a rainbow being, who has wings of white brilliance. This image appears in a cloudless sky and is completely self-radiant. Gnostic initiates invoke Tzadkiel with the intonement of El and the chant Maggid Ha-El Elyon Tzadkiel, while holding this image in mind.

There are a couple more things we can say of Tzadkiel in conclusion. Tzadkiel is the great angel of the luminous assembly and, therefore, is good to invoke when one is seeking contact with a disincarnate tzaddik. The invocation of Tzadkiel will ensure that one's connection is, in fact, with a true spirit of God and not some other sort of spirit. Likewise, Tzadkiel can also help an aspirant find a living tzaddik and spiritual community. The image of the great angel implies knowledge of another secret mystery—the rainbow body attainment. That, however, is the subject of another day and another book.

The Speaking-Silences

In Yetzirah, the world of angels, Hesed manifests as the order of the Hashmalim. *Hashmal* literally means "speaking-silence," hashmalim (plural), the "speaking-silences." The term hashmal appears in Ezekiel, at the culmination of Ezekiel's vision, when it says God speaks to him out of silence— hence a "speaking silence." Some hint as to what a speaking silence might look like is given in Exodus 20:15, where it is written: "and all the people saw the sounds." It suggests the experience of synesthesia, which can occur in deep meditation and represents a radically altered state of consciousness. In the experience of synesthesia, one might see sound, hear a smell, touch or smell a color, and so forth. One cannot help but think of the Zen Buddhist phrase, "the sound of silence" in this context.

The idea of radical alterations in consciousness is the key to understanding the hashmalim, for among other things, that is exactly what the speaking-silences do. They are angels of God that alter consciousness and facilitate metanoia (spiritual transformation or conversion). This is integral to the other primary function of the hashmalim, which is manifesting blessings. In order for a blessing to manifest, there must be a change in consciousness, for everything manifests with, in, and through consciousness, and everything is, in its true substance, consciousness. A change in consciousness brings about a corresponding change in the plane of one's experience or in the flow of circumstances, situations, and events of one's experience. Therefore, as a hashmal imparts the blessing, it must also inspire a change in consciousness.

The name speaking-silence reveals that the hashmalim are the blessings God gives, as when we pray and bring about change in our consciousness and God answers our prayer, giving us exactly what we asked for. God often speaks directly through blessings. Thus, when we receive a blessing from God that we asked for, we call it "God's answer to our prayer."

The word hashmal suggests something more. Ever notice how in your dreams no one ever really says anything out loud? Rather, you inwardly know what the characters in your dream are saying and what they mean. God and the holy angels tend to speak like that. They speak directly within our own thoughts and emotions. God and the holy angels are perfectly silent, and yet we hear them inwardly. Thus, the hashmalim are angels of divine communication or transmission, specifically, direct knowing.

The order of Hashmalim remind us of something rather important. When the mind is silent, the heart is still, and we are completely open and sensitive, then the tzaddikim, maggidim, and the Spirit of God speak in us. How they speak is a transmission of direct knowing. Prayer is more than speaking; it is also listening and hearing. Therefore, the difference between true prayer and holy meditation vanishes in the experience of a mystic.

Spiritual Practices for Hesed

The Transcendental Center—The Silent Witness

> ➤ Gather yourself inward, within behind your heart, letting go of the surface. Envision the spiritual sun of Christ indwelling behind your heart and gather yourself into that light-presence. Let go of the dream-like past and all thoughts of the future. All tension, stress, and negativity let melt away in the light of the spiritual sun (radiant awareness). Just let go and let be, and abide in the spiritual sun within behind your heart.

➤ As you sit in meditation in this way, shift your focus to a point above your head—the transcendental center about twelve inches above the head. Centered above the head, become the silent witness. Whatever thoughts and emotions occur, do not follow after them, grasp at them or identify yourself with them. Do not do anything with them at all, neither invoking them, banishing them, nor judging them. Merely watch the radiant display of the mind and heart, uninvolved as the silent witness without any judgment whatsoever. This is the whole aim of the practice.

➤ Begin with a short period of practice, perhaps ten minutes twice a day. Then, as your capacity grows, you can extend the period of your practice, cultivating the ability to abide as the silent witness for longer periods of time. If we can learn to abide in this way for an hour, it is a wonderful thing. First, we experience an innate peace. Second, we create the conditions necessary for the transformation of thoughts and emotions. For as long as we remain identified with our thoughts and emotions, we can do little to change them. Therefore, the first step to transforming thoughts and emotions is learning how to become detached or uninvolved. Third, through the practice itself, once we develop our capacity as a silent witness, we may then use the same method as a way of contact with the luminous assembly of the tzaddikim.

Mind to Mind Contact with the Holy Tzaddikim

Only when you have cultivated the capacity to abide as the silent witness for a prolonged period of time can it be used as a method for contact with the holy tzaddikim and maggidim—for the mind must be silent, the vital still, the consciousness clear.

➤ Go to a place where you will not be disturbed. Light a candle and some incense. Then follow the steps of the silent witness meditation. While your consciousness is inwardly gathered into the spiritual sun, pray that God sends a holy tzaddik to commune with you mind to mind and heart to heart—that divine grace might flow and a strong and true connection might be formed. Pray that God gives a host of forty holy angels charge concerning you, to come and form a matrix of light around you so that the environment is completely positive and good, and no deceiving spirits or klippotic forces can enter into it. Pray that the divine presence purify and bless you and abide with you in your meditation. Let your heart pray as you are inspired.

➤ Then be silent and shift your focus to the center above the head—become the silent witness. Instead of turning downward to watch the mind and heart, turn upward and open yourself to the Holy Shekinah and the luminous assembly. Listen and hear, and let yourself be completely receptive to the divine presence and power that manifests. Perhaps there will only be silence, or perhaps there will be a heavenly voice. The aim of this method is not a vision, but rather a mind-to-mind and heart-to-heart transmission. It may well be that only after the meditation you become aware of a transmission having occurred. In any case, at the close of the meditation, give thanks and praise to the Holy One of Being for what you have received—whether something or nothing.

➤ For any practice like this to truly be effective, it must be part of a daily continuum of prayer and meditation. It is best to use this method in conjunction with other practices, like meditations on the Mother, Yeshua, or the holy Bride, using another meditation as a daily practice and this meditation one to three times a week. As with any true spiritual practice, it may take some time to bear fruit. One must be patient and consistent, and learn to wait upon the Spirit of the Lord. "All good things come to those who wait."

NINE

GEVURAH, POWER,
THE DARK FACE
OF GOD

Attributes

Thirty-Two Paths of Wisdom: Rooted Consciousness (Sekhel Nishrash); it is called this because it is the essence of the homogenous Unity; it is unified in the essence of Understanding, which emanates from the domain of Original Wisdom

Gevurah: Severity or Rigor; also Din, Judgment

Place in the Tree of Life: The center of the Pillar of Severity

Divine Name: Elohim Givor

Alternative Divine Names: Ha-Ash Ha Gedulah, Great Fire; Elohim Amet, God of Truth; Shafet, Judger; Dayyan, Judge; Ish Miylchamah, Man of War; Elohim Nisah, God Testing and Trying

Partzuf Above: Zer Anpin, as the Great Warrior in the Chariot of Fire

Partzuf Below: Lord Yeshua exorcising demons and liberating souls; Lord Yeshua delivering souls in Hades and Hell; Isaac and Rebekah

Divine Image: A Spiritual Warrior riding the Merkavah; Yeshua the Exorcist; Michael and the armies of heaven

Archangel: Kamael and Samael

Order of Angels: Seraphim

Celestial Attribute: Madim, Mars

Titles Given to Gevurah: Pachad, Fear or Holy Awe; Tzimtzum; the Day
   of Reckoning; Judgment Day; the Wrath of God; the Dark Face
   of God; the Dark Face of the Mother; Consuming Fire; Sphere
   of the Angels of Wrath; Plagues of God; the Angel of Death; Red
   Mother Seed; The Left; Depth of North; Power of the Adepti;
   Strength of God; The Holy Law; Peacekeeper; the Second Day
   of Creation; Place of Sacrifice; the Agent of the Fall; the Other
   Side; the Scapegoat

Level of the Soul: Ruach, Human Spirit, or Divine Intelligence (specifically, the Upper Ruach)

Heavenly Abode: Makom, the Sixth Heaven—Place of Meeting

Spiritual Experience: The Vision of Power; the Ordeal of Power; Gnosis
   of the Law; Power of Discernment-Judgment

Virtues: Self-empowerment; courage; passion; resolution of conflicts;
   strength of character; integrity; leadership; conscious action; good
   coordination

Vices: Bullying; tendency to be overbearing; cruelty; oppression and
   exploitation of others; warmongering; anger; hatred; bigotry; violence; cowardice; rape; unbalanced male sexuality; tendency to be
   accident-prone or clumsy

Symbols: The wild rose of five petals; the chain; the scourge; the
   sword of truth; the upright and the inverted pentagram; the spear;
   the purifying fire or alchemical fire; the bow and arrow

Commandment: Honor your father and your mother (Exodus 20:12)

Sermon on the Mount: Blessed are the pure in heart, for they will see God
   (Matthew 5:8)

Angel of the Apocalypse and the Churches: The Second Star and Lampstand; the message to the angel of the church in Smyrna (Revelation 2:8–11)

The Self-Restraint of God and the Human One

Before the beginning, as we have seen, the light of the Infinite filled endless space and there was no "space" in which creation could come into being as a distinct reality from God and the Godhead. The quality of Hesed held dominion and there was nothing but God and only God—primordial grace. The first action opening the way for creation was the tzimtzum in which God withdrew into Godself, creating an infinite sphere of space—the primordial void—which became the womb of creation.

In the beginning, when God emanated God's infinite light into the primordial void, through the power of tzimtzum, God exercised self-restraint upon Godself, measuring and limiting the flow of Hesed-mercy with Gevurah-severity. With each gradation of the infinite light, God exercises a greater degree of self-restraint—each Sefirah representing a greater limitation or concealment of God's light and glory. As previously indicated, at the level of Adam Kadmon, the Sefirot are almost completely pure grace or Hesed, but at the level of Asiyah, the Sefirot are mostly Gevurah, which is to say most restricted. God's progressive restraint of the Shekinah from one universe to another means a greater possibility of free will and individuation of creatures with the generation of each successive universe, the universe of Asiyah representing the realms and worlds of the greatest possible free will and individuation.

In the same way that God restrains Godself in creating and relating to creation, as creatures seek to draw near to God and reach out to God, they must exercise self-restraint. In the descent or involution of God's presence and power, God progressively restrains Godself to make the Shekinah accessible to creatures—hence, God exercises Gevurah (severity). However, in the ascent or evolution of life-forms to the highest of life (conscious unification with God and the Godhead), Gevurah becomes the self-restraint of creatures, the negation of all negations of the sacred unity that God is. Descending-involving, God must restrain Godself; ascending-evolving, we must restrain ourselves. To enter into the upper Olamot, we must become more and more like unto God, as in the upper Olamot only that which is in God and is something of Godself exists.

This self-restraint or negation of what is not God in ascent, however, is truly no restriction or limitation at all, but rather is a progressive enlightenment and liberation of the soul, for as we have seen, the inmost part of the soul is in God and is of God, and our true freedom to be ourselves is in the ascension. In restraining ourselves, we give greater freedom to the presence and power of God in us. This is directly reflected in the mystery of the crucifixion and resurrection of the Christ-bearer, in which, fully self-restrained, the Christ-bearer becomes fully Christ.

According to the Thirty-Two Paths of Wisdom, Hesed is rooted in Keter-Hokmah, the supreme grace or mercy of God, and Gevurah is rooted in Hokmah-Binah, which serve to measure the flow of the Light of God into countless gradations. As we saw in our contemplation of Hokmah, Hokmah represents the creative utterances upon which creation is founded. As we discovered in our exploration of Binah, Binah represents the supernal or archetypal patterns based on those creative utterances, which form the matrix of creation. The creative utterances and archetypes are the supernal expression of the Torah (law). Gevurah, thus, has its roots in these utterances and archetypes and is the active execution of the law in creation.

The law is the self-restraint God exercises on Godself in God's interaction with human beings and creation, and it is the self-restraint that human beings exercise upon themselves in order to draw near to God and unite themselves with God. Gevurah-rigor, which is the law, represents the vehicle or covenant through which we are connected to God in a harmonious and conscious relationship. Hesed-love, which is the fulfillment of the law, represents the fruition of that relationship in the unification of ourselves with God.

The Awesome Power of God

At the level of Atzilut, the Sefirah Gevurah manifests as Elohim Givor, which means strong, mighty, or powerful God. Elohim as Binah represents the archetypal forms or supernal patterns the one life-power assumes. Elohim as Gevurah represents that actual manifestation of distinct and individual divine powers, which have their origin in Hokmah and Binah— hence the measured grace of God through which the seven Sefirot of construction manifest. How these divine powers appear, whether peaceful, blissful or wrathful, is determined by the law, specifically the law of karma. Basically, the divine powers assume an appearance according to the balance of karma, whether appearing to an individual soul or to a collective of souls (as in collectives of souls grouped together in regions, nations, or even worlds).

An example of the different appearances divine powers assume according to the law of karma is the story of the Red Sea. Pharaoh and the hosts of Pharaoh went in pursuit of the children of Israel, cornering the children of Israel at the shores of the Red Sea. The Shekinah, however, parted the Red Sea, allowing the children of Israel to escape, but when Pharaoh and his hosts attempted to follow them across, the Red Sea swallowed Pharaoh and his hosts. This is a story of Elohim Givor and the appearance of Elohim according to the karma of peoples. On the one hand, to the children of Israel, Elohim Givor was the manifestation of God's power delivering them from bondage and destruction; on the other hand, to Pharaoh and his hosts, Elohim Givor was the manifestation of God's power as judgment and wrath.

Pharaoh and his hosts represent the egoistic self and fragmented consciousness of the unenlightened individual, specifically souls linking themselves with the dominion of the klippot—the titanic and demonic forces. Moses and the children of Israel represent an integrated and awakened individual who is established in a degree of enlightenment, specifically, souls linking themselves with the Sefirot—the divine powers. To the unenlightened soul that cleaves to klippotic forces, Gevurah appears as judgment and wrath, but to the enlightened soul that cleaves to the Spirit of Yahweh, Gevurah appears as the divine power redeeming and delivering the soul from bondage.

According to the Tradition, God and the holy angels in heaven took no pleasure in the destruction of Pharaoh and his minions, but mourned the sorrow and suffering of the unenlightened. Yet, at the same time, God and the holy angels rejoiced over the enlightenment and liberation of the children of Israel, experiencing great joy in the deliverance of souls from the dominion of the klippot. Understanding the transmigration of souls, in truth, all souls were liberated on that day—the children of Israel to their pursuit of a greater degree of enlightenment, and the minions of Pharaoh to new incarnations in which they, too, might seek enlightenment and draw nearer to God. Gevurah always acts to transform and liberate.

The appearance of Elohim in creation, according to the law of karma is indicated by Givor, which is spelt with the Hebrew letters Gimel (ג)-Bet (ב)-Vau (ו)-Resh (ר). Gimel means "camel" and connotes travel and commerce, specifically, travel through the wilderness of the desert. It represents the travel of the soul based upon the principle of cosmic memory—the karmic matrix.

The letter Bet means "house" and connotes a dwelling or abode and the center of life, specifically, the body and the world to which the body joins the soul. As the first letter of the Book of Genesis, Bet represents the matrix of creation (the spiritual forces indicated by Elohim), incarnations, and the spiritual forces at play within and behind them, which correspond to the karma of the soul.

Vau, as we saw in our study of the Tetragrammaton, means "nail" or "hook" and connotes binding together, linking, or connecting. As the number six, it represents the six Sefirot between Binah and Malkut. Vau represents the various spiritual forces to which a soul can link itself, which in turn determines how God or reality appears to the soul. Spiritual forces act as the mediating principle between God and the human soul and, thus, determine the relationship of the soul to God.

Resh means "head" or "face," and connotes appearance, communication, and relationship. It alludes to the state of consciousness determining appearances and the nature of communication and relationships that form. Resh is how God or reality appears to us.

Elohim Givor, then, reflects what we have previously said—that God (Elohim) does not change, but the appearance of God's presence and power (Givor) changes corresponding to changes in our own state of consciousness. Givor indicates that our souls are bound to the cycles of endless transmigration by karmic conditioning and that each incarnation is a karmic matrix, so that every circumstance, situation, and event of life, and our relationship with life and God, is the product of karma, whether positive, negative, or neutral. Essentially, our life, dreams, visions, and afterlife experiences are all the radiance of our soul-being or the face of Elohim as Elohim appears to us.

Elohim Givor also indicates that God has dominion over all spiritual forces and that all spiritual forces are sustained by God's power and are the manifestation of God's power. The best way to understand how God's power manifests as all spiritual forces, whether divine, titanic, or demonic, is in terms of human life. The life-power is the same in all human beings, whether godly or ungodly. The one life-power manifests as average human beings, whom are neither particularly good and saintly nor wicked and evil. The same life-power sustains and manifests as those who are good and righteous persons and those who are wicked and evil-doers. Whether good, admixed, or evil, every human being is sustained by the one life-power and is a manifestation of the one life-power. The same is true of spiritual beings-forces in the more subtle dimensions of Asiyah, Yetzirah, and Beriyah, whether angel, titan, or demon.

The Nature of Karma and Tikkune

Today we understand that life-forms have evolved within the womb of the earth for millions of years, as though waves of life arising from within one another, ever moving toward greater intelligence and self-awareness. Essentially, greater intelligence and self-awareness has manifest as the life-forms that are able to support and embody it come into being. Humanity, as it is, represents the pinnacle of intelligent life on earth. Yet according to the Kabbalah and Gnosticism, there are further levels of intelligence and self-awareness to be developed within humanity from which a divine or super humanity is destined to arise.

This alludes to grades of evolution within the race of humanity itself, proposing that within humankind there are various levels of development and evolution, specifically on the level of the soul-being. When we speak of intelligence and self-awareness, we are actually speaking of the soul or consciousness. In Kabbalistic terms, the evolution of life-forms is the evolution of Nefeshim and the evolution of intelligence, which generates self-awareness, is Ruachot.

Until the dawn of humankind on earth, all evolution transpired on a subconscious level, quite apart from any real conscious exertion on the part of species. It was essentially a secret operation of God's Spirit within nature and transpired on a very deep and hidden level. As we have indicated, humankind marks a significant transition in evolution, for unlike previous life-forms, humankind has a capacity for a conscious evolution because of the greater intelligence that is in it. The present humanity is, basically, the transitional being in the twilight zone between the unconscious and conscious evolution.

In the previous chapter we spoke of a gift that God seeks to give to us, namely Godself, and in the Scriptures we hear of a "chosen people" or the "elect" to whom God gives Godself. Exoterically, this has been taken to mean the Jewish peoples. However, esoterically, the elect are souls of sufficient evolution who are able to receive the gift—hence souls of a higher grade of self-awareness. The nature of this gift is a fiery or divine intelligence, specifically, the fiery light of supernal consciousness. As we have seen, it is through this gift that a human being may experience a conscious unification with God and Godhead.

The Kabbalah says that vessels or universes were created and destroyed many times in the process of forming this present universe. In speaking of the evolution of life-forms and souls—Nefeshim and Ruachot—we see the same process reflected. Life-forms are formed and destroyed in the process of evolution, and souls are generated and reabsorbed in the process of reincarnation. It is a wave-like motion of progress and regress in a spiral ascent.

Karma, in essence, is this dual-action of evolution: progress and regress. It is the cosmic law of cause and effect, the aim of which is a creative evolution toward the highest of life. Although we may speak of karma in terms of positive, neutral, and negative actions, basically, it is all a question of whether a given action facilitates or retards the soul's development and evolution—hence whether our actions lead toward a progress to a supernal or divine humanity or a regress back into our bestial past.

Evolution occurs through a process of progression and regression, much like the incoming tide of the ocean. Every progress moves a little further forward and every regress recedes a little less backward, so that, in fact, it is one motion of ascent when viewed over the course of time. In speaking of the liberative quality of creation, it is this that Kabbalah is indicating. While we can speak of the backward pull and tendency to bind that is inherent in the cosmic law, which is often referred to as negative karma, in truth, it is merely a regression in which souls are able to work out whatever hinders and obstructs further progress in evolution. In other words, whether a seeming progress (positive karma) or regress (negative karma), everything in our experience represents an opportunity for progress in conscious evolution. Spiritual practice and spiritual living from a Gnostic and Kabbalistic perspective is nothing other than working out whatever is necessary for the development and evolution of the soul-being.

This process of working out what is necessary for continued progress in a conscious evolution is called *tikkune* in the Kabbalah, which means correction, repair, mending, or healing. According to the Tradition, both the metaphysical structure of the universe—the Sefirot and Olamot—and the human soul are in a process of evolution and in need of tikkune: the working out and healing of whatever is necessary for the ultimate fruition of creative evolution. Because human souls are microcosms of the macrocosm (the metaphysical universe), the tikkune of human souls brings about the tikkune of the Sefirot and Olamot.

The primary agent of this tikkune is Gevurah—the holy law or principle of evolution itself. It is the agent of the tzimtzum through which series of Nefeshim and Ruachot come into being as individuations of the one life-power. Likewise, it is the agent that tries and tests every development in the process of creative evolution to see if it is strong, good, and true. When it is ready, it passes into the next cycle of progress; what is not ready goes into a cycle of regress to work out what is needed for progress—all according to the law. It is in this sense that we may understand the title of Gevurah as Din, which means judgment.

Three Visions

At our ordinary level of consciousness, we tend to be bound by what is called the vision of ignorance, which is karmic vision. Souls occupying similar life-forms all share a basic common karma. In that we have human bodies, we share human karma. This is what is called the human kingdom, and being human, we all represent something of the soul of the human one.

In the human kingdom, we all have individual karma, reflecting our previous lives and our personal history in this life. Each of us is born in a certain country, a region, and community, under certain conditions, and into a specific family. We each experienced a different upbringing and education and different influences, life experiences, and beliefs. All of this

forms our individual karmic condition, reflecting our previous evolution
through past lives. In essence, we are all a complex accumulation of habits
and past actions. Consequently, each of us has our own world-view and
unique perspective on things. We might look a lot alike, but we are all
very different in how we see things. In effect, we all tend to live in our
own individual and separate worlds, and to what degree these worlds ever
really meet is a great question. Karmic vision is based primarily upon our
own subjective projections—our preconditions, preconceptions, and expectations. Because our view is inherently limited and partial, and our self-
image is inherently flawed, this vision is a mixture of truth and falsehood.
Essentially, it's a story we have made up, based upon our personal history
and a delusion of separation, and it represents karmic conditioning—
hence the vision of ignorance.

In the vision of ignorance, everything is based upon past developments
in evolution, and without some sense of potential future developments, it
binds us to the past—the repetition of history. To break through this
karmic vision, we need some spiritual or mystical experience that produces the vision of faith—hence, initiation.

The vision of faith is essentially a vision of experience—a revelation of
the truth and light in our own experience, which we then are able to enact
in our spiritual practice and spiritual living. Obviously, there can be many
different levels of manifestation to the vision of faith. However, in Gnostic Christianity, it ultimately comes by way of the light transmission and
direct perception of the light continuum—the sacred unity of God that
underlies all existence. To the degree we recognize, realize, and embody
this spiritual truth, we enter into the vision of gnosis, which is the vision
that arises in the attainment of Chris- consciousness.

These three modes of vision are reflected in the threefold body of
Melchizedek discussed in the previous chapter. The vision of ignorance
allows the perception of the emanation body of a tzaddik; the vision of
faith manifests through the perception of the glory body of the tzaddik;
and the vision of gnosis comes with the perception of the truth body—
the state of pure radiant awareness. These three visions thus reflect progress
on the path to self-realization.

The Ordeal of Power and Tikkune of the Soul

The nature of the Gnostic path is a quickening of the evolution of the soul-being and a swift ascent to supernal or Christ-consciousness. An evolution of consciousness that could take hundreds, or even thousands, of lives by ordinary means of gradual development can occur in three to seven lives by way of Christian Gnosticism and the practice of Kabbalah. This assumes, of course, that one fully sets oneself on the path and that one receives initiation into the light-continuum.

Essentially, reception of the light transmission invokes the full karmic force of a soul so that the process of tikkune is sped up, and thus, the ascent to Christ consciousness transpires more rapidly. The path of initiation is not the path of least resistance, but is, in fact, the path of most resistance. It is akin to climbing straight up the face of a mountain rather than spiraling round and round to eventually reach the peak. This is reflected in the saying of Lord Yeshua: "Enter through the narrow gate; for the gate is wide and the road is easy that leads to destruction, and there are many who take it. For the gate is narrow and the road is hard that leads to life, and there are few who find it" (Gospel of St. Matthew 7:13–14).

One should not be put off from setting oneself on the path of initiation because of fearing an invocation of the full force of one's karma. The full force of one's karma does not manifest at the outset of the path, any more than does the full manifestation of divine power. At the outset of the path, one must learn to meet the challenges already present within one's life. As one progresses from one grade of the enlightenment experience to another, one learns to meet more subtle and sublime challenges, having developed the capacity to meet them. The path is the work of a lifetime, perhaps several lifetimes, and one's capacity at each stage is equal to the challenges one faces. Likewise, one is not alone in the great work. There is always the divine grace of guidance, assistance, and empowerment in the face of every challenge for all who take up the divine life and actively engage in spiritual practice and spiritual living. The truth is that the invocation of the full force of our karma is what leads to the ultimate healing of our soul in enlightenment and liberation.

The greater adept is the Rosicrucian grade that corresponds to Gevurah, and it is at the level of the greater adept that an initiate experiences the full force of his or her karmic continuum. It arises as the full influx of the divine presence and power. If the disciple is a well-prepared vessel when this radical influx of divine power occurs, then it will be a completely wonderful and blissful experience. However, whatever imperfections or impurities might remain will be swiftly revealed. If those imperfections are many and unresolved, then the adept is likely to shatter under the psychic pressure created by the inrush of great force. This is called the ordeal of power and typically leads the adept into the second dark night of the soul, which is the most severe challenge on the path.

Although psychism and occultism in the New Age often mistake magic-powers as indicative of a higher grade of soul or an actual enlightenment, this is not necessarily true. Power, in and of itself, is not self-realization, although it is, indeed, a by-product of the self-realization process and the ability to manage greater power is part of actual attainment. The truth is, one must have faith, hope, and love to endure the ordeal of power, and the knowledge, understanding, and wisdom necessary to properly use it in the great work. It is this that indicates actual enlightenment. This is well reflected by the saying of Yeshua: "Not everyone who says to me, 'Lord, Lord,' will enter into the kingdom of heaven, but only one who does the will of my Father in heaven. On that day many will say to me, 'Lord, Lord, did we not prophesy in your name, and cast out demons in your name, and do many deeds by the power of your name?' Then I will say to them, 'I never knew you; go away from me, you evildoers'" (Gospel of St. Matthew 7:21–23). It is also reflected perfectly in the myth of the temptation and the questions put to Master Yeshua by the adversary, Satan (Matthew 4:1–11), all of which surround the use of divine power.

Here, we are speaking specifically of the manifestation of various spiritual gifts or magic-powers that naturally arise at a certain point in the enlightenment experience; yet the ordeal of power is common to all realms of evolution. This is clearly demonstrated in the development of humanity in modern times, with our growing access to various forms of power through our science and technologies. More and more, as we develop our intelligence, we have access to greater material powers. The question becomes whether or not we have the level of maturity in our mental and vital being to manage these powers and use them wisely to facilitate further progress in our evolution. Quite obviously, the material knowledge and powers humanity is accessing could be used to radically quicken the pace of human progress or equally to cause a radical regression in human life on earth. According to the masters of the Tradition, our whole species and whole world has entered into the ordeal of power—hence the season of the apocalypse.

While the ordeal of power, as it is experienced by the greater Adept, may be somewhat distant to many of us, the question of how we use power is relevant to all human beings in these times and is certainly important to the spiritual aspirant long before the grade of the greater adept. Frankly speaking, we all have access to power. One need only consider such material powers as the money-power, sex-power, social-power, fame-power, or any other form of life-power in one's ordinary life. On a practical level one can ask oneself, "Who does this power serve?" Essentially, in the practice of Christian Gnosticism, it is the aim of the initiate to uplift all powers to the divine, whether material, psychic, or spiritual powers, and to restore all powers to the service of the divine will and kingdom. This is the very essence of the tikkune of the soul and the world.

On a fundamental level, we are the world and the world is us; we are the society in which we live and the society is us. Therefore, if we seek to bring about a change in our societies and the world, we must bring a change about in our own consciousness. Our redemption and healing (tikkune) is the redemption and healing of the world. This is the very foundation of the great work.

The Love of the Lord and the Fear of the Lord

There are three sorts of individuals who might walk up to a wild tiger in the forest and pet the big cat upon its head. One is the perfect tzaddik, who is filled with the Spirit of Yahweh, and peace and love, to whom the tiger is no threat. The other two are the idiot and the fool. The idiot is too stupid to understand the danger of the tiger and thus too stupid to fear it. As for the fool, he is too arrogant and reckless to acknowledge his fear. While the perfect tzaddik may pet the tiger and go unharmed, the idiot or fool will most likely be dinner or simply good sport!

"A tiger is a great and powerful beast, indeed, but God is far greater and more powerful than a mere tiger, and potentially far more dangerous! One who seeks to draw near unto the Lord would do well to be aware of this and proceed with mindfulness and alertness. Life is composed of great beauty and great danger, and Yahweh is the life-power. Those who are wise fear the Lord as much as they love the Lord, and on account of fear they preserve their life" (Tau Elijah Ben Miriam).

This was a favorite saying of my beloved tzaddik when he would give teachings on Gevurah, which is also called *pachad* (fear). Confronting our fears and walking through them is an important part of the path to Christ consciousness, and as my teacher was also fond of saying, "Where there is no fear, there is also no courage." It takes courage to live life fully, and yet more courage to embark upon the mystical journey. Just as there are material dangers in the world, so also there are psychic and spiritual dangers in the path to self-realization.

Pachad is not a childish and superstitious fear of God's punishment, as though God was some sort of tyrant or abusive parent, nor is it fear of the obscene fiction of eternal damnation in hell. Such things, as we have seen, are all ignorant projections upon God. By "fear" is meant holy awe, which, coupled with love, is also eyes of wonder. Holy awe and wonder fills the soul that draws near unto God and the Godhead, and where there is no awe and wonder, the soul is far removed from the Holy Spirit. Quite simply, awe and wonder are the natural human experience of God's presence, as anyone who has ever had a direct experience of the Shekinah will tell you.

Most initiates early on the path are taken by surprise at their own reaction to the first time there is a larger movement of energy in the subtle body, or when they first experience contact with one of the archangels. Before fully embracing the spiritual or mystical experience as it unfolds, more often than not, the young initiate reacts with a vital recoil and fear. This is true even when an aspirant may have worked for a long time to bring about such a development. While the novice will frequently feel that there is something wrong with him or her, or as though he or she failed some sort of test, in the eyes of an experienced adept or master of the Tradition, it is a sign of health and success, for the fear tells the tzaddik that the novice was conscious and had some awareness of the real power moving within and behind the experience, and that the novice had an understanding of what they were experiencing or contacting.

It is only natural that we experience some degree of fear, along with other emotions, upon entering into new and unfamiliar experiences. This is true in mundane circumstances and it is equally true in supramundane circumstances. While being dominated by fear or paralyzed by fear would certainly be unhealthy and represent a severe imbalance, the presence of fear itself is quite natural and to be expected, and oftentimes it serves as a guardian early on so that we do not overshoot our capacity. Dealing with fear is part of the sacred quest. In truth, sometimes it is our friend, invoking mindfulness and alertness in us, while other times it is our adversary and must be dealt with in kind. We must learn to discern the difference and to respond consciously based upon that discernment, understanding that, ultimately, we must learn to walk through all fear and to transform all fear into focused awareness.

In terms of human emotions, fear and love typically move together. Anyone who has ever had the experience of truly falling in love will also speak of the fear that gripped them in the process. Ask anyone in love who has realized that they have met the person they will marry! Thus love and fear hang out together, and where there is no fear there is also no real love.

Fear is typically a form of resistance to something—resistance to something new and unfamiliar, something uncomfortable, something overwhelming or that takes us out of control (as in love). It is often a great teacher, revealing weaknesses, impurities, and imperfections to be worked out before we are able to move forward. When fear is allowed to turn into anger, anger is allowed to become hatred, and we are ruled by our fears and insecurities. Fear leads to the dark side and evil, yet fear can also be recognition of darkness and evil, and lead us away from evil.

If so many different things can invoke fear, if fear has so many different faces and is part of our early spiritual or mystical experiences, along with other emotions, then how could we draw near unto the Lord and experience the awesome and terrible power of God without some degree of fear and trembling? Encountering the presence of God directly, we will experience the full range of human emotions, and fear will be among them. Thus, Gevurah is also called Pachad, and it is written: "The fear of Yahweh is the beginning of knowledge" (Proverbs 1:7). As my teacher often said, "Those who love the Lord, and are drawn to the Lord, also fear the Lord, for they are aware of the great and awesome force that we call 'God.' It is the power of life and death, and the whole universe."

The True Nature of Sacrifice

The word "sacrifice" comes from a root meaning "to make sacred" or "to sanctify," and connotes purification and consecration. Something sacred or sanctified is something set apart from mundane use and dedicated to supramundane use. Something is made sacred because of the meaning we give to it, how we use it, and our reverence for it.

The Hebrew word for sacrifice means "to draw near," specifically, to draw near unto the Lord, and connotes a vehicle of drawing near or of unification with God. As we have seen, drawing near to God happens through self-restraint, and thus sacrifice is an act of restraint, whether the restricted use of a sacred or holy object or an act of self-restraint through which we ourselves are made sacred or holy.

By self-restraint is meant purification, which is a letting go of anything that does not have a place in God or that is not of God. If God is truth, then it is a letting go of ignorance and falsehood; if God is love, then it is letting go of anger and hate; if God is good, then it is letting go of anything evil, and so on. One might say that the entire mystical journey is a path of purification in that, when all things obstructing the truth and light are removed, our innate divinity naturally and spontaneously shines from the depths of our being, and we realize all along we have been at one with God, the source of all life. Understanding the principle of sacrifice in this way, rather than the primitive idea of an appeasement of a deity or soothing the arbitrary whims of a tyrannical god, sacrifice is a letting go of something inferior for something superior—a release of something lesser for something greater. Sacrifice is not a loss but rather a gain!

Offering-up is often a term for sacrifice, which suggests an uplifting of something or the transformation of something from a lower form to a higher form, specifically, the translation of something mundane to something supramundane. This was the significance of burnt offerings in the primitive mind, in that, through burning a sacrifice, one transformed something material into something spiritual, and thus it could then be received by deity, which is spiritual. It is also the idea behind cremation, which is intended to swiftly release the spirit from the body and thus deliver it into the embrace of the great Spirit, God.

All of these ideas of sacrifice relate to the function of Gevurah, and thus Gevurah is called the place of sacrifice. As the temptation has a correspondence with Gevurah, as well as with Yesod, so also does the night of passion and the crucifixion. While the mystery of the Crucifixion as divine revelation corresponds to Tiferet, as an action of self-restraint and holy sacrifice, it corresponds to Gevurah, as does Isaac who was willing to make a sacrifice of himself unto the Lord.

The mystery of the crucifixion and resurrection itself reveals the true nature of sacrifice, for through the Crucified One, all negative karma is dispelled (all klippot shed), and through the Risen One, all are drawn near unto the Lord and unified with God. This holy act of sacrifice is the ultimate tikkune—the shattering of all husks of darkness (klippot) and the release of the holy sparks contained in them to unification with Christ in God. Far from a death or a loss, the crucifixion represents a letting go of a lower plane of existence to ascend to a higher plane of existence, specifically, an ascent to the supernal being.

The name for the rite of the Holy Eucharist in Christian Gnosticism represents well the true nature of sacrifice—the wedding feast. This alludes to sacrifice as an action of mystical union and specifically an act of love and delight. A true sacrifice is an act of love that brings into union, the fruition of which is pure joy or delight. The same holy rite also reveals the transformation power of sacrifice, for in the rite, the bread and wine are transformed into the body and blood of Christ, specifically the presence and essence of the Christos, which when eaten joins the body and soul to the Soul of the Messiah. Sacrifice is inherently a mystical and magical act.

While in Gnostic worship flower offerings, light offerings, incense offerings, food offerings, and such are given as symbols of sacrifice, the true sacrifice is the offering-up of ourselves and our lives to the holy Shekinah and the great work. Spiritual study and contemplation, prayer, and meditation, and sacred ritual are holy sacrifices, for through these we draw near to our Neshamah and the Lord. So also are mundane activities, when they are dedicated to the evolution of the soul-being and we are spirit-connected while performing them. Even the sexual act of love-making is considered a vehicle of holy sacrifice in Gnosticism, when lovers embrace one another as the Lord and the Shekinah or as the Bridegroom and holy Bride. Ultimately, the aim of the Gnostic initiate is to transform the whole of life into the divine life, leaving nothing out, and thus embody the Christos in life—making life a true and holy sacrifice before the presence of the Lord.

The Patriarch and Matriarch of Gevurah

Isaac and Rebekah are the patriarch and matriarch of Gevurah, and thus their story is the story of Gevurah. The life of Isaac begins with a conception by divine intervention of grace, so that Isaac is born by way of Hesed in the same way Gevurah emerges from Hesed. When, as a young man, Isaac allows himself to be bound on the altar as a sacrifice before the presence of the Lord, exercising self-restraint he reflects the activity of Gevurah. In that through his act of self-restraint God provided another sacrifice, Isaac reflects the action of Gevurah, setting a flow of measured grace in motion.

Isaac does not choose his own wife, as do the other patriarchs; a servant of his father's house finds Rebekah, once again reflecting self-restraint, as does Rebekah herself. When Rebekah conceives and becomes pregnant, she is pregnant with twins—Esau representing the bestial soul and evil inclination and Jacob representing the godly soul and good inclination. This reflects the dual quality of Gevurah and the opposing archangel and arch demon attributed to it.

The two brothers wrestle in Rebekah's womb and Esau, being stronger, emerges as the firstborn. When it comes time for Isaac to impart the patriarchal blessing, he intends to give it to the first-born son, Esau. However, like Justice herself, Isaac is blind. With Rebekah's help, Jacob poses as Esau and takes the blessing, as ordained by heaven, reflecting the karmic balance in Gevurah. Esau had sold his birthright to Jacob for some food and, according to the law, the blessing belonged to Jacob. Everywhere one looks into this story, Gevurah appears.

The Purifying Fire of God

In Beriyah, the Sefirah Gevurah manifests as archangel Kamael, whose name literally means the "burner of God" or "fire of God." The image of Kamael reflects his name. He appears as a human form composed of intense fire and heat, not in robes, but in armor as the great guardian of God's presence and the angel of judgment. With the name of Elohim Givor and the chant *Ah Ya Ko Ma Kamael*, initiates invoke this great and powerful angel for the sake of Divine justice.

The archangel Michael is said to be the commander of the armies of heaven, but Kamael is said to be the champion of God, who subjugates all Titans to the divine will according to the law of perfect justice, and who is victorious over all evil. When the Scripture speaks of Yahweh as a man of war, it is speaking of the archangel Kamael, before whom no evil can endure. Yet, Kamael does not engage in war but is a fire consuming fire, making all like unto itself, the mere presence of which is the "end of darkness and evil."

To one who is on fire with the Spirit of Yahweh, who cleaves to the Spirit of the Lord and has put on the image of the Lord, the presence of Kamael is pure bliss; yet to one who is removed from God and does not come in the name of the Lord, the presence of Kamael is dread and terrible—a great fire that burns and consumes. This description, of course, depicts a personification of the law in Beriyah—for in essence, Kamael is the appearance of the soul's karma.

We may gain some understanding of Kamael from the words of St. Paul, when he says, ". . . through the law I died to the law, so that I might live to God." He also says, "And we have come to believe in Christ Jesus, so that we might be justified by faith in Christ and not by doing works of the law, because no one will be justified by works of the law" (Galatians 2:16). The meaning is this: the body and surface consciousness are bound by the law and cannot liberate itself from the law. Nefesh and Ruach are bound to the matrix of karma because they are the product of karma, but the Neshamah and the inner and higher self (Christ-self) is not bound to the law. Thus, through faith in our divine nature and the indwelling Christ, we are liberated from the law of karma. Kamael, the burner of God, burns away all klippot, including the klippot of our old and unenlightened self, thus revealing the soul of light and Christos in us. Such is the function of Kamael-Gevurah.

Kamael conveys divine power upon the faithful and elect in the same way that Tzafkiel conveys divine blessings. Essentially, Kamael acts to help remove obstructions to the flow of grace and to measure out grace so that we might receive God's blessing-power. Likewise, this great angel helps us understand our karma and therefore the nature of tikkune to be performed. Kamael reveals the weaknesses, impurities, and imperfections in consciousness so that we might understand what needs to be worked out in order to progress in self-realization. At the same time, Kamael is the angel of divine protection, serving as the guardian of the assembly of the faithful and elect, and is said to defend against psychic assaults of dark and hostile forces, as well as assaults of black magic and "the evil eye." When an elder or tau seeks to uphold oaths, it is Kamael who is invoked.

The Adversary of God and Humanity

The arch-demon Samael (Satan) is also said to be the manifestation of Gevurah at the level of Beriyah. Samael, which as you will recall means the "poison of God," is the personification of the evil inclination or the inclination to self-destruction and violence, which is called *sitra ahara* in Hebrew. While, indeed, we may speak of cosmic forces of evil (dark and hostile forces), in the Kabbalah, evil is primarily understood as cosmic ignorance and the evil inclination in us. After all, if there is any external agent of evil, it only has power over us to the degree that we have not put an end to the inclination of violence in ourselves.

Pride and arrogance (selfishness), lust and greed, jealousy and envy, anger and hate, insecurity and doubt—every form of negativity—are by nature a poison and generate negative karma, leading to death and destruction. The same mind that generates positive thought and emotion also generates negative thought and emotion; the same imagination that envisions the divine powers also envisions darkness and evil; the same life-power through which good and noble things are enacted also is the life-power through which wickedness and evil is done. Understanding this, we understand the relationship of Kamael and Samael.

If one wishes to gain insight into the adversary, the evil one, or the dark face of God, one need only consider the meaning of the name Samael and contemplate the ultimate outcome if humankind continues to poison the environment of this good earth. How "good" will planet earth be in future generations if we continue to live in our present selfish, greedy, and hateful manner that pollutes and poisons the environment? Will the water be good to drink or the air good to breathe? Will the beauty of nature reflect the glory of the presence of God? Indeed! Satan will be cast down upon the earth, as said in the book of Revelation, and it is we who are bringing him to earth!

The same can be said of war, terrorism, and every form of evil we enact upon one another and the creatures of this good earth. What is true upon a material level is also true upon psychic and spiritual levels. The balance of good and evil is dependent upon the human being. The choice is up to each and every one of us whether we are visited by God or the devil.

The Angels of God's Power and Glory

Gevurah manifests at the level of Yetzirah as the order of the Seraphim. Seraph literally means "fiery serpent" or "burning angel." Seraphim appear in the vision of Isaiah, and the great Seraphim are said to be holy angels that abide directly in the presence of the Lord, continually in worship of the Lord. These seraphim are said to appear like the light of the sun, on fire with the Spirit of Yahweh, and are described as having six wings— two to cover the face, two to cover the feet, and two with which to fly. Their function is to conceal the one-who-sits-upon-the-throne and yet, at the same time, to reveal the glory of the Holy One.

Isaiah says that the Seraphim are in attendance above the image of the glory of Yahweh and that they call to one another saying, "Holy, holy, holy is the Lord of hosts; the whole earth is full of His Glory" (Isaiah 6:3). The masters of the Kabbalah say that, when the great Seraphim worship in the presence of Yahweh, they perspire fire and light, and this fiery-light pours down through the heavens, becoming the river of fire surrounding the third heaven, called Shehakim, meaning "clouds of grace," or "sky-like." This same river is said to pour out into the hells, becoming the fire of hell. You will recall that, according to the Kabbalah, the Holy Spirit is the light of heaven and fire of hell. Thus, it is the power of the Holy Spirit that pours out through the great Seraphim, which is called their "perspiration from worship." This indicates that the Seraphim are angels of the Holy Spirit and specifically are angels of divine illumination and divine power. Thus, as the hashmalim grant blessings, or are blessings; the seraphim grant illumination and power or are illuminations and powers.

According to the Tradition, based upon the literal meaning of Seraph as a fiery serpent, there are two other forms of Seraphim besides the great seraphim described by the prophet Isaiah. One is alluded to in the Sefer Yetzirah in the Mishna that speaks about Theli, the celestial dragon. Certain esoteric interpretations of the Mishna speak of Seraphim that are great dragons, which are said to be personifications of cosmic forces that are neither good nor evil but rather are pure energy.

The other form of Seraphim is depicted as a plague of fire snakes or venomous serpents that the Lord sent among the children of Israel, the bite of which was lethal (Numbers, chapter 21). Moses sought a remedy from the Lord for the bite of these Seraphim. The Lord told Moses to fashion a bronze image of a Seraph and to put it on top of a pole in the center of the Israeli camp. Anyone who was bitten by a fire snake would be saved if they looked up and gazed upon this image. There are many esoteric teachings in the Christian Kabbalah regarding this form of Seraphim; however, the most significant is the interpretation of these Seraphim as the secret power of the Holy Spirit in the spine and, specifically, in the channels of the subtle body—what in Eastern Traditions is called "Kundalini," or "Dakini," or "Shakti Power." It is said that if this fire snake is awakened prematurely, it can cause illness and even death. Rather than a blissful experience, it could be a hellish one. However, awoken in due season, sublimated and directed up through the central channel of the spine, this serpent power leads to divine illumination and magic-power. Thus, the teachings say that there is a Seraph within each of us—the serpent power, which is the Holy Spirit power. It is the aim of the Gnostic initiate to awaken this divine power and to direct it inward and upward—Godward.

Spiritual Practice for Gevurah

Divine Protection

➢ When you feel in need of divine protection, it is good to chant the divine name of Elohim Givor. As you intone the name, let the vibration fill your body and the entire space around you, and let the name fill your mind so that your mind merges completely with the name. When your chant is complete, let your heart pray for divine protection and the grace of the Lord—and so it shall be.

➢ Alternatively, chant the name, let the vibration of the name fill you and the space around you, and visualize a circle of great fire magically appearing around you, into which no darkness or evil can enter. Envision a burning angel appearing, with a sword of flashing fire in his hands, as a guardian of the sacred circle. Wherever you go, the circle of great fire and the burning angel will be with you. When you no longer have need of the burning angel, give praise and thanks to God for divine protection, and pray the holy angel be released from its charge concerning you. If you perform this practice for someone else, simply envision them in the circle rather than yourself.

➢ In the same way the burning angel is invoked, the archangel Kamael can be invoked when the need for divine protection is great. Chanting the divine name, chant the chant of Kamael and envision the divine image of Kamael magically appearing in the space before you, with his great sword of truth in hand. Pray for divine justice and tikkune in the situation for which you have invoked the great angel and offer the situation up before the Lord in prayer, letting go to the divine will. This invocation is typically performed by initiates in response to greater injustice in the world beyond themselves.

➢ Equally, one may simply envision the spiritual sun in one's heart and one's whole body transformed into the spiritual sun—a fiery light that transforms everything it touches into itself (the light-presence). No evil or darkness can draw near to one who abides as the spiritual sun—the Spirit of Messiah.

TEN

TIFERET,
DIVINE BEAUTY
AND SUN OF GOD

Attributes

Thirty-Two Paths of Wisdom: Transcendental Influx Consciousness (Sekhel Shefa Nivdal); it is called this because through it the influx of Emanation (Atzilut) increases itself; it bestows this influx on all blessings, which unify themselves in its essence

Tiferet: Beauty or Harmony

Place on the Tree of Life: The Center of the Pillar of Compassion (Middle of the Middle Pillar)

Divine Name: Yeshua; also Yahweh Elohenu

Alternative Divine Names: Yeshua Messiah; Adonai Yeshua; Yahweh Eloah Ve-Da'at; Ben Ha-El, the Son of God

Partzuf Above: Zer Anpin, proper

Partzuf Below: Yeshua Messiah teaching and initiating; Yeshua healing the people; the Risen Messiah; Jacob, Leah, and Rachel

Divine Image: The Holy Child; the Christ-bearer Crucified; the Risen One; the Light of the Cross; Melchizedek

Archangel: Raphael

Order of Angels: Malachim

Celestial Attribute: Shemesh, the Sun

Titles Given to Tiferet: Melekh, the King; the Spiritual Sun; the Sun of
   God; the Anointed; Adam, the Human One; Son of Adam, Son of
   the Human One; the Great Seth; Good Serpent; the Serpent-Sun;
   the Son; the Mother's Child; Holy One; the Beginning of Life; the
   Light of the World; the Light of Life; Light in Darkness; Secret
   Sun; the Crucified One; Indwelling Christ; Lord of the Sabbath;
   Depth of East; Self-Made-Perfect

Level of the Soul: Ruach, proper (Union of the Upper and Lower Ruach)

Heavenly Abode: Ma'on, the Fifth Heaven—Dwelling Place

Spiritual Experience: Gnosis of Yeshua Messiah; Gnosis of the Mystery of
   the Crucifixion and Resurrection; the Vision of the Pattern-That-
   Connects

Virtues: True individuality; vitality; empowerment; divine pride; positive
   motivation; self-determination; strong will; drive; courage; dignity;
   strong spirit; self-awareness; devotion to the Great Work; living the
   Holy Gospel

Vices: Lack of true individuality; lack of motivation—apathy; power-
   lessness; lack of energy or enthusiasm; weak will; arrogant pride;
   selfishness; low self-esteem; shyness; lack of faith and devotion;
   distracted; lack of self-awareness

Symbols: The Crucifix; the Cross; the Rose Cross; the Cube; the trun-
   cated pyramid; the Seal of Faith; the Lamen of Adept; the Double-
   Sided Seal; the Seal of Amet; gold; the upright pentagram, as a
   symbol of the Christed Human Being; Star of David or hexagram

Commandment: You shall not murder (Exodus 20:12)

Sermon on the Mount: Blessed are the merciful, for they will receive mercy
   (Matthew 5:7)

Angel of the Apocalypse and the Churches: Third Star and Lampstand, and
   the message to the angel of the church in Pergamum (Revelation
   2:12–17)

The Pattern-That-Connects

The Tree of Life glyph is composed of Sefirot and the paths that connect them. The paths of the Tree of Life are represented by the twenty-two letters of the Hebrew alphabet, the aleph-bet. Tiferet (beauty) is the center of the Tree of Life and, as such, it is the sacred heart of the tree. In the simplest terms, we may understand the function of Tiferet on the tree akin to the heart in the body, which distributes blood and therefore oxygen throughout the body. In terms of the Tree of Life, the Sefirot would represent organs or various limbs of the body and the paths would represent the arteries and veins, as well as the nervous system. The blood and oxygen, of course, would be the shefa (everflow) and ruhaniyut (radiant breath).

In the Judaic Kabbalah, the Sefirah Tiferet shares the same divine name as Hokmah, the Tetragrammaton, but is pronounced with different vowels. This represents the Son as the image of the Father, and specifically alludes to the metaphor of the Tetragrammaton as the trunk of the tree. While Abba-Hokmah is the trunk proper, Keter being the root, as the sacred heart of the tree, Ben-Tiferet is the trunk in function. Abba-Father is completely realized in Ben-Son.

Hebrew letters are also words and numbers. By spelling out the letters as words, spelling out every new letter that appears, and, through a play number associations, there is a way to draw out all twenty-two letters of the aleph-bet from the Tetragrammaton, so that, as it is said to contain all divine names, it contains the whole aleph-bet also. The letters represent twenty-two energy intelligences, which are forms that ruhaniyut and shefa assume. The attribute of the Tetragrammaton to Tiferet alludes to all of these energy-intelligences being contained in Tiferet in perfect balance and harmony—hence the title of the Sefirah: beauty or harmony.

If the divine names are the Sefirot at the level of Atzilut, then the universe of Adam Kadmon is the universe of holy letters from which the names and language are derived—hence the power of the human one to name things and to speak the word of God. For this reason, Adam is attributed to Tiferet where things are named and the word of God is spoken. It is this metaphysical understanding of the aleph-bet that is alluded to in the Judaic Kabbalah when Hebrew is called the language of God and the holy angels. To know the energy-intelligences represented by the twenty-two letters is to know the spiritual forces and spiritual principles upon which creation is founded, and thus to gain gnosis of the mysteries of creation.

This provides insight into the esoteric meaning of the word of God. For these twenty-two energy-intelligences are emanations of the word, combinations of which are the energy-intelligence behind all things in creation—every creature and everything in creation being a unique individual manifestation of the word, which is formed according to God's wisdom. Adam Kadmon is the universe of the primordial word-wisdom (Logos-Sophia). Tiferet is the realized word and the actual sacred unity underlying creation—the pattern-that-connects.

This idea of the word that is the source and sustenance of all life is reflected in the attribute of the sun to Tiferet, which as a celestial body is the light and life of the worlds that orbit it, and specifically is the light and life of all life-forms on earth. Apart from the sun, nothing can come into being. Life is in the sun and life is the light of all creatures (consciousness of all creatures). Such is the nature of the word through which "all things came into being," and "without which not one thing came into being," and in which is "the life" that is "the light of all people," according to the Prologue of the Gospel of St. John. Thus Tiferet, which is the word of God, is quite distinctly the spiritual sun, which is the light and life of all worlds.

The term aleph-bet itself proves an interesting contemplation in conjunction with the word Adam. As we have seen, Adam is Aleph-Dam, spirit in the blood; aleph-bet means spirit in the house or house of the spirit. On one hand, aleph-bet is creation or the macrocosm, which is the house of the spirit. On the other hand, it is Adam, the human one or the microcosm, that is the house of the spirit. The aleph-bet, the power of the word, is in the human one, which is reflected in the self-awareness and capacity for sophisticated and complex language in races of intelligent-life (human beings). It is the power of the word that separates the human kingdom from the animal, vegetable and mineral kingdoms. Likewise, it is the knowledge and understanding (Gnosis) of the spiritual or metaphysical dimensions of the power of the word that separates the human kingdom from the superhuman kingdom, as we see in the person of Yeshua Messiah. In speaking of the Gnosis of Yeshua Messiah, it is this knowledge and understanding of the spiritual power of the word that is meant in the Christian Kabbalah. This divine Gnosis is Tiferet—the word of God, the Sun of God.

Following Hesed and Gevurah, Tiferet is the measured grace of God, the dynamic balance and harmony of mercy and judgment, which is called rahamim (compassion). It is directly connected to every Sefirot on the Tree of Life by way of the paths-letters, except for Malkut, to which it is said to be connected through a secret path only under certain conditions. As we have seen, too much severity or too much mercy is not compassion at all. Where there is too much severity, there is cruelty, oppression, destruction, and death; where there is too much mercy, darkness and evil reign and there is a unity of unconscious oblivion. Likewise, compassion is a dynamic balance and harmony of all energy-intelligences and all divine powers. Tiferet is the divine fullness of all energy-intelligences in a dynamic balance and harmony—"the harmony of all spheres of influence" that acts as the mediating intelligence, which is another common translation of Sekhel Shefa Nivdal.

This is the function of Zer Anpin (the little face) in relationship to Arik Anpin (the daughter) and Nukva (the little face). Zer Anpin is the mediator or interface between the two, and through the agency of Tiferet, Keter and Malkut are united in perfect harmony. In this aspect of the teachings, one must bear in mind that Zer Anpin is actually all six Sefirot between Aima and Nukva, the Sefirot Hesed, Gevurah, Netzach, Hod, and Yesod being extremities of Zer Anpin. Tiferet, as the six, is the Vau of the Tetragrammaton, through which the upper He (Aima-Binah) and the lower He (Nukva-Malkut) are united. As the tip of the Vau is Yod, Zer Anpin is the extension of Abba and is the manifestation of Arik Anpin below the great abyss. It is this mystery of the Son that is the revelation of the big face, the image of the Father, the union of the Mother and Daughter, and the Bridegroom and the Bride that plays out in the Gnostic Gospel. For in the Christian Kabbalah, Tiferet is the Christ-center, and Yeshua Messiah is the incarnation of the power of the word, which is the Partzuf Zer Anpin above.

The Lord Your God—The Way of the Soul

At the level of Atzilut, the Sefirah Tiferet manifests as the divine name of Yahweh Elohenu, which literally means the "Lord your God." As we have seen, "Lord" indicates the transcendental aspect of God, while "your God" indicates the immanent aspect of God. It also indicates the mystery of two aspects of the divine in our experience—the impersonal and personal. In our experience, the divine manifests as an impersonal force, specifically energy-intelligence; but the divine also manifests in our experience as Divine being or a person, assuming personas (Partzufim) through which we can experience a personal relationship. On the one hand, God is a completely impersonal force; on the other hand, God is distinctly a person with whom we experience a personal relationship, both force and being representing modes of consciousness.

Initiates also experience this in terms of such things as "angels." For angels can manifest as spiritual beings or as spiritual forces—it really all depends upon the individual to whom they appear. Some individuals are more inclined to view them as forces, while others are more inclined to view them as beings, and some encounter them as both beings and forces. The same is true of God. We experience God as impersonal or personal, all according to the angle of our view. In truth, God is impersonal divine force and the person of Divine being. Rather than either/or, God is and/both. This is one level of the meaning of Yahweh Elohenu.

Yahweh Elohenu as Tiferet indicates that, at the level of Tiferet, we are able to know and understand God, and know and understand the spiritual forces at play within and behind creation. This is the meaning of Tiferet's alternative name of Yahweh Eloah Ve-Da'at, which literally means "Lord God and knowledge" or the "Lord God as God is known." Yahweh Elohenu is God as each individual knows and understands God. Thus, God is completely accessible at the level of Tiferet on the Tree of Life, specifically through Ruach, which implies one's own self-awareness.

In the Christian Kabbalah, the name of Tiferet is the name of Yeshua. Yeshua is the Aramaic pronunciation of the Hebrew name Yehoshua (Joshua) or the Greek name Jesus. Sometimes initiates pronounce the blessed name as Yeheshuah, to place emphasis on the letters that form the name. Most commonly, the Aramaic pronunciation is used because it is the actual language the Master spoke and it was the actual pronunciation of the Master's name at the time of the Gospel. Through the pronunciation of the name as Yeshua, we directly connect ourselves to the perfect tzaddik, the apostles and the Gospel.

The name of Yeshua, as we previously indicated, is the Tetragrammaton with the addition of the letter Shin (יהשוה), and literally means "Yahweh delivers." Yahweh literally means "That Which Was, Is, and Forever Shall Be," which alludes to the being of the becoming or to reality as it is—hence the truth. The name of Yeshua, therefore, literally means "the truth that sets free" or "the truth will set you free."

Yeshua is, thus, the embodiment of the truth that enlightens and liberates, and the term Messiah is, therefore, akin to the Eastern term "Buddha"—enlightened one. While much of Christendom has come to the degraded belief in Yeshua Messiah as isolated to the person of the Master and thus as something outside of oneself, Gnostic Christianity holds the belief in Yeshua Messiah as the divine presence and power within oneself—an enlightened nature within us. Obviously, the Gnostic has faith in the incarnation, as well as the crucifixion and resurrection; however, the Gnostic has faith in his or her own divine destiny to become Christ or Messiah—to be Christed as Jesus was Christed. This self-realization is depicted by Tiferet on the Tree of Life—hence the title Christ-center.

As the name Yahweh Elohenu alludes, this divine presence is within us and beyond us; thus Tiferet specifically represents the Gnosis of the indwelling Christ and the cosmic Christ. Yeshua is therefore the name of our inner and higher self, the Christ-self; and Messiah is the divine nature of our Soul. Our Neshamah is, in essence, a unique individual emanation of the Soul of Messiah, and embodying our Neshamah we embody something of Messiah, the Sun of God.

Shin is a significant letter. It is the letter indicating the fiery intelligence or the power of the Holy Spirit, which, as we have seen, is the spirit of the prophets, the spirit of the initiates, and the Spirit of the Messiah. The shape of this holy letter alludes to this threefold spirit, the power of which manifests as the threefold body of Melchizedek and, as we shall see, the presence of which manifests as the threefold sanctuary of divine Gnosis. It is through the gift of the fiery intelligence, which is the power of the word, that one becomes a true initiate and is able to draw upon the shefa and ruhaniyut of the great name *Yahweh* and all the other divine names. Yeshua is the name of any true initiate in whom this fiery intelligence has awakened and who has realized the fiery intelligence in him- or herself to some degree, more or less. For this reason, it is called the name of names, because, through the name of Yeshua, the power of all divine names is in the Christed human being.

The Divine Life of Yeshua

In the Gnostic Tradition, an important distinction is made between the Christ-bearer (person of Yeshua) and the actual Christ-presence (soul of Messiah). According to the Gnostic Tradition, although the soul of Yeshua was, indeed, a great soul of light, he was not born an enlightened being or the Christ, but rather, like all of us, was born a human being in bondage to cosmic ignorance. While some might think such a belief degrades the perfect Master, in truth, it exalts the Holy One all the more. Because he was fully human and then became fully enlightened, he is a true image of divine illumination, and the glory and grace of God is revealed even more through the person of Yeshua Messiah.

The Gospels of St. Matthew and St. Luke both tell stories of the virgin birth. If studied, neither relate the same story but are radically different. Thus, Gnostics understand these stories as metaphors and do not make the mistake of taking them literally. According to both the Gospel of St. John and the Gospel of St. Mark, Yeshua becomes the Messiah through the initiation of baptism imparted by the prophet John the Baptist. This is the Gnostic view of Yeshua becoming Messiah.

In the Gnostic Gospel, Yeshua is a spiritual prodigy as a boy and studies with two different teachers: one who teaches him the Judaic faith, along with the mystical Kabbalah of the time, and another who teaches him the magical Kabbalah as he matures. It is said that Yeshua learned swiftly, that various attainments came easily to him, and that as a very young man his knowledge and ability exceeded his teachers, yet always he remained a true and faithful disciple. It was not until he met John the Baptist that he encountered his true holy tzaddik. It was John who taught him the union of the mystical and magical Kabbalah and who initiated him into the mysteries of the Baal Shem (the master of the name) and the inmost secret level of the Kabbalah. We gain insight into the love of Yeshua for his tzaddik in the Gospel of St. Matthew, when Lord Yeshua speaks a disciple's praise for his master, saying, "Truly I tell you, among those born of women no one has arisen greater than John the Baptist . . ." (Gospel of St. Matthew 11:11). Even if one believed the virgin birth to be literal and historical, Yeshua himself was born of a woman, and he praises John even above and beyond himself in saying this. Although a disciple may excel his or her teacher, in the eyes of the disciple, his or her teacher is always the teacher, the holy tzaddik. Thus, in saying this, Yeshua refers to John the Baptist as his tzaddik.

According to the Tradition, the relationship of the tzaddik and disciple was not new to the soul of John the Baptist and the soul of Yeshua. For the soul of John was the soul once incarnate as the prophet Elijah and the soul of Yeshua was Elisha, the protégé of Elijah who became his successor. In 2 Kings, we hear the story of a promise Elijah made to Elisha before the ascension of the prophet. Along the way to where the ascension would take place, Elijah puts his disciple to the test three times by asking Elisha to turn aside and stay behind. Elisha refuses to leave the presence of his tzaddik, however, and continues in the journey with the prophet. Then, after parting the Jordan River and crossing over to the other side, Elijah says to Elisha, "Tell me what I can do for you, before I am taken from you?" Elisha responds, saying, "Please let me inherit a double portion of your spirit." Elijah then says to him, "You have asked a difficult thing; yet, if you see me as I am taken from you, it will be granted you; if not, it will not" (2 Kings 2:9–10). As it turned out, Elisha did see the ascension of Elijah. However, the promise was not fulfilled in the incarnation of Elisha, but was fulfilled in the incarnation of Yeshua. According to the Tradition, it was fulfilled in the baptism of Yeshua by John at the same point where the Jordan River was formerly parted by Elijah and the original promise was made. And so it is written:

> In those days Jesus came from Nazareth of Galilee and was baptized by John in the Jordan. And just as he was coming up out of the water, he saw heaven torn apart and the Spirit descending like a dove on him. And a voice came from heaven, "You are my Son, the Beloved; with you I am well pleased." (Gospel of St. Mark 1:9–10)

The Spirit of the Messiah then entered into Yeshua, which is "a double portion of the Spirit of Elijah," for the Spirit of the Messiah is the union of the spirit of Elijah (the prophets) and the spirit of Enoch (the initiates). In this, we understand that Yeshua was not born the Messiah, but became the Messiah through a spiritual quest. We also understand that the soul-being of the Master passed through a series of incarnations in the human life-wave, creating the conditions necessary for the divine incarnation.

Yeshua, the Christ-bearer, became joined to the Christ-presence at the baptism, yet the complete unity of Christ and the Christ-bearer does not occur until the resurrection, when the body and the person of Lord Yeshua are fully transformed into the solar body of Christ. There are many points in the Gospels where this is reflected, but the most obvious is the statement of Lord Yeshua on the cross, when he says, "Eloi, Eloi, lema sabachthani?" which means, "My God, my God, why have you forsaken me?" (Gospel of St. Mark 15:34). These are words of the Christ-bearer when the Christ-presence has withdrawn in the final dark night of the soul, indicating a subtle division between Christ and the Christ-bearer before the grace of the resurrection.

In Gnostic tradition, what is significant about this distinction between the Christ-bearer and Christ is that Lord Yeshua is understood as continually evolving into the divine fullness of Christ throughout the Gospel, in the same way we ourselves progress from one grade of self-realization to another throughout our own lives. In the case of Yeshua Messiah, however, this progress transpires far more rapidly than is typical because of the former attainment of his holy soul. Thus, at birth Yeshua was a human being like any other, and following his death and resurrection, he is fully Christ, the Sun of God. The journey of Lord Yeshua is the journey of every soul that consciously labors to evolve to Christ consciousness—a journey that typically takes place through several or more lives.

This distinction is not so simple and clear-cut as it might seem, however. For in the progress of the Gospel, as Yeshua actively engages in the light transmission, he is constantly shifting from one level of consciousness to another, at times being completely transparent to the Christ-presence, while at others being quite distinct from the Christ-presence. As the Gospel progresses and Lord Yeshua unfolds self-realization in Christ consciousness, more and more he is at one with the Christ-presence and thus inseparable from the Christos. In reality, on the one hand, Lord Yeshua is the image of the human one coming into being in Christ consciousness. Yet, on the other hand, Yeshua Messiah is the Christos communicating itself to the world. It is in this latter sense that the experience of Yeshua will be completely different from our own, in that the soul of Yeshua was the Christ-bearer to humanity on earth and, within behind the appearance of separation and union, was all the while Christ. Ultimately, the divine incarnation transpired in a mystery, which is only understood in our soul when we ourselves become established in Christ consciousness.

The Serpent and Savior—The Great Seth

No one has ascended into heaven except the one who descended from heaven, the Son of Man [Adam]. And just as Moses lifted up the serpent in the wilderness, so must the Son of Man be lifted up, that whosoever believes in him may have eternal life (Gospel of St. John 3:14–15).

While Lord Yeshua rarely speaks of himself as the "Son of God," he often refers to himself as the son of the human one (Adam). In so doing he calls himself the great Seth, for according to the Scriptures, after Cain slew Abel and was exiled, God blessed Adam and Eve with another son, called Seth, who is said to be the image and likeness of Adam. This image and likeness is said to be androgynous—hence the human one before the separation into male and female, Adam and Eve. Thus, this is the image and likeness of Yahweh Elohim.

The name Seth is significant because it is composed of the last two letters of the Hebrew aleph-bet, Shin (ש) and Tau (ת). Shin, as we know from our previous discussion, is the letter representing the Holy Spirit and Shekinah. Thus, it represents the fiery intelligence. Tau is the cross and represents completion, perfection, and fulfillment. As the cross, it indicates the union of male and female, Logos and Sophia—hence the androgynous state of the human one. Seth literally means the "light of the cross," but also alludes to the unification of Logos and Sophia in one body of light. This is the meaning in Gnosticism of the "second Adam."

If one contemplates the story of Moses and the fiery serpents (Numbers, 21) and the image of a bronze serpent set on top of a pole in the center of the Israeli camp, the image is the shape of Tau—the cross. This image directly suggests the source of light in the perfect Master and the true nature of the light of the cross.

As we have said, Hebrew letters are also numbers. Therefore, every word in Hebrew also represents a number. In the Kabbalah, whenever two words share the same number value, they represent manifestations of the same consciousness-force. The word "Messiah," which means the anointed, and the word "Nechash," which is the serpent in the Garden of Eden, both equal 358. Thus, the serpent and the Savior represent one and the same spiritual force, and in essence, the Messiah is the serpent redeemed. In the above verse, the nature of the serpent is a fire snake. Thus, the source of light in the Master is the fiery serpent, which in Eastern schools is called "Kundalini."

This numerical correspondence between the serpent and the Savior means that the fiery intelligence that manifests as Messianic consciousness also manifests as the unenlightened condition—hence, "the force that binds is the force that liberates." This gives us deeper insight into the fiery intelligence spoken of in Christian Gnosticism. For we understand the power of the Holy Spirit as a secret power hidden within us, the awakening of which leads to supernal or Messianic consciousness (Christhood).

According to the masters of the Tradition, it is this divine power that is activated in the reception of the light transmission; the power of the Holy Spirit descends from above, awakening itself below. The union of the descending and ascending force of the Holy Spirit manifests a third force— the supernal light-force. Hesed represents the descending force and Gevurah represents the ascending force. Tiferet represents the manifestation of the supernal light—hence the state of supernal illumination, which is called the spiritual sun and the serpent sun in Christian Gnosticism.

In the Gnostic Gospel, there is a threefold baptism: a baptism of water, of fire, and of the spirit—an outer, inner, and secret rite of baptism. The first represents the self-purification necessary to properly awaken the serpent power; the second represents the awakening and uplifting of the serpent power, guided in its ascent by the inner or Christ-self; and the third represents the fruition of self-realization in supernal or Messianic consciousness.

Quite literally, one in whom this divine power is awakened is on fire with the Spirit of Yahweh—the spirit of the one life-power. Like Tiferet, which is called the mediating intelligence, one in whom this power is awakened embodies the light-presence and unites heaven and earth—the material world and world of supernal light—and is a vehicle of the light transmission in the world—hence Seth, the tau of light. Essentially, all divine names associated with Tiferet point to this attainment, the Rosicrucian grades from Tiferet to Keter all representing various degrees of the divine illumination that comes in the awakening of this fiery intelligence.

The Mystery of the Crucifixion and Resurrection

In Gnostic Christianity, the purpose of the divine incarnation is the revelation of the light continuum and awakening the fiery intelligence within humanity. The crucifixion and resurrection is understood as the central act in a mystery drama performed by Master Yeshua in order to open the way for the full light transmission and to put the wisdom teachings he gave to his disciples into their proper context. It is one thing to speak of the development of consciousness beyond the body and an ascent to higher planes of existence; it is another to actually demonstrate truth-consciousness and to impart the inner and secret teachings of the Gospel from the solar body of the resurrection.

Orthodox forms of Christianity found their dogmas and doctrines almost exclusively upon the outer teachings Lord Yeshua gave during his life and ministry, specifically, the interpretations of those teachings by St. Paul, who ironically refers to himself as the "least of the apostles." Gnostic Christianity, however, focuses primarily upon the inner and secret teachings given after the resurrection by the Risen Christ. This is well-reflected in many of the books of the Nag Hammadi library, which purport themselves to be secret teachings imparted to the inmost disciples by Lord Yeshua after the drama of the crucifixion and resurrection was enacted. While orthodox Christianity places the most emphasis upon the crucifixion as a "sacrifice for the sins of the world," Gnostic Christianity places greater emphasis upon the crucifixion and resurrection as a vehicle of divine revelation.

Christos, the light-presence, cannot be crucified; rather, it is the Christ-bearer that is crucified. Essentially, at the time of the crucifixion, there is a distinct separation that occurs between Christ and Christ-bearer. In the Gnostic vision of the crucifixion, the Christos is envisioned as a light-presence above the image of the crucified one, with only a most subtle and sublime connection with the Master in the form of clear light. At the instant of death, Yeshua, as the Christ-bearer, shifts the center of his consciousness into the light-presence, demonstrating the way of transference of consciousness beyond the body. Essentially, identifying himself with all of humanity, he uplifts all who form a spiritual connection with him into the light continuum.

On a certain level, the crucifixion was a great mystical and magical act—perhaps the greatest feat of divine magic ever performed. In submitting to the crucifixion, Lord Yeshua made his body the talisman of the karmic continuum of the world, and thus made his body a magical talisman of liberation. In effect, cosmic ignorance, the law, and karmic matrix were crucified (suspended), so that anyone who identifies with Lord Yeshua and mystically unites him- or herself to Yeshua might experience liberation from karmic bondage. As we have seen, the true meaning of sacrifice is "drawing near," and Yeshua made himself a vehicle through which others might draw near to supernal being.

This action was specifically on behalf of the disciples of the Master— disciples of the past, present, and future—whose karmic vision prevents the pure vision of the light-continuum. This is reflected in the story of the transfiguration when Lord Yeshua attempted to impart the light transmission, only to have the disciples who were with him fall unconscious due to karmic conditioning. Thus, he enacts the crucifixion and resurrection to dispel all karmic obstructions to the light-transmission.

Part of the dispelling of karmic vision happens by the Lord shedding the physical body and putting on a body of light, just as one might remove one set of clothing and put on another. In so doing, he demonstrated the illusory nature of dualistic consciousness and death, and revealed the true meaning of his wisdom teachings. Thus he prepared the proper ground for the root, heart, and essence transmission of the supernal light, which correspond to Malkut, Tiferet, and Keter, respectively, as well as the emanation body, glory body, and truth body of Melchizedek. However, the true purpose of the crucifixion and resurrection was the actual light transmission and the secret gnosis associated with it.

While we might speak of the crucifixion and resurrection as a process of uplifting souls toward the world of supernal light, at the same time, the world of supernal light is brought down upon the earth, so that the disciples of the Master might know the matrix of supernal light both above and below, within and all around themselves. This was the purpose of the crucifixion and resurrection—divine revelation.

This activity of uplifting and bringing down is reflected by Tiferet, the Christ-center on the Tree of Life. For on the one hand, Tiferet uplifts Malkut (the world) into union with itself and therefore union with the supernals. On the other hand, Tiferet brings down the light of the supernals into Malkut. Essentially, Yeshua Messiah, as the Risen Christ, is the embodiment and revelation of Tiferet—the Transcendental Influx Consciousness.

The Bridegroom and Holy Bride

In the Gnostic Gospel, the Soul of the Messiah is incarnate as the Bridegroom and the Holy Bride—Lord Yeshua and Lady Mary Magdalene. As we have said, Lady Mary is seen as the copreacher with Lord Yeshua and as codivine with him. In every way, she is his soulmate, Christ the Sophia in union with Christ the Logos. Therefore, in Gnostic Christianity, it is impossible to talk about Lord Yeshua without talking about the Holy Bride. To speak of one is to speak of the other, for spiritually they are inseparable.

The majority of Christendom does not view Yeshua as having been married or having had sexual relations. However, Gnostic Christians believe that St. Mary Magdalene was the consort and wife of Yeshua. According to the Scriptures, husband and wife are "one flesh" and are united in body, spirit, and soul. Thus, everything that transpires in the life of Lord Yeshua also transpires in the life of Lady Mary.

If one is familiar with teachings on Vajra Guru and Vajra Dakini in Tantric Buddhism or Shiva and Devi in Hindu Tantra, one will have a good idea of the Gnostic view of the relationship of Yeshua and Mary— the Lord is the supernal being and our Lady is the supernal consciousness-force. In essence, the entire magical display of the Master is the Holy Bride. It is through her that the disciples receive the transmission of the fiery intelligence, both that of the serpent power and the supernal light. This is reflected in the relationship of Tiferet and Malkut on the Tree of Life. Tiferet transmits the supernal ruhaniyut and shefa, via Yesod, to Malkut, and Malkut distributes the ruhaniyut and shefa in creation. In fact, Malkut is the holy Shekinah. In the same way, the Bride is the personification of the holy Spirit power in creatures and creation, even as the Bridegroom is the personification of the divine self of all creation.

According to Gnostic masters, on an inner level, the story of the first miracle at the wedding in Cana (Gospel of St. John 2:1–11) is actually an esoteric allusion to the awakening of the Christ-presence in Lady Mary and the mystical union of Yeshua and Mary. The supernal light-presence had already descended upon Lord Yeshua and the serpent power was already fully awakened and uplifted in him. Thus the wedding feast of Cana is symbolic of the same initiation occurring in St. Mary Magdalene. The author of the Gospel of St. John also places Lady Mary as the first apostle to receive the Risen Christ and as the person chosen to communicate the good news to the disciples, following which the disciples receive the visitation of the Master and the initiation of the radiant holy breath.

While on one level the light-transmission is said to occur through the mystery of the crucifixion and resurrection, on the inmost level it is said to occur through the mystical embrace of the Bridegroom and Bride. This is also reflected in the Kabbalistic teaching concerning the relationship of Tiferet and Malkut, for it is said that, when there is a coupling below of the King (Tiferet) and the Holy Bride (Malkut), there is a corresponding coupling of Abba and Aima above. This union of Abba and Aima, as we have seen, forms Arik Anpin (the big face), and through this coupling above and below, the supernal light-force flows and pours out upon the world via the Bridegroom and Bride. Thus, within and behind the light transmission that transpires through the enactment of the crucifixion and resurrection, is the light transmission via the mystical embrace of Christ the Bridegroom and Christ the Bride (Logos and Sophia). One might say that the crucifixion and resurrection is an outer manifestation of this inner mystery of mystical union between the Bride and Bridegroom, which would be unseemly to openly depict!

When Yeshua Messiah is called the second Adam (Bet Adam), the perfection of Adam Ha-Rishon, it is an allusion to this mystical embrace between Lord Yeshua and the Holy Bride, for as the first Adam was male and female in one body, so the second Adam is male and female in one body of light. Apart from mystical union with the Holy Bride, Lord Yeshua cannot resemble Adam Ha-Rishon, and thus could not reveal the true supernal glory of the divine kingdom. Thus, as the Holy Bride is fulfilled in Lord Yeshua, Lord Yeshua is fulfilled in the Holy Bride. They are one divine presence and power, the one anointed with the supernal light of God.

The Holy Threefold Sanctuary— Outer, Inner, and Secret

Through the incarnation of the Soul of Messiah in Lord Yeshua and Lady Mary and the light transmission embodied in the apostolic succession, a holy sanctuary of faith and gnosis is established. The sanctuary is composed of objects of refuge through which the faithful and elect receive sanctuary from the negative influences of klippotic forces. These objects of refuge also act as vehicles of divine grace.

Initiates receive sanctuary and the blessings of divine grace through faith and self-identification with the objects of refuge—unification of oneself with the divine images of the holy sanctuary. When we direct our mind, heart, and life toward the sanctuary, our thoughts, feelings-emotions, words, and actions are naturally uplifted and filled with the blessings and goodness of the sanctuary. This tends to shelter us from negativity and dispels negativity, dispelling negative karma and generating positive karma in its place.

The threefold sanctuary has an outer, inner, and secret manifestation, each representing more subtle and sublime dimensions of the sanctuary that are increasingly nearer to the spirit and truth. The outer sanctuary is called the sanctuary of the faithful, the inner sanctuary is called the sanctuary of the elect, and the secret sanctuary is called the sanctuary of the divine Gnosis.

Outer Sanctuary

The outer sanctuary is composed of three objects of refuge: Yeshua Messiah (Christ), the Gospel (teachings of Christ), and the Gnostic circle (spiritual community founded on the teachings of Christ).

As we have seen, through faith in the divine incarnation, and specifically faith in the mystery of the crucifixion and resurrection, we are spiritually connected to Yeshua Messiah. Through this spiritual connection, we are liberated from the karmic matrix and bondage to the dominion of the klippot and, likewise, we are established in the path of the great resurrection and ascension. Yeshua Messiah is the first object of refuge because he is the center of the divine incarnation in the first coming and, therefore, all blessings flow from him.

The second object of refuge is the Gospel, which is the spiritual teachings and initiations imparted by Lord Yeshua. The Sermon on the Mount, which appears in the Gospel of St. Matthew, is often considered the heart of Yeshua's teaching. In the Sophian Tradition of Gnosticism, the Gospels of St. Thomas, St. John, and St. Mark are the main focus of study and contemplation, along with the Letter to the Hebrews and Book of Revelation. However, in Gnosticism, the Gospel is something far more than things written. It includes inner and secret oral teachings. Thus, there is the written Gospel and the oral Gospel. In Gnosticism, by "Gospel" we actually mean an initiate's knowledge and understanding of the Gospel and, specifically, the truth and light as it is revealed in the experience of the initiate. More than this, we mean the continuum of spiritual practice and spiritual living through which an initiate makes him- or herself "Christ-like" and is able to progress toward Christ consciousness. One who lives the divine life of the Gospel abides in the holy sanctuary.

The third object of refuge is the Gnostic circle or spiritual community. We gain strength, support, and encouragement from spiritual community and the opportunity to receive from others and give to others. We transcend ourselves through healthy spiritual fellowship. In the Gnostic circle, we receive teachings and initiations into the secret wisdom of the Gospel—the circle being a Mystery School from which we receive our spiritual education. Going to school, we are educated and become knowledgeable and skilled practitioners of a spiritual science and art. Community is essential to Gnostic Christianity, and participating in spiritual community, we are received into the holy sanctuary.

Inner Sanctuary

The inner sanctuary is composed of the tzaddik (spiritual teacher), the great angel (the light transmission), and the Holy Bride (the fiery intelligence of the light transmission). Hence, it is the sanctuary of discipleship. Essentially, this is the energy dimension of the holy sanctuary experienced in spiritual practice and spiritual living itself—the divine life.

The first object of refuge is the tzaddik, one's spiritual teacher and guide, through whom something of the light-presence is embodied and manifest to oneself. While this could be a disincarnate tzaddik, as previously explained, it is ideally an incarnate tzaddik with whom one can more easily and objectively experience interaction. Through the tzaddik, one is directly linked to the light transmission manifest as the apostolic succession—to all tzaddikim, past, present, and future, and to the holy Mother, Lord Yeshua, and Lady Mary. Thus, the tzaddik is a physical gate of the holy Shekinah and serves as a vehicle through which the light transmission is imparted in the form of teachings and initiations of secret wisdom. There is a distinct living presence and field of spiritual energy around an authentic tzaddik, which naturally and spontaneously transmits blessings and serves to protect us during periods of spiritual or psychic vulnerability. Thus, an authentic tzaddik is a true object of refuge through which we experience sanctuary.

In speaking about the tzaddik, however, we are not actually speaking about the personality of the tzaddik but rather the light-presence that manifests within and behind the appearance of the holy person, which directly reflects the indwelling Christ within ourselves. In truth, the external teacher is an outer manifestation of our inner teacher and guide—our Neshamah and Christ-self. In the process of self-realization, we discover the outer and inner teacher are one and the same light-presence. Thus, as an object of refuge, the tzaddik represents the indwelling Christ, which is the true object of refuge at the level of the inner sanctuary in Christian Gnosticism. The whole objective of a spiritual teacher, incarnate or disincarnate, is to bring forth the light of the indwelling Christ.

The holy apostle also represents the descending force we experience and realize through our spiritual practices, which is esoterically understood as the Bridegroom. When this force moves, we have true sanctuary in the tzaddik—the one who will guide the ascent of the fire snake.

The second object of refuge is the great angel, which is the way the tzaddik transmits the fiery intelligence to the disciple and reflects the unique individuality of the disciple. The great angel, therefore, represents the initiate's way upon the path. On one level, according to the Christian Kabbalah, the four great archangels (Raphael, Gabriel, Michael, and Uriel) represent specific ways on the path to Christ consciousness. Raphael personifies the way of knowledge; Gabriel personifies the way of devotion; Michael personifies the way of power; and Uriel personifies the way of work. According to the nature and temperament of the initiate, he or she will be naturally inclined to one of these ways and it will be the central focus of his or her spiritual practice and spiritual living—the way of the initiate on the path. There is a fifth way, represented by Metatron-San-dalfon, which is the weave of all four ways. This is the ideal way in Sophi-an Gnosticism and is the basis of the teachings and initiations of the Tradition. The Tzaddik will teach and initiate each aspirant according to the way he or she is naturally inclined.

Esoterically, the great angel also represents the product of the union of the descending and ascending force of the serpent power and the Gnosis of the Gospel we acquire through direct experience of the spirit and truth. In this regard, one might consider the great angel that speaks the Revela-tion to St. John. The great angel personifies the reception of the light transmission and what St. John writes is essentially his own experience of the Gnosis of Christ. In a similar way, every initiate will have his or her own experience of the light transmission or Gnosis of Yeshua Messiah—a direct spiritual experience of the Gospel, through which knowledge, un-derstanding, and wisdom are attained.

In early stages of development, the great angel is called the "holy guardian angel of the initiate." It is called this because, early on, an aspi-rant's experience of the spirit and truth is largely subjective and relative to him or herself alone. However, as an aspirant progresses in the Gospel, unfolding self-realization of higher grades, the great angel is called "the angel of the Lord" because the spiritual experience of an aspirant is no longer so subjective and relative to him- or herself alone, but is nearer to the actual experience of supernal or Messianic consciousness. Ultimately, the great angel is the personification of the initiate established in the ex-perience of Christ consciousness to one degree or another, whether at the level of cosmic consciousness or supernal consciousness.

The third object of refuge is the Holy Bride, which is the radiant dis-play of the holy Shekinah within and around the tzaddik and the Gnostic circle that forms around the tzaddik. The tzaddik and the Gnostic circle are essentially a vehicle of the Holy Spirit or holy Shekinah in the mate-rial world, as is oneself as a member of the mystical body of Christ. It is the Holy Spirit that is the foundation of the Gnostic circle and through which light transmission is ultimately received and imparted.

The Holy Bride also represents the ascending force of the serpent power or the fire snake proper, which, when awakened and uplifted, establishes the conditions necessary for reception of the supernal light and full attainment of Messianic consciousness. Thus, the inner sanctuary is the mystical embrace of the Bridegroom and Holy Bride—the great angel being the divine image of the self-made-perfect in Christ consciousness.

Secret Sanctuary

The secret sanctuary is composed of the threefold body of Melchizedek—the truth body, glorified body and manifestation body. Thus, essentially, the secret sanctuary is the attainment of supernal or Messianic consciousness—complete enlightenment and liberation. When the soul-being is completely established in Christ consciousness and liberated from the cycles of the transmigration, the supreme or ultimate sanctuary has been attained. In attainment of the secret sanctuary, one becomes the holy sanctuary for other souls that are as yet in bondage to the karmic web and the dominion of ignorance.

The outer sanctuary corresponds to Malkut, the inner sanctuary corresponds to Yesod, and the secret sanctuary corresponds to Tiferet on the Tree of Life. Thus, Tiferet is the very essence of the holy sanctuary in our experience—the indwelling Christ.

Wrestling with the Angel and the Grade of Lesser Adept

It is written: Jacob was left alone, and a man wrestled with him until daybreak. When the man saw that he did not prevail against Jacob, he struck him on his hip socket, and Jacob's hip was put out of place as he wrestled with him. Then he said, "Let me go, for the day is breaking." But Jacob said, "I will not let you go, unless you bless me." So he said to him, "What is your name?" And he said, "Jacob." Then the man said, "You shall no longer be called Jacob, but Israel, for you have striven with God and with humans and have prevailed." Then Jacob asked him, "Please tell me your name." But he said, "Why is it that you ask my name?" And there he blessed him. So Jacob called the place Peniel, saying, "For I have seen God face to face, and yet my life is preserved" (Genesis 32:24–30).

Much could be said of the correspondences in the story of Jacob, Leah, and Rachel to the Sefirah Tiferet. However, at the center of the story is this event, which depicts the dark night of the soul that must transpire before any real entrance into Tiferet or actual realization of the indwelling Christ. Essentially, this story represents the integration of the outer self with the inner self, or the transformation of Nefesh Behamit into Nefesh Elokit, which then serves as the holy vessel for the Ruach and Neshamah.

When the Scripture says that Jacob was left alone, it means that the Shekinah departed from him. This departure of the Shekinah represents the first dark night of the soul, which follows the first cycle of progress on the path. Early on the path we experience great zeal as we find our spirit-connectedness and begin to have some spiritual or mystical experiences. The teachings we receive uplift us, the initiations energize us, and we begin to experience some inner guidance. As this stage of the path unfolds, however, we eventually find a conflict arising between the emerging divinity and our old self. We begin to see how much work on ourselves we must do in order to follow the inner guide. Very swiftly, our zeal fades and a struggle ensues amidst great psychic tension. It is the first real challenge on the path and, frankly, many well-meaning aspirants succumb to it and do not endure to pass beyond.

The "man" with whom Jacob wrestles is actually an angel. On the one hand, it is the angel of Esau, Jacob's brother, who personifies Jacob's Nefesh Behamit—the outer and unenlightened self. On the other hand, Peniel is an angel of God, specifically the truth and light revealed in the experience of Jacob or the voice of the inner guide. In other words, Peniel is the personification of Jacob's inner demons and, at the same time, is the personification of his holy guardian angel—the dualism of Jacob's own consciousness in conflict. Jacob's victory represents the resolution of this conflict through a work on himself that unites the outer and inner self in harmony, so that the personality and life-display (Nefesh) become the vehicle of the inner and higher self, or the Ruach and Neshamah. In Christian terms, Jacob takes up his cross and follows the indwelling Christ. Jacob is, therefore, no longer the same person but has truly become a holy person, a man of God, and thus he receives a new name—Israel. Israel literally means "one who strives with God and is victorious" and is the name of any initiate who passes through the first dark night of the soul, from the assembly of the faithful into the assembly of the elect.

This transition from the assembly of the faithful into the assembly of the elect is represented by the Rosicrucian grade associated with Tiferet, the lesser adept. Essentially, an initiate who is a lesser adept has passed through the first dark night of the soul, making his or her personality and life-display a vehicle of the indwelling Christ, so that he or she lives from within the Christ-center. In the eyes of the lesser adept, he or she is the servant of the indwelling Christ in all activities of life, and thus does not live for him- or herself, but lives in Christ and for Christ in all things. The life of the lesser adept is devoted to the great work—the enlightenment and liberation of him- or herself and the uplifting of others. The lesser adept is, in Rosicrucian terms, a "true Christian"—a person who is like Christ.

From the foregoing, you will understand how being a true Christian is not isolate to those claiming to be "Christian," for a person of any faith could well be a true Christian—just look at Yeshua, he was Jewish and such a true Christian that he became Christ! In essence, a true Christian is one who lives according to the divine will of the inner and higher self— hence the person who is enacting his or her true will. Understanding this as a Gnostic Christian is extremely important, because recognition of the spirit of truth in all world wisdom traditions is essential to Gnosticism. It is the universal spirit of truth that is the cosmic Christ. Thus, wherever truth is found, Christ is found, regardless of the name by which truth is known.

Fundamentally, Tiferet represents the spirit of truth at the heart of any faith or the central object of devotion in any faith. One who lives according to the spirit of truth of his or her faith is a lesser adept of the tradition. In so doing, the person has recognized something of that truth and light within him- or herself and is actively realizing it through his or her life. Krishna, the Buddha-nature, the indwelling Christ, or other names may be used, but it is the same light-presence, which on the Tree of Life is represented by Tiferet. There are many branches of the true faith and many faces of the beloved.

The Healing Power of God

At the level of Beriyah, the Sefirah Tiferet manifests as the archangel
Raphael, whose name literally means the "healing power of God." As mentioned above, Raphael personifies the way of knowledge on the path and,
thus, we may understand that the healing arts of the Kabbalah are founded upon knowledge (gnosis). Conversely, we may understand that illness
and dis-ease are the products of cosmic ignorance, which, when dispelled,
naturally results in healing.

Healing implies "to make whole," "to make well," or "to restore balance
and harmony," specifically "a restoration to the unity of being." The healing arts applied in the material world certainly aim at physical healing and
the preservation of life in the body. Yet it is in the aura and subtle body
and soul that the origin of illness and dis-ease is found; therefore, true
healing is psychic and spiritual in nature. This is reflected in the Gospels,
for, above all, the Master Yeshua was noted for his ministry of healing and
was perhaps the greatest spiritual healer to ever walk upon the earth. All
healings in the Gospel were of a psychic and spiritual nature. Lord Yeshua
often alludes to the cause of illness and dis-ease in the mind, heart, and
soul, when he says to those who are healed, "Go and sin no more," hence
"do not entertain negativity or create negative karma anymore." Similarly,
Lord Yeshua often directed individuals he healed to present themselves at
the temple and to make the corresponding "sin offering" and the offering
of thanksgiving, reflecting the need to dispel the inner cause of the illness
or dis-ease. Any time Lord Yeshua did not say, "Go and sin no more" or
"Go present yourself to the priests and make the necessary offering," he
would say, "Your faith has healed you." All of these sayings directly express the psychic and spiritual nature of the healings the Master performed. His way of healing reflects tikkune of the soul—correcting,
mending, or healing wounds of the soul from negative karma, and damage
to the aura and subtle body resulting from negative karma.

Essentially, the subtle body is a body of consciousness, specifically, a
body of energy, and the aura is the field of energy around the matrix of
the physical and subtle body, which are joined together as one body in
incarnation. As a body of consciousness, this subtle body is composed of
our thoughts, feelings-emotions, imaginations, words, and deeds. As a
body of energy, it is formed by the spiritual forces with which we link

ourselves through our thoughts, feelings-emotions, imaginations, words, and deeds. Healing, therefore, comes about through a shift in consciousness and the spiritual forces with which we are connected in consciousness. Positive thought, feeling-emotion, visualization, word, and action are, thus, the means through which all true healing transpires—tikkune in the heart and soul, the mind and life.

Self-healing, like self-initiation, is certainly possible to one who has this knowledge and understanding—and has the power of faith to enact it. However, as we have said, in the case of most ordinary individuals, the subtle body has only minimal energy and, in these modern times, the power of faith is often lacking. Positive thought, feeling-emotion, visualization, word, and deed, generate energy and link us to divine spiritual forces. Primarily, it takes energy to bring about healing, just as it takes energy to truly pray, meditate, and perform sacred ritual. Therefore, the help of a healer is often necessary, much like the help of a spiritual teacher and guide. The nature of this invisible assistance is the generation and transmission of energy-intelligence needed to bring about healing. In the case of Lord Yeshua, his subtle body was a great body of light—a solar body—so that, indeed, he was the light of the world like the sun. It was on account of this body of light that he was able to perform so many phenomenal healings. Energy is transmitted from the body of light of the healer to the subtle body of the person in need, and in this way, the healing transpires. However, to actually receive the healing power, the person seeking healing must have faith—be completely positive—to form the necessary psychic and spiritual link that acts as a circuit through which the energy is transmitted. The presence of faith within the person being healed is the "ground" forming the circuit that allows the healing energy to move and flow.

In the process of healing work, one who knows the healing way of the Kabbalah draws down the shefa and ruhaniyut of the Sefirot into the subtle body, making him- or herself the vehicle or channel of the life-power, and then, through various methods, transfers that spiritual energy to the subtle body of the person in need. Sound, visualization, gesture, and touch often play a key role, and the laying-on-of-hands is common. On some occasions, the initiate in the healing arts will actually transfer his or her consciousness fully into the body of light, project the body of light independent from the physical body, and then merge his or her body of light with the subtle body of the person to be healed. This is done when greater energy is needed or when a healing is to be performed at a great distance.

This healing art reflects the gnosis of the true Gospel, which is the gnosis of the name of Yeshua Messiah in the context in which we have been speaking of the name. Because this divine knowledge is at the very heart of Gnostic Christianity, the Rosicrucian initiate is told that the only proper claim of an initiate of the Rosicrucian order is "to heal gratuitously." A true Rosicrucian initiate is therefore a spiritual healer, like the original disciples of Lord Yeshua, and the true Rosicrucian order is a healing body.

It must be understood, however, that all healing does not necessarily happen in one of these material bodies. Often the healing of the soul happens when the subtle body separates from the physical body and the subtle body dissolves into the divine nature of the soul in what we call "death." Thus, as much as serving to heal and preserve life, the Gnostic initiate as a healer also serves as a guide of souls in "the crossing" or in the process of death in the same way that healing is performed. Adepts of the Tradition are thus able to render assistance to the dying and the dead. Just as the adept of the Tradition can transfer his or her consciousness into the light-body, so also can the adept or master of the Tradition help others transfer their consciousness into a light-body and help energize that subtle body. The transference of consciousness to a body of light is the very essence of the mystery of the resurrection and is the ultimate form of spiritual healing.

Understanding these things concerning spiritual healing will give you insight into the archangel Raphael, which is attributed to Tiferet and is the great angel of Christ, the spiritual sun. Everything we have spoken concerning spiritual healing is personified by Raphael and is reflected in the image of Raphael. Raphael appears as a human form composed of pure sunlight, as though the body of the great angel is formed of the sun itself. This spiritual or solar being shines in a crystal-clear blue sky as the "sun at dawn" and is the light of our world, specifically, the light of the world-to-come. With the intonement of the divine name of Tiferet, and the chant *Ar Iyah Raphael*, the great solar angel is invoked, which in attainment is said to be the light of one's own solar body.

Initiates who seek deeper intimacy with Raphael make it a habit in their daily practice to greet the rising sun at dawn in remembrance of the great resurrection and the archangel Raphael, who appears in the eastern quarter of the sacred circle. One common practice in greeting the sun at dawn is taking a glass of fresh water, invoking the spiritual sun and Raphael to bless the water and imbue it with the healing and illuminating power of the spiritual sun. Drinking the water, the initiate takes the power of the divine blessing into him- or herself. This is considered a good practice for self-healing.

Raphael teaches the way of knowledge and the healing arts, and grants understanding of true compassion. When there is strife in a situation, the invocation of Raphael will bring harmony and peace. According to the masters of the Tradition, Raphael was one of the holy angels at the ascension of the Lord, the other being Gabriel. Therefore, Raphael holds secret knowledge concerning the great ascension. In Rosicrucian teachings, Raphael is the archangel of the second coming, having a secret connection to the Holy Bride and New Jerusalem, and is considered the angelic presence behind the sun that illuminates our solar system. In other words, Raphael is a very accessible angelic presence, as is the order of the Malachim under Raphael's dominion.

The Messengers of God

Tiferet at the level of Yetzirah manifests as the order of the Malachim. Malach means "messenger," thus the Malachim are the messengers of God. The idea of a messenger connotes a message, whether communicated in symbolic imagery, written or spoken, and specifically alludes to intelligence and word. Essentially, the Malachim are angels of divine intelligence and the word of God, and communicate the knowledge of God and will of God. When we pray for knowledge of God or the will of God in a specific situation and intuitively receive an awareness of God's presence or the will of God in that situation, it is typically a Malach that has communicated the awareness to our mind and heart. Any communication of God to creatures or creation happens through the agency of the Malachim.

We encounter the Malachim often in our prayers and meditations. Every time we receive some message from the divine, whether through a direct intuition, vision or dream, we are encountering the Malachim. In circumstances in which we may not be getting the message, the Malachim may use others to bear the message to us—sometimes our tzaddik, a friend or family member, and oftentimes little children, as most children are especially open and sensitive to the contact of angels. According to the masters of the Tradition, a Malach may even use an animal to bring a message to us—simply making a certain animal appear at a specific moment when we might notice it and open ourselves to the meaning of the sign. Malachim often speak through signs and omens, whether in waking consciousness or in dream. As the term "messenger" applies to a prophet in the Tradition, we know the Malachim are messengers of prophecy.

Whenever God wants to communicate God's word, God sends a Malach in order to do so. As we know that every creature is a word of God, we know the Malachim often help us gain insight and understanding of the mysteries of the soul. Because the Messiah is called the word of God, we also know the Malachim give insights into the Christos, specifically the indwelling Christ in the soul.

The most common experience of the Malachim among Christian initiates is in the form of what is called a "word of knowledge." A word of knowledge comes in the form of a direct intuition or knowing in the mind and heart—such a word of knowledge could be an intuitive insight into a great mystery or it could just as easily be an intuitive awareness of something about to happen in the physical plane. For example, one evening some years ago I was in a mentoring session with a student and we were discussing deep things of the Kabbalah. At the time, I also worked at a hospice for AIDS patients as a volunteer and chaplain. My thoughts were not at all directed toward the hospice in that moment, but all of a sudden I knew a certain woman was dying and that I had to go and be present with her. There was a spiritual practice I was to do and I knew exactly what it was and what would transpire that night. Everything came to pass exactly as "I" knew it would. This was a word of knowledge imparted by the Malachim.

It is not so much that we must actively invoke the Malachim, as much as make ourselves open and sensitive to the Holy Spirit and to contact with the angels of God. In the vision of Jacob's ladder, it specifically says that Jacob saw angels ascending and descending upon the ladder. By saying that angels were ascending before saying that they were descending, the Torah is saying that angels are among us and that they are in the subtle dimension of the earth all of the time. The only reason most ordinary people in modern times to not *see* them or experience conscious contact with them is that modern people tend to close their minds to the holy angels and do not believe in them. The angels are crafty, however, and do not easily give up. They will use any means and assume any form necessary to carry out the divine will with which they are charged. In a technological era when people are more likely to believe in higher forms of extraterrestrial life than in God and the angels, guess what? They will appear in exactly those forms ordinary people might accept them in! Many an extraterrestrial contact is actually an experience of angelic beings, according to modern masters of the Tradition, and the darker contacts in which people feel they are in some way abused or harmed by aliens is often contact with demons. Welcome to the universe of Yetzirah—the world of the angels!

Our experience with angels makes it perfectly clear that the Olamot of which the Kabbalah speaks all occupy the same space at the same time, so that the world of angels exists as an inner dimension of the material world. In fact, the world of angels, titanic spirits, and demons is actually the matrix of spiritual forces within and behind the appearance of the material world. In truth, we live in a mystical and magical universe, which is inherently spiritual as much as material. Understanding this and connecting ourselves to divine and angelic powers consciously, the seemingly impossible becomes quite possible and many wonderful things can happen—real magic!

Spiritual Practices for Tiferet

According to the oral tradition, a man once came to Lord Yeshua at night, in secret, and the Lord received him. The man was deeply troubled, and said to the Lord, "Adonai, I see you have come, yet I myself am not ready. I am encumbered by mundane life and encrusted with klippot. It will be no different on the day I die. How shall I ever be received by you? Tell me, Lord, what can I do?" The Lord felt compassion for the man and could see that he was bound to sin. Seeing the spark of holiness in the depth of the man's heart, he said to him, "As you have come to me this night, so come to me in your death. When you lay down on your deathbed to die, envision your heart as a spiritual sun and gather yourself into it. Then see my image above you and project yourself as the light into my light-image, and I will receive you. Tell no one what I have spoken to you, but let it remain between us before the Father. I will meet you on the other side of that which men call death."

This is an essential method for transference of consciousness into a subtle body of light, which if practiced in life will transpire at the time of death. The practice appears in many methods of Gnostic meditation, and it appears in Eastern schools as well. First, one must learn to envision his or her own body becoming light, and then learn to envision oneself as light pouring into the body of light that forms the divine image of the meditation. Through such practices, many initiates have experienced healing and other wonders. It is the way Gnostic initiates establish themselves in the path of the great resurrection and ascension.

Essential Meditation upon the Risen One

> Envision within behind your heart the image of the spiritual sun and gather yourself into it. Let your whole mind and body be filled with this light-presence, all darkness or negativity passing away. From within the sun in your heart, see a ray of light shoot forth and magically appear in the space before you as the image of the Risen One.

> His inner robe is white brilliance, and his outer robe is amethyst. His body shines as though composed of sunlight and there is a rainbow aura surrounding him, the red band near his body and the violet band at the outermost edge.

> See the Lord smile upon you and let your heart pray. As you pray, see the Lord smile upon you, and see him bless you. Envision his blessing as streams of light pouring out of his heart upon you, making your body, heart, and mind shine brighter and brighter—like unto the image of the Lord.

> When your prayer becomes silence, open your mind, heart, and life completely to the presence of the Lord, making yourself completely transparent before him. As you chant his blessed name, envision the divine image of the Risen One dissolving into fluid light, pouring down into you through the crown center on top of your head, and reappearing in your own body of light.

Adonai Yeshua, Yeshua Messiah.

➤ Chanting, your mind becomes the mind of Christ; your heart becomes the sacred heart of Christ; your body becomes the mystical body of Christ; and you are at one with the Lord. There is light upon light in the space of the meditation, and that light is the light of the world. Abide at one with the Lord as long as you can. When you depart the space of meditation, walk in the world as a Christ-bearer.

➤ It is good to meditate in a special room set aside for it or in front of a shrine in your home. When praying and meditating, it is good to offer up incense and candles, all as one is inspired. Do as you like in this regard. After some time of daily practice with this essential meditation, then it would be good to try the transference of consciousness method.

➤ Basically, the meditation is the same, except the divine image magically appears on its own and, when you chant the blessed name, instead of visualizing the image of the Lord dissolving into fluid light and pouring into you, envision yourself dissolving into fluid light and pouring into the image of the Risen One—projecting your consciousness as light up through your crown center into the presence of the Lord, thus uniting yourself with the Lord in this way. This can give one freedom to engage in inner-plane workings and prepares one for the transference of consciousness at the time of death. There is not enough space to cite the great virtues of this practice or how it is used in conjunction with the wonder-working arts—but those who practice it faithfully will come to understand the greater vistas.

Healing Meditation with Yeshua

This meditation is used to receive healing energy or to impart healing energy to others. In general, healing energy is envisioned as golden light, corresponding to the spiritual sun or Tiferet, which is the source of all healing. However, in advanced healing practice, specific colors are used corresponding to the nature of the illness or dis-ease and the Sefirah in which the subtle cause is found. The image of Lord Yeshua used in this practice is envisioned as more dense or material because the method aims at bringing about healing grounded in the physical body. As with most of the practices given in this book, it is designed for the novice practitioner and should prove effective for anyone willing to use it.

➤ Pray to the Lord for healing. As you pray, envision the image of Yeshua the healer magically appearing in the space before you. He wears a white robe of a soft ivory shade and over his head has a white shawl made of the same cloth. He has an olive complexion and deep brown eyes, filled with love and compassion. His smile is subtle and comforting, and his presence fills one with faith and confidence. There is a subtle golden light all around him and a feeling of a great angelic presence.

➤ Chant the name of the healer—*Ah Da Na Ya Yeshua, Adonai Raphael* ("Lord Yeshua, Lord healing power of God"). As you chant, envision the golden light around the image of the Lord increasing and growing brighter. When you come to the end of the chant, envision the hands of the Lord as hands of light, and see him come to you and lay hands on you. Envision him reaching into your body with his hands of light and touching your pain or discomfort, the healing light flowing to the cause of your pain. The place of pain in the body is a darkness, which the Lord fills with golden light, healing you. When the Lord has shared the healing power and removes his hands from you, listen inwardly for the word of the Lord. Listen to what the divine presence instructs you to do or to the blessing the divine presence imparts. There is often a word of knowledge or message given. Then envision the image of the Lord magically disappear as he appeared. Give thanks and praise to God for the divine incarnation and the healing power.

➤ In the same way, you can perform this healing meditation for others. Simply see the Master lay hands on the person to be healed. If a person is open to it, it is best to perform the practice with them, praying with them and guiding them through it. Sometimes initiates of the Tradition will envision themselves becoming the image of the Lord, envisioning the healing power as golden light within and around themselves, and then lay hands on a person, enacting the same process by making themselves the vehicle of the divine presence and power of Yeshua, the healer. The greatest healing comes to oneself when one acts as a holy vessel of the healing power for others. It is always a priceless blessing to have the opportunity to share and give what you receive.

ELEVEN

NETZACH,
THE DIVINE
DOMINION

Attributes

Thirty-Two Paths of Wisdom: Hidden Consciousness (Sekhel Nistar); it is called this because it is the radiance that illuminates the transcendental powers that are seen with the mind's eye and with reverie of Faith

Netzach: Victory or Dominion

Place on the Tree of Life: The base of the Pillar of Mercy

Divine Name: Yahweh Tzavaot

Alternative Divine Names: Sar Shalom, Peaceful Ruler

Partzuf Above: Zer Anpin as the Prophet

Partzuf Below: Yeshua Messiah Opening the Way; Moses and the Greater Prophets

Divine Image: The Image of the Human One in the predawn sky; a naked and beautiful woman who is crowned

Archangel: Haniel; or sometimes Uriel

Order of Angels: The Elohim

Celestial Attribute: Nogah, Venus

Titles Given to Netzach: Day Star, Sun of the Morning; Door of the Inner Sanctum; Sphere of the Creative Spirit;

Place of the Martyrs; Victorious One; Ruler of Dominions; Depth of Height; Clear Mirror of Prophecy; Light-bearer; Sphere of Philosophers and Mystics; Mystic Abode; Nature's Grace; Sphere of the Lesser Gods; House of the Mighty Ones; the Portal; Star of the East; Herald of Christ; Sign of the Eternal Day

Level of the Soul: Ruach (Lower Ruach or Ordinary Human Intelligence)

Heavenly Abode: Zebul, the Fourth Heaven—Dwelling

Spiritual Experience: Vision of the Divine Dominion; Awareness of the Presence of God in Creation; Vision of God's Glory; Inspiration of the Creative Spirit

Virtues: Inspiration; artistic talent; appreciation of beauty and art; harmony; cooperation; passion; refinement; selflessness; comprehension of values; monetary stability; social graces; affectionate; positive self-expression

Vices: Lack of creativity or inspiration; dispassionate; lustfulness; unfaithfulness; poor socialization; unattractiveness; disharmony; negative self-expression; frivolous with money; lack of appreciation for artistry; debauchery

Symbols: The Secret Garden; the rose; dew of the morning; the holy lamp and lampstand; the girdle; peacock; the Fire in the Sacred Circle

Commandment: You shall not commit adultery (Exodus 20:14)

Sermon on the Mount: Blessed are those who hunger and thirst for righteousness, for they will be filled (Matthew 5:6)

Angel of the Apocalypse and the Churches: Fourth Star and Lampstand, and the message to the angel of the church in Thyatira (Revelation 2:18–29)

The Hidden Realm of Action

There is a veil between the moral triad and the action triad, which is called the Veil of Paroket. It is the reflection of the principle of relativity of Da'at below, representing the causal plane, which divides the spiritual and supernal planes above from the higher vital, mental, astral, and material planes below. While the cosmic illusion power comes into being at the level of Da'at through the agency of Gevurah, and thus the binding force of the karmic matrix has its root in Da'at, the actual matrix itself is the causal plane or what is called the veil of paroket in the Kabbalah.

Because the universe of Adam Kadmon is completely beyond the comprehension of mental being and present humanity, it is often not spoken of in the transmission of the teachings of Kabbalah, but rather focus is given to Atzilut, Beriyah, Yetzirah, and Asiyah. When teachings on the Sefirot and Olamot are given without reference to Adam Kadmon, the supernal triad corresponds to the universe of Atzilut, the moral triad to the universe of Beriyah, the action triad to Yetzirah, and the Sefirah Malkut to Asiyah. In this system of attributing the Olamot to the Sefirotic triads of the tree, we are able to see the interconnection between the Olamot and the inner planes of consciousness. The supernal planes correspond to the universe of Atzilut and the supernal triad. The spiritual planes, which contain the upper heavens, correspond to the universe of Beriyah and the moral triad. The higher vital, mental, and astral planes correspond to the universe of Yetzirah and the action triad, and the material plane corresponds to the universe of Asiyah and Malkut. The causal plane or veil of paroket thus serves as a great divide or gulf between the higher vital and the spiritual planes. In that the veil of paroket is the actual karmic matrix, we understand that the higher vital, mental, astral, and material planes appear according to karmic conditioning and therefore correspond to karmic vision.

In this sense, they are planes of cosmic illusion and are inherently deceptive, being reflections of the light of the supernal and spiritual planes within consciousness bound to cosmic ignorance. Reference to these lower planes as "planes of cosmic illusion" is not to suggest that they are in any way unreal or illusory in and of themselves, but that our own subjective perceptions of reality at these levels is illusory in nature—that our karmic vision tends to prevent true seeing and knowing.

The supernal planes are not perceived by the mind proper, but rather are perceived by the metamind of pure radiant awareness, which cannot be described or explained in terms of our linear and finite reason. The spiritual planes cannot be perceived or known through the concepts of our mental being; they are perceived by way of pure intuition. Therefore, everything we have spoken of so far in our exploration of the Sefirot and

Tree of Life can actually only be *known* and understood via intuitive perception and pure radiant awareness, to the degree we are able to establish ourselves in the vision of faith and evolve toward the vision of true gnosis.

In truth, we have been speaking of the mysteries in terms of the lower planes in order to indicate the greater reality of the mysteries as they are in the upper planes. Whatever we have been able to glean of the actual mysteries is dependent upon the degree to which we have been able to intuitively grasp something of the greater truth and form concepts, emotional associations, and images that are more or less in harmony with the greater truth. Thus, what we have are mental and vital illuminations of the mysteries (transcendental powers) seen with our mind's eye and the contemplations of faith, as the text of the *Thirty-Two Paths of Wisdom* indicates in speaking about Netzach.

Netzach, Hod, and Yesod compose the triad of action. It is impossible to speak of one of these Sefirot without speaking of the others, as they act together as an integral unit, although each of their functions is distinct. The same is true of the Sefirot composing each triad, the pillars, and the whole tree. The Sefirot exist as a sacred unity of the one being-consciousness-force that is God and creation. Essentially, Netzach is the energetic quality of consciousness or the mind, which generates feelings-emotions, thoughts, and images, and it is the energetic quality of divine consciousness that generates the forces, patterns, and actual forms of creation. Netzach is the creative spirit-energy generating the subtle dimensions of actual existence or life.

Netzach appears in our immediate experience as the spontaneous creativity of our consciousness, specifically as instincts, feelings, and emotions, and the creative imagination. At the level of Netzach this energy does not have any well-defined boundaries or forms, but is more fluid and flowing, interpenetrating and interacting in a synthetic way. It is only through the agency of Hod and Yesod that it is clearly defined and established in actual forms of thoughts and images. The same is true of the divine consciousness-force at the level of Netzach. It is more akin to the pure force or energy within and behind the subtle forms than anything distinct, individual, and independent. Therefore, in Netzach, rather than distinct individuation, everything exists more in terms of collectives or what could be called "group souls."

Netzach emanates directly from Tiferet—and, in turn, emanates Hod and Yesod—and thus contains the potential for distinct, individual, and independent formations and tends to generate them. How Netzach generates such forms is through Hod, the subtle forms appearing in Yesod, which is the subtle substance of consciousness—hence, the astral light and astral planes.

Netzach and Hod essentially act upon one another to shape the form of the images that appear in Yesod. This interaction may be understood in the following way. Instincts, feelings, and emotions correspond to Netzach, while thoughts or concepts correspond to Hod. On the one hand, instincts, feelings, and emotions shape our thoughts; yet, at the same time, our thoughts shape our instincts, feelings, and emotions. Thus, feeling-emotion and thought shape one another, and those shapes or forms appear as images to our mind's eye or imagination. Everything in the human world has come into being in this way—first through feelings-emotions, thoughts, and images in the mind, and then into actual manifestation in the material plane. We, ourselves, are the product of the feelings-emotions, thoughts, and images in our parents' minds, which led to the physical sexual encounter through which we were conceived. Through this same process in the inner planes of consciousness, everything of the human world has come into being and, in fact, everything in creation. Everything is conceived and formed in the inner dimensions before actually manifesting in the physical or material plane—hence the universe of Yetzirah (formation) is attributed to the triad of action.

Knowledge of things conceived, formed, and transpiring in the inner dimensions before actual manifestation in the material plane is the key to understanding prophecy, as well as the science and art of divine magic. One who is able to look and see the movements of force and form in the inner dimensions of consciousness is able to see what will come to pass in the material world. One who is able to consciously direct this flow of spiritual forces and forms has the ability to change what actually manifests in the material world—and therefore can work wonders. In truth, there is no such thing as a miracle, only a science of consciousness, which, by way of the application of certain principles or laws in higher planes of consciousness, is able to bring about a corresponding affect/effect in the lower planes. It is this that is called wonder-working or divine magic. For this reason, prophecy is attributed to Netzach and magic is attributed to Hod, and Netzach is called the clear mirror of prophecy and Hod is called the hazy mirror of prophecy.

Everything According to Its Kind

At the level of Atzilut, the Sefirah Netzach manifests as Yahweh Tzavaot, which means the "Lord of Hosts." Tzavaot in Netzach represents kinds or types of creatures, as in the group souls of the various kinds of animals, orders of angels, legions of demons, and the spirits of various dominions, such as the planets or elements. You will recall that, on the great Tree of Life, Netzach in a higher universe is the Hokmah of a lower universe. Therefore, Netzach of Yetzirah is Hokmah of Asiyah and thus manifests as the twelve signs of the zodiac—the twelve kinds or types of human souls.

When a spirit or soul passes down from the supernal and spiritual planes through the causal plane, moving toward incarnation, the kind or type of creature it will become is determined by its previous development and evolution—karma. In the case of a human soul, it will enter through the gate of one of the zodiacal signs, which will determine the kind or type of human incarnation through which it will come into being. At the level of Netzach, the kind or type that soul will assume is established, but it is not until the soul passes through Hod that it will become a distinct and individual entity of its kind. Thus, Yahweh Tzavaot is the divine power that generates the infinite diversity of all kinds of creatures in creation, and Elohim Tzavaot is the divine power that generates the infinite diversity of unique and individual creatures—all according to their kind or type.

We may understand this in terms of human incarnation. Adam Ha-Rishon is the group soul, as it were, of humanity, and there are twelve kinds or types through which human souls manifest. Passing into incarnation, the human soul is shaped by one of the kinds or types of the human being—entering the domain of one of the zodiacal signs. This takes place in the higher vital planes and represents the generation of a human Nefesh of the corresponding zodiacal sign. At this point, the Nefesh is pure energy of that gate, existing in an undifferentiated unity, having no specific form or individuation apart from that gate, which is akin to a field of energy. The Nefesh becomes a ray of pure energy passing from Netzach to Hod (the mental plane), or from the higher vital plane to the mental plane, and through the matrix of Hod , the Nefesh assumes a subtle form, becoming a unique and individual Nefesh of that zodiacal gate. This energy form then emerges and appears in the astral planes (Yesod), which are the lower vital planes, becoming yet more distinct and individual, and then passes from the astral into physical incarnation in the material plane. The position of the sun, moon, planets, and stars at the time of actual birth reflects the karmic matrix through which the unique individual Nefesh was generated. This matrix is a specific configuration of the energy-intelligences of the Sefirot, which is represented by the divine name of Netzach and Hod joined together—Yahweh Elohim Tzavaot.

In the same way individual Nefeshim are generated and come into being, whole realms and worlds are generated, for realms and worlds are aggregates of countless life-forms, including both animate and inanimate forms. Because everything in existence is a form of the one being-consciousness-force, everything is alive and therefore considered a life-form in the eyes of the Kabbalah. In the same way every Nefesh is distinct and individual, so is each realm or world unique and individual, being the product of the collective karma of the countless spirits and souls of which it is composed. Thus, Yahweh Elohim Tzavaot is the matrix of spiritual forces in the subtle dimensions within and behind the material plane, which forms the foundation of the material universe.

Much like the idea of progressions in one's birth chart, representing the movement of the celestial influences forming new configurations and relationships, and thus creating cycles of ebbs and flows of spiritual forces, the matrix of spiritual forces in the subtle dimensions is active and dynamic, ever changing and reconfiguring itself. Therefore, in the same way an astrologer might speak of conjunctions, oppositions, squares, trines, and such in an astrological chart, so, too, is there a constant play of spiritual forces in the subtle dimensions, creating ebbs and flows of the life-power and, thus, inauspicious and auspicious manifestations in realms and worlds.

When there is a full and free flow of spiritual forces manifesting auspiciously, it corresponds to the function of Yahweh Tzavaot; when there is a restriction of the flow of spiritual forces or there is an inauspicious manifestation, it corresponds to the function of Elohim Tzavaot. Therefore, Yahweh Tzavaot corresponds to mercy or grace and Elohim Tzavaot corresponds to severity or judgment in the play of spiritual forces. As we saw in our exploration of Gevurah, the balance of mercy and judgment is not determined by God but by creatures, all according to their development and evolution—hence, the karma of beings. In worlds in which human beings (intelligent life-forms) exist, the balance in the play of spiritual forces is primarily determined by them. On earth, it is we who determine the array of spiritual forces in the inner dimensions of the earth.

Essentially, the spiritual forces that manifest in the higher vital, mental, and astral planes are determined by our creative imagination, which is the primary faculty of the creative spirit of God in us. Our emotions, feelings, and desires are the energy; our thoughts, words, and deeds are the forms that the energy assumes. Emotion-feeling-desire and thoughts shape one another and produce images in the imagination. These images become vehicles in the astral planes for spiritual forces corresponding to the nature of the desires and thoughts forming them, and through our words and deeds, we become vehicles of those spiritual forces in the material plane. When our feelings-emotions, thoughts, words, and deeds are in harmony with the divine presence and power of the supernal and spiritual planes, then we connect with the divine powers and create vehicles of the divine powers in the lower planes, thus bringing the divine powers down to earth. When our feelings-emotions, thoughts, words, and deeds are not in harmony with the divine presence and power in the higher planes, then we connect with the klippotic forces of the other side, and forming vehicles for them, we bring the klippot into the world. In this way, the collective thoughts, feelings-emotions, words, and deeds—the creative imagination—of humanity determine the balance of spiritual forces in the lower planes, specifically in the astral planes. This, in turn, determines the circumstances, situations, and events that play out in the material plane, and thus the fate or destiny of the earth and all that is in it.

The power of the human mind and imagination is great, the power of many human minds and imaginations is greater still, and the images or forms we generate in the subtle dimensions are very real powers having very real influence for better or for worse. The life span of the spiritual beings-forces we bring into the astral earth is dependent upon the emotional charge and form given to it by thought. Once a spiritual being-force is brought into the astral earth, it has power to influence the minds, hearts, and lives of humankind for the duration of its life span, and it can act independently according to its nature—whether divine, admixed, or demonic—until the life-force in the astral form dissipates and the connection vehicle dissolves. Some spiritual beings-forces brought into the astral plane exist only for moments, representing a swiftly passing thought and emotion in the mind. Other spiritual beings-forces, however, can exist for long durations of time, even for many ages, as generations of humanity strengthen the life-force and astral form with their thoughts, feelings-emotions, words, and deeds—essentially *feeding* the spiritual entity. While some spiritual beings-forces have only a little power to influence, some have far more power, and others have levels of magic power that would be unimaginable to most ordinary human beings—such as those spiritual entities we call archangels and archdemons.

There is a key principle taught in the magical Kabbalah: "If you create the conditions or environment necessary for something to transpire, it will naturally and spontaneously manifest." While the astral forms we generate through our thoughts and emotions are, in essence, illusory, initially having no real life or power of their own apart from our minds, the spiritual forces they depict, and that enter into them and act through them, are very real. Any time we create an astral form corresponding to a spiritual force we have created the necessary conditions or environment for that spiritual force to manifest on the inner planes. Eventually, it will enter into the astral image and act through it. These forms are talismatic representations of the spiritual forces that appear to psychic vision or the mind's eye, and not the actual forces themselves. Thus, the appearance of spiritual forces in the lower planes is inherently deceptive and only through intuition can the true nature of any force be perceived. Nevertheless, these spiritual entities are quite real in their own plane of existence and have very real power to influence how things manifest in the material plane.

While we are constantly bringing spiritual beings-forces into the astral earth and these entities are influenced and fed by our thoughts, emotions, words, and deeds, likewise, these entities influence and feed us, so that we are completely interdependent and interconnected with the play of spiritual forces. Because most ordinary human beings are completely unaware of the play of spiritual forces and unaware of the light-presence of their

Neshamah and Christ-self, humanity is, for the most part, unconsciously compelled by the spiritual forces. However, when human beings realize the light-presence within them and become conscious of the play of spiritual forces and the law upon which it is founded, then all spiritual forces are subject unto the human one, who is the image and likeness of Yahweh Elohim, thus having the power of Yahweh Elohim Tzavaot.

The Work of Creation and the Work of the Divine Chariot

Ma'aseh Bereshit (the work of creation) is a term applied to the mysteries of the soul and Creation. Ma'aseh Merkavah is a term applied to the mysteries of God and divine revelation or prophecy. These terms are also used to denote two distinct stages in the development of spiritual practice and progress upon the path to self-realization.

When we first take up a spiritual practice, the actual practice itself is completely the product of our own mind, specifically our creative imagination. We generate sounds, colors, lights, and images in our mind and the spiritual practice is akin to a flight of fantasy, although ideally a controlled one. It has no life or power apart from that which we give to it. Essentially, we are cultivating the faculties for progress in self-realization and we are creating a vehicle (chariot) for spiritual or mystical experience. However, at the outset, we are nowhere near self-realization and little, if any, authentic spiritual or mystical experience occurs in our practice. We are merely practicing prayer, meditation, and ritual, cultivating the necessary skills and vehicles through which spiritual or mystical experience will eventually unfold. This stage of generation is called Ma'aseh Bereshit in the Kabbalah.

At some point, our experience in spiritual practice will shift. It will not be merely a practice generated by our own mind, but the spiritual beings-forces depicted in our practices by sound, color, light, and symbolic images will enter into the spiritual practice and our practice will take on a life and power of its own—the divine presence and power. The divine presence will communicate with us in our spiritual practices and we will experience communion with the divine powers—various spiritual and mystical experiences will unfold. This is the shift toward fruition stage, when our spiritual practices generate good fruit, and it is this that is called

Ma'aseh Merkavah in the Kabbalah—when our spiritual practice becomes an actual vehicle of the divine presence and divine powers.

Ma'aseh Bereshit expresses the work of the assembly of the faithful or initiates of the outer order and corresponds directly to the outer threefold sanctuary. Ma'aseh Merkavah expresses the work of the assembly of the elect or the adepti of the inner order and corresponds directly to the inner threefold sanctuary—hence, the actual great work. From what we have discussed above, you will understand that the shift from Ma'aseh Bereshit to Ma'aseh Merkavah not only benefits the individual initiate but all humanity and the world—for when Ma'aseh Merkavah manifests, divine grace flows from the supernal and spiritual planes through the lower planes and into the material world. Initiates who labor together in this way are thus able to shift the balance in the play of spiritual forces in the astral earth, balancing the forces of darkness with forces of light, and therefore serve to act as conscious agents of the divine will and divine kingdom on earth (Keter-Malkut).

It is in this context that we come to understand what Christian Gnosticism means when it says that "there is no such thing as personal salvation," or what the Kabbalah means when it says that "the faithful and elect do not practice for themselves alone, but for the sake of heaven." Indeed! In spiritual practice we not only uplift and enlighten ourselves, we uplift and enlighten humanity, the world and all that is in it. We practice for the world and for the sake of the kingdom of heaven. Such is the work of the divine chariot—the great work of perfecting and completing creation according to the divine will.

The Way of Divine Rapture

The very heart of mysticism is an inner experience of union with the divine. Thus, at the heart of the mystical Kabbalah is what is called *devekut*—cleaving or attachment of oneself to the divine, which leads to a rapturous union. According to the Kabbalah, there are many gradations of devekut, but on the most basic level, it is the cultivation of joy and energized enthusiasm.

The sages of wisdom say that the Shekinah cannot come to rest upon a depressed person and, likewise, the divine spirit cannot enter where darkness is allowed to dwell. In order to experience the holy Shekinah or entertain the divine spirit, one must let go of negativity and uplift one-self—hence, increase the vibration of one's consciousness. Essentially, negativity represents lower and discordant vibrations. Positive thought, feeling-emotion, word, and deed represent higher and harmonious vibra-tions. It is through our vibration that we link with spiritual forces and de-termine our experience in life, whether positive or negative.

Anything we might do to cultivate joy and energized enthusiasm is de-vekut. A perfect example familiar to all is music. According to the Scrip-tures, King Saul frequently called upon David to play his instrument and sing to uplift the spirits of the king. Most of us have experienced feeling down and put on a favorite piece of music to energize and uplift us. Whether we knew it or not, we were engaging in a most basic practice of devekut!

First and foremost, our practice of devekut must be in simple things—finding moments in life through which we might experience a taste of rapturous union. Such joy can be found in a sunrise or sunset, a beautiful flower, a subtle crescent moon in the starry night sky, or in the sound of children at play. The delight taken from fine art, scientific discovery, or closing an important business deal can lead to devekut. Enjoyment of a shower or bath, good food, the feeling of the breeze upon one's face, the warmth and beauty of a campfire, making love, and so many other daily events are all opportunities for devekut. One merely need open one's heart and mind to the sacred unity underlying all life and the mystery of the source from which life flows, and actually enjoy the moment with gratitude and appreciation for life. This is the most basic level of devekut.

Many wisdom traditions focus on eliminating attachments to the world and seek to completely dispel passionate emotions. The Kabbalah, how-ever, teaches us to cultivate passion and desire, and to transform our at-tachments into vehicles of divine rapture. Hence, Kabbalah encourages us to live life fully and to enjoy the blessings of life. Only, in the midst of life, we must remember the source of all blessings and, with our awareness and enjoyment, give thanks and praise.

Devekut in daily activities is the ground for devekut in our spiritual practice—prayer, meditation, and sacred ritual. Through knowledge of the Sefirot—divine names and Partzufim, the names of prophets and apostles, archangels and angels, mysteries of creation, the soul, and God—we have many vehicles through which we might uplift ourselves and experience more intense levels of rapturous union. All one needs to do is to fill one's mind and heart with the object of devotion and allow one's thoughts, emotions, words, and actions to completely reflect the object of devotion. In so doing, one will experience unification with that aspect of the divine.

When my tzaddik would speak of devekut, he would say, "Seek to know Yahweh, the one life-power, in all of your ways." Of the ultimate state of devekut, he said, "It is the most intense and passionate love in which you are not separate from the beloved, not even for an instant." This, in essence, is the aim of devekut—to experience the love of God and the awareness of God in all things. The ultimate experience of devekut is conscious unification with God, specifically, unification with one's supernal soul, Christ within and beyond oneself, and the light continuum.

The Fire Philosophers

Philosophus is the Rosicrucian grade that corresponds to Netzach. It means "one who contemplates wisdom and is wise." This term is somewhat deceptive because, in the conventional wisdom of profane society, the idea of a philosopher suggests a person who is an intellectual and is primarily mental. Yet the title philosophus is attributed to a Sefirah representing emotions, intuitive feeling, and creative inspiration—in a word, art. In esoteric wisdom, however, the philosopher is more the artist than the scientist and, specifically, is associated with the heart, not the head. By the title "philosophus," what is meant by the masters of the Tradition is a person who knows his or her heart—one's inmost heart's desire—and seeks to fulfill that holy desire.

In ancient times, the philosopher was called a sage—the wise person—and philosophy was the contemplation of morality and ethics, as well as theology and theosophy—contemplation of God and wisdom. It is in this sense—the idea of the sage—that the term Philosophus is used by Gnostic initiates.

In ancient times, it was the heart, not the head, that was considered the seat of intelligence, and intelligence was conceived as the activity of the heart and mind joined together, through which the light of the spirit and soul shined forth. The same is true in esoteric wisdom today, for the heart is the seat of the indwelling Christ and our divine intelligence. Thus,

Philosophus represents a state of devekut-attachment to the indwelling
Christ and to our Neshamah through the agency of the upper Ruach. The
nature of this cleaving manifests as what is often called the Divine Genius,
which, on the one hand, implies a certain knowledge and understanding
of things that are invisible and hidden and, on the other hand, connotes a
flow of creative inspiration. In other words, the philosophus is an educated initiate, and by education is meant "one who is bringing forth that
which is within him- or herself." This bringing forth is a giving birth to
the divine genius or Christ-self within oneself and one's life. The fullness
of this birth, of course, marks the transition from the grade of the philosophus to that of the lesser adept.

Just as it is difficult to distinguish the magister templi from an elect
adept, so it is equally difficult to distinguish between the lesser adepti and
the philosophus. However, what is stirring in the philosophus is in full
motion in the lesser adept, and whereas the heart of the philosophus is on
fire with the Spirit of Yahweh, the whole consciousness-being of the lesser adept is on fire with the Spirit of the Lord. The difference is one of degree—the degree of divine passion with which the initiate attaches him-
or herself to Christ indwelling and thus identifies him- or herself with the
divine genius.

This quality of being on fire with the Spirit of Yahweh and the state of
devekut is what has generated the term "Fire Philosophers" as a title for
Rosicrucian initiates. Yet, as we saw in our exploration of the Gnosis of
Yeshua Messiah in Tiferet, this term implies the awakening and uplifting
of the fire snake, the heart center being the bridal chamber in which the
descending and ascending forces are united as one divine presence and
power. Thus, we understand the various grades of devekut as a direct reflection of stages in the awakening of the serpent power, the higher states
of devekut being the result of the full awakening of the serpent power

Philosophus is the highest grade of the outer order or the assembly of
the faithful, and marks the transition from Ma'aseh Bereshit to Ma'aseh
Merkavah, as discussed previously. Essentially, the fire snake is awakening
in the philosophus and he or she is experiencing increasingly higher states
of devekut with the indwelling Christ, which tends to manifest in various
forms of mystical experience and outbursts of creativity. At the level of
the philosophus, the divine illumination is typically unstable and unpre-

dictable, and long dry spells may occur between flows of divine grace. Nevertheless, the initiate of this grade is a victorious one and is rightly called a noble sage. When devekut is kindled to a blaze, he or she will be among the fire philosophers and enter into the adepti of the inner order.

The Devekut of the Prophets and the Apostles of God

Previously, we explored the distinction between the greater prophets and the lesser prophets. According to the Tradition, the lesser prophet is able to look into the holy law and, based upon knowledge and understanding of the law, is able to see what will come to pass. The greater prophets, however, are the holy ones who are Baal Shem, masters of the name. Through the holy name, the greater prophets are able to attach themselves completely to God's Shekinah and thus to unite themselves with the law. Therefore, not only does the greater prophet have the ability to look into the law and see what will come to pass, but having the power of the name, everything comes to pass as the greater prophet speaks it. Thus, the greater prophet sees in the clear mirror of prophecy, and the lesser prophet beholds his or her visions in the hazy mirror of prophecy. The distinction between the greater and lesser prophet is therefore one of direct intuitive knowledge (complete gnosis) and indirect psychic vision (partial gnosis). Specifically, the distinction is one of devekut-attachment, the lesser prophet experiencing prophetic consciousness through lower grades of devekut and the greater prophet through higher grades of devekut.

The Rosicrucian grades of the philosophus, lesser adept, and greater adept represent the lower degrees of devekut and, thus, the attainments of the lesser prophets. The grades of elect adept, magister templi, and magus represent higher degrees of devekut and, therefore, the attainments of the greater prophets. The grade of ipsissimus represents the supreme state of devekut—complete unification with God and Godhead, as embodied in Yeshua Messiah. Thus Yeshua Messiah is rightly called "Adonai," having the power of the essential name, Eheieh ("I am").

As we have said, the hazy and clear mirrors of prophecy correspond to

Hod and Netzach, respectively, and Hod and Netzach are directly below Tiferet on the Tree of Life. Therefore, the light-presence reflected in the mirror of prophecy is the spiritual sun, Tiferet. Netzach represents the imagination, feelings, and emotions of the mind; Hod represents the thoughts of the mind. Yesod, which is the union of Netzach and Hod, represents desires that come into being by way of the activity of the mind. Thus, by the attribute of the mirror of prophecy to the action triad, the Kabbalah is saying that the mirror of prophecy is the human mind and heart and that prophecy is a response to human desire, specifically, the revelation of God's ratzon, so that the human will-desire might reflect God's will-desire.

While Netzach, Hod, and Yesod reflect Tiferet and transmit the ruhaniyut and shefa of Tiferet to Malkut, the triad of action, along with Malkut, emanate from within Tiferet, so that not only do they reflect Tiferet, they are also the emanation of Tiferet on the lower planes. Tiferet is, thus, that which is reflected in consciousness, and it is the consciousness within which it is reflected. That is to say, the light-presence that is reflected in consciousness is consciousness itself—pure radiant awareness.

This realization is the difference between the prophetic succession and the apostolic succession. For although the greater prophet was able to attain complete unification with the holy law, and thus the power of the great name of Yahweh, the greater prophet did not recognize and realize the inseparability of his or her own consciousness from the light-presence. Therefore, the greater prophet always experienced him- or herself as separate and distinct from the light-presence. The prophet was able to more or less reflect the supernal light-presence and to experience the Shekinah resting upon him- or herself, but he or she was not able to attain unification with the light-presence or to experience the Shekinah indwelling him- or herself. Essentially, believing the peak of cosmic consciousness to be the supreme and ultimate attainment possible for a human being, the greater prophet did not conceive of a superior attainment and therefore did not know to strive toward self-realization in supernal consciousness. Lord Yeshua, however, recognized the inseparability of the supernal light-presence and the consciousness within him, and therefore he passed beyond the peak of cosmic consciousness, embodying the self-realization of supernal or Messianic consciousness. In Yeshua Messiah and the apostolic succession, we have become aware of this superior attainment and how to accomplish it. Thus, we are able to consciously evolve toward supernal consciousness. It is this holy awareness that fulfills the law and the prophets, and through which the holy apostle draws upon the essential name of Eheieh—I am or I shall be.

Psalms, Prophecy, and Wonder-Working

In exoteric faith, both Jewish and Christian, the Psalms are viewed as praise to God—songs and melodies of worship. Yet, if one is aware of the various terms in the Scriptures for meditative states that lead to higher levels of consciousness and prophecy, one finds that many of them appear frequently in the psalms. This suggests that the Book of Psalms has an important place in meditative and prophetic disciplines. While the Hebrew word for psalms, *Tehillim*, which comes from the root *halal*, is often translated "to praise," it also has two other possible meanings that reveal the deeper spiritual intention of the psalms.

The first alternative meaning of halal alludes to the idea of brightness or shining. Halal appears in this context in Job 25:5, "If even the moon is not bright and the stars are not pure in his sight . . ." and Job 29:3, ". . . when his lamp shone over my head, and by his light I walked through darkness . . ." The second alternative meaning comes from the word *hode-lut*, which shares the root halal, and denotes madness or a radically altered state resembling something demented. This would suggest that the word halal indicates a condition in which one departs from his or her ordinary state of consciousness and experiences divine illumination. Specifically, halal connotes praise intended to bring one into the enlightenment experience through a state of self-abandon or self-transcendence.

The state of divine madness or divine intoxication is commonly associated with the experience of mystics and prophetic states. Rumi, who was perhaps the greatest Sufi poet, speaks of this often in his spiritual poetry. On the day of Pentecost, when the fire of the Holy Spirit descended upon the apostles and they went out to preach in a state of divine illumination, they were accused of being drunk. Yeshua, himself, was accused of being a drunkard or demented by demonic possession. There are many places in the Old Testament in which the Bible specifically relates prophecy to a state of madness. The idea of divine madness directly relates to being carried away by divine passion or being possessed by the Spirit of

God. One appears crazy to the unenlightened because one is oblivious to the conventional wisdom of unenlightened society and to oneself, instead being directed by the Holy Spirit according to divine wisdom.

Tehillim, from the root halal, therefore designates the psalms as vehicles through which one might enter into a state of divine illumination or prophetic consciousness, which is exactly how the Kabbalah views the Book of Psalms. According to the Tradition, the psalms are invocations of the spirit of prophecy and they are magical incantations or spells, each having a specific intention.

While many psalms represent prayers or meditations which direct the mind and heart toward a higher state of consciousness, others represent inspired utterances from the mind and heart of a person already in a state of divine illumination. For this reason, according to the masters of the Tradition, those psalms that begin by saying "A Psalm of David" are psalms of aspiration toward a state of higher consciousness; those psalms that begin by saying "Of David, A Psalm" are psalms spoken or sung when David was already established in a state of illumination. Psalms 24 and 110 are good examples of the latter, clearly reflecting deep insight into the depth of the mysteries spoken and having a prophetic quality.

In the study and contemplation of the psalms, we see three distinct forms of invocation or incantation, corresponding to mercy, severity, and compassion, thus representing the three pillars of the Tree of Life. Those of mercy represent the devekut-attachment of the soul to the corresponding Sefirot or divine attributes invoked. Those of severity represent invocations to dispel or banish klippotic forces, while those of compassion represent both banishing of klippotic forces and invocations of the divine powers.

In the Tradition, the psalms are spoken of in conjunction with Netzach because of their relationship to devekut, prophecy, and mysticism, which correspond to Netzach. However, on the outermost level, the psalms are creative expressions and Netzach represents the energetic quality behind all forms of creativity and creation.

Nothing New Under the Sun

In contemplation of science and art, which are attributed to Hod and Netzach, respectively, an interesting observation arises. Science is clearly a process of discovery of things already present, although previously unrecognized, while art seems to be the creation of something new. Yet in the actual experience of creative inspiration, one finds that art is not really the creation of something new but, like science, is a process of discovery.

The idea of discovery directly suggests the true nature of the action triad. There is nothing new in the triad of action; rather, the triad of action is actualizing the spiritual potential of the supernal and moral triads. In essence, Netzach, Hod, and Yesod are discovering or revealing the divine potential beyond the veil of Paroket. It is this quality of discovery that is alluded to in Ecclesiastes when it says, ". . . there is nothing new under the sun" (Ecclesiastes 1:9).

Adam (humanity) is given the task of naming things. Naming connotes recognition or discovery and the realization or actualization of potential. For what is named already existed before it was named; yet without the name recognition, that which is named is not realized and actualized. To this very day, Adam is still naming things—recognizing or discovering the hidden depths of creation and realizing and actualizing the exhaustless divine potential of the life-power. In this sense, human beings are cocreators with God, drawing out the unmanifest potential of creation, realizing it, and actualizing it.

We may consider this principle in terms of the development and evolution of the soul-being through the process of gilgulim (transmigration). Although the potential of the Neshamah and upper Ruach exists within every human being in every incarnation, until the divine nature of the soul is recognized and realized, in effect, the potential of Neshamah and Ruach does not actually exist but remains unmanifest. Essentially, until the indwelling Christ and the divine intelligence are realized, they are not part of a person's experience and do not exist in the world for that person. The same is true of all cosmic forces in creation, whether spiritual, psychic, or material. Until they are discovered, realized, and actualized, they remain unmanifest potential. When the masters of the Kabbalah say that activity below in the material world stirs activity above in the spiritual world, it is this principle of actualization they are indicating, for although the divine powers exist in potential, until they are actualized and realized by humanity, they remain unmanifest, both in the spiritual and material world.

The attributes of science and art, along with prophecy, to Netzach and Hod reflect that the scientist, artist, and prophet share a kindred spirit—the discovery and revelation of the truth and light within creation through which humanity is uplifted Godward. While a prophet is not necessarily a scientist or artist and a scientist or artist is not necessarily a prophet, there is science and art in prophecy and there is something prophetic in true science and art. According to the masters of the Tradition, the role of the prophet is to give direction to scientific exploration and artistic expression. The role of the scientist and the artist is realization and actualization of the divine will and divine kingdom beheld in the vision of the prophet. Science, art, and prophecy are meant to work hand-in-hand for the fulfillment of humanity and the divine plan in creation.

Dogmatic religion has caused a great division between prophetic, scientific, and artistic exploration. However, in the eyes of the Gnostic Christian, all truth discovered is God's truth, whether prophetic, artistic or scientific. For the ultimate fruition of the divine plan on earth, the prophet, scientist, and artist must all work together for the conscious preservation and evolution of humanity and this good earth. Spirituality alone does not hold all the keys to the fruition of the divine plan on earth, and science and art apart from spirituality tend to become destructive and perverse. To understand this, one need only consider fundamentalism in religion, the use of science to create weapons of mass destruction, or the darker and perverse side of modern art and entertainment.

The prophet, scientist, and artist are, indeed, kindred spirits. When science and art are vehicles or channels of the human soul, the light of the creator shines through them, as surely as it shines through the prophet and prophecy. We can say this of any human endeavor—to the degree that it acts as a vehicle of the human spirit and soul and is linked to the Shekinah, any activity can be a channel of the supernal light and serve the divine will and kingdom.

The Creative Spirit, the Mystic, and the Artist

In our present dualistic condition, there is a great distinction between the objectivity of science and subjectivity of art. Largely, it is this distinction between the objective and the subjective that separates the scientist from the artist. While science aims to tell us exactly how things are, art aims to provide interpretations of things. Both, in their own way, seek to open our eyes to new vistas. The same is true of mysticism. However, in mysticism, the distinction between the objective and subjective tends to vanish, so that, in the experience of the mystic, the subject and object merge together; the knower (subject) and that which is known (object) become one and the same. When science or art leads to an awareness of the unity of subject and object, science or art becomes mystical.

Since the time of Einstein and the breakthrough of the Theory of Relativity, many scientists have found a mystical dimension in their respective sciences, in which the objective and subjective seem to overlap. For example, the scientist is now aware that the observer changes the experiment and may even change the outcome of the experiment. This became especially obvious when scientists sought to discover the subatomic level of matter, one segment of researchers thinking they would find particles at the subatomic level and another segment thinking they would find waves. As it turned out, the scientists that went looking for particles found particles and those that went looking for waves found waves. This discovery alludes to the truth that matter and consciousness, the objective and the subjective, are interconnected and thus that consciousness can change how things manifest. While modern science remains greatly resistant to this truth, nevertheless, as science progresses, it stumbles across it more and more.

If the observer changes things merely by observing, by interpretation, and by angle of view, then there is more power in art than most modern artists might realize. If an artist is able to capture a different view of things and is able to convey that new view to others, uplifting the consciousness of the people and opening their minds to new possibilities, then it is quite possible that an artist can change the human world as much as the scientist. For if things manifest as we expect them to manifest, then changing our expectations may well change what actually manifests. An artist who is aware of this creative power is a mystic and magician.

The science of magic is attributed to Hod. However, without some realization of Netzach, the mystical and artistic truth of the creative spirit, there is no such thing as magic or the magician. The full power of the wonder-working science is dependent upon full mystical realization and the same creative inspiration as good art. Indeed, according to masters of the Tradition, one must first attain some degree of spiritual or mystical realization and explore creativity before one can practice the magical Kabbalah and become a mage of light. While the knowledge of magic is in Hod, the power of wonder-working is in Netzach. For this reason, as much as being called a science, magic is also called an art, and the mage of light must be well established in Netzach.

Science and magic aside, art and creativity hold the best potential for many individuals to draw near to God and to experience the Spirit of God. Art and creativity are more likely to lead to the cultivation of one's humanity and drawing out the light of the soul. Likewise, development of our feelings-emotions and imagination is more likely to lead us into an experience of conscious unification with God than merely the generation of concepts and intellectual analysis. Therefore, art, creativity, and development of our feeling-emotions and imagination are central to the mystical journey, as much as development of the intellect and other aspects of intelligence. In terms of Netzach, it is through music, song, dance, poetry, and other forms of art that one may most easily contact and experience the divine power it represents. God is the creator, and the Spirit of God is a creative spirit. Thus, becoming creative naturally draws us closer to God.

The Divine Mother and the Nature Sphere

Not everyone is an artist. We all have our own unique talents and abilities, but that does not preclude our capacity to be creative or to engage in creative expression. Although all of us are not artists—songwriters, musicians, poets, painters, and such—we can all gain inspiration from the art of others and experience creative expression of our own via the talents of those who truly are artists. In a similar manner, we can all gain inspiration from the supreme artist or creator—God—via God's art, which is nature and creation. In the same way we can easily draw upon the divine power of Netzach and draw near unto God through creativity and artistic expression, we are all able to do so through nature and the recognition of God's glory in creatures and creation. While manifestation of creation, Mother Nature, and this good earth on the material plane is Malkut, the creative spirit, the forces of nature, and life of the earth have their root in Netzach. Therefore, any time we experience awe and wonder, a feeling of connectedness through nature, or are moved or inspired by creatures and creation, we are experiencing contact with Netzach.

According to the Tradition, nature is a secret operation of the Holy Spirit, and as we have seen in the Christian Kabbalah, the Holy Spirit is the Mother Spirit. Thus, nature is conceived of as a manifestation of the divine Mother. As much as Gnosticism speaks of our heavenly Father, it also speaks of our earthly Mother, understanding nature herself as the manifestation of God's glory—God's presence and power. Likewise, while Gnosticism teaches about the angels of the heavenly Father, it also teaches us about the angels of the earthly Mother. On the one hand, the angels of our earthly Mother are the forces of nature, specifically, the spiritual or cosmic forces within behind the natural forces. On the other hand, her holy angels are everything that appears in creation—oceans and deserts, mountains and valleys, rivers and streams, and even such things as rocks, vegetation, and creatures. In other words, God's Spirit is constantly speaking to us through nature and as nature, and thus the prophets and apostles of God often go out into the wilderness to commune with God. With this in mind, one cannot help but reflect upon the story of the ravens that fed the prophet Elijah when he was fleeing persecution, or Daniel emerging from the lion's den unharmed. Likewise, one cannot help but remember the prophets of God wielding the great forces of nature, the revelations of God's Spirit to holy men and women on mountains and in caves, and the numerous occasions that the Shekinah or angels of God appeared to shepherds tending flocks in the wilderness, all reflect the earthly Mother and her holy angels, as much as the heavenly Father and the angels of the heavens.

Where the angels of our heavenly Father end and the angels of our earthly Mother begin, no one knows. In our experience, they are completely interdependent and interconnected and thus inseparable. Yet, we distinctly experience the earthly angels, the heavenly angels, and all manner of good spirits of God. As much as the Gnostic seeks contact and communion with heavenly angels, he or she seeks contact and communion with the earthly angels too. Within every place in nature there is an earthly angel—there is a spirit and power. Within everything that appears in nature, there is an earthly angel—a spirit and power. In the same way that orders of heavenly angels are within the dominion of a heavenly archangel, many lesser earthly angels are within the dominion of a great earthly angel, such as a mountain, river, desert, and the like. As the Hermetic saying goes, "As above, so below; as below, so above." While the Sophian Gnostic seeks a rapturous connection with God's Spirit through nature, the Gnostic initiate also seeks knowledge of the earthly angels and of all the spirits that are hidden in nature. Much like our Native American brothers and sisters, we, too, find that the Great Spirit sends messengers in the form of animal peoples and natural phenomena, along with messengers of the other world or the heavens. Unlike the pagan faiths, however, the Gnostic does not worship the forces of nature or the angels of our earthly Mother. The Gnostic embraces the earthly angels as brothers and sisters, and directs his or her worship to the Most High.

As we have said, nature is a secret operation of the Holy Spirit. Nature is becoming conscious of herself in humanity, and the forces of nature are becoming conscious. The power of the Holy Spirit is awakening with, in, and through the human one. For a little while, human beings exist under the dominion of the holy angels, who are akin to elder brothers or sisters. Yet the human spirit is destined to ascend beyond the holy angels, both the heavenly angels and the earthly angels, and in ascending, the human one draws the holy angels in ascent with him- or herself. Nature, our earthly Mother, and the angels of our earthly Mother are thus redeemed from cosmic ignorance through humanity, when humanity abides in the awareness of sacred unity and cleaves to God most high (El Elyon). In so doing, humanity joins heaven and earth in mystical union and creation is made perfect and complete. This is the Netzach-victory which is the spiritual aim of the great work at the heart of Sophian Gnosticism.

The Divine Muse

In the universe of Beriyah, the Sefirah Netzach manifests as the archangel Haniel, which means the "Glory of God," or "Grace of God," or "one who sees God." According to the Tradition, Haniel has a close relationship with the archangel Uriel, which means the "Light of God," who is the archangel associated with the element earth, the planet earth, and the northern quarter of the sacred circle. According to the Tradition, Yeshua Messiah embodied the power of seven archangels, which are said to be the great angels of the Sefirot from Binah to Yesod; however, in the attribution of the seven archangels of the Christos, Uriel is often put in the place of Haniel.

Haniel and Uriel are two distinct archangels, but the substance of God's glory and grace is light, and it is through this light that one sees God. Therefore, these two great angels are interconnected and both personify something of divine illumination. In a certain respect, one might say that Uriel is like the medium—the substance and embodiment—of creative expression, and Haniel is like the creative expression or inspiration itself.

While Uriel is connected with Eretz (the earth), Haniel is connected with Nogah. Nogah means "brightness" and represents one of the forms of light beheld in prophetic vision. At the same time, it means the "bright morning star" or Venus. The connection between the "light of God" and the idea of brightness is obvious, although there are more subtle and sublime esoteric connections that may not be quite so obvious. First of all, when the bright morning star appears in the east, it heralds the coming of dawn and light upon the earth. When it appears in the west, it heralds the sunset and departure of light from the earth. A bright star is said to have led the three magi to the birthplace of Christ. Likewise, the bright morning star is said to have dawned at the conclusion of the temptation of Christ and at the dawn of the enlightenment of the Buddha. According to the Sophian Tradition, the same star appeared at the resurrection when the Holy Bride greeted the Risen Yeshua. You will recall in our discussion of Da'at the correspondence of the star Sirius with the order of Melchizedek and that, according to Gnostic Tradition, Venus is said to be the transmitter of the spiritual energy of Sirius in our solar system—hence the vehicle of the light transmission to planet earth. All of this alludes to the secret relationship of Uriel and Haniel, and specifically to the inmost nature of Haniel, who is said to be the great angel of the light transmission on earth. While Uriel acts as the guardian of the earth and specifically the human life-wave, Haniel is the guardian of enlightenment upon the earth. It is in this context that the mission of Uriel and Haniel overlap.

In the Book of Jude, we hear of a holy book that does not appear in the canonized Scriptures—the Book of Enoch. The Book of Enoch, as the name suggests, is said to have been written by Enoch, giving an account of Enoch's ascent into the heavens and all of the mysteries, heavenly abodes, and angelic beings he encountered along the way. According to the Tradition, Haniel is the archangel who guides Enoch in the ascension. Thus, among the great angels of God, Haniel is called the opener of the way and guide of the elect. In the process of guiding Enoch, Haniel also explains to Enoch the visions that he sees. Therefore, Haniel is said to know the mysteries of all the holy angels, the heavens, and, specifically, the path of the great ascension.

Haniel is also called the divine muse by masters of the Tradition—the archangel who inspires all forms of craftsmanship and artistry. Accordingly, we read in Exodus:

> . . . *See, the Lord has called by name Bezalel the son of Uri son of Ur, of the tribe of Judah; he has filled him with divine spirit, with skill, intelligence, and knowledge of every kind of craft, to devise artistic designs, to work in gold, silver, and bronze, in cutting stones for setting, and in carving wood, in every kind of craft. And he has inspired him to teach, both him and Oholiab son of Ahisamach, of the tribe of Dan. He has filled them with skill to do every kind of work done by an artisan, by a designer, or by an embroiderer in blue, purple, and crimson yarns and in fine linen, or by a weaver—by any sort of artisan or skilled designer.* (Exodus 35:30–35)

It is through the agency of Haniel that Yahweh transmits this knowledge, skill, and inspiration to Bezalel and Oholiab and to any creative person who makes him- or herself a holy vessel of divine artistic inspiration.

The image of Haniel is that of a most beautiful androgynous being, robed in translucent emerald-green light. His-her face shines with golden light and brilliant white light shines from his-her heart, sparkling with all colors like a diamond. His-her wings are a clear transparency barely perceived in vision, and the words of this great angel of God are as the music of pure and unadulterated inspiration. Many have heard the harmony of the celestial spheres in the presence of Haniel. Holding this image in the mind's eye, initiates invoke Haniel by intoning the divine name of Netzach and the chant, *Hal Al Ha Na Haniel.*

My teacher once said, "If one abides in the love of the Lord and invokes the archangel Haniel, one will see the face of the God of Jacob, which is the vision of Zer Anpin. We know this from Psalm 24 of which it is said, 'Haniel inspired David to write.'"

Principalities, Dominions, and Authorities

Netzach in Yetzirah manifests as the order of elohim. When elohim is not capitalized, it designates this order of angels, which contains the angels called *Dominions, Principalities,* and *Authorities.* You will recall, when we spoke of the Aralim associated with Binah, that we indicated the close association of the thrones and dominions, as in the idea of a throne and a kingdom. Thus, among the elohim are the dominions that are intimately connected to the thrones. One might contemplate the thrones as the knowledge and the dominions as the skill and power through which a specific kind of knowledge is manifest. This will give some sense of what the dominions among the elohim are and how they manifest in our experience. Yet the dominions are something more. They are also abodes—realms or worlds—which, in mystic vision, we discover are actually spiritual beings or matrixes of spiritual forces. In this sense, the elohim represent spiritual beings, which are the realms and worlds that appear in creation, and they are the matrixes of spiritual forces behind the realms and worlds that appear.

According to the Tradition, the dominions are ruled by the principalities and authorities, the principalities specifically representing personification of the divine principles upon which a dominion is established, while the authorities are chieftains that have authority in a dominion by way of the principalities. We may gain some insight into this arrangement through a teaching given in the Zohar. The Zohar says that there is a chieftain that rules over every nation on earth. A "nation" represents an earthly dominion. Every nation is founded upon certain principles (principalities) through which the nation is governed. The chieftain, then, is the governing authority, which operates within the parameters of the principality and dominion over which it presides. According to the Zohar, an authority, principality, and dominion are in charge of every nation, and they are governed by divine providence and determine the karmic balance of those who dwell in them. Thus, a chieftain can only act according to divine authority and can only act beyond its boundaries (such as in the invasion of another chieftain's dominion) according to the balance of the law. By speaking of this in terms of earthly dominions, the Zohar reveals the truth of all dominions, as the same triad of spiritual beings-forces applies to all realms and worlds in all planes of existence. All three of these classes of angels are within the order of elohim.

Dominions can be relatively limited and small or they can be vast. Correspondingly, principalities can have more or less influence, and may or may not reflect the divine will and divine kingdom. Among the authorities or chieftains, there are greater and lesser chieftains, and the greater chieftains can have incredible power. You will recall that the name elohim can mean "gods" and "goddesses." Thus, the greater chieftains have often been called gods and goddesses and have been worshipped as such. The lesser gods and goddesses of pagan worship are, in fact, among the angels of the order of elohim, which includes cosmic and natural forces that form the actual matrix of creation. One might wonder what sort of angel would seek to be worshipped in place of the one God; yet one must understand that among the elohim are those cosmic forces which are called the demiurgos and archons, the false creator and rulers bound to cosmic ignorance. In effect, this class of the elohim believe they are responsible for creation and are unaware that they are dependent upon a higher cause, the one life-power (Yahweh). The cosmic illusion-power not only affects creatures on the material plane, but affects all manner of beings-forces below the causal plane.

While the chieftains have their authority by way of divine providence and the holy law, this does not mean that all chieftains are necessarily holy angels of God or that they seek to serve the divine will and kingdom. Like the Beni Elohim in Hod, many of the elohim are not divine powers proper, but are titanic and dark beings-forces. One must always bear in mind that, at the level of Beriyah, one-third of the cosmic forces are titanic and dark forces, and at the level of Yetzirah, the Tradition says about one-half of the spiritual beings-forces are admixed or dark. Thus, associated with every angelic order are also titanic and demonic beings. St. Paul reminds us of this when he speaks of chieftains and principalities that are "spiritual forces of evil in heavenly places." In giving teachings on the elohim and the Beni Elohim, the elders of the Tradition always remind us that we must put all spirits to the test, to see if they are from God or from the other side.

Among the order of elohim, there are angels associated with the heavenly Father under the dominion of Haniel, which like Haniel are inspirations or are muses; likewise, among the elohim are the angels of the earthly Mother, as mentioned above. That angels of the order of elohim are often mistaken for gods by mediums and psychics is reflected in the story of Saul visiting the medium or witch of Endor when she speaks of her vision, saying, "I see a god (elohim) coming up out of the ground" (1 Samuel 28:13). As it turns out, of course, it is a vision of the prophet Samuel that the medium is seeing and not a god or an angel. That the Torah uses the word elohim reveals that among the elohim are all manner of spirits associated with psychism and spirits that grant magical powers. The reason the Scriptures speak strongly against psychism or mediumship is that, in a lust for magical power or psychic powers, a person may well link him- or herself with the wrong sort of spirits and not labor for authentic spiritual development. Likewise, those seeking psychics or mediums are typically seeking answers only to mundane questions of petty desire, and this tends to invoke the wrong sort of spirits. While the use of spiritual astrology to gain insight into one's personality and character, the journey of the soul, and the soul's tikkune is considered beneficial according to the Kabbalah, because of the dangers inherent in psychism, fortune telling is avoided.

Spiritual Practices for Netzach

Riding Upon the Melody

➤ Sometimes prayer does not come easily. Perhaps we are a bit down or not in the right mood. In such cases, music can prove very helpful. Likewise, listening to music itself can become prayer, meditation, and worship, all depending upon one's intention. Riding upon the melody can uplift our heart, and minds so that we might be inspired to prayer, and it may become a way of prayer, meditation, and worship in itself.

➤ Choose music that is uplifting and inspiring and that has a spiritual connotation to you. Play the music and let your mind and heart ride upon the melody. Let the music fill your mind and heart and carry you in ascent into the embrace of the beloved.

> In the same way, you can take the inspiration drawn from the music and let it become prayers of your heart, giving praise and thanks to God and rejoicing in the presence of the Holy One. Where there is joy, the Shekinah is swift to come upon those who invite and welcome her, and the Holy Spirit is naturally attracted to a heart filled with light and gladness.

> Through gesture and the body, one can also pray and worship. Letting good music fill you, your prayer and worship can be spoken through gesture and dance. All that is necessary is conscious intention. While you entertain the sacred dance, you can also visualize Lord Yeshua and Lady Mary Magdalene dancing with you, and the spirits of holy saints and angels gathered with you in the presence of God, worshipping the Lord your God in spirit and truth. Alone at home, you can easily find yourself in the midst of a luminous congregation!

TWELVE

HOD, THE
SPLENDOR
OF GOD

Attributes

Thirty-Two Paths of Wisdom: Perfect Consciousness (Sekhel Shalem); it is called this because it is the Original Arrangement; there is no root through which it can be pondered, except through the chambers of Greatness, which emanate from the essence of its permanence

Hod: Splendor, Submission, Empathy

Place on the Tree of Life: The base of the Pillar of Severity

Divine Name: Elohim Tzavaot

Alternative Divine Names: Ash Adumah, Red Fire; Elohim Tzavaotainu, God of our armies

Partzuf Above: Zer Anpin as the Mage of Light

Partzuf Below: Lord Yeshua as the Wonder-Worker; Aaron and the Lesser Prophets

Divine Image: The Image of the Mage in the Circle of Light; a hermaphrodite

Archangel: Michael

Order of Angels: Beni Elohim

Celestial Attribute: Kokab, Mercury

Titles Given to Hod: Swift Justice; Depth of Depth or Depth of Below; Hazy Mirror of Prophecy; Sphere of Psychic Vision; Thunder Mind; the House of Perdition; the Abode of Science; House of the Alchemist; Sphere of the Titans; Light of Splendor; Light of Truth; Swift Messenger

Level of the Soul: Lower Ruach

Heavenly Abode: Shehakim, the Third Heaven—Clouds of Grace or Sky-like

Spiritual Experience: Vision of Glory; Gnosis of the Wonder-Worker; Quickening of the Mind

Virtues: Sound logic; skilled communication; clarity of mind; honesty; clear perception; good ability to solve problems; productive curiosity; knowledge

Vices: Dishonesty; unclear mind; misperception; confusion of information for knowledge; idle curiosity; dullness of mind; inability to communicate; over talkative; poor problem solving skills; illogical

Symbols: Priestly vestments; names; books and verses; writing materials; water in the cup; the metal mercury

Commandment: You shall not steal (Exodus 20:15)

Sermon on the Mount: Blessed are the meek, for they will inherit the earth (Matthew 5:5)

Angel of the Apocalypse and the Churches: Fifth Star and Lampstand, and the message to the angel of the church in Sardis (Revelation 3:1–6)

Relating with the Human One and God

Earlier, we spoke of the Universe of Chaos and Void that came into being when the original unity of Adam Kadmon was shattered—a primordial state in which the Sefirot had no way to connect with one another and therefore no relationship to one another. The mending of this first shattering came by way of Atzilut and the divine names and Partzufim of Atzilut, which created a new order of relationships among the Sefirot. This same process repeated itself in the generation of Beriyah, Yetzirah, and Asiyah. The new order of relationships at the level of Beriyah is formed by the archangels; at the level of Yetzirah, it is formed by the orders of angels; and at the level of Asiyah by the configuration of the sun, moon, planets, and stars.

The Sefirot and Olamot themselves were created as the vehicle through which the Infinite One might be in relationship with creation without complete negation of creation and by which human beings might be able to form relationships with God. The divine names and Partzufim, the archangels, orders of angels, and celestial bodies form connections between the Infinite One and finite creation and thus are the basis of the sacred relationship between God and the human one. In a word, the Sefirot and Olamot are all about *relatedness.*

This is especially true of the six Sefirot of the moral and action triads, which are gradations that connect the supernal abode of the infinite to finite creation (Malkut). These two triads of Sefirot essentially represent the two primary modes of relationship, nonreciprocal and reciprocal.

The moral triad represents the human relationship that is not reciprocal. Hesed is the all-giver and Gevurah is the all-receiver. A Hesed-Gevurah relationship is akin to that which forms between a student and a teacher in which the student must exercise full self-restraint to allow the teacher to fully impart his or her knowledge. Tiferet would therefore represent a primarily one-way relationship of the student receiving and the teacher giving. In essence, Tiferet is an imposing of one's giving on another person in a situation in which there is no possibility of reciprocity. There are circumstances in which such a relationship is right and proper; however, outside of the appropriate circumstances, the same sort of relationship could equally be unhealthy and improper.

The triad of action represents a relationship that is reciprocal, the most basic example of which is the relationship between a man and a woman. Netzach is a word derived from *menatzeach,* which means "to overcome," "to conquer," or "to dominate." Some men think that they must totally control and overwhelm a woman in relationship, to the extent that she completely loses her own individuality and personality. Likewise, some women completely dominate their husbands to the extent that the husband is never allowed to be himself. In an exclusively Netzach relationship, one person dominates over the other and there is no true reciprocity.

Hod is the total opposite. Hod means "splendor," but it is also related to the word *hoda'ah*, which means "empathy" or "submission." In a Hod relationship, the person holds onto the idea that he or she must completely annul him- or herself, in effect completely losing him- or herself in the relationship. While the Netzach relationship tends to be mean-spirited and oppressive, the Hod relationship tends to allow and encourage evil. Both the Netzach and Hod relationships, whether between two lovers or two friends, are unhealthy, as neither create the possibility of reciprocity, which corresponds to Yesod-foundation. Essentially, the Yesod-foundation of such imbalanced relationships is faulty, and thus the relationships are dysfunctional.

For a truly reciprocal relationship to exist, the individuals involved in the relationship must alternate between dominance and submission, allowing a give-and-take in the relationship. A good conversation is an example of this. While a one-way conversation in the form of a lecture given by a teacher to his or her students is fine, in actual conversation there must be both speaking and listening. While one person speaks, the other must listen, and listening and hearing must alternate back and forth between the individuals involved in the conversation. This leads to reciprocity and a good conversation. A person who is too talkative and does not give others the opportunity to speak would have too much Netzach. The person who is too quiet and does not engage in the conversation would have too much Hod—either would make good conversation impossible. Any time there is a balanced flow of giving and taking between people on any level, it represents a Netzach-Hod relationship and the exchange between them represents Yesod. The ideal example of a perfectly reciprocal relationship is a man and woman involved in sexual intimacy based upon mutual love in which both partners are receiving mutual pleasure at the same time. The delight of one is the delight of the other and, in their shared delight, unification happens. The Hod-Netzach relationship brings about unification on one level or another, whether of the mind, heart, or body.

Most healthy human relationships and the psychology involved in them represent a balanced Hod-Netzach relationship. Even those relationships that are properly Hesed-Gevurah, as between a student and a teacher, aim at an ultimate fruition in the triad of action. For when the student learns the subject completely, he or she then becomes the teacher. In so doing, he or she can give to the teacher by way of sharing new insights into the subject or by way of sharing what he or she has learned with others and thus propagate the teachings.

In terms of human relationships, the balance between Hod and Netzach determines the nature of the psychic and spiritual forces brought into play in the relationship. Yesod is the inner and psychological aspect of the relationship and Malkut is the external manifestation. When there is a proper balance between Hod and Netzach, and the desire of the holy soul and Christ-self is served by the relationship, then something of Tiferet-beauty is revealed in the relationship. In this light, we may contemplate the saying of Lord Yeshua, "Whoever welcomes one such child in my name welcomes me," and ". . . where two or more are gathered together in my name, I am there among them" (Gospel of St. Matthew 18:5 and 18:20).

While we may speak of Netzach and Hod in terms of relationships that form between human beings, we can also speak of Netzach and Hod in terms of our relationships with other creatures and creation. According to the Torah, as human beings created in the image and likeness of God, we have dominion over all creatures and our environment, the good earth. According to the Gospel, as human beings established in the Christos, we also have dominion over all spiritual beings-forces. This Netzach-dominion, however, must be exercised with Hod-empathy, which is to say, with an understanding that what we do to other creatures and to our environment we do to ourselves and thus we must act with respect for all life. We have, indeed, been granted dominion as cocreators with God, but that dominion is for the sake of the divine will and kingdom and the welfare of all living spirits, visible and invisible. As human beings created in the image and likeness of God, as much as having a capacity to dominate, we also have a capacity of empathy and awareness of our interdependence and interconnectedness with all that lives. This must coincide with the dominion we exercise.

In the same way we are to build Netzach-Hod relationships with one another as human beings, we are also to develop Netzach-Hod relationships with other creatures and creation, through which we actively tend to the welfare and well-being of other creatures and fulfill God's plan on this good earth. Netzach-dominion does not mean exploitation and oppression, but rather indicates a sacred trust for the sake of the greater good. Creatures and the earth support the life of humanity; in turn, humanity is to support the life of the earth and its creatures. The same may also be said of our relationship with invisible spirits. While many forms of ceremonial magic are merely the exploitation and oppression of spirits to serve the will of the magician, in the divine magic of the Kabbalah, the mage of light seeks the enlightenment and liberation of the spirits as much as seeking their help in the great work. Hod-Netzach therefore indicates our proper relationship with one another and with creation when our minds, hearts, and lives are aligned with God's will (our true will).

In our relationship with God, Hod and Netzach mean something quite different than in terms of our relationships with one another or our relationship with creation. God is God, and the proper relationship between the human being and God is one of complete empathy or submission. As we have said many times, God's will is not something outside of us or anything separate and apart from us, but rather is the true desire of our holy soul and divine self—our own true will.

Empathy is the ability to experience the feelings and emotions of others as one's own, and telepathy is the ability to experience the thoughts of others as one's own—both telepathy and empathy correspond to Hod. By Hod-submission to God, the Kabbalah means becoming telepathic and empathic to God—to experience the feelings-emotions and thoughts of God as one's own and to live according to that holy awareness. While religion is founded upon an external submission to God according to an external authority, true spirituality or mysticism is founded upon an internal submission to God's presence experienced inwardly and is therefore surrender to an inner guidance or authority. This is the way of the prophets and apostles of God, and it is the way indicated by Hod-Netzach on the Tree of Life.

Essentially, our relationship with God is designated by the moral triad, for in our relationship with God, we are the all-receiver and God is the all-giver. It is basically a one-way relationship in which there is no real reciprocity. Thus, the moral triad corresponds to our relationship with God, while the triad of action corresponds to our relationship with one another and creation. Yet, mysteriously, God has ordained a creation in which we can give something back to God. Because of the cosmic illusion of separation and the free will produced by it, we are able to seek God and to reunite ourselves with God, as it were, essentially giving ourselves to God. In our seeking God and uniting ourselves with God, we unfold a process of self-realization. Thus, we give God's presence a dwelling place, embodying something of God, and we give back something new, a realized self. In this sense, we have a reciprocal relationship with God, reflecting Godself to Godself and thus completing the creative process.

God and the Hosts of Creation

At the level of Atzilut, Hod manifests as Elohim Tzavaot, the God of hosts. We spoke a great deal about Elohim Tzavaot in connection with Yahweh Tzavaot, yet there is more to be said of these two names and, specifically, of the divine name Tzavaot itself. If we take Tzavaot to mean all hosts, both heavenly and earthly creatures, then Yahweh Tzavaot would indicate the dominion of God over all creatures and creation directly, while Elohim Tzavaot would suggest the dominion of God over all creatures indirectly via creative powers such as archangels. Yahweh Tzavaot therefore indicates times in which God directly intercedes in creation and directly interacts with creatures. Elohim Tzavaot represents times in which God indirectly intercedes and indirectly interacts with creatures through intermediaries (specifically, archangels and angels).

This is suggested by the attribute of the hazy mirror of prophecy to Hod and the clear mirror of prophecy to Netzach. Accordingly, when the lesser prophet is visited by the Lord, it is through the agency of archangels and angels. When the greater prophet is visited by the Lord, it is not by way of an intermediation of angelic beings; the Lord speaks directly with the prophet. "Lesser" and "greater" in this regard represent degrees of intimacy and transparency in the consciousness of the prophet.

It is interesting to note that the most spectacular prophecies from our perspective are, in fact, those of the prophets beholding their vision in the hazy mirror of prophecy at the level of Yetzirah, for in them are elaborate descriptions of angels and heavenly realms. These are the prophecies that most often truly catch hold of the human heart and imagination, which reveals something about them. They represent something of the word and wisdom of God brought down nearer to humanity, which is exactly the function of the world of angels (Yetzirah). In this sense, the hazy mirror of prophecy and the intermediation of the holy angels represent God's Hod-empathy for humanity—God reaching out to humanity by way of lower gradations.

God does not only reach down, however; God also draws humanity up toward him- or herself. While we may not relate to the experience of the greater prophet as easily as that of the lesser prophet, to the degree that we cleave to the word of the Lord spoken by the greater prophets, we are drawn in ascent with them Godward. Thus, Hod and Netzach relate to the twofold action of divine revelation—the bringing down of the light to humanity and the uplifting of humanity into the light. When it is said that the Torah and the prophets were fulfilled through the incarnation in the person of Yeshua Messiah, it is the complete unification of this twofold action of divine revelation that is meant. As one holy apostle puts it, in the person of the Lord Yeshua, God becomes fully human so that the human being might become fully divine. God entered into humanity so that humanity might enter into God. In the same way that the visions of heavenly realms and angelic beings move us, so the idea of an incarnation of God moves us. Likewise, in the same way we are drawn in ascent with the greater prophet when we cleave to the word of the Lord that the prophet has spoken, so in cleaving to the divine incarnation are we taken up in divine rapture. Not only are we carried in ascent through the divine incarnation; we experience complete unification with God. For the action of Yahweh Tzavaot and Elohim Tzavaot are one and the same in the Spirit of the Messiah.

At the heart of Gnostic Christianity is the gnosis of the Christos in all things and all things united with God through Christ—hence, Christ as the pattern-that-connects. Tzavaot as a divine name alludes to the Christos in all creatures, both heavenly and earthly. Yahweh Tzavaot alludes to the presence of God in all creatures and Elohim Tzavaot alludes to all creatures as a manifestation of God's presence and power, each according to their kind. In terms of humankind, we are specifically sons and daughters of God—children of light. Of all the kinds of creatures on earth, we have the greatest capacity for the light and we have the ability to draw out the light from within one another and from within the whole of creation. While relating with the Infinite One directly may seem remote to us in our present condition, in our relationships with one another and with God's creatures, we experience a relationship with God to the degree that we are aware of Christ in others and Christ in creation. Developing our relationships founded upon this holy awareness, we draw out the light from within ourselves and all our relations. In the Christian Kabbalah, Tzavaot represents this holy awareness.

Tzavaot is spelled with the Hebrew letters Tzaddi (צ)-Bet (ב)-Aleph (א)-Vau (ו)-Tau (ת). Tzaddi, as a word, means "fishhook." One is reminded of Yeshua speaking of his disciples as fishermen and of the symbolic meaning given to the Greek word for fish, *Ichthos*, which was considered an anagram for "Jesus Christ, God's Son, Savior" in the early Church. A fishhook implies a drawing out of something and, given the Christian context, specifically a drawing out of the light-presence (Christos). Bet means "house" and connotes creatures and creation, thus a drawing out of something from within creatures and creation. That something is designated by the Aleph, which connotes the spirit (Christ-spirit). Vau, which as we have seen connotes a link or connection, suggests the drawing out of the spirit through relationships. Tau means "cross," specifically the idea of being Christed, thus made perfect and complete. This is the natural result of drawing forth the Christos from within oneself, God's creatures, and creation—oneself and all things become Christed or anointed with the supernal light of God. Tzavaot therefore indicates the very purpose of creation, specifically, the human being in creation. It suggests that, when we develop proper relationships with one another, God's creatures, and our environment, we naturally experience God's presence and power in our lives and unite ourselves with God in creation (Elohim).

There is another distinction to be made with regard to Elohim Tzavaot and Yahweh Tzavaot. While Elohim Tzavaot represents our ability to cleave to God in creation (on earth), Yahweh Tzavaot represents our ability to cleave to God beyond creation (in heaven). Thus, when we cleave to God in creation and to God beyond creation, we join creation with God and unite heaven and earth. It is through the Neshamah that we are able to cleave to God above, and through Nefesh Elokit that we are able to cleave to God below. It is through Ruach that the Neshamah and Nefesh are joined together as one soul of light. When it is said that the human one is created in the image and likeness of Yahweh Elohim, by the image of Yahweh is meant Neshamah, and by likeness of Elohim is meant Nefesh Elokit. When it is said that Yahweh Elohim breathed the spirit into the human one, by spirit is meant Ruach, which is the capacity to unite the heavenly and earthly soul. According to the Kabbalah, it is this capacity that makes us truly human and when we unite heaven and earth in us, we are, indeed, manifest as the image and likeness of God—and thus have dominion over Tzavaot as the great Seth.

Mental Being and the Thunder Mind

Netzach-dominion corresponds to the higher vital planes, while Hod-empathy corresponds to the mental planes. It is through the higher vital and mental being that we are able to consciously direct the spiritual forces in the astral planes, which correspond to Yesod. Prophecy and the magical art therefore necessitate the development and mastery of the mental and vital being—the mind, heart, and life.

Mind in the Kabbalah means something far more than the ordinary mind of the intellect and finite reason. The intellect and finite reason are merely the surface mind. Beyond the surface, there is the higher mind, illumined mind, intuitive mind, and the universal mind or cosmic consciousness. Although, indeed, the aim of the Gnostic is transcendence of the mental being altogether, this transcendence comes through the full development of the mental being from one level or gradation to another, until, at the level of the universal mind, one is able to pass through the great threshold called "cessation" into the metamind state of supernal consciousness. It is this latter development that is called the "perfect thunder mind" in Christian Gnosticism, which in fact is beyond the mental being altogether.

The base of the mental being is found in Hod, although the peak is in Binah as we have previously discussed. In terms of the Olamot, the vital being corresponds to Yetzirah and the mental being corresponds to Beriyah, Atzilut representing the supramental or supernal being. Thus, the supramental being corresponds to the divine names, our mental being corresponds to the dominion of the archangels, and our vital being corresponds to the universe of angels. In the same way, the Sefirot are channels or vehicles of the supernal light, our mental being, vital being, and even our physical being are to be channels or vehicles of the supernal consciousness-force. However, the vital being must be purified and the mental being fully developed from base to peak, every level of the mental and vital consciousness being linked together in a state of integral being.

We are all familiar with the ordinary mind and, from time to time, most of us experience something of the higher mind and illumined mind. The higher mind is experienced as flashes of insight, whether into things mundane or supramundane. The illumined mind is something more than flashes of insight; it is experienced as streams of inspiration in which insights are linked together, forming a flow that may continue for a shorter or longer period of time. The intuitive mind is less common. It is the experience of whole fields of knowledge and understanding appearing in the mind, as though knowledge and understanding of a whole subject suddenly fills the mind. What we call "genius" tends to be the function of the intuitive mind. In the way we use this term in conventional wisdom, it is usually indicative of only those forms of genius that can be exploited for the interests of unenlightened society, thus excluding many forms of genius that go unacknowledged. Likewise, in terms of recognized genius, oftentimes links between lower levels of the mental being and vital being are not established; therefore, the genius is often a partial and disbalanced state—hence the psychological dysfunctions commonly associated with many geniuses.

The universal mind or cosmic consciousness is something beyond what we typically would call a genius, and one might say represents a state of "greater genius." Essentially, the universal mind represents knowledge and understanding of multiple fields of knowledge and combines both supramundane and mundane knowledge. While the intuitive mind can manifest in either mundane or supramundane matters, the universal mind always includes the spiritual and metaphysical. One could well be an atheist and attain something of the intuitive mind. But in the development of the universal mind, there is an awareness of the sacred unity underlying existence and knowledge of the source in reflection. Whether one is a theist or nontheist, the universal mind is innately spiritual and one is compelled by love and compassion. In one way or another, one becomes aware of a cosmic intelligence in the universe and aware that nothing is truly separate from it. This cosmic intelligence is reflected within one's mind, thus the state of greater genius that manifests.

Because love and compassion are innately present with the state of the universal mind, we understand the inseparability of the vital and mental being in the full development of mental consciousness. In fact, in terms of a spiritual-mental development, cultivation of the higher levels of vital being is absolutely essential, for the mental being cannot be universalized without it and any super humanity conceived by way of will apart from love is the hallmark of what can only be called "black magic," which leads to a titanic or demonic state of being. This is well reflected by way of the modern philosopher Nietzsche versus the way of Buddhism. Love and compassion were not included in the philosophy of Nietzsche, and consequently Nietzsche did not attain any real superhuman state, but ended his life in an insane asylum. On the other hand, Buddhism teaches a path that puts emphasis upon the development of love and compassion and has led many souls to enlightenment and liberation.

The development of the higher levels of vital being corresponds to Netzach and the development of the mental being corresponds to Hod. As we indicated in terms of healthy human relationships above, there must be a dynamic balance between Hod and Netzach, and if dysfunction is to be avoided, the two must function together as a single unit.

Although many people experience something of the higher mind and illumined mind, and a few even experience something of the intuitive mind, the experience of these higher states of mental consciousness does not necessarily reflect actual attainment. Actual attainment implies that one is able to enter and exit a higher state of consciousness at will, whether it is a higher vital or mental consciousness. While many people may experience higher levels of vital and mental consciousness from time to time, for the most part it is a random or inconsistent experience that is not under the conscious control of the person. In most cases, the person does not know how it happened and cannot consciously invoke the experience again. Therefore, he or she has not realized or attained it. To actually realize a higher level of mental or vital being, we must develop the capacity to consciously shift into it and form a link between the higher and lower levels. In order to do this, we must develop spiritual self-discipline and, specifically, the power of concentration or focused awareness (*kavvanah*).

Contemplation and Meditation—
Conscious Evolution

There are many terms in Hebrew for states of contemplation and meditation that appear in the Scriptures. The key to all of them is what is called *kavvanah*, which is translated as "concentration," "feeling," and "devotion." The word kavvanah comes from the root *kaven*, which means "to aim," and connotes a state of directed consciousness toward a specific goal or the idea of conscious intention. That feeling and devotion are associated with kavvanah indicates that it is a concentration of the heart and mind together, and it alludes to the intimate connection between kavvanah and devekut. If we were to designate contemplation and meditation as "controlled thought and emotion," then kavvanah would be the most basic overall term for any practice of contemplation or meditation.

Kavvanah is often used as a term to denote prayer and worship, so as to say that, where there is actual concentration or conscious intention, one's prayers and worship are effective. Designating deeper states of contemplation and meditation, as well as prayer and worship, kavvanah suggests that the line between prayer-worship and meditation is a very fine one and often vanishes altogether. In methods of Gnostic worship, there are many points specifically designed to be used as contemplations or meditations to enter higher states of consciousness. These points are called kavvanot and they aim at various states of devekut through which yichudim (unification) is accomplished. For example, in the Shema (*Shema Israel, Adonai Elohenu, Adonai Achad*, "Hear, O Israel, the Lord is your God, the Lord is One"), when an initiate chants "Shema Israel," he or she focuses on Malkut and thus cleaves in his or her soul to Malkut-kingdom. When the initiate chants "Adonai Elohenu," he or she elevates his or her mind and heart to Tiferet, attaching the soul to the Christ-center. Chanting "Adonai Achad," the initiate concentrates completely upon Keter, unifying him- or herself with the most high or the Divine I Am. Thus, there are three kavvanot in the Shema, which are three rungs of ascent into Yichud and the divine rapture that comes from at-onement.

Kavvanah is also associated with good works, such as actions of charity or other good deeds. Essentially, any action performed with kavvanah may be an act of devotion or worship of the beloved, which is to say any act in

which one clears one's mind of all extraneous thoughts and emotions, concentrating oneself completely on the task at hand. This capacity to remove
all distraction and focus one's mind, heart, and life completely upon a single action is crucial to prophetic states and real magic.

In addition to the general concept of kavvanah, the word is often used
in the Kabbalah to denote devotional works of a mystical nature that are
composed of collections of kavvanot meditations, or works of a magical
nature that are composed of collections of kavvanot rituals. These kavvanot are used to direct consciousness along inner and secret pathways
that are defined by the meditation or ritual, which has a very specific goal
in mind.

Kavvanah is linked to another term for contemplation and meditation,
hitbonenut. This word literally means "self-knowledge" or "self-understanding." If one were to look at a flower and appreciate its beauty and fragrance,
one might be relatively unaffected and unmoved by the experience—completely unchanged. Just because one examines a flower very closely and
enjoys the flower for a few moments does not necessarily mean that one
will find a passage into higher consciousness through the flower. However, if one were to contemplate and meditate upon the flower with the intention of using it to attain a higher level of awareness or as a means of
attaining some degree of self-understanding, then this activity would be
hitbonenut meditation.

Hitbonenut is often a term for meditation while contemplating God's
creation and, specifically, meditations on the mysteries of creation and the
presence of God within it. One can easily experience a strong devekut
and love of God through such contemplation and perhaps even gain
glimpses of worlds within and beyond nature's sphere. What comes from
this form of hitbonenut is something more than the awareness of God's
presence in creation. It naturally leads to awareness of God's presence
within oneself and the awareness of one's own place in creation—hence
the depth of love and sense of connectedness love tends to invoke.

Hitbonenut, however, is something more than meditation through the
contemplation of nature. It is meditation through the contemplation of
anything. It could be the contemplation of a starry night sky, a stone, a
bird in flight; or it could be contemplation of a sacred object or symbol, a
verse from the Scriptures, a Sefirah, or any number of other things through

which one might gain knowledge and understanding of oneself in the context of a greater reality or the light of God. Essentially, hitbonenut is contemplative meditation in which one completely fills one's mind and heart with the object of meditation. In hitbonenut, one concentrates one's mind on a single object of meditation, allowing nothing else to enter one's mind. This quite naturally leads to a state of kavvanah and higher levels of mental and vital consciousness.

There is another key term associated with kavvanah, which goes beyond the states attained by hitbonenut. It is called *hitbodedut* and literally means "self-isolation." Basically, there are two forms of hitbodedut, external self-isolation and internal self-isolation. External self-isolation involves physical seclusion or retreat in which one withdraws to be alone with oneself and God. Such spiritual retreat is an important part of spiritual practice and spiritual life and, at times, is crucial for progress upon the path. While the Gnostic initiate does not entertain any sort of permanent withdrawal from the world and mundane activities, initiates of the Tradition do take periods of spiritual retreat, whether in their own home for a few days or by a journey out into the wilderness to pray, meditate, and perform sacred ritual. This is one form of hitbodedut.

Internal self-isolation consists of removing the mind from all outward stimulation, and even from one's own thoughts and emotions. Essentially, it is the complete emptying of the mind or rising above the level of thoughts and emotions. When we speak of the silent mind and still vital, we are speaking of hitbodedut, which is the true meditative state proper. The ability of hitbodedut is crucial to the attainment of any higher degree of the enlightenment experience, for it is through the hitbodedut state that we are able to pass into cessation and thus enter into supernal consciousness.

Hitbonenut is any method of meditation in which one fills the mind with the contemplation of an object, while hitbodedut is any method of meditation in which one completely empties the mind altogether— whether by fullness or by emptiness, higher states of consciousness are the natural result of such kavvanah.

Hitbonenut can be likened to our directing our mind toward a single object of focus, and hitbodedut can be likened to our consciousness and the object of focus merging completely together so that the subject (meditator) and object (meditation) become one and the same. In this sense, hitbonenut and hitbodedut are stages in meditation itself, hitbonenut being the entrance into the meditative state and hitbodedut being the actual meditative state. Hitbonenut would thus represent one level of kavvanah, and hitbodedut would represent a much deeper (or higher) level of kavvanah. In this sense, our practice of meditation is hitbonenut; when we actually experience the meditative state, it becomes hitbodedut.

Yeshua speaks of hitbonenut-meditation when he says, "Consider the lilies of the field, how they grow; they neither toil nor spin, yet I tell you, even Solomon in all of his glory was not clothed like one of these." Likewise, he very clearly indicates the practice of hitbodedut meditation when he says, "But whenever you pray, go into your room and shut the door and pray to your Father who is in secret; and your father who sees in secret will reward you" (Gospel of St. Matthew 6:6, 6:28–29).

What is the reward of prayer and meditation? It is the experience of higher states of consciousness, both vital and mental consciousness, and the experience of a Spirit-connectedness. Ultimately, the rewards of prayer and meditation are enlightenment and liberation—the experience of supernal or Messianic consciousness. In a word, the reward is a conscious evolution.

The Mage of Light and Magical Kabbalah

The art of divine magic corresponds to Hod, specifically in the form of ceremonial or ritual magic. From our previous discussion on the gradations of divine magic, you will recall that the highest form of magic transpires purely through a silent volition or mere thought in the mind of the initiate, and that a master of the magical art does not need to rely upon anything external to bring about a magical result or what some might call a miracle. The next highest form of divine magic is commonly called *inner plane working*. In this method of magic, the adept transfers his or her consciousness into a body of light and performs the magical act on the inner planes, typically at the level of the astral planes. The lowest level of divine magic is ceremonial or ritual magic, which is dependent upon the regalia of the art—the magical circle, magical weapons, talismans and amulets, incantations, and such; hence, an actual physical ritual of magic.

Kavvanah—concentration of the mind, heart, and life—is the key of all magic, and the purpose of ceremonial magic is to facilitate and develop the power of kavvanah. Essentially, everything in the sacred space of a magical ritual corresponds to the kavvanah-intention of the ceremony. Everywhere the initiate might cast his or her gaze, there is this one thought, this one conscious intention, and nothing but that thought. Thus, the environment of the ceremony and the magical ritual itself all serve to focus the mind of the magician upon one thing—the magical intention for which the sacred ritual was created.

The ability to transfer the center of one's consciousness into the subtle body and perform the magical art on the inner planes, and the ability to perform the magical art through a silent will or mere thought, represent higher grades of kavvanah. In the study and practice of the magical Kabbalah, the initiate first learns the art of ceremonial magic as a method to support and develop kavvanah. As higher grades of kavvanah are developed, the initiate shifts more and more to methods of inner plane working.

As we have said, things tend to manifest as we expect them to, and whenever the circumstances and environment are present for something to manifest, it will naturally and spontaneously come into being. This is the very principle upon which ceremonial magic operates. A skilled ceremonial Magician is an expert in correspondences, and using this esoteric knowledge he or she is able to create the circumstances and environments necessary to manifest things according to his or her desire. In the case of the mage of light, his or her desire is the divine will and kingdom, and thus it is not his or her own personal will that is served but rather a greater good and God's will.

To understand how ceremonial magic works, one must realize that there are inner dimensions corresponding to any material space, the subtle dimensions nearest to the physical plane being called the astral planes. The astral planes are formed of an energetic substance called the astral light, in which things take form much as they do in the physical plane, except the substance of astral forms is far more subtle than material forms. This astral dimension is essentially the subtle matrix within and behind the material plane and acts as a receiver-transmitter of spiritual forces of the higher planes. Thus, the astral dimension links the material world with the world of spirits and worlds beyond. Everything in the material world has a corresponding manifestation in the astral planes that reflects the spiritual beings-forces to which things in the material world are connected. The astral planes are shaped by thought and emotion, and changes can be made on the astral level by a corresponding change in our thoughts and emotions. When we move in the material plane, we also generate movement in the astral plane, and spiritual beings-forces move with us corresponding to the thoughts and emotions we entertain. Typically, this is something that happens quite unconsciously. However, in the magical art, we move with kavvanah—concentration and conscious intention—and thus are able to affect/effect changes in the astral dimension that bring about corresponding changes in the physical dimension. Until one is able to gather one's consciousness inward and upward without reliance on anything external to support one's kavvanah, ceremonial or ritual magic proves a powerful method.

Although this explanation is somewhat simplistic and partial, it does give us an idea of how magic is possible. It also suggests that what is called magic is not exclusive to what we might typically think of as magical. Anything we might do in life can be a magical act if the action is performed with kavvanah, which is to say, with the full force of concentration and conscious intention. When our center of concentration is the divine and our conscious intention reflects the divine will, then the magical act is divine. For this reason, my teacher was fond of saying, "The magician never acts without clear and conscious intention in anything he or she does, and in everything, the mage of light seeks divine guidance, waiting upon the Spirit of the Lord before he or she acts. Any action in which there is kavvanah is inherently magical, and any action performed in harmony with one's true will shall bring about a magical result."

To illustrate the idea of a magical act that does not necessarily appear as what one might think of as magical, we may consider the example of a modern saying in schools of business—"dress for success." This is inherently a magical idea, for, although perhaps not yet successful, the person who dresses as though he or she is successful is more likely to succeed. Dressing well, a person will feel better about him- or herself, and he or she is more likely able to feel and think he or she will be successful and therefore believe in his or her ultimate success. Likewise, it will inspire similar thoughts and feelings from others, and others will be more likely to believe in that person's ability to succeed and perhaps actively help the person succeed. The way one dresses thus becomes a magical talisman and acting with a positive attitude of success becomes a magical ritual.

Obviously, mundane applications of magical principles, such as in our example, do not necessarily make one a magician, let alone a mage of light. Divine magic proper is specifically concerned with the spiritual be-ings-forces moving within and behind what transpires and with the mani-festation of the divine kingdom. Essentially, the magician is aware of the play of spiritual forces through which what we call reality is manifest, and consciously seeks to participate in the play of spiritual forces and to bring about a balance among the cosmic forces. In the case of the mage of light, he or she labors to banish dark and hostile forces from the psychic sphere of humanity and the earth and to actively invoke the divine powers. Like-wise, the mage of light seeks to heal every form of illness or disease, whether psychic or spiritual, and restore others to health and happiness— to accomplish the tikkune of the world. The ultimate intention of the mage of light is to act as a holy apostle—seeking the enlightenment and liberation of all living spirits and souls.

Without the development of kavvanah, real magic is impossible. Like-wise, without the generation of positive merit or energy, one cannot ef-fectively perform a magical ceremony. For this reason, one famous book on magic, *The Book of the Sacred Magic of Abramelin*, advocates acts of charity before engaging in the magical art. In the magical tradition of the Kab-balah, the art of ceremonial magic is intimately connected to spiritual or mystical attainment and a continuum of daily prayer and meditation. Prayer and meditation develop kavvanah and naturally generate positive merit or energy. More importantly, through daily prayer and meditation, the initiate abides in a state of spirit-connectedness, and thus the initiate experiences divine guidance in the magical art.

The need for a continuum of daily spiritual practice and spiritual living is reflected by the Rosicrucian grade associated with Hod, called *Practicus*, which denotes an initiate who integrates the path into his or her life through actual spiritual practice. Spiritual practice is essentially a work on oneself, seeking a refinement and perfection of one's humanity and, yet more, the realization of divinity in oneself. The term practicus suggests

the idea of a consistent effort until one succeeds, or continued experimen-
tation until eventual discovery. As the saying goes, "If at first you don't
succeed, try, try again." The only real failure in any endeavor comes when
a person gives up hope of success and gives in to negativity and doubt,
thus giving up his or her efforts toward eventual victory. Practicus, therefore, connotes perfect success, understanding any failure as part of a
process working out whatever might hinder or obstruct one's success. This
view of perfect success is integral to any spiritual practice and, most especially, to the art of divine magic.

The Great Angel of the Holy Mother and Messiah

Hod manifests in Beriyah as the archangel Michael, whose name is actually a question: "Who (*Mi*) is like unto God?" According to the Tradition,
the archangel Metatron is the greatest of all the angels, as Metatron is the
angelic image of Enoch, the human being who ascends beyond the highest heavens to the world of supernal light, and is thus exalted above the
angels. However, among angelic beings proper, it is Michael who is said
to be the highest angel, whose true image is "like unto God." In this respect, Michael is the guardian angel of humanity, for Michael is the supernal pattern of Adam, who is created in the image and likeness of God.

Raphael, Michael, and Gabriel are said to be the three archangels who
visit Abraham and Sarah. According to legend, Raphael is sent to heal the
wound of Abraham; Gabriel is sent to bring justice to Sodom and Gomorrah; and Michael is sent to announce the conception of Isaac. When
Abraham was about to sacrifice Isaac, the sages of wisdom say it was
Michael who stayed his hand and directed Abraham's attention to the ram
caught in the thicket.

Michael is the angel of the Lord who appears to Moses as the burning
bush, and thus is considered the forerunner and herald of the Shekinah.
He is also said to be the Maggid Cohen Ha-Gadol of the celestial temple
and the great angelic minister of the order of Melchizedek. While
Michael appears with the Messiah in the seventh heaven and appears as
the glory of the Messiah in the third heaven, his dominion is in the fourth
heaven. In the fourth heaven, it is said that he offers up the souls of the

righteous as a burnt offering before Yahweh, thus transforming souls into pure spirit and facilitating their ascent into the upper heavenly abodes.

On the sacred circle, the archangel Michael stands in the south and is the great angel who holds dominion over the element of fire. Likewise, he is the archangel of the summer solstice and the feast of the ascension, which is celebrated on summer solstice in Christian Gnosticism.

Michael is sent as the guardian angel of the Holy Mother while she is pregnant and serves as the guardian angel of the Yeshua Messiah in his mission. When it was time for the ascension of the Mother, it was Michael who announced it and Michael who led the Mother in her ascent. According to the Tradition, it was Michael who set the holy crown upon her head. When Yeshua Messiah ascended, Michael became the great guardian of the apostle of the apostles, the Holy Bride, and when St. Mary Magdalene departed with her son to travel to a distant land, Michael accompanied them. Michael is said to be the guardian of the royal blood and present with every incarnation of the soul of the first apostle. Accordingly, in the Tradition, the secret order of initiates who protect the descendants of St. Mary Magdalene and the incarnations of the Holy Bride is called the order of St. Michael.

Archangel Michael appears with the woman of light in the Book of Revelation, where it says, "And war broke out in heaven; Michael and his angels fought against the dragon. The dragon and his angels fought back, but they were defeated, and there was no longer any place for them in heaven" (Revelation 12:7–8). Michael is the commander of the armies of heaven and is the great angel who holds dominion over the spirit of the dragon. Because of this association, Michael is the chief archangel invoked in Gnostic rites of exorcism and is said to be "the great guardian of those who stalk the fallen."

Michael is associated with Kokab (Mercury) and therefore with communication and travel. In the esoteric system of planetary attributes to the seven interior stars or centers of the subtle body taught in the Rosicrucian tradition, Mercury corresponds to the crown star on top of the head—the seat of the cosmic Christ. This center is the threshold to supernal consciousness and, thus, Michael is said to resemble the supernal image of the self. More profoundly, this is the center through which the adepts and masters transfer their consciousness into the body of light at the moment of death. According to the teachings of the Christian Kabbalah, if one has not developed this capacity but is dying, he or she may call upon Michael to guide and protect his or her soul in the transition. Thus, Michael is often invoked as the guardian of those who are dying. Similarly, it is said that, if one finds oneself in a dark dream or is plagued by darkness in an afterlife state and one can remember to call upon Michael, one will be instantly delivered from the darkness.

The image of Michael is sometimes envisioned similar to that of Kamael—a human form in armor bearing a great sword or spear—except that, with Michael, his whole body is formed of brilliant light as though it were the sun. More commonly, however, Michael is envisioned as a great angel who appears as a human being, whose body is solar light and whose face is white brilliance, with great wings that are formed of translucent ruby-red light and tinges of emerald green. Other times, Michael is envisioned as the burning bush, for the masters of the Tradition say that the image of Michael cannot be described in human terms and, in truth, he does not appear as anything close to our conception of a human being. Holding one of these divine images in mind and intoning the divine name of Hod and the chant *Ya Mi Ha Michael*, this great angel is invoked by initiates.

Michael is associated with the way of power and therefore divine magic. Thus, along with things corresponding to the aspects of Michael mentioned above, Gnostics often invoke Michael to gain deeper knowledge and understanding of the magical art. Michael may also be invoked in matters concerning courage, strength of faith, and force of will, as well as scientific discovery and technological advancement (specifically, the right use of science and technology).

Sons of Light and Sons of Darkness

Hod in Yetzirah manifests as the Beni Elohim, which literally means "sons of God." Yet among the Beni Elohim are angels that may rightly be called sons of light and those that properly are called sons of darkness—for among the Beni Elohim are many angels of wrath, as well as titanic and demonic beings of great power. The first appearance of the Beni Elohim in Scripture is in the Book of Genesis where it is written:

When people began to multiply on the face of the ground, and daughters were born to them, the sons of God saw that they were fair; and they took wives for themselves of all that they chose. Then the Lord said, "My spirit shall not abide in mortals forever, for they are flesh; their days shall be one hundred twenty years." The Nephilim were on the earth in those days—and also afterward—when the sons of God went into the daughters of humans, who bore children to them. These were the heroes that were of old, warriors of renown. (Genesis 6:1–4)

According to legend, the Beni Elohim that descended out of the heavens are the fallen. While the term "fallen" may refer to all titanic and demonic beings, it is often used to refer to the Beni Elohim who entered into the earth sphere and, specifically, to a certain class of demon said to have been among them. A movie by this title was made that depicted the mythical powers attributed to this extremely potent class of demons.

What is unique to the Beni Elohim among the orders of angels is their ability to assume an actual physical incarnation and, in the case of certain otherworldly beings of this order, their ability to swiftly and completely possess and control incarnate creatures. Most angelic, titanic, or demonic beings operate primarily by way of influence. In the case of demonic beings, most are only able to obsess or possess a person over a period of time or are only able to enter swiftly through individuals whose psychic sphere is fractured. The dark beings that come from the order of the Beni Elohim, however, can do so instantaneously to almost any ordinary human being or animal at will.

The reason the Beni Elohim have such power is that they are angelic beings that have the most intimate knowledge of the mysteries of Asiyah—the material plane, material forces, and material forms. While the Beni Elohim are said to possess great magical knowledge, they are also said to be the angels behind all scientific and technological developments. According to the Zohar, those Beni Elohim that are called the "sons of light" inspire divine magic, science, and technology that uplift humanity, advance the evolution of life on earth, and serve the divine kingdom. Those Beni Elohim that are called the sons of darkness teach arts of sorcery and inspire science and technology used for warfare and corruption of life on earth.

In essence, one could say that any scientific or technological knowledge is a Beni Elohim, as is the form of cosmic force that is mastered through the corresponding knowledge. In this sense, one could speak of the Beni Elohim as something neutral, which becomes good, evil, or something admixed, dependent upon what human beings do with the knowledge and power. There is a hint to this in another place where the order of Beni Elohim is mentioned in the Scriptures, where it is written:

> One day the heavenly beings came to present themselves before the Lord, and Satan also came in among them. The Lord said to Satan, "Where have you come from?" Satan answered the Lord, "From going to and fro on the earth, and from walking up and down upon it." (Job 1:6–7)

These heavenly beings are Beni Elohim—that Satan or Samael is among them alludes to the evil or violent inclination, which tends to pervert or corrupt the natural order of creatures and creation. This suggests that the appearance of the Beni Elohim, and whether the knowledge and power they represent serves the good or evil inclination, is determined by the karmic balance of the observer.

All angelic orders are composed of a vast array of different classes of angels, and the Beni Elohim are no exception. Along with those described above, there are also sons of God who are angels of wrath said to wield powers of pestilence, plagues, and ill fortune, and there are numerous classes among them that are exclusively dedicated to worship of God. In the classes of the Beni Elohim dedicated to worship are those who inspire and lead creatures to worship. These sons of God bless those who worship with kavvanah, enacting worship above corresponding to the worship below—thus uniting the worship on earth and in heaven.

The name "sons of God" is typically applied to this order of angels associated with Hod; however, it also appears as a title of human beings, specifically the faithful and elect. You will recall Lord Yeshua's blessing upon the peacemakers, whom he says will be called Beni Elohim—children of God. In the Gospel of St. John, Lord Yeshua indirectly alludes to the association of the term Beni Elohim with human beings and the idea of the children of light and children of darkness when he says,

"And this is the judgment, that the light has come into the world, and people loved the darkness rather than the light because their deeds were evil. For all who do evil hate the light and do not come into the light, so that their deeds may not be exposed. But those who do what is true come to the light, so that it may be clearly seen that their deeds are done in God." (Gospel of St. John 3:19–21)

This association between the order of angels called Beni Elohim and human beings also called Beni Elohim reflects the nature of the human being as a vehicle or channel of spiritual forces in the material world. It is not a question whether or not human beings will channel or embody spiritual forces; rather, the question is always what kind of spiritual forces we will attach ourselves to—whether divine, admixed, or demonic.

As we have seen, among the orders of angels all three forms of spiritual beings-forces exist and all three forms seek to influence and draw near to human beings, because it is through humanity that spiritual beings-forces gain dominion in the material plane. It is this knowledge that motivates the Gnostic initiate to study and practice divine magic, so that he or she is no longer unconsciously compelled by the play of spiritual or cosmic forces, but rather is a conscious participant for the sake of the divine kingdom. In the beatitude that links human beings to the term Beni Elohim, the Master teaches us the aim of this divine magic—to bring peace.

Spiritual Practices for Hod

Contemplative Meditation

The contemplative Kabbalah is founded upon methods of contemplative meditation, in which one fills one's mind completely with the subject/object of contemplation. It is a principal method through which initiates seek to experience the inward revelation of secret mysteries. One can perform contemplative meditation upon the Sefirot (spheres), Olamot (universes), or Netivot (paths) of the Tree of Life. Likewise, one can do so with correspondences of letters, numbers, and words, passages from the Scriptures, Sepher Yetzirah, Bahir, Zohar, or any number of sacred texts. Anything at all may be a source of contemplative meditation, which is a form of hitbonenut that naturally develops kavvanah.

The aim of contemplative meditation is to access the divine intelligence to gain new and deeper insights into the mysteries or to receive divine guidance on a matter—for the methods of contemplation can be applied to circumstances, situations, and events in one's life as well. Essentially, through contemplation, initiates seek gnosis and the basic method proves a powerful way to gain insight and knowledge of almost anything.

> ➢ When you wish to engage in contemplative meditation, choose the subject/object of contemplation and sit down in a place where you will not be disturbed. Let your body find its own natural rhythm of breath and relax while remaining alert. When you are centered, fill your mind with the subject-object of contemplation, systematically going over every detail you know on the subject/object, thinking of nothing other than this one subject/object. When you have exhausted everything you know about the subject/object, let go of it completely and abide in silent meditation, as though leaving it to your holy soul. If your mind begins to wander, engage in the contemplation again, going over it completely and then once again letting go of it in silent meditation. Do this several times and, whether something comes or not, conclude the session of contemplation and go about other business of your day. Once seeding your deeper mind—your subconscious—in this way, it will continue the contemplation.

> ➢ It is like fishing: the contemplation is baiting the hook and the silent meditation is throwing the line into the water. Sometimes you will gain new insight and knowledge quickly, while on other occasions something will come only after a period of time passes. There will be other times when you will go away having caught nothing. It is not uncommon that insight and knowledge may flood the mind at another time when you are not actively practicing the contemplative meditation. Sometimes, the new insight or knowledge might even come by way of a dream. One may have to contemplate and meditate upon a subject/object many times before any response comes from the divine intelligence. Whether knowledge and understanding comes swiftly or takes some time, practice contemplative meditation frequently upon the subject-object until insight and knowledge comes. If you contemplate the subject-object consistently, you will always gain what you seek in due season.

Those who master the art of contemplative meditation are able to direct their mind to a subject/object and gain knowledge and understanding instantly, as though something from nothing.

> If one desires to, one can light a candle and a stick of incense while one practices contemplative meditation, and one can pray beforehand that God might empower one's meditation. Likewise, it can be helpful to chant divine names that correspond to the subject-object of one's meditation or to invoke the spirits of the saints and holy angels (tzaddikim and maggidim) into it. However, the method of contemplative meditation remains the same and can be used alone without any supports.

THIRTEEN

YESOD, THE FOUNDATION OF ALL

Attributes

Thirty-Two Paths of Wisdom: Pure Consciousness (Sekhel Tahor); it is called this because it purifies the Sefirot; it tests the decree of their structure and the inner essence of their unity, making it glow; they are then unified without any cutoff or separation

Yesod: Foundation or Reciprocity

Place on the Tree of Life: Near the base of the Pillar of Compassion, between Tiferet and Malkut

Divine Name: Shaddai; El Shaddai; Shaddai El Chai

Alternative Divine Names: Kol, All; Brit, Covenant; Kodesh Tzaddik, Holy Righteous One

Partzuf Above: Zer Anpin as the Holy Tzaddik

Partzuf Below: The Holy Apostle; John the Baptist; the Patriarch Joseph

Divine Image: Yeshua Messiah laying-on-hands in transmission; the Holy Apostle in a Robe of Rainbow Light; a beautiful naked young man

Archangel: Gabriel

Order of Angels: Kerubim

Celestial Attribute: Levanah, the Moon

Titles Given to Yesod: The Passage Way; the Gates of Heaven and Hell; the Matrix; Sphere of Vision; the In-Between; House of Enchantments; House of Mirrors; Astral Sea; the Holy Member; the Silver Orb; Domain of Forces; Abode of Images; the Dragon's Lair; Depth of West; the Dream Center; Sign of the Covenant

Level of the Soul: Ruach and Nefesh (Lower Ruach joined to the Nefesh)

Heavenly Abode: Rakiya, the Second Heaven—the Firmament

Spiritual Experience: Vision of Forces in the Astral Earth; Vision of the Matrix or Grid; Vision of the Secret Mechanisms of the Universe

Virtues: Emotional stability; visionary ability; independence; strong imagination; mutability; good memory; receptivity; reciprocity; sensitivity; awareness of cycles; intuition; feminine strength; good rhythm

Vices: Overly emotional; inability to perceive reality; extreme subjectivity; gullibility; instability; lunacy; impractical dreams; weak personality; faulty memory; idleness; radical mood swings; insensitive; obsessive tendencies; compulsive tendencies

Symbols: Diffused light; silver; a mirror; incenses; a bowl of water; dagger; fan; essential oils; triangle of evocation

Commandment: You shall not bear false witness against your neighbor (Exodus 20:16)

Sermon on the Mount: Blessed are those who mourn, for they will be comforted (Matthew 5:4)

Angel of the Apocalypse and the Churches: Sixth Star and Lampstand, and the message to the angel of the church in Philadelphia (Revelation 3:7–13)

The Foundation of Creation

The word Yesod means "foundation" and connotes reciprocity. Yesod appears on the Middle Pillar in between Tiferet and Malkut. Much like the idea of a foundation of a building, which serves as an interface between the earth and the structure, Yesod serves as the foundation of the Tree of

Life—the interface of the Sefirot above with the Sefirah Malkut below. According to the Kabbalah, it is called the foundation of the palace of lights, and just as the foundation of a building lends stability to the structure, so Yesod-foundation gives stability to the palace of lights.

Yesod receives the influx of ruhaniyut and shefa from all the Sefirot above it and distributes it to Malkut, imbuing Malkut with the life-power. The Thirty-Two Paths of Wisdom says that it "purifies the emanations," which is to say that it acts as a filter, diffusing the supernal light so that Malkut can receive it without being overwhelmed. The force of the influx of the supernal light and spiritual energies of the Sefirot flowing into Yesod is too intense to be received directly by Malkut; thus, Yesod absorbs the force of the influx and serves to measure the flow of ruhaniyut and shefa into Malkut.

This process of filtration and diffusion, according to the Thirty-Two Paths of Wisdom, "tests the decree of their structure and the inner essence of their unity, making it glow." What is received by Yesod is ideal and the ideal must be adjusted and refined before it can be practically applied and actualized. We may understand this within our own experience in terms of ideas formed in the mind. There is typically a vast difference between an initial idea conceived in the mind and its actual manifestation in the material world. In order to actually manifest an idea, it must first be developed and refined before it can be implemented. When it is actually manifested, it is not the idea itself that manifests, but a representation of the idea that has its roots in the original conception. In the same way, in the process of filtering and diffusing the supernal light, Yesod refines and develops the ideal into actual manifestation—the culmination of the triad of action.

As we discussed previously, Yesod represents the astral planes and, specifically, the subtle substance of the astral planes, which is called the astral light. This is a curious substance that shares in the nature of both mind and matter. Essentially, it is the substance of consciousness itself at the point of transition between what we call mind and matter—matter simply being a denser manifestation of consciousness. Thus, the astral light is the subtle substance within and behind matter—the subtle substance within and behind all material objects and the material universe (Asiyah). The astral planes are, thus, the matrix of light upon which the material universe is founded—the level of consciousness where mind and matter merge.

Fundamentally, the astral light is the subtle medium in which spiritual forces from the higher planes take shape and come into substantial being on an inner level, which then becomes translated into actual manifestation on an outer level in the material plane. Everything that comes into being or transpires in the material plane first comes into being and transpires in the astral planes; thus everything in the material plane has a representation in the astral light. Although the concept of the Zelem, our ideal or heavenly image, typically refers to the supernal image of our Neshamah, it may also be used as a reference to our ideal image in the astral light or the astral body. It is this subtle body that is the foundation of the body of light and that serves as the subtle matrix of the material body.

Knowledge and understanding of Yesod, and the ability to consciously bring about changes at the level of the astral planes, is therefore the secret key to any form of magic designed to take effect in the material world. It is also the basis of prophecy, for if one is able to look and see what is occurring in the astral, one will know what is going to transpire in the material world.

In the provisional teaching on the inner planes, the astral planes are divided into the upper, middle, and lower astral planes. The upper astral represents worlds and realms under the influence of the divine powers, and the first two heavens appear in the upper astral, Vilon (the veil) and Rakiya (the firmament). The worlds and realms of the upper astral are inhabited by the spirits of saints, holy angels, and all manner of righteous spirits that serve the divine will. The worlds and realms of the upper astral are radiant and glorious and are a delightful experience in consciousness.

The middle astral is also luminous, although less luminous than the upper astral. Its worlds and realms are under the dominion of the admixed or titanic powers, such as the lesser gods and goddesses of pagan faith. They are inhabited by mythical beings, planetary spirits, elementals, and spiritual beings-forces of similar natures. These spiritual beings-forces are neither exclusively good nor evil, as they do not necessarily facilitate or oppose the divine will. They act according to their own self-interests, sometimes in harmony with the divine plan and other times opposing it.

In this sense, the worlds and realms of the middle astral are very similar to our human world, which may or may not serve the divine kingdom.

The lower astral is a darker region of the astral, composed of worlds and realms dominated by demonic and chaotic powers. The lower astral is populated with evil and unclean spirits, dark and hostile forces, chaotic beings and the various monstrous apparitions of dark legends (hungry ghosts, dark wraiths, goblins, vampiric spirits, and such). The abodes of hades, the seven hells, and all of the dominions of chaos exist in the lower astral, some dimensions of which are akin to an anti-astral universe, and are said to be "outside of this cosmos." In terms of the darker abodes of the lower astral, as the saying goes, "Fools rush in where angels fear to tread!"

According to the masters of the Tradition, there is a constant friction between the spiritual beings-forces in the astral, especially between the beings-forces of the middle and lower astral, which struggle with one another to dominate the minds and hearts of human beings and, thus, to hold dominion over the material world. As the upper, middle, and lower astral planes all intersect in the astral earth, this conflict of cosmic forces transpires constantly in the astral dimension of the earth. Specifically, it takes place in the human mind and heart that remains under the influence of cosmic ignorance. The weave of interrelationships and interactions between these spiritual beings-forces and their dominions can prove quite complex and confusing, as can the politics, alliances, and struggles between human peoples and nations all striving for their own self-interests and ambitions. Their movements are, on the one hand, directly reflected in the masses of unenlightened humanity who tend to live unconsciously under their dominion; and, on the other hand, their movements are determined by the thoughts and emotions entertained in human minds and hearts. Thus there is something of a reciprocal relationship between the beings-forces in the astral dimension and beings-forces in the material dimension.

According to the Kabbalah, the balance of spiritual forces in Yesod is determined by the thoughts, feelings-emotions, words, and deeds of human beings. Thus, the astral planes are essentially the radiance of human consciousness, and specifically, the product of the creative imagination in humanity. If one realizes that mind and matter are not as separate as many might think and that radical changes in the material world can be brought about purely through the mind itself, then one will understand that the secret behind prophecy and magic is in the creative imagination. More importantly, one will understand that it matters a great deal what thoughts we entertain in our minds and what imaginations we entertain in our hearts, for by these little nothings our own fates and fortunes, and the fate of the world, are determined. The foundation of creation is the power of desire-energy in us and the creative imagination that directs it.

The One-Who-Lives

Understanding the Sefirah Yesod as the astral light, which ebbs and flows, and as the astral planes, which span the upper, middle, and lower astral, one will realize that the appearance of Yesod is constantly changing. The association of Levanah with its cycles reflects this, as do the three variations of the divine name corresponding to Yesod—Shaddai, El Shaddai and Shaddai El Chai.

Shaddai means "Almighty," El Shaddai means "God Almighty," and Shaddai El Chai translates as "Almighty Living God." Shaddai is the holy root of all three names by which Yesod is known, and it is spelled with three letters in Hebrew, Shin (ש)-Dalet (ד)-Yod ('). Shin, as we have seen, is the glyph of the fiery intelligence or Shekinah. Dalet is a door or passageway, suggesting a point of entrance and an exit. Yod is a window through which light and air passes, and is the number ten, representing the essence of the ten Sefirot.

Shaddai as Yesod therefore indicates that Yesod is the door or passageway through which the divine presence and power enters into actual creation and that the appearance of the divine presence is dependent upon the flow of spiritual energies from the Sefirot. Shaddai equals 314, as does the name of the archangel Metatron when the Nun is counted as fifty. This correspondence alludes to the connection between Da'at and Yesod and the idea of the supernal light as the secret source of the astral light. Essentially, the ultimate purpose of Yesod is to reflect and transmit the supernal light into creation via the astral planes. However, Yesod is only able to directly reflect and transmit the influx of the supernal light when there are holy vessels in Malkut able to receive it. The vessels in Malkut are human beings and, thus, the appearance of Yesod is determined by the state of humanity—specifically, the state of human consciousness.

You will recall the legend of Enoch who is said to have been transformed into Metatron—according to Genesis, "Enoch walked with God." The divine name used in this verse is Elohim, corresponding to Binah and the upper Shekinah. When it is said that Enoch "walked" with God, what is meant is that he was able to bring down the supernal presence and power of the Sefirot and embody it, and being transformed by that fiery intelligence, he was taken up in divine rapture. This indicates the power in human beings to invoke the spiritual energies of the Sefirot, which only manifests when there are human beings who make themselves vessels of the supernal light-presence.

As we have seen, the three pillars of the Tree of Life represent three different modes in which the divine presence can appear—mercy (peaceful), judgment (wrathful), and compassion (blissful), corresponding to Hesed, Gevurah, and Tiferet, respectively. The appearance of Yesod as Shaddai is the manifestation of Yesod under the influence of judgment (wrathful), and the appearance of Yesod as El Shaddai is the manifestation of Yesod under the influence of mercy (peaceful). When there is a dynamic balance between judgment and mercy and Yesod is under the influence of compassion (blissful), it is called Shaddai El Chai.

We may understand this in terms of the upper, middle, and lower astral planes and the spiritual forces with which human beings link themselves. When human beings invoke the divine powers and attach themselves to the divine spirit, Yesod is established as El Shaddai, God Almighty, and the divine powers flowing through the upper astral hold the balance of dominion in the astral earth. When human beings do not invoke the Divine powers, but rather link themselves to spiritual beings-forces of the lower astral (the klippot), then Yesod appears as Shaddai, the Almighty, and the dark and hostile forces come into dominion in the astral earth. Yesod is established as Shaddai El Chai, the Almighty Living God, when among human beings there is a balance between those who seek the light and those who live in darkness, and neither the forces of light nor the forces of darkness hold dominion in the astral earth. In the present state of human evolution, this latter is the ideal, for mass humanity cannot endure a complete dominion of darkness and, as yet, is incapable of withstanding the full influx of the supernal light. For this reason, the tzaddikim labor to maintain the balance between the forces of light and darkness on earth and seek to preserve the human life-wave until such time as a larger segment of humankind is ready to receive the fullness of the supernal light.

As we have said, the divine name of a Sefirah is the manifestation of the Sefirah at the level of Atzilut, the archangel is its manifestation at the level of Beriyah, and the order of angels is its manifestation at the level of Yetzirah. Therefore, when initiates of the Kabbalah seek to shift the balance in the play of spiritual forces in the astral planes, they chant the divine names and invoke the archangels and orders of angels that correspond to the change they wish to bring about. This forms links between the universes and planes, for the power of the divine name is brought down into the archangel, and the power of the archangel is brought down into the order of angels—thus forming a flow from the supernal and spiritual planes into the higher vital, mental, and astral planes. The initiate is the link or channel in the material plane, and, thus the flow of divine presence and power is linked or channeled from Atzilut into Asiyah, and miracles happen.

We may consider this method in terms of the three divine names of Yesod. When an initiate seeks to invoke justice or judgment, he or she will chant the divine name of Shaddai, and this will shape the manifestation of Gabriel and the Kerubim, which, as we shall see, have both peaceful and wrathful appearances. When invoking the flow of the divine presence and power through the Middle Pillar, the initiate will intone Shaddai El Chai, seeking a dynamic balance of mercy and severity. But when an initiate seeks to invoke mercy or grace, he or she will chant the divine name of El Shaddai. If greater force is needed or the initiate has a specific aim in mind for which the spiritual energy of other Sefirot are needed, then he or she will join the invocation of Yesod with the invocation of other Sefirot. When the divine name of Yesod is used in Sefirotic invocations, it quite literally serves as the foundation of the invocation and determines its basic nature, whether of the Pillar of Mercy, Pillar of Severity, or Pillar of Compassion.

According to the Tradition, from the time of Enoch until the time of the prophet Moses, no one called upon the name of Yahweh; God was called upon by the name of El Shaddai. Thus, El Shaddai is the name by which the patriarchs and matriarchs invoked the divine presence and power and, among the divine names of the Sefirot, it is said to be the most accessible, along with the name of Malkut, Adonai.

There are specific spiritual gifts associated with every divine name so that, if an aspirant chants a divine name frequently, he or she may acquire the corresponding spiritual gifts. The spiritual gifts associated with Shaddai are prophetic dreams and the ability to interpret dreams, as we see with the attribute of the patriarch Joseph to Yesod. Because it is said that El Shaddai was the primary name called upon until the time of Moses and the prophets and we are told the name is associated specifically with dreams and dream interpretation, we know that, before Moses, prophecy occurred primarily through dreams and not waking visions. When it is said that Shaddai is the most accessible of the divine names, it indicates that all human beings can receive divine guidance through dreams and that the astral planes are the first and primary experience of the inner planes in early stages of development upon the path. One could say that Shaddai El Chai is the one-who-lives in our dreams and who speaks in our dreams when we call upon the name.

The Delight of Dreams

Yesod is called the "dream center" and, as we know, is intimately connected with Da'at, the hidden Sefirah, which represents our ability to communicate our intelligence. Yesod is also associated with the genital region of the human body, which indicates that Yesod is fundamentally desire-energy. Thus, dreams are a communication of our intelligence and are the expression of our desire through our creative imagination.

Dreams are a great mystery and they are many things. Everyone dreams, although not everyone remembers his or her dreams. Many dreams are of a purely personal subconscious nature, reflecting mundane life, our desires and fears in the mundane sphere, yet all dreams have a connection with the astral. What we would call nightmares and our darker dreams are linked with the lower astral, and those that are somewhat brighter are linked to the middle astral. When dreams take on a more spiritual content and there is greater lucidity in dreams, it is often linked to the upper astral. Sometimes dreams can become portals through the astral planes to the higher planes; when this happens, they are called visions.

The Kabbalah says that, when we sleep, our soul departs the body much as at the time of death. However, in sleep a subtle and vital connection remains between the body and soul, whereas in death the connection between the body and soul is completely severed. For this reason the sages of wisdom have said that sleep and dream are "one-sixtieth the power of death." When the soul departs the body in sleep, it passes into worlds and realms beyond the physical and comes into contact with spiritual beings-forces, just as it does in the afterlife states. There is also a similar dissolution in consciousness and shift into a more subtle body of consciousness, as in death. Accordingly, the souls of the faithful and elect who worship God in spirit and truth, and who invoke the divine powers and attach themselves to the Spirit of the Lord, are drawn in ascent toward the heavenly abodes and the embrace of the beloved. On the other hand, those who cleave to the other side or are attached to the sphere of the lesser gods cannot ascend beyond the lower planes and are bound below. Thus the Kabbalah speaks of spiritual beings-forces that seek to deceive the soul and prevent its ascent into the heavenly abodes and world of supernal light in dream and sleep, as at the time of death.

The astral and all planes of consciousness below the causal plane are inherently deceptive, as they are the product of the cosmic illusion-power. To pass beyond the dominion of cosmic ignorance and the cosmic forces of ignorance, the soul must first pass through the astral and lower planes, which are their domains. As the cosmic forces of ignorance dominate the mundane sphere, if one's desire is only for things of the world, then the soul cannot pass beyond the dominion of cosmic ignorance that manifests as the lower planes—the astral, mental, and higher vital planes.

Understanding this, one will realize that schools of thought are mistaken that propose that all dreams inherently convey deeper wisdom or that all dreams represent the communication of the inner or higher self. Rather, dreams reflect the state of the soul or the state of consciousness. Unless the divine intelligence and Neshamah are part of one's life, they are not part of one's dreams. Death reflects life and dream reflects life. The spiritual beings-forces we encounter in dream and death correspond to those with which we link ourselves in waking consciousness or life. Death and dream are merely shifts into the more subtle dimensions of the same consciousness; thus, afterlife experiences and dreams are radiant expressions of consciousness, whether enlightened or unenlightened.

It is the upper Ruach or divine intelligence that is able to enter and abide in the higher heavens and spiritual planes, and it is the Neshamah that is able to enter and join herself to the world of supernal light and experience the most intimate embrace of the beloved. When we link the lower Ruach and Nefesh with the upper Ruach and Neshamah, then the Christ-self and God speaks in our dreams and we experience contact with the tzaddikim and maggidim in our dreams. Such dreams are pure delight and open the way for the delight of delights—conscious repose of the soul in God and Godhead.

The visionary experience of the spiritual and supernal planes is a great blessing and most wonderful thing; yet the ability to maintain the continuity of self-awareness in the deepest state of sleep represents the essence of the supreme attainment, for the highest meditative state and the deepest sleep state are one and the same. Therefore, the deepest sleep state is an experience of the most subtle and sublime level of consciousness. However, in the deep sleep state the ordinary person falls unconscious and is unable to recognize this inmost nature of being. The inmost nature is Ain Sof—the infinite or bornless one—and in recognition and realization of the inmost nature of being, we are united with the Infinite.

The recognition of the inmost nature of being corresponds to the truth body of Melchizedek. Thus, the truth body corresponds to the deepest sleep state, the glorified body corresponds to the dream state, and the manifestation body corresponds to waking consciousness in the experience of the tzaddik. As the perfect Tzaddik abides in the body of truth, it is said that the perfect tzaddikim no longer have a need to dream, just as they no longer have a need to incarnate. Such is the nature of enlightenment and liberation—the resurrection and ascension of Gnosticism.

The ability to shift one's center of consciousness into the subtle body, consciously enter into the astral planes, and ascend into the higher planes, takes a great deal of kavvanah-concentration and energy, and thus to do so at will consistently takes much time and practice. The same is true of lucid dreaming and visionary dreams in which one is able to pass through dream into the inner planes. Long before one develops the capacity to transfer one's consciousness into a subtle body in meditation and ritual, one is likely to experience lucid dreams and visionary dreams. As a matter of fact, it is quite common that lucid and spiritual dreams naturally arise the more one engages in daily spiritual practice and spiritual living. Likewise, with consistent spiritual practice and some understanding of the esoteric dimension of the Scriptures—the Kabbalah—through one's dreams, one will be able to look and see the movement of spiritual beings-forces within and behind the circumstances, situations, and events of one's life. Even the most unenlightened dreams communicate tikkune to be done upon the soul if one knows how to interpret them, and those who seek the indwelling Christ and follow in the way of Christ-presence will find divine guidance appearing more and more in their dreams. In the experience of initiates, dreams are often the first conscious contact they have with the tzaddikim and maggidim of the inner planes, and the answer to prayers and the revelation of secret mysteries often come through dreams. It is simply a matter of opening oneself to divine grace.

Methods for development of consciousness beyond the body or transference of consciousness into a subtle body and methods for generation of lucid and visionary dreams are typically practiced together in the Tradition, as the development of one corresponds to the development of the other and they tend to facilitate one another. In such practices the role of the magical art assumes a significant place in the unfolding of self-realization, for whether in dream, or astral projection, one must know how to put all spirits to the test to see if they are from the divine or if they come from the other side. In the passage of the soul through the lower planes, this is essential for, as we have said, the lower planes are inherently a sphere of deception. It is the magical rituals of the Tradition that teach initiates how to test the spiritual beings-forces they encounter, and how to banish unclean and evil spirits and invoke the divine powers.

The foundation of these practices is spiritual study and contemplation, prayer, and meditation, through which the mind and heart are filled with heavenly and divine things and our desire is directed toward the kingdom of heaven, which is to say inward and upward—Godward. All developments of higher consciousness are dependent upon the direction of our desire-energy. To the degree we are able to shift the balance inward, we naturally and spontaneously experience higher levels of consciousness. As the masters of the Tradition have said, we must learn how to be in the world but not of the world, which is to say that we must learn to live from within the Christ center and no longer live only on the surface, grasping at limited name and form. One who is able to do this will not experience the sting of death, but will consciously be able to ascend to a higher plane of existence when the time of transition comes. It is this that is meant when Lord Yeshua says to us that we must acquire the resurrection while we live if we are to experience it when we die. All wisdom traditions agree on this point—although the term for the resurrection may differ from one tradition to another.

Dying, Death, and the Afterlife— The Apocalypse of the Soul

Yesod is called Depth of West. On the sacred circle, the western quarter is associated with dying and death. According to the Zohar, the Tree of Life holds dominion by day, and when the sun sets in the gate of the west and night comes, the Tree of Death rules the world. This alludes to the correspondence of sleep and death, both of which are understood as the departure of the soul from the body. It also alludes to the intimate connection between Yesod and Da'at, as Da'at is the gate in between the Tree of Life and the other side, or the tree of death.

With Da'at, you will recall our discussion of the apocalypse, which actually means "revelation." Apocalypse is an apt term for dying and death, as the process of dying and death is a progressive revelation of our inmost being when the gross and subtle levels of consciousness dissolve, which are akin to veils that conceal our true nature. Essentially, we die as we have lived and the afterlife experience reflects the life our soul has departed from. More than our exterior life, death and the afterlife experience reflect our interior life—our intentions in life and our state of consciousness. Up until the actual event of death, it is always possible to bring about a change in consciousness and, thus, a change in our experience of death and the afterlife states. More than anything else in life, it is our state of consciousness at the moment of death that holds the greatest influence upon the afterlife experience.

It is curious that "apocalypse," the Greek word for revelation, has come to mean darkness, horror, and destruction in our language—as originally it was meant as a promise of redemption and a deeper revelation of the path of the great ascension. That the apocalypse implies something negative to us merely reflects that we tend to value and identify ourselves too much with the wrong things and do not understand who and what we truly are. The same may be said of the great fear of death in our culture. We fear death because we value and identify with name and form too much, and with the material world and material possessions. Consequently, we do not know the soul of light in us and our bornless nature, and death appears to our eyes as a great adversary or evil.

The idea that death is the ultimate end and that there is nothing after death is mistaken, just as is the idea that all souls automatically enter the light. In truth, death is but a transition into a new level of experience—a new beginning—which can be a passage into the light or through great darkness, all depending upon the state of the soul or consciousness. As we said of Da'at, that it assumes an appearance relative to the observer or the one experiencing it, so it is with death. In the same way life, holds many possibilities, so also do death and the afterlife.

The teachings of the Kabbalah on dying, death, and the afterlife experience, along with sleep and dreaming, could fill an entire volume, and most likely there would be much left unsaid. Here, we may give only a brief outline of the most basic ideas upon which these teachings are founded. Essentially, dying and death is a process of the dissolution of gross and subtle elements of consciousness into the primordial nature of consciousness. This primordial nature of being-consciousness is Ain Sof. Thus, dying and death is a return of the soul to God and Godhead. If the soul is able to recognize Ain Sof, specifically Ain Sof Or, and to realize its unity with the Infinite, then the soul attains repose in God and the Godhead. However, if the soul is not able to recognize and realize the sacred unity, then this process of dissolution leads to a process of reincarnation once again, and the cycles of gilgulim continue. Because dying and death is a process of return to God and Godhead and holds the potential of the enlightenment and liberation of the soul, it can be transformed into a vehicle of self-realization through an understanding of the process and spiritual practice. In the eyes of the Gnostic initiate, it presents a wonderful opportunity and is viewed as the final adventure life offers.

According to the Tradition, the process of dying begins the instant we contact the cause of our death. The process of dying can be short or long, depending on the cause. The process of dying from a sudden accident is very brief, while in the case of some forms of terminal illness, it can span a larger segment of one's life. That the Tradition says dying begins at the moment we contact the cause of our death indicates that what we call life and death overlap and are interwoven, and it alludes to the overlapping and interweaving of the universes and planes of consciousness. It also indicates the true nature of our experience of reality—that we are always in transition from one state of consciousness to another. The reality of our experience is always changing and we are always changing—nothing is static or fixed in creation.

In the case of a prolonged terminal illness, we see the process of dying most clearly. As the person becomes increasingly ill, the physical life ebbs away. The person can engage in fewer and fewer physical activities, often material possessions are progressively falling away from them and, unfortunately, fewer friends come to visit. Activities, possessions, friends, and such, these are all extensions of the body and life, and as the process of death unfolds, they fall away and dissolve. It is as though the world of the dying person is shrinking—the circle of life closing in on its center. By the time the day of death comes, in effect, the world of the dying person is the size of the room in which his or her deathbed is found.

On the deathbed, when the actual dying process unfolds, what transpires is the final dissolution of the gross and subtle matrix that joins the soul and the body—dissolution of the gross and subtle elements. These are the elements of earth (form), water (feeling), fire (perception), air (intellect), and spirit-space (consciousness). Earth dissolves into water, water into fire, fire into air, and air dissolves into spirit-space. Then spirit-space dissolves into itself, which is to say it dissolves into its inmost nature (Ain-nothingness). The dissolution of earth, water, fire, and air represents the outer dissolution or dissolution of gross elements, and the dissolution of spirit-space represents the inner dissolution or dissolution of the subtle elements.

The Outer Dissolution

When the earth element dissolves into the water element, the body loses strength and all energy is drained out of it. It becomes difficult to move and the body feels very dense and heavy. One cannot get up or sit up on one's own; it becomes impossible to even hold up one's head. The pallor of death sets in and it becomes difficult to open and close the eyes. The mind is agitated and may become delirious, but drowsiness comes over us and offers some peace. This means that the energy of the earth element is shifting out of the body and is no longer providing a foundation for consciousness in the body. Inwardly, one may experience visions of shimmering mirages and it is not uncommon to see spirits or images of those who have died.

When the water element dissolves into fire, we experience a loss of control of all bodily fluids. One might experience a runny nose, tears may form in the eyes, and one might become incontinent. Then dryness of the mouth, throat, eyes, and nose follows, and one might experience a great thirst. A tremor or twitching may come into the body, and bodily sensations begin to fade away. One may experience an oscillation between pleasure and pain, hot and cold, and the mind may become frustrated, cloudy, anxious, and irritable. One might see visions inwardly of ethereal wisps of a mist-like substance swirling in ascent, much like smoke from a stick of incense.

When the fire element dissolves into air, the experience of dryness intensifies, and all warmth moves from our extremities to the heart. There is no more drinking and eating. Our memory of our family and friends fades; we forget their names and are unable to recognize them. Sight and sound become increasingly confusing, and we no longer perceive things outside of us. Some inwardly behold the flight of sparks departing, like the sparks ascending from a campfire that is stoked.

When the air element dissolves into spirit-space, it becomes more difficult to breathe. It seems as though breath is escaping us. We may begin to pant and our breath may become raspy. Inhalations become increasingly shorter and exhalations increasingly longer; the eyes may roll upward and all volitional movement ceases. The mind is no longer aware at all of the external world. The feeling of contact with the world vanishes and the mind becomes dazed. Visions tend to arise in the mind. For those who have a great deal of negativity in their lives, dreadful and terrible images may appear, and darker moments of life may be reflected in the mind. For those who have lived in a loving and merciful way, the visions may be heavenly, radiant, and blissful, and they might meet loved ones, saints, and angels in their visions. When this dissolution is complete, it is the point at which clinical medicine would pronounce a person "dead." However, on a psychic and spiritual level, actual death does not occur until after the inner dissolution that follows this outer dissolution, typically about twenty or so minutes following clinical death.

The Inner Dissolution

The inner dissolution corresponds to the dissolution of our most subtle thoughts and emotional states—the inner mental and vital being. Essentially, it is the reversal of the moment of our conception, when the white father seed united with the red mother seed and our soul-being was drawn into the womb through the play of karma (the law). According to the masters of the Tradition, the energy-essence of the father seed becomes rooted at the top of the head as the fetus develops and the mother seed becomes rooted in the base of the spine. These correspond to the descending and ascending force of the serpent power, the father seed being gentle and cool and the mother seed fierce and hot. In the process of dying, these seeds of energy move into the heart center of the subtle body, and the subtle body dissolves into that center point.

When the father seed moves down the central channel into the heart center, there is an experience of brightness, as though the light of a full moon shone in a crystal-clear sky. The mind becomes extremely calm and clear—completely lucid—and all thought-forms resulting from fear, anger, or hate dissolve. Profound peace comes over the soul and there is no fear. When the mother seed moves up the central channel into the heart center, it is as though a brilliant sun shines in a clear sky and the soul experiences great bliss. All thoughtforms resulting from desire, lust, and greed vanish completely and no desire remains whatsoever. The experience of profound peace deepens all the more. The movement of these two seeds is called the white and red path, respectively, and corresponds to Hesed and Gevurah.

Once the father and mother seed meet in the heart center, what is called the black path unfolds. It is as though one becomes enshrouded in an abyss of blackness, akin to a cosmic womb, and the mind becomes free of all thoughts; ignorance and all forms of delusion come to an end. This is said to be Tiferet passing through Da'at into union with Keter (Ain). The black path is called perfect peace and culminates in the spontaneous dawn of the transparent light, like the light of the predawn sky. The entrance into the black path is the actual point of death and thus the conclusion of the dying process.

Although the description of the dying process may seem somewhat complicated, if one is aware of it and understands it, one can transform the dying process into a vehicle of self-realization, and thus experience the resurrection and ascension at the time of one's death. According to the masters of the Tradition, if at any point in the dying process one is able to merge oneself with the Holy Mother, the Son or the Bride, one can attain supernal or Messianic consciousness in that instant and be taken up in divine rapture. However, to do so, one must practice meditations of mystical union and the transference of consciousness in life, or have formed a vital link with an adept or master who might be able to help one accomplish it.

The Afterlife Above

The black path is akin to the void of primordial space that came into being from the tzimtzum at the outset of creation, and the afterlife states that arise following it reflect the emanation of Or Ain Sof in the process of creation. According to the masters of the Tradition, the soul abides in the black path three or four days before the afterlife states actually begin to unfold. In the case of the ordinary person, the first, most subtle states arise unnoticed. They correspond to the Olamot of Adam Kadmon, Atzilut, and Beriyah. Unless a soul has formed some connection with these higher levels through spiritual practice in previous lives, the person remains unconscious when these most subtle levels appear. Thus, the initial states in the afterlife experience arise only for initiates who have labored to experience them in life through daily spiritual practice, specifically, the practice of meditation.

The first and most subtle state that arises is the inmost essence of the supernal light, which is called the transparent light state. This state corresponds with Keter and the initial phase of the universe of Adam Kadmon—the primordial human one. It is said to be like the light of the predawn sky and is the inmost essence of the soul of light, which emanates from Or Ain Sof. No one can describe this light of primordial awareness, but a master of the light transmission who embodies something of this most subtle aspect of the Christ presence can help a practitioner recognize it in meditation. The experience of the transparent light state can last as long as an initiate is able to abide and rest undistracted in this pure primordial awareness. This is the secret essence of the truth body of Melchizedek and the ultimate fruition of the resurrection and ascension—the highest grade of enlightenment, corresponding to the grade of the Ipsissimus. In the recognition of this transparent light as the radiant nature of one's holy soul, the soul is joined to God and the Godhead in perfect repose and becomes Christos in full. Yeshua Messiah speaks of this state of self-realization in the Book of Revelation when he says, "I am the Alpha (Aleph) and the Omega (Tau), the first and the last, the beginning and the end" (Revelations 22:13).

If the initiate becomes distracted or falls unconscious, then the soul passes out of the transparent light state and another less subtle and sublime afterlife state arises. The transparent light becomes a brilliant white light, and the white light condenses into points of light, which become spheres of light. The spheres of light give off emanations in the form of rays of light. Thus the essence of the world of supernal light appears filled with rainbow glory—a universe of endless light, sound, and color. This does not arise apart from the practitioner, but rather from within the heart center of the body of light in which the soul manifests in the initial afterlife states. The initiate is a being of light-energy in a universe of light-energy, and if he or she is able to recognize this vision of pure radiant awareness as the radiant nature of his or her holy soul, then he or she will experience the attainment of the divine fullness and be liberated through unification in Christ with God. The vision of pure radiant awareness corresponds to the rectification of the universe of Adam Kadmon and the inner matrix of the truth body of Melchizedek, and it corresponds to self-realization of the grade of magus.

If the initiate is not able to attain recognition in this state, another afterlife state unfolds, which is called the great vision of the light-presence. The matrix of light becomes the light-forms of the divine names and Partzufim. The divine images of the Holy Mother, Yeshua Messiah, and the Bride appear, along with images of the holy ones—the prophets and apostles of God. Then the archangels and orders of angels appear, and the seven heavens—the whole divine kingdom and great luminous assembly. It is a vision of the world of supernal light, the mystical body of Christ. This great vision of the light-presence corresponds to Atzilut and the outer matrix of the truth body, which is the glorified body of Melchizedek. It is the self-realization of the grade of magister templi, and the initiate who is able to recognize the sacred unity of his or her holy soul and the world of supernal light is liberated from the cycles of the gilgulim and taken up into the supernal abode.

This divine vision is a dazzling brilliance and the sound vibration is incredibly tremendous. It is like the light of billions of suns and the sound of tens of thousands of thunders. Unless the soul is able to attain unification, dread and terror may set in and the soul will fall unconscious. Then the great vision of the light-presence will transform into the vision of dark radiance. This is a vision of the tree of death and fierce divine presence. The angels of wrath appear, the seven hells and abodes of chaos, and all of the legions of the great void and chaos. It is the very same divine presence, but beheld by the mind and heart filled with fear. If the initiate is able to recognize the nondual nature of the light and the darkness, and that this vision is the radiant nature of the holy soul, then he or she will be delivered and taken up into the abode of supernal light. This vision corresponds to the universe of Beriyah, where the dominion of darkness comes into being, and to the inner matrix of the body of glory, the secret of which is the union of the light and the darkness.

The vision of dark radiance can easily be overwhelming, and if the soul is overwhelmed, then the vision of the infinite arises. The divine kingdom and the demonic kingdom appear together, and all worlds and realms in between the world of supernal light and the dominion of darkness—the whole matrix of creation fills the vision of endless space, and the initiate *sees* with the light of Adam Ha-Rishon from beginning to the end of creation. This divine vision is completely beyond mortal imagination. Every possibility of creation is present in it—from the light and great ascension to darkness and the pit of destruction. It is much like the vision of the apocalypse of St. John, except it is not centered upon the planet earth but rather the entire universe and all worlds and realms that are in it.

The soul is endowed with a great power of clairvoyance in this vision, and is completely empathic and telepathic. The soul can *see directly* into all mysteries of the soul, creation, and God, and is able to perceive all past and future incarnations. Every teaching, initiation, or instruction of spiritual practice one has ever received is clearly recalled, and the initiate may even intuit secret mysteries never before disclosed. The vision of the infinite is also called the vision of the great name of God, for all of the Olamot from Adam Kadmon to Asiyah appear, which correspond to the four letters of the holy name.

This divine vision represents a great opportunity for enlightenment and liberation for souls that have established themselves in the holy sanctuary in previous lives. If a soul is able to recognize this great magical display as the radiance of the soul of light and, thus, unify itself with Christ in God, then the soul will be liberated from the gilgulim and taken up into the abode of supernal light. Likewise, divine grace may empower remembrance of the holy soul and an initiate may experience divine rapture through grace at this point in the afterlife states. This vision corresponds to the outer matrix of the glorified body of Melchizedek, which is the body of manifestation or emanation. If this divine vision passes without recognition, then the soul assumes an astral body akin to the image of itself in the life from which it has departed, moving once again into the currents of the gilgulim.

In the case of most ordinary human beings, the initial cycles of the afterlife experience are like a lightening flash in the mind, passing away the very instant they arise. The positive karma generated by spiritual practice and spiritual living that will allow the soul to attain self-realization has not been developed in previous lives. These states primarily relate to the faithful and elect who have sojourned the path to enlightenment as taught by one of the world wisdom traditions and who have labored for the development and evolution of their soul-being. The appearance of these visions, of course, will reflect the knowledge and understanding of the individual experiencing them and will assume forms corresponding to his or her respective Tradition.

The Afterlife Below

The afterlife experience for most souls begins in the universe of Yetzirah or the astral planes, specifically, the astral dimension of the earth. Arising out of the black path, the soul passes into the brilliant white light, falls unconscious, and regains consciousness in the astral earth where it assumes an astral body. The experience is much like ordinary dreaming in which a person falls asleep and, from the deep sleep state, dreams arise, but the person forgets that they are asleep and dreaming. In a similar way, when the soul first arises out of the black path and appears in the astral earth, the person does not remember that he or she has died.

This astral body is far less energetic and luminous than the body of light in the previous afterlife states, although it possesses all senses and is extremely light, subtle, and very mobile, and is said to be ten times more lucid than the physical body. It has a basic capacity of clairvoyance and is empathic and telepathic to a certain degree, though the clairvoyant capacity is not under conscious control. Until the afterlife experience, called the judgment, this body resembles the person of the former life in the prime of youth. It is in perfect health without any defect whatsoever (even if the person suffered a physical disability in life). Because it has no physical basis, this body can pass through solid objects, and in it one is able to transport oneself to a person or place by merely thinking of it. Unaware one is in this subtle body, however, and unaware that one has died, most movement is not under one's conscious volition. In this sense, this phase of the afterlife experience is dream-like, for just as dreams occur outside of an ordinary person's conscious control, so also does this afterlife experience.

Essentially, this cycle of the afterlife experience is the wandering of the soul in the astral earth parallel to the material earth, so that the person sees the events transpiring in the material dimension but is unable to interact with the material world. The soul tends to go to places that are familiar and tries to visit loved ones and friends. However, except perhaps for some children or rare individuals endowed with psychic perception, one cannot be seen by the living. The person will try to be seen and noticed by people and try to touch those who are friends and family, but to no avail. The person will try to affect things in the material plane or to use their material possessions and find that he or she cannot. Powerless, he or she will witness the mourning of family and friends, and see preparations for his or her funeral and the dispensing of his or her possessions. Many individuals swiftly realize that they are dead, but for others, a powerful denial may set in. In extreme cases, the spirit of the dead can linger around the body and possessions for many weeks, sometimes even for many years. While in this state a person will visit every place they ever traveled in life and will recall events of life with great clarity as though they were there.

This experience is extremely intense, for with the clairvoyant power of this astral body, one experiences the thoughts and emotions of others. If one has lived a kind and compassionate life, this could be a very pleasurable experience. However, if one has caused a lot of trouble to others and harmed others, it can be a distinctly horrible experience. One is extremely sensitive in this state and one feels the effects of everything one has done to others—all the pleasure and pain amplified.

In the astral earth, there are all manner of spirits, including the spirits of others who have died, and thus one comes in contact with spirits as well. One is also equally sensitive to the energy of spirits and the kind of spirits one encounters directly corresponds to the spiritual beings-forces one is habitually linked with in life. This, too, can be either a wonderful or horrible experience, all depending upon the karmic continuum of the soul-being.

During this cycle of the afterlife experience, it is said that, every seven days, the soul relives its dying and death. The average duration of this cycle is said to be forty-nine days to one year, although it could be significantly shorter or far longer than that. Some souls become earthbound for many years and some for centuries before moving on. Essentially, this cycle lasts until the soul lets go of the past life and is ready to move on. When this happens, the soul passes into the afterlife experience called the judgment.

At this point, the soul encounters a great light-presence that assumes a form relative to the individual soul-being. This light-presence is accepting, warm, loving, and forgiving—it is all good. Essentially, it is the divine radiance of the Christ-self that is at one with God and Godhead. In this divine presence, one relives one's whole life in one's mind, integrating all knowledge and experience gained, while giving an account. If there is judgment, it does not come from the light-presence but from within oneself. If there is anything that cannot be forgiven, it is one's own inability to forgive oneself and others. This is well reflected in the Lord's Prayer and the saying of Lord Yeshua, "Blessed are the merciful, for they will receive mercy."

The judgment need not be a judgment; it all depends upon how we have lived. What it becomes is completely determined by the life we have lived. If we have acquired knowledge, understanding, and wisdom, served to uplift the human spirit, and have been loving, then it could well be a most blissful and wonderful experience. Conversely, if we have enacted evil and clung to darkness, we may encounter a presence of great wrath. Peaceful, blissful, or wrathful, it is all the radiance of our soul-being, the state of our own consciousness that we behold. From the judgment, some souls are taken up into the heavenly abodes, while others may enter into worlds and realms of the middle astral. Some wander in an astral dimension of the earth, in what might be called a *purgatory* state, and may then be taken up into one of the heavenly abodes or be reborn in the world once again. Some souls pass through one of the hells or abodes of chaos to purify the soul before the next incarnation. All of these states represent transitions toward the next material incarnation. Most souls return to the earth for physical incarnation; however, some souls pass into other worlds beyond this earth. Although a soul may pass into the highest heaven—the seventh heaven—until a soul attains supernal self-realization, it will eventually return to a material incarnation to continue its development and evolution.

Unlike the initial afterlife experiences in which the divine power spontaneously appears, once the soul enters into the astral phase of the afterlife, the divine powers only appear if the soul focuses his or her mind on them and invokes them. One must remember the divine powers to invoke them, which means that one must have formed a vital link with them in one's previous lives. The astral cycles of the afterlife offer many opportunities for enlightenment and liberation, for if one does invoke a divine name or Partzuf, an archangel, or an order of angels, they instantly appear and one's soul can be carried in ascent. If one has engaged in spiritual practice and spiritual living, such invocations will be a natural part of the afterlife experience and may potentially result in supernal consciousness. We also find the great virtue in having an incarnate tzaddik—for if the soul visits family and friends, then it will draw near unto the holy tzaddik who is likely to perceive the soul and render assistance.

While some initiates experience fruit in life from their spiritual practices and are granted many spiritual gifts or magic powers, some initiates experience very little in the way of fruition during their lifetime. For many, fruition of their life's labor in the great work comes only at the time of death and in the afterlife states that follow. This is reflected in the title of the Rosicrucian grade associated with Yesod, which is called Theoricus, implying knowledge without the generation of talents or spiritual gifts. According to the Zohar, there is great merit generated by one who seeks to acquire knowledge and who engages in spiritual practice without seeing any fruit in life, for it may well lead to a greater fruition at the time of the transition of the soul beyond the body. Death and the afterlife is the real revelation of the development and evolution of the soul-being, and as the Scriptures say, "To one who lives by faith, it will be accounted to him or her as righteousness."

The subject of dying, death, and the afterlife properly belongs to Yesod because the bulk of the afterlife experience is principally astral and corresponds to Da'at-Yesod on the Tree of Life. Essentially, the entire afterlife experience occurs within one's consciousness, but then so also does this life! Thus, the recognition of what appears as the radiant nature of one's holy soul is as much a part of Gnostic practice in life as it is in the afterlife states. This process we speak of in terms of death and the afterlife occurs in sleep and dreams; it is happening on a subtle level all the time, even in waking consciousness. If one wonders where the heavens and hells are, and all the worlds and realms of the inner planes, they all exist in the same space at the same time, right here and now. We exist in them and they exist in us. It is simply a matter of becoming fully conscious and developing a continuity of self-awareness throughout all states of consciousness. Then one will realize the metadimensional nature of creation and the sacred unity underlying it. This is, in essence, what Gnostics mean when they speak of the resurrection and ascension—an awakening to a greater reality.

The Prophet of the Apostle of Light

As it is written in the prophet Isaiah, "See, I am sending my messenger ahead of you, who will prepare your way; the voice of one crying out in the wilderness: 'Prepare the way of the Lord, make his paths straight.'"

John the Baptizer appeared in the wilderness, proclaiming a baptism of repentance for the forgiveness of sins. And people from the whole Judean countryside and all the people of Jerusalem were going out to him, and were baptized by him in the river Jordan, confessing their sins. Now John was clothed in camel's hair, with a leather belt around his waist, and he ate locusts and wild honey. He proclaimed, "The one who is more powerful than I is coming after me; I am not worthy to stoop down and untie the thong of his sandals. I have baptized you with water; but he will baptize you with the Holy Spirit." (Gospel of St. Mark 1:2–8)

The Kabbalah says that one does not have to withdraw from the world in order to seek higher states of consciousness and self-realization. In fact, in the case of most souls among the faithful and elect, the mission of their Neshamah demands a strong contact with the world as much as with the divine powers above. Yet the Kabbalah also says that there are souls of higher grades who enter that are not meant to have much contact with the mundane world, but whose mission is otherworldly and who are destined to withhold themselves from the mundane sphere. These latter are very rare and special tzaddikim who qualify for the title "maggid" (angelic) because their mission is akin to that of a great angel and their soul abides more in the heavens than in the body. According to the Tradition, John the Baptist was a holy tzaddik of this class, and thus he is often called the maggid of the Holy Gospel.

As we have said, the soul of Elijah was reincarnate as John the Baptist, and the Christian Kabbalah says that all of the great prophets sent forth a holy spark of their Neshamah into the soul of John, so that the divine fullness of the Baal Shem—the master of the name—would be incarnate in him. He was, himself, a great light-presence in the world, embodying the light of the succession of prophets who went before him, and yet it is written of John: "There was a man sent from God, whose name was John. He came as a witness to testify to the light, so that all might believe through him. He himself was not the light, but he came to testify to the light. The true light, which enlightens everyone, was coming into the world" (Gospel of St. John 1:6–9). According to a Christian midrash (story, myth, or legend) associated with this set of verses, John not only came to bear witness to the incarnation of the supernal light, the soul of the Messiah, but to serve as the opener of the way and midwife.

John was only six months older than Yeshua, and from his earliest youth was set apart and given to a Baal Shem of an assembly of prophets to be raised. He dwelled always in the wilderness, apart from mundane society and, until his imprisonment by Herod, never set foot in a town or city of the profane human establishment. Whatever teachings he received, he remembered from the very first instruction, and the way of the Merkavah came easily to him, as though it were child's play. Who else could be the holy tzaddik of the one who was to be first among humankind to be anointed with the supernal light of God?

When John and Yeshua stood together at the River Jordan, the great angels Metatron and Sandalfon stood with them, the seven archangels of the Christos formed a circle about them, the corresponding orders of holy angels formed a circle outside of that inner circle, and the souls of the righteous and spirits of the prophets also gathered around. It was as though John and Yeshua became a gate of supernal light in the material world. This is the visionary dimension of the baptism of Yeshua by John that is envisioned in Gnostic meditation upon the advent of the Messiah entering into the world.

A Christian midrash, which speaks of the baptism, says that, when the Spirit of the Messiah entered into Lord Yeshua, it awoke in St. Mary Magdalene too, and that the union of Lord Yeshua with the Holy Spirit was the union of the Bridegroom and Holy Bride on an inner level. Thus in the baptism, John is as a tzaddik presiding at a wedding. Accordingly, the wings of the great angels of Keter and Malkut are said to be the wedding canopy, and when *Mazzal Tov* (good luck) was proclaimed, it was good fortune for the world, completing the blessing of creation in the beginning when God said, "It is very good."

In the Christian Kabbalah, John the Baptist is the Partzuf (Partzuf below, personification or embodiment) of Yesod. First, because he is the tzaddik of the perfect master and Yesod is the Sefirah of the holy tzaddik;

second, because he is the tzaddik who presides over the wedding of the Bridegroom and Bride, and Yesod represents the union of the Bridegroom (Tiferet) and Holy Bride (Malkut). When Malkut is united with Tiferet, the supernal light of Keter is brought down. This is the very essence of holy baptism.

John the Baptist plays as central a role in Gnostic Christian invocations as do the Holy Mother and Bride. The Mother is often invoked and asked to help give birth to Christ in us, and the Holy Bride is invoked and asked to join our soul in complete unity with Christ. The spirit of John the Baptist is invoked to open the way and to serve as the midwife in our process of giving birth to the Christ consciousness. Likewise, when we seek knowledge of the way of the prophets and prophetic consciousness, John the Baptist is called upon. Many Gnostic meditations focus upon the image of John the Baptist in much the same way as upon the image of the Mother, Son, and Bride; the maggid of the Gospel is viewed inseparable from the divine incarnation, just as Yesod is inseparable from the Pillar of Compassion.

In Judaism, the spirit of Elijah is said to visit every rite of Milah (circumcision), and the soul of Elijah is said to come among the faithful at every Passover feast. In Gnostic Christian tradition, the Spirit of John is said to be present at every rite of baptism, and the Soul of John is said to attend every feast of the resurrection.

The Strength of the Almighty

The archangel Gabriel is the manifestation of Yesod in Beriyah. Gabriel literally means the "strength of God" or "God is my strength." Perhaps more than any other archangel, Gabriel reveals the enigmatic nature of angelic beings. Although we often project human ideals upon the archangels and angels, and all too often sentimentalize the angels, in truth they are other than human, and are otherworldly in nature. The motivation of the angels cannot be understood in human terms or mortal values. Although, at times, angels can be very helpful to human beings, they can also be very dangerous and even harmful. While they may serve human interests that are aligned with the divine will, just as often they may oppose human interests. Essentially, what angels are to us depends entirely upon our relationship with the divine.

Gabriel stands in the western quarter of the sacred circle, and while associated with love and devotion, Gabriel is also associated with darkness, death, and destruction. According to the Tradition, it was Gabriel who wrestled with Jacob at Peniel, wounding him on his thigh, and Gabriel enacted the destruction of the cities of Sodom and Gomorrah. When it says that the Lord sought to kill Moses following the revelation of the burning bush (Exodus 4:24), it is Gabriel who is said to have stalked Moses, assuming the form of a great dragon, akin to Leviathan. Yet, Gabriel is the archangel of the annunciation, who brings glad tidings to the Holy Mother and who proclaims the birth of the Holy Child to the shepherds. Gabriel is also said to be one of the two holy angels present at the resurrection and ascension. In the vision of Daniel, Gabriel is the man in white linen helped by Michael, and according to the Kabbalah, he is the man clothed in linen in the vision of Ezekiel. When St. Mary Magdalene was lost and wandering before her awakening, Gabriel acted as her guardian angel and is said to be the holy angel that bound the demons away when she was exorcised by the Lord. Gabriel is also credited with saving three holy men from a fiery furnace. Gabriel is said to be the guardian of the patriarch Joseph and, according to Islamic tradition, is the angel that spoke to the prophet Mohammed.

Gabriel is known as the Prince of Paradise (Tebel-Vilon), the first heaven, and is the ruler of the guardians of paradise and the great guardians of the continuum-covenant. He-she also has dominion over the cycles of the moon and the element of water, and is said to be a giver of dreams and visions. Gabriel is also said to be the watcher who stands guard at the gates of the abyss and the great angel who holds the keys to the pit of Abaddon (destruction). These attributes of archangel Gabriel well portray the enigmatic nature of angelic beings. The teachings on Gabriel are meant to remind initiates that the true nature of angelic beings will always be something of a mystery—a thing wise to remember when invoking them.

There are several images used in invocations of Gabriel. Perhaps the oldest is the image of a human, clothed in linen of brilliant white, with a body composed of pure fire. Another is the image of a great winged angel, in robes of amethyst with wings of rainbow glory. Gabriel is also envisioned in robes of blue with subtle hints of orange when invoked in correspondence with the elemental force of water. In a certain form of invocation, Gabriel is also envisioned in the image of a great dragon. All of these divine images allude to mysteries of Yesod in Beriyah. In the most basic invocations of Gabriel, the divine name of Shaddai El Chai is used and the chant *Gya Ko Ho Ge Ba Gabriel.*

Gabriel is often called to bring about divine revelation through dreams and visions, and for a deeper understanding of the prophets. In the Gnostic ritual most commonly used to consecrate the Holy Eucharist, the invocation of Gabriel plays a key part. He-she is also invoked to facilitate justice and for the guardianship of the continuum. Associated with the moon, Gabriel is also frequently invoked in lunar rites. As one of the four great angels of the sacred circle, Gabriel has many roles in the continuum.

The Guardians and the Gates

At the level of Yetzirah, the Sefirah Yesod manifests as the order of Kerubim. The word *Kerub* is closely associated with merkavah and *rakhav*, which means "to ride." Thus, Kerub connotes a vehicle, mode of transportation, or something ridden. This idea plays out when it is written, "God rode on a Kerub, and flew; he swooped down on the wings of the wind" (Psalm 18:10).

The images of two Kerubim appear on the ark of covenant in the holy of holies of the temple. In a verse mentioning them, there is another association of the Kerubim to the word Merkavah: ". . . also his plan for the golden chariot of the kerubim that spread their wings and cover the ark of covenant of the Lord" (1 Chronicles 28:18). When the ark of the covenant stood in the tabernacle and in the temple of King Solomon, it is said that the space in between the Kerubim was a point of focus for prophetic meditation. In speaking of the ark of the covenant, the Lord said to Moses, "There I will meet with you, and from above the mercy seat, from between the two Kerubim that are on the ark of covenant, I will deliver to you all my commandments for the Israelites" (Exodus 25:22). The images of the Kerubim had "little faces," which is to say the faces of children; the Kerubim faced one another and their wings stretched out to one another, so that they formed something of a gate. The ark contained the two stone tablets of the law, the original Torah scroll (which is called the "Tree of Life"), Aaron's rod that bloomed, and a portion of the heavenly manna that fed the children of Israel in the wilderness. The powerful spiritual emanations of the holy objects were focused between the Kerubim, so that a gate or portal was formed into the spiritual dimension. Thus, concentrating his or her mind in this space between the Kerubim, a prophet was able to enter into prophetic consciousness. With knowledge of the divine names, a prophet would even be able to bring spiritual powers of the upper worlds through this gate or portal.

This indicates that the Kerubim are gates from one dimension to another or from one world or realm to another and, as such, that they serve as vehicles between one dimension and another or as connections between dimensions, worlds, and realms of creation, but the Kerubim not only form the gates, they are also the guardians of the gates they form. This is indicated in the Scripture by the kerub that is said to be placed at the gate of the Garden of Eden, in whose hands is said to be a flaming sword that turns this way and that, so that no one should enter into paradise apart from God's will. Thus, the Kerubim are the gates and they are the guardians, the gate and guardian being one and the same. What is the nature of their guardianship? In passing through the gate, the soul will either endure the greater spiritual force on the other side of the gate or it will not. Such is the true nature of the divine protection of a gate or portal.

In the vision of Ezekiel, the Kerubim are said to be the appearance the Hayyot Ha-Kodesh assume, which indicates a very close association between the Hayyot and the Kerubim. This is reflected in the correspondence between Yesod and Da'at on the great tree, and the teaching that Da'at represents what is revealed of Keter. While the Kerubim on the ark of the covenant have one face each and their faces are those of little children, others among the Kerubim have four faces like the Hayyot—the face of a human being, the face of a lion, the face of an eagle, and the face of an ox. This alludes to the Kerubim as the "star gates" and "earth gates" through which emanations from the spiritual world are said to enter into the astral earth, and it places them in association with both the Ofhanim and Aralim.

In contemplating the Kerubim before the gate to the Garden of Eden and the Kerubim on the ark of the covenant, when it is said that John and Yeshua formed a gate of light at the time of the baptism, one cannot help but think of the Kerubim. Likewise, when one looks at the Tree of Life one cannot help but see the Pillars of Mercy and Severity as great Kerubim, the Pillar of Compassion being the gate of the ascension formed in between them. Accordingly, it is said by the masters of the Tradition that a kerub of mercy and kerub of judgment must stand together to form a gate, as the passage between dimensions, worlds, and realms requires both mercy and judgment.

Any time there is a shift or projection of consciousness from one dimension, world, or realm to another, the order of Kerubim is involved. As watchers in between worlds, the Kerubim are said to hold great knowledge of secret mysteries, like unto the Aralim (thrones). Because gates or in-betweens compose the matrix of creation and connect various parts of creation to one another, the Kerubim are said to have the power of uniting things and to reveal the proper order of things. It is from the Kerubim that initiates gain knowledge of the keys necessary to invoke and pass through gates and it is Kerubim that are invoked as guardians of the continuum and holy places. Although it is common to primarily speak of the Kerubim as gates in space, to properly understand them one must also consider them as gates in time, as space-time is inseparable. This alludes to the powerful role of Kerubim in prophecy and their invocation in divine magic dealing with space-time.

Apart from the higher classes of Kerubim that serve as gates and guardians, according to the Tradition there are also classes of Kerubim that perform divine intercession and others that abide continually in prayer and work wonders through their communion in God's presence. Besides these, there are said to be classes of Kerubim that are extremely dark and wrathful, which are not frequently invoked by initiates on account of their unpredictability and ferocity. Much like all the other orders of angels, the Kerubim are also represented by a great diversity in classes and types—certainly more than space allows to be described in this present work. However, the above discussion should put one well on track as to what is meant by the Kerubim in the Kabbalah.

Spiritual Practices for Yesod

The Invocation and Meditation of John the Baptist

> ➢ Much insight into the Holy Gospel and divine incarnation can be gained by meditation upon the maggid, John the Baptist. Likewise, through invocation of the spirit of John, knowledge of the prophets and the way of the prophets can be acquired. When gnosis of deep

mysteries is sought, it is not uncommon for an initiate to enact the rite of baptism and go on retreat in the wilderness to invoke the spirit of the prophets and practice meditation on the maggid.

➢ Pray the Invocation:

Eheieh, Yahweh, El Shaddai, Adonai—O Holy One of Being, grant me the blessing of communion with the spirit of the prophets. In the name of Moses, Samuel and Nathan, and Isaiah, Jeremiah, and Ezekiel. In the name of the Anointed, the Bridegroom, and Holy Bride, O Spirit of the Prophets, Spirit of John the Baptist, come and be with me. Appear in my mind, speak in my heart, and illuminate my life—impart the blessing of your presence upon me, and let us commune in the Spirit of Holiness.

➢ Having invoked, envision the divine image of the maggid magically appearing in the space before you, clothed in a camel's hair garment with a leather belt, his hair disheveled and his eyes wild and piercing. One foot is upon a flowing river and the other upon the earth, and the whole image is radiant with glory—the image of the prophet being formed of translucent light.

➢ Sometimes names of God and of the prophets are chanted, and other times the meditation remains in silence, all according to inspiration. Perhaps the spirit of John will speak to you, or perhaps he will touch you and bless you. A word of knowledge might come or a secret mystery might be disclosed; sometimes one might see a vision. Whether something or nothing at all, let whatever happens happen. When the meditation is complete, envision the prophet baptizing you with light and glory, your own body-mind radiant with light, and the image of the maggid vanishing as he appeared. Then give thanks to God for the divine revelation that transpires through the prophets and praise the Lord. This is the most basic meditation with John the Baptist.

The Middle Pillar Meditation

The practices used from one initiate to another can vary greatly in a Gnostic circle. However, the Middle Pillar Meditation is typically a point in common in the continuum of spiritual practices among initiates of the

Tradition. It is the base method used to awaken the serpent power, establish key centers in the subtle body, and to circulate spiritual energy through the subtle body and aura. At the same time, it is an essential method for drawing upon the ruhaniyut and shefa of the Middle Pillar of the Tree of Life and, specifically, for drawing down supernal light into the subtle body—a method for the generation of the body of light. Thus, it is something more than a practice to awaken the fire snake, being an invocation of the Spirit of Messiah and the divine powers. While in the basic practice only the divine names of the Middle Pillar are used, after performing the Middle Pillar, initiates may also invoke the archangels of the Tree of Life and the orders of angels, or they may invoke a Partzufim such as Yeshua Messiah, the Mother, or the Bride. It is often joined to other practices.

The Middle Pillar meditation is used to generate spiritual energy necessary for projection of consciousness into a subtle body, for healing work, and for divine magic. If we were to describe the Middle Pillar in the simplest terms, it is the energy generator of an initiate's continuum of spiritual practice and, thus, serves as a cornerstone upon which a continuum of daily spiritual practice is built. It is an excellent practice for self-healing and is at the heart of the healing way in the Holy Kabbalah. All practices of healing are developed by modification of the Middle Pillar. It is also a primary method of psychic and spiritual defense. For energizing the subtle body and the aura, it makes it impossible for klippotic forces to form links or engage in psychic assaults to cause harm. When one is like the spiritual sun, then darkness, and negativity can find no roost. It is a powerful and versatile spiritual practice, and it is easy to learn and to use. It is good for the beginner and the adept alike, and is often the very first practice given to a novice initiate.

> ➤ Sit or stand, as you like, and set your mind upon your breath, letting your body find its own natural rhythm of breathing. Gather your consciousness within behind the heart and calmly abide for a few moments—just be.

> ➤ Shift your focus to the top of your head and envision on top of your head a sphere of brilliant white light—diamond-like light that sparkles with the colors of the rainbow, as though crystalline. Imagine that you are breathing through this center on top of the

head and breathe at least three cycles of inhalation and exhalation through the center. Then bring the center to life with the intonation of *Eheieh* at least three times. (Three cycles of breath and intonations of the corresponding divine name is the minimum number for each center in the practice.)

➤ Envision that a channel of light descends through the top of your head down to your throat and that a center of translucent lavender light forms at the throat. Breathe through the center. Then bring this center to life with the intonement of the divine name of *Yahweh Elohim.*

➤ Envision that the light continues its descent to the center of the torso at the solar plexus and forms a center of translucent golden light there. Breathe through this center. Then awaken the center by intoning the divine name of *Yeshua* (alternatively, *Yahweh Elohenu* can be used).

➤ Envision the light progressing in descent down to your groin region and forming a center of translucent violet light in the groin. Breathe through the center and then bring it to life with the divine name of *Shaddai El Chai.* (For a special flow of grace, the name of *El Shaddai* may be used, or for special divine protection, the name of *Shaddai.*)

➤ Envision the line of light going down to your feet and forming a center of radiant darkness at your feet—like translucent obsidian light. Breathe through the center and then intone the divine name of *Adonai.* (For a stronger grounding of energy and oneself, the divine name of *Adonai Ha-Eretz* may be used; for a more devotional practice, the divine name of *Adonai Melekh* can be used. Devotees of the Holy Bride often use the divine name of *Kallah Messiah.*)

➤ Envision a fiery energy kindled in the Malkut sphere (the black sphere at your feet) and imagine a great stirring and pressure building until a thread of fiery energy shoots up the channel of light formed by the Middle Pillar. Envision the fiery energy and light mingling in each center in ascent and the combined energy of fiery light rushing up out of the top of your head, as though you have become a great fountain of fiery light. See this light pouring over you and washing through your sphere of sensation or aura.

➢ Imagine the flow of light becoming linked to your breath, so that in breathing and envisioning you can consciously direct this fiery light. As you exhale, envision a current of fiery light descending down the front of your body, and as you inhale, the same current flowing up the back of your body, thus creating a circuit flowing around you.

➢ Once you establish the first current, then envision another current going down the left side of your body and up the right side, also linked to your exhalation and inhalation.

➢ Now envision a translucent sphere of the fiery light around you and these currents moving independently in the sphere. Envision your body as translucent fiery light and see all the centers in their place in the body of light, and the descending and ascending force flowing. Abide in meditation with this vision of awareness as long as you can. This concludes the practice. (Sometimes the practice is opened and closed with the Kabbalistic Cross. If the Middle Pillar is performed to defend against negativity, the outer sphere of light may be envisioned becoming solid and impenetrable, as though becoming crystal that is self-radiant.)

➢ At first the idea of breathing through the centers or moving energy through the aura and subtle body by breathing might seem somewhat strange. However, within and behind the ordinary breath there is another *spiritual breath* or *energetic breath*—the radiant holy breath. In fact, there are five distinct winds or breaths within the radiant holy breath in the subtle body, corresponding to the five elements. The practice of breathing through the centers is a gentle way to become conscious of this breath of the soul and, thus, is included as part of the basic practice. In advanced practices, specific breath exercises are given to further actualize and realize the power of the holy breath.

FOURTEEN

MALKUT, THE
DIVINE
KINGDOM

Attributes

Thirty-Two Paths of Wisdom: Scintillating Consciousness (Sekhel MitNotzetz); it is called this because it elevates itself and sits on the throne of Understanding; it shines with the radiance of all the luminaries, and it bestows an influx of increase to the Prince of the Face

Malkut: The Kingdom

Place on the Tree of Life: The base of the Pillar of Compassion

Divine Name: Adonai

Alternative Divine Names: Adonai Ha-Eretz; Adonai Melekh; Kallah Messiah

Partzuf Above: Kallah, the Bride; Nukva, the Daughter

Partzuf Below: St. Mary Magdalene; also King David

Divine Image: The Image of the Holy Bride, St. Mary Magdalene; the Maiden of Light crowned and enthroned

Archangel: Sandalfon

Order of Angels: Ashim

Celestial Attribute: Holem Ha-Yesodot, Sphere of the Fundamental Elements; Eretz, the Earth

Titles Given to Malkut: The Community of Israel; the Gnostic Circle;
the Body of Christ; the Gate; Valley of the Shadow of Death;
Gate of Death; Daughter of the Living One; Holy Bride; Matrix
of Life; Maiden of Light; Lower Shekinah; Tree of Death; Dove
of Peace; Jerusalem; Promised Land; The Land Flowing with Milk
and Honey; Gate of Prayer; Depth of Evil; Gate of Tears; Gate of
Justice; Sophia Nigrans; the Kingdom of Heaven; the Princess; the
Queen; The Virgin; the Mistress of the Wilderness; Holy Abode;
Garden of Eden; the Spirit of the Prophets

Level of the Soul: Nefesh, Vital Soul (Nefesh Behamit and Nefesh Elokit)

Heavenly Abode: Vilon, the First Heaven—the Veil; Tebel, Earthly
Paradise

Spiritual Experience: Gnosis of the Kingdom of God; Rapturous Union
with Mother Nature; Vision of the World To Come; Vision of the
Lady in Red; Vision of New Jerusalem

Virtues: Grounding; harmony with nature; comfort with the body; joy
in life; sense of adventure; discrimination or discernment; awareness of surroundings; awareness of abundance

Vices: Lack of focus; disharmony with the environment and nature;
disregard for the body; greed; delusion of lack or poverty; poor
discernment; dullness; inertia; lack of joy and vitality in life; bad
neighbor

Symbols: The Sacred Circle or Magical Circle; the Sanctuary of Holy
Temple; the Place of Meeting; the House of the Tzaddik; square;
equal-armed cross; Maltese cross; any sacred place; nature; a stone
or crystal; the Holy Pentacle or Coin of Redemption; any currency;
sandals or shoes

Commandment: Do not covet (Exodus 20:17)

Sermon on the Mount: Blessed are the poor in spirit, for theirs is the kingdom of heaven (Matthew 5:3)

Angel of the Apocalypse and the Churches: The Seventh Star and Lampstand,
and the message to the angel of the church in Laodicea (Revelation
3:14–22)

The Holy Kingdom

A tree becomes mature when it is fertile and able to bear good fruit—which is to say, fruit that contains seed. The life of a tree is in its fruit and, in essence, a tree exists for the sake of generating fruit, which in turn creates new trees. The same is true of the Tree of Life and the Sefirah Malkut, which is the holy fruit of the tree. The Sefirot, from Keter to Yesod, exist to bring about Malkut, which is the holy vessel that receives all of the spiritual energies of the Sefirot. Malkut (kingdom) contains the spiritual energies of all the Sefirot above it and is composed of the spiritual energies of all the Sefirot, thus representing the immanent matrix of spiritual forces manifest as creation.

Malkut is represented by the final He in the Tetragrammaton, which indicates the sovereignty of the divine presence and power in creation and connotes the idea of receiving. As we have seen, the first He in the Tetragrammaton represents Binah-Aima and the upper Shekinah. Sharing the same letter of the great name, Binah and Malkut are intimately connected. Malkut is called Nukva, the Daughter, and is the lower Shekinah. Binah-Aima is the transcendental matrix of forces on an archetypal level; Malkut-Nukva is the matrix of forces in actual manifestation. This matrix of creation is, in essence, one and the same—the Mother representing the ideal and the Daughter representing the actual. Thus, the divine Mother, as the upper Shekinah, is the presence and power of God beyond creatures and creation, and the Holy Daughter, as the lower Shekinah, is the presence and power of God within creatures and creation.

Because Malkut is complete receptivity, it is said that "she has no light or life of her own" but has only the light and life she receives from the supernal Mother via the six Sefirot between Binah and Malkut. Thus, the appearance of the Shekinah in the lower planes and in the world is dependent upon the divine powers that are invoked and the degree to which the ruhaniyut and shefa of the Sefirot are brought down into Malkut, which on the most fundamental level represents the material world. Accordingly, the Shekinah may appear bright or dark, as a manifestation of mercy or judgment, all dependent upon the balance of the divine powers that are invoked or evoked by human beings. Life on earth can be heavenly or hellish, all depending on the actions of human beings.

As all life is a manifestation of the Shekinah—the divine presence and power—how life unfolds and everything that transpires in it is how the Shekinah appears.

Malkut is Nukva, the Daughter, but she is also Kallah, the Holy Bride. You will recall that Tiferet (the six) manifests as the Son and Bridegroom. When the supernal light is brought down into Malkut and she is filled with the ruhaniyut and shefa of Tiferet (the six), she is united to Tiferet. When Tiferet and Malkut are united, the Son becomes the Bridegroom and the Daughter becomes the Holy Bride. This corresponds to the bright appearance of the Shekinah and manifestation of divine providence according to mercy. Conversely, when the flow of supernal light and the ruhaniyut and shefa of the six is impaired and Malkut is separated or divorced from Tiferet, Malkut is called the divorced woman, the widow, or the Shekinah in exile. This corresponds to the dark appearance of the Shekinah and the manifestation of divine providence according to judgment.

Essentially, Malkut represents the power that God gives to us to receive from him (or her) and the idea of the human being and creation as a holy vessel of God's grace—specifically, as a holy vehicle through which the divine presence and power might be realized and embodied. In Malkut, the purpose of giving and of creation is fulfilled. It represents the relationship in which the one who receives can reciprocate and become the "giver," and in which the human being becomes the embodiment of God's presence and power. This is how the Malkut of God is manifest in the material world.

The highest manifestation of Malkut is at the level of Adam Kadmon. In the universe of Adam Kadmon, the Sefirot are composed of clear or transparent light—the pure light of the Infinite, which is the inmost essence of the supernal light. This is the light of the Soul of the Messiah, and Malkut of Adam Kadmon is the body of the primordial human being—the anointed one of God—which is composed of transparent light. Malkut of Adam Kadmon thus corresponds to the full realization of the truth body of Melchizedek and is called the supernal light-presence or clear-light joy.

At the level of Atzilut, the transparent light appears as white brilliance, which is said to be akin to a spiritual nuclear fire. This fiery light is the glory that pours forth from the mystical body of the Messiah and manifests as Malkut of Atzilut, which is the world of supernal light. In essence, the supernal light-presence (Malkut of Adam Kadmon) and the world of supernal light (Malkut of Atzilut) are inseparable, and yet there is a most subtle and sublime distinction between them that allows the universe of Beriyah to come into being.

In Beriyah, the white brilliance manifests as rays of rainbow glory, the aura of the Messiah, as it were, which represents the emanation of the cosmic Christ and all spiritual forces of creation. The aura of the Messiah is called the light of the heavens and Malkut of Beriyah is called the kingdom of heaven, for, receiving this light of the cosmic Christ, Malkut of Beriyah gives birth to the seven heavens and all of the celestial abodes. This level of Malkut corresponds to the realization of the glorified body of Melchizedek—the angelic or heavenly body.

The kingdom of heaven is the light of the universe of Yetzirah, of which the Lord has said, "I formed the light and created the darkness..." From this light, the holy angels and all spirits of righteousness were formed and, thus, Malkut of Yetzirah is called the world of angels. It is the light of the world of angels that is the light of the material world. Malkut of Asiyah is the material universe and world, specifically this good earth, to the degree the kingdom of heaven is reflected in it and the world is established upon the divine order that Malkut represents. Basically, Malkut represents the culmination of the process of creation that transpires in each of the Olamot and is the divine order as it manifests in all five universes.

Associated with the final He of the Tetragrammaton, which represents the universe of Asiyah, Malkut is primarily spoken of as the material world and the matrix of spiritual forces within and behind the material dimension. The idea of Malkut as the purpose of the whole Tree of Life—the holy fruit of the tree—and its primary correspondence to the material universe and the material world, reflects the importance the Kabbalah places on the material world for fulfillment of the divine plan. In the Christian Kabbalah, life in the material world is considered a precious gift, because only in the material plane can the soul-being develop, evolve, and make actual progress toward full self-realization. Afterlife states are merely the integration of experience acquired during incarnation. Until the soul-being evolves beyond the need for physical incarnation, the material plane serves as the principal vehicle for enlightenment and liberation. While, indeed, there is great darkness and evil in the world, and death and destruction reign in it, nevertheless the material world is the ideal realm for progress and is necessary. If one examines Kabbalistic teachings closely, whether Jewish or Christian, one will even find suggestions that the material world itself is destined to be transformed by the supernal light into a world of supernal light—every particle of matter is said to contain this light of the Infinite. Essentially, the message of Malkut is that this life is sacred and that its purpose is ultimately enlightenment and liberation of the soul. It is like a holy womb giving birth of our soul to eternal life.

The Presence of the Lord

At the level of Atzilut, the Sefirah Malkut manifests as the divine name Adonai, which translates as "the Lord." In Judaic Tradition, the Tetragrammaton was pronounced only by the high priest in the holy of holies or by a prophet in seclusion seeking to invoke prophetic consciousness. Thus, the name of Adonai was created to be spoken in place of the Tetragrammaton, so that, anywhere the name of Yahweh appeared in the Torah, it would be pronounced Adonai. In the same way that Malkut is a vessel for the spiritual energies of all of the Sefirot, so the name of Adonai is a vessel for the name of Yahweh and serves as a shield to preserve the holiness of the great name of God.

You will recall that, in the Judaic Kabbalah, the divine name of Binah is "Yahweh pronounced as Elohim." The same is true of Malkut; the name of Malkut is "Yahweh pronounced as Adonai." This reflects the intimate connection between Binah and Malkut, the Daughter being the manifestation of the divine Mother in creation or what is called created wisdom in the Christian Kabbalah. The name Adonai itself indicates the idea of created versus uncreated wisdom in the sense that it is a name created as an outer vessel of God's true holy name—Yahweh—which is emanated and not created.

Malkut is the most restricted gradation of the supernal light. It is for this reason that Malkut is called a "depth of evil" in the Sefer Yetzirah. As we have seen, tzimtzum creates the possibility of darkness and evil. Thus, with the Sefirah that is most constricted comes the possibility of the greatest darkness and evil. The name Adonai, therefore, represents the manifestation of God's presence and power in a more diffused and limited way than any other divine name. The virtue of this is that the name Adonai is accessible to anyone who seeks to call upon the name of the Lord, even if the person is in a state of impurity or encumbered by klippotic influence.

As we saw in the previous chapter, Yesod has three variations of the name Shaddai to designate manifestation of the Sefirah under the influence of mercy, judgment, or compassion. Malkut, however, has only the proper name of Adonai; thus Adonai can indicate peaceful, wrathful, or blissful manifestations of the Divine. This alludes to the truth of God as the source of all life and of all spiritual beings-forces, whether good or evil, and to the divine providence that holds dominion over all spiritual forces. Adonai is the presence and power of God in any appearance it might assume—Lord of the light and Lord of the darkness, Lord of life and Lord of death.

Given the broad range of the divine name Adonai, this name reminds us that everything transpires according to divine providence and the holy law. Nothing happens without a reason—a greater purpose and meaning in the divine plan. As we have said, even darkness and evil, death and destruction have a place and purpose in creation and ultimately serve the divine will. While the greater purpose and meaning of certain events in life may remain a complete mystery to us, nevertheless, it is important as Gnostic initiates that we know and understand this fundamental truth— for only then will we realize the divine presence and power that manifests with us and as us in this life.

Adonai is the name of life as it is—good and evil alike—and the name reflects the very process of life. Adonai is composed of four Hebrew letters: Aleph (א)-Dalet (ד)-Nun (נ)-Yod (י). Aleph is the "yoke of the Spirit," the one life-power. Dalet is the "door of life." Nun is the opposite of Dalet, being the "gate of death." Yod is the "holy spark" or "seed of light" being realized through the process of birth, life, and death. Thus, Adonai means the individuation and self-realization of the spirit-power through the process of birth, death, and rebirth, until the divine fullness of Yechidah is awakened and realized. As much as the name of the Shekinah, it is also the name of self-realization. It is in this sense that the divine name Adonai is often given to Yeshua Messiah, for he represents the first human being of supernal self-realization.

There are two common variations of Adonai associated with Malkut—Adonai Ha-Eretz and Adonai Melekh. Adonai Ha-Eretz means the "Lord of the Earth" and Adonai Melekh means "Lord King." These two divine names represent the sovereignty of God over the earth and creation. Adonai Ha-Eretz specifically indicates Malkut as this good earth when the kingdom of heaven is reflected in it and Adonai Melekh specifically indicates Malkut as the manifestation of the divine will in creation. Other names are formed from Adonai as well, such as Adonai Ha-Olam, "Lord of the Universe," or Adonai Messiah, "Lord Anointed." However, the essential meaning of Adonai always remains the same—all are the name Adonai, and Adonai is everything.

The Rainbow Veil

The veil of the abyss divides the supernal and moral triads and the veil of Paroket divides the moral and action triads. These "veils" are reflected in the veil of Qeshet, which is between the action triad and Malkut. Qeshet is the Hebrew word meaning "rainbow," and the veil of Qeshet represents the refracted light of the supernals passing through the astral planes.

This is the light of fantasy, false dreams, and visions that are reflected into the astral, but do not bear the necessary conditions and energy to actually manifest. Likewise, the veil of Qeshet represents misperceptions of the metaphysical dimensions and all manner of strange doctrines engendered by them, from atheism to the most outlandish cultic teaching. Essentially, the veil of Qeshet is what hinders and obstructs the true opening of mystical or spiritual consciousness. On the one hand, we could speak of the veil of Qeshet as the product of seeking a spiritual view that agrees with us or composing a spirituality of ideas that we like, versus seeking gnosis of the truth, whether it agrees with us or not. This phenomenon is common in so-called "modern spirituality" and prevents the manifestation of the spirit of truth. On the other hand, we could speak of this veil as psychism and mediumship at their worse, which tends to lead completely astray from any authentic spirituality. If the veil of the abyss is cosmic ignorance, and the veil of Paroket is the karmic matrix, then the veil of Qeshet is karmic vision—specifically, the vision of ignorance.

In Rosicrucian Tradition, the grade of theoricus is attributed to Yesod and the grade of zelator is attributed to Malkut. The titles of these Rosicrucian grades give us a clue as to how the veil of Qeshet can be parted so that we can pass beyond it, for zelator is a novice initiate who is zealous, enthusiastic, and excited with all the new possibilities that arise with the dawning sense of the mystery; however, he or she is ignorant of the mystery. The theoricus is a novice initiate who has recognized his or her ignorance and therefore seeks a spiritual education—one who studies, contemplates, prays, and meditates, seeking true knowledge of the metaphysical dimensions and the mysteries. Thus, to pass beyond the veil of Qeshet, one must go to school—study in an authentic wisdom tradition or Mystery school—and receive initiation. Obviously, a well-educated spiritual teacher and experienced guide is the best way to liberate oneself from the veil of Qeshet to experience a true spiritual or mystical awakening, and a spiritual community provides the ideal environment for mystical attainment. This is the basic message of all teachings on the veils.

Spiritual education, however, is not something imposed from the outside, but, as we have said, is a drawing out of what is within oneself. It is not so much that an initiate is going to tell you the truth as much as to teach you how to look and see it for yourself. The message of Malkut is that the spirit of truth is within you and that it is reflected everywhere in nature. One need only learn how to look and see, and to listen and hear it. In a valid wisdom tradition, all teachings are taken as provisional and meant to be proved in one's own experience. This is the education that dispels the veil of Qeshet.

Qeshet means something more, however, for it is not only a veil of the cosmic illusion-power, but is also a symbol of promise. The rainbow is the sign of the covenant that God made with Noah and his family (humanity) when they emerged from the ark after the flood. It is written: "God said, 'This is the sign of the covenant that I make between me and you and every living creature that is with you, for all future generations: I have set my bow in the clouds, and it shall be a sign of the covenant between me and the earth'" (Genesis 9:12–13). On the one hand, this is said to be the promise of the preservation of the human life-wave on earth until the dawn of a supernal or supramental humanity. On the other hand, it is said to be the establishment of the kingdom of heaven as a sanctuary of the faithful and elect in their journey to enlightenment.

The dual attribute of the veil of Qeshet might at first seem something of a contradiction—the idea of karmic vision and the idea of the promise of enlightenment. However, if one understands karma to mean evolution, and one understands the role of cosmic ignorance for the sake of individuation and free will, then one will realize that karma is as much a vehicle for enlightenment and liberation as it is for ignorance and bondage. After all, the veil of Qeshet is in the mind, and it is the same mind that is enlightened or unenlightened.

The Life of St. Mary Magdalene—
The Incarnation of the Holy Bride

The oral tradition of Christian Gnosticism is replete with myths and legends of St. Mary Magdalene, including esoteric teachings attributed to her. As we have seen, she is believed to have been the consort and wife of Yeshua Messiah, copreacher and codivine with him. She is the apostle of the apostles, the Holy Bride and incarnation of Christ the Sophia. Basically, Lady Mary represents the embodiment of the Partzuf of Malkut in the Gospel—Nukva, the Daughter, and Kallah, the Bride.

According to the Tradition, the soul of Lady Mary was previously incarnate as Rachel, Jacob's most beloved wife, and as Rahab, the prostitute who helped the spies of Israel to escape from Jericho. Rachel was the mother of Joseph and Benjamin and it is said that her soul took on the karma of incarnating as Rahab in order to help the children of Israel enter into the holy land. Were it not for Rahab saving the two men sent to spy out the city of Jericho and had the two men not returned, it is likely that the Israelites would not have had the courage to enter the holy land and fulfill the promise of God. Thus, as Rahab, the soul of Rachel acted as a secret tzaddik.

You will recall that, according to the Tradition, the soul of Lord Yeshua was incarnate as Jacob and as Elisha. It is said that Jacob and Rachel were soulmates, which is to say that they shared the same Neshamah. The correspondence between Jacob and Rachel and the incarnation of Lord Yeshua and Lady Mary therefore indicates that Yeshua and Mary are soulmates, the male and female aspects of one soul of light. Accordingly, when the Tradition says that the soul of Yeshua attained supernal consciousness amidst an elder race before entering into the human life-wave on earth, the same is true of St. Mary Magdalene.

The life story of Lady Mary is quite the opposite of Lord Yeshua, and the difference well reflects the distinction between the Bridegroom (Tiferet) and the Holy Bride (Malkut). While being fully human, Lord Yeshua was never a man of this world and did not directly involve himself in mundane affairs. From his earliest youth, he was set apart and given a spiritual education, including the esoteric knowledge of the mystical and magical Kabbalah. His family was relatively poor, but deeply spiritual. The situation into which Lady Mary was born was quite different. Her family was very wealthy and was unspiritual. Her father was a merchant and trader, and her mother enjoyed the finer things of life. She received no spiritual education, although, like Yeshua, she was a spiritual prodigy. Because of her family, her spirituality was deeply buried as she grew up and she became completely immersed in the mundane world. Lord Yeshua was always fairly clear about why he entered into the world, but Lady Mary became lost and aimlessly wandered for some time. There are a few among the elect whose experience is akin to Lord Yeshua, who never became immersed in unenlightened society and the establishment. For most of us, our experience is more akin to St. Mary Magdalene—souls that become lost and immersed in great darkness before realizing the light that is in us. In this sense, the experience of Lady Mary is closer to us and, for many Gnostic initiates, it is through her that they experience the deepest intimacy with the Christ-presence.

The otherworldliness of Lord Yeshua and the worldliness of Lady Mary are an expression of Tiferet and Malkut, respectively. Tiferet is beyond the world and Malkut is the world, and Malkut manifests as the divine kingdom only when joined to Tiferet. The same is true of Lady Mary as the Holy Bride. She awakens and becomes Christ the Sophia only when she meets Lord Yeshua in life and is joined to him as a disciple and consort— then she becomes the divine kingdom. Until that time, she is lost and wandering, like the Shekinah in exile, and experiences the extremes of light and darkness, as all of humanity does while bound to cosmic ignorance. The enigma of the Holy Bride is the enigma of all humanity and the material world—how, on the one hand, humanity and the world are divine and, on the other hand, how humanity and the world come to be dominated by ignorance and darkness.

It is said that Mary Magdalene was a beautiful baby and an exquisite little girl, and that her beauty grew from year to year as she matured. Her beauty and grace were almost otherworldly, so that it is said it was angelic and unimaginably enchanting. Men and woman alike noticed her. Wherever she went, she was the center of attention. At the same time, it is said that Mary dreamed dreams and saw visions and that the spirits of prophets and angels visited her, but she would not speak of these things for fear of being branded a witch or heretic. Her incomprehensible beauty, the worldliness it invoked, and her spiritual depth created a vast struggle in Mary, so that inwardly she was truly torn and greatly troubled. Because she had no one to confide in who might understand and she herself was confused about her experience, her deep troubling became torment.

Mary's father arranged for her to marry a very wealthy Jewish man living in Babylon who was also a merchant and trader. In so doing, her father hoped to get more business through new family ties and to acquire greater wealth for himself. This became a greater torment to Mary, for she had dreamed of her beloved and it was not this man, and in her heart of heart's she did not want to leave the holy land. However, under ancient law, a daughter could not refuse her father's wishes and she had no choice but to marry whomever her father arranged for her to marry. Thus, Mary and her handmaid were placed with a caravan going to Babylon.

It is said that Mary's inner struggle became so great during the journey to Babylon that she began to lose her mind. Dark visions and nightmares replaced her heavenly visions. She felt as though her soul was ebbing away as the caravan moved further and further out of the holy land. On the way, the caravan Mary traveled in was attacked by a large band of robbers. Mary was taken, raped, and sold into slavery in Babylon. The man who bought Mary turned her out as a prostitute for wealthy men, and Mary was a broken woman—rage, hatred, and darkness filled her. Here and there bright dreams would come, but feeling completely lost and abandoned, they seemed to her like taunting and they fueled the darkness that consumed her. It was as though she had descended into the depths of Hades and the abodes of Gehenna (hell).

Because of her unimaginable beauty, she attracted the attention of very wealthy and powerful men, and it was not long until one of them bought her freedom. Yet she continued as a prostitute, as she could conceive of nothing else to do and had no love for men. Having the ear of powerful men, she acquired power. Consorting with wealthy men, she accumulated wealth. She became immersed in political and social intrigue, manipulating men and women alike. It is said that, at one point, she instigated a conspiracy to murder on account of her hatred, seeing the man killed who once owned her as a slave and made her a prostitute. Deeper and deeper she sank into darkness, and it was as though she became an empty and soulless shell animated only with an inner fury cloaked by an outward beauty and charm.

At the point of greatest darkness in the experience of Mary Magdalene, Lord Yeshua underwent the baptism and the temptation in the wilderness. The influx of supernal light into the world awoke something within Mary. She remembered the dreams and visions of her youth and the image of the beloved she had known in her heart. Her rage turned into despair and sorrow. She turned to God and called upon the Spirit of the Lord for deliverance, repenting of the negativity and darkness. God heard Mary's prayer and sent a holy man to her—a guide to set her on the path. When the holy man came to her, her heart and mind were opened and she received him. He told her that her father had died and that the Spirit of the Lord called her to return to the holy land. He said to her, "In dreams and visions, the Lord has shown you the path of your soul, and now the Lord calls you to follow your dreams that you might pass from darkness into the light. Seek out the Anointed One, for he will deliver you and heal your wounds." So Mary made arrangements and set out for the holy land with a caravan the very next day. On the same day that Lord Yeshua performed the first miracle at the wedding feast of Cana, it is said that Lady Mary entered into the holy land.

Although something of the light-presence was awakening in Mary, it was not an easy journey, for having entertained such darkness, she had formed links with seven powerful demons and they plagued her along the way. Once she entered the holy land, she straightaway sought out the Anointed. She found him preaching to peoples gathered around him. She hid herself in the back of the crowd and listened to him. His voice was as the cooing of a dove, soothing and comforting to her, and yet his words burned her to the core. At one point, he glanced at her, caught her gaze, and he smiled. She felt something enter her—an energy or vibration that pervaded her whole body. When Lord Yeshua finished teaching the people, he sent two disciples to bring Mary to him, and he waited for them on the edge of the wilderness near the River Jordan.

According to the Gospel of St. Mark, Lord Yeshua exorcised the seven demons from Mary. Gnostic Tradition says he then charged the two disciples to baptize Mary Magdalene, and when they had baptized her, he took her out into the wilderness to teach and initiate her in secret. When they returned, Yeshua announced that Lady Mary was to become his bride and he gave instructions for the preparation of a wedding feast. The wedding took place three days later. From that day on, Lady Mary was always in the company of Lord Yeshua, and she was copreacher and codivine with him—one in body and soul.

Lady Mary was like a divine muse to Lord Yeshua and embodied the pure desire to receive that fulfilled his holy desire to give. Through her presence, Lord Yeshua was inspired to impart the inner and secret teachings of the Gospel and the light of the Christ-presence increased in him a hundredfold. In private, he gave her the inmost secret teachings, which only she and her brother St. Lazarus received, so that the whole mystery of the Gospel of truth was revealed to her. Alongside Lord Yeshua, she preached the Gospel and worked wonders; she taught and initiated the women disciples and led them in the way, truth, and light. Grace upon grace, light upon light, came through St. Mary Magdalene. Lord Yeshua drew forth the supernal light that was in her and she drew forth the supernal light that was in him.

Within and behind every miracle and significant event in the life story of Lord Yeshua, there are stories of St. Mary Magdalene and the role she played in the mystery drama of the Gospel. According to Gnostic Christianity, the Gospel of truth emerges from the love-play of the Bridegroom and Holy Bride, and, in their union, they fulfill and complete one another. He is the Son of the heavenly Father, Christ the Logos, and she is the Daughter of the earthly Mother, Christ the Sophia—the Soul of the world. Through Lady Mary, the Holy Bride, humanity and the world are joined to Yeshua Messiah and, in her redemption, all souls are redeemed.

As we said in our exploration of the mystery of the crucifixion, Lord Yeshua made his body a magical talisman of the negative karma of the world, so that, in submitting himself to be crucified, the negative karma of the world was crucified in him. It was through his union with the Holy Bride that he was able to do this, for it is through her that he becomes intimately connected to the world and the darkness that rules in it. Incarnating in an unenlightened family and submitting herself to the dominion of the establishment, her experience of rape, slavery, prostitution, and her fall into the depths of darkness are all talismatic acts through which Lady Mary takes the darkness of the world upon herself. In the covenant of marriage, husband and wife become "one flesh." Thus, just as the experience of Lord Yeshua became the experience of Lady Mary, so did Lord Yeshua take upon himself the experience of Lady Mary and the great darkness she had bound to herself. In essence, in Gnosticism, the early life of Lady Mary is integral to the mystery of the crucifixion and resurrection, for she also undergoes the same heroic act of allowing herself to be a holy sacrifice for the enlightenment and liberation of souls. If one considers her experience, it is as though she, too, was crucified and experienced the descent into hades and the depths of hell and was raised to eternal life from among the dead. Because she descends into the depths of darkness, Lord Yeshua also descends into the pit to deliver souls bound to the dominion of darkness—the Holy Bride leading the way.

This great mystery is reflected in the story of Lady Mary anointing the body of Lord Yeshua with ointment or perfume—different variations of which appear in the canonized Gospels. According to the Gospel of St. John, it is written:

> *Six days before Passover Jesus came to Bethany, the home of Lazarus, whom he had raised from the dead. There they gave a dinner for him. Martha served, and Lazarus was one of those at the table with him. Mary took a pound of costly perfume made of pure nard, anointed Jesus' feet, and wiped them with her hair. The house was filled with the fragrance of the perfume.* (Gospel of St. John 12:1–3)

The masters of the Tradition say that, in this mystical/magical act, Lady Mary consecrated Lord Yeshua's body as a talisman of the negative karma of the world and imparted an initiation, preparing him for his journey through death and darkness. At the same time, it was an act of devotion or worship—a sensual and erotic act of love-play between divine consorts, prophetic of what was soon to transpire.

However exoteric Christianity might attempt to explain away and dismiss this story of St. Mary Magdalene, it is clear that she had knowledge and understanding of the divine revelation of the Gospel that eluded the male disciples, and it is equally clear that she had a more intimate relationship with Lord Yeshua than any other disciple. According to the Tradition, although it is not mentioned in the canonized Gospels, Lady Mary was present at the transfiguration and while the men fell unconscious she remained awake and, therefore, received the light transmission in full. That night it is said that she took three of the women disciples into a cave and was transfigured before them. The images of Mother and Grandmother Israel appeared with her, and she revealed to the women the mysteries of what was to come and the world of supernal light.

On the night of passion, when the male disciples went out to the garden in the Kidron Valley with Lord Yeshua, Lady Mary remained in the upper room with the women disciples and held vigil with them through the night. Lady Mary felt the trial and tribulation of Lord Yeshua in her soul as the pains of giving birth and all of the women with her, so that their prayers were amidst tears and wailing, and yet in the depths of their being, they knew the peace and joy of life eternal being born among them.

In the morning, Lady Mary, the Holy Mother, and an old woman, along with St. John, went to the Mount of Golgotha and stood by Lord Yeshua in his crucifixion, suffering inwardly with him the anguish of dying and death. With her knowledge and understanding of the resurrection, Lady Mary experienced the height of joy and yet, with the suffering of her beloved, she experienced the depth of sorrow—a greater torment in the soul than in her own journey through darkness.

Lady Mary carried with her the cup of blessing. When the Lord had died and the centurion thrust his spear into Yeshua's side, Lady Mary collected some of the blood and water that flowed out into the cup. When she did this she prayed that the cup would become a holy vessel of Christos, and through the power of the blood and the light-presence that was in her, she consecrated the cup and it became the Holy Grail. From that time on, whoever drank from the Grail was healed of all wounds and their life was extended—and thus Lady Mary became the Mistress of the Grail.

Every morning and evening, Lady Mary visited the tomb of Lord Yeshua, mourning his death and praying for the resurrection. On the third day, she was the first to behold the Risen Christ and she witnessed the first ascension to the Father. It is written of this eternal moment:

> *Jesus said to her, "Do not hold on to me, because I have not yet ascended to the Father. But go to my brothers and say to them, 'I am ascending to my Father and your Father, to my God and your God.'"* (Gospel of St. John 20:17)

As the first to bear the good news of the resurrection, St. Mary Magdalene was ordained the first holy apostle—the apostle of the apostles—and it is through her that the apostolic succession is sustained.

According to the Tradition, before the final ascension of the Lord, Lady Mary swore a vow to continue to incarnate in a woman's form until the time of the second coming of Christ in glory. Thus Gnostic Christians believe that the soul of St. Mary Magdalene is incarnate somewhere in the world in every generation and that she is the matrix of the true apostolic succession.

This is reflected in the Gnostic tale of the day of Pentecost. The Bridegroom ascended into heaven, but the Holy Bride remained upon the earth, and it was through the Holy Mother and Bride that the holy fire of Pentecost poured out upon the apostles. The Holy Bride is the fiery light poured out upon them. When the men were driven out of the upper room to bear forth the living presence, the women remained in the upper room with the Mother and Lady Mary—abiding as the matrix of hidden light.

Legend says that St. Mary Magdalene conceived a child with Lord Yeshua seven days before the crucifixion and resurrection, and that she gave birth to a son, whose name was Michael. Until her son was old enough to travel safely, Lady Mary retreated to the hills of Galilee—some say to a town called Safed. There she taught those who came to her, and initiated them into the inner and secret mysteries of the Gospel. Many came to drink from the Grail and be healed and to learn the ceremony of the Grail, which was known to her alone. However, Lady Mary was not well received and accepted, as most of the male disciples were jealous of her knowledge and understanding of the mysterie—only a few among the apostles believed in the Bride. Thus, a division began between the outer and the inner church in the first circle—those who believed in the Lord exclusively and those who believed in the Bridegroom and Holy Bride.

Lady Mary feared for the life of her son, Michael, as there were men who sought to kill him. An angel of the Lord appeared to her, warning her of coming danger and directing her to travel to a distant land, where she would be received and accepted and her son would be safe. Joseph of Arimathea is said to have traveled with her, both as a holy witness of the Gospel of truth and guardian of the Holy Bride. With them they took the Holy Grail and traveled to southern France.

In the new land, Lady Mary preached the Gospel of truth, along with her son and Joseph. She soon became known as a wonder worker, healer, and prophetess, and people sought her out for advice and comfort. Men and women alike became her disciples, and many faithful who believed in her followed her from the holy land. Because she gave birth to the son of Lord Yeshua, she became known as the mother of the royal blood, her son St. Michael being the first heir and initiate in the lineage of the royal blood. Thus, while the true apostolic succession is spiritual, founded upon the light transmission and the attainment of Christ consciousness, there is also said to be a physical talisman of the apostolic succession in the royal blood via the son of the Holy Bride. Some would say that the lineage of royal blood, along with the Sophian Tradition of Christian Gnosticism, has continued to exist in an unbroken succession since the time of St. Mary Magdalene to the present day.

There are many stories of St. Mary Magdalene's death. It is said of Mother Mary that her body was translated into pure light and that she was taken up in divine rapture in her death; but it is said of the Holy Bride that she left her body behind as a blessing upon the earth and departed the world in the same way as ordinary souls so that she might honor her vow to swiftly return. Nevertheless, the spirits of the holy saints and angels attended the death of the Bride, and those who witnessed her death beheld a great light-presence visibly manifest. When her soul departed her body, it was as though a shooting star passed from the body of the Bride to another womb. Because her body was laid to rest in France, it has often been called the second holy land by those who are faithful to her.

The life story of St. Mary Magdalene that we have given here is but an overview. It is in nowise complete and does not include any of the esoteric teachings attributed to her. There are also other life stories that are given in the Tradition, some that are radically different from the one we have provided. However, this outline of her life story does convey an idea of how St. Mary Magdalene is viewed in the Sophian Tradition and the central role she plays in the Gnostic Gospel. Space does not allow a more detailed account of her story or an analysis of the deeper esoteric meaning contained in it. Our purpose here is a basic exploration of principles of Gnostic Christianity and the Tree of Life in the Christian Kabbalah. In the Sophian Tradition of Christian Gnosticism there is no Gospel without the Holy Bride, and in the Christian Kabbalah her story conveys teachings on Malkut. It is for this reason that an outline of her story has been given.

The Bride's Reception and the Second Coming

You will recall our exploration of the promise made by Elijah to Elisha that was fulfilled by the same great souls incarnate as John the Baptist and Yeshua—a promise fulfilled in a future incarnation. According to the Gnostic Gospel as told in the Sophian Tradition, a similar promise transpired between Lord Yeshua and Lady Mary. Yeshua promises her that she will be received, saying, "I have come, most beloved, and I am coming; and I will come again in you and you will be received, even as the Son of Adam has been received. And you will bear twice the power of the Son of God, for you are the Daughter of the Most High who shall give birth to the holy ones in the end of days."

When Lord Yeshua speaks this promise, Lady Mary is said to have responded with a holy vow, saying, "I will run and return, and continue to incarnate in a woman's form until the end of days so that all things might be fulfilled. Few are those who embody the person of light in the woman's form, yet it is woman who gives birth to the new generation and until she is known in her fullness, surely the light of the human one shall not be manifest in full. May it come to pass as my Lord speaks."

According to the Tradition, the Christos was embodied by both Lord Yeshua and Lady Mary. Yet because she was not fully received, the full

power and glory of Kallah Messiah—the anointed Bride—was not manifest. In the Sophian view, the first coming was the implanting of a seed of
light in human consciousness, which is akin to the womb of the Holy
Bride. The second coming represents the fruition of that holy seed when
larger segments of humanity enter into supernal or Messianic consciousness. This is reflected by the saying of the prophet Joel:

> *Then afterward I will pour out my Spirit upon all flesh; your sons and your*
> *daughters shall prophesy, your old men shall dream dreams, and your*
> *young men shall see visions. Even on male and female slaves, in those days,*
> *I will pour out my Spirit.* (Joel 2:28–29)

Masters of the Tradition say that the dawn of supernal or Messianic
consciousness is the same, whether in a man or a woman, and that both
men and women equally can attain it. In the Spirit of the Messiah, there
is no distinction between gender, class, or race groups, for the light-presence enters anyone who desires to receive it. Thus, St. Paul writes:
"There is no longer Jew or Greek, there is no longer slave or free, there
is no longer male or female; for all are one in Jesus Christ" (Galations
3:28). Yet, the masters of the Tradition also say that when Christ consciousness dawns in a woman, the light-presence is more powerful, for
women have an innate capacity to naturally and spontaneously transmit
the light-presence to others in their environment. Essentially, the Christed man tends to impart the light transmission to select individuals, while
the Christed woman tends to impart the light transmission to whole
groups of individuals.

Because the second coming is the dawn of Messianic consciousness in
larger segments of humanity and because of this innate capacity associated with womanhood, the second coming is believed to be an advent of
supernal consciousness that will be sparked by a holy woman who incar-
nates the soul of St. Mary Magdalene and embodies the divine fullness of
the Soul of the Messiah. This is the vision of the second coming held by
Sophian Gnostics, and distinctly reflects the mysteries of Malkut on the
Tree of Life, which is called the Daughter and the Bride, and is the holy
fruit for which all Sefirot were generated.

Today, as we witness the struggle for equality between manhood and
womanhood in the world, this vision of the second coming perhaps makes

even more sense than in previous generations. For the co-equality and co-enlightenment of men and women alike is necessary for the emergence of a new humanity and new world order. We cannot speak of the redemption of humanity apart from the redemption of womanhood. Likewise, we cannot speak of the evolution of a higher form of human being except through the matrix of womanhood. Thus, in the eyes of Sophians, the second coming is dependent upon true womanhood and, specifically, the incarnation of Christ in a holy woman who, in effect, will give birth to a new and enlightened humanity and a new world order—the divine kingdom.

This idea is reflected in the Book of Revelation, where the image of the woman of light appears giving birth to a holy child (Revelation 12). Although the holy child is spoken of as male, the masters of the Tradition say that this child is the androgynous one, who is like unto the holy angels, both male and female in one body of light; hence, this child is the union of the Bridegroom and Bride, Christ the Logos and Christ the Sophia.

There is much more that could be said about the vision of the second coming as it is taught in the Sophian Tradition. However, time and space do not permit us to go any further into this mystery. Yet this mystery is considered a key message of Malkut in the Christian Kabbalah and it is at the heart of Sophian Gnosticism.

The Black Bride—Sophia Nigrans

The Daughter and Holy Bride is the image of the divine Mother below; the lower Shekinah is the reflection of the upper Shekinah. Everything we might say of Binah regarding the divine feminine, we may also say of Malkut, for Malkut is the manifest power of the divine Mother. Just as the divine Mother is both bright and dark, so also is the Daughter and Holy Bride. For though we may speak of the upper and lower Shekinah, in truth, there is but one Shekinah above and below. The Shekinah-power manifest in the holy saints and angels and the Shekinah-power manifest in the evil-doer and demons, in essence, is the same Shekinah. The whole of creation and all creatures are sustained by God's presence and nothing exists apart from God's presence.

The Holy Bride is the maiden of light, the mother of the royal blood, and the crone of ageless wisdom; yet she is also the mistress of the night,

the queen of demons, and the hag of chaos. The bright bride is personified by Eve, but the black bride is personified by Lilith, who is said to
have been the "first wife of Adam." According to legend, before Eve was
created, the Lord gave Lilith to Adam as a partner. He was the image of
God by day, she was the image of God by night, and they were ordained
to be co-equal and to shine with the same supernal light.

Essentially, Lilith was the divine emanation of feminine power in all of
its glory and strength—awesome and wonderful. Adam could not deal
with Lilith, however, and felt overwhelmed by her, so he sought to subju-
gate her to himself. This played out in Adam and Lilith's attempts at love-
making. Adam always wanted to be on top, but Lilith thought, as equals,
they should lie side by side or that they should alternate who was on top.
Much to Lilith's frustration, however, Adam refused to allow it. This created strife between Adam and Lilith, so that they could find no happiness
or satisfaction with one another. As the story goes, eventually Lilith had
enough of Adam's attempts to dominate her, so she spoke a magic name of
God, rose into the air, and flew away into the wilderness of the desert
near the Red Sea. This was a place of ill-repute, said to be the haunt of
ancient demons, and there Lilith stayed.

Enraged, Lilith emanated her wrath in the form of Naamah, and Naamah engaged in unbridled sexual relations with the ancient demons, giving birth to hundreds of demons every night. Thus, the wrathful darkness
of Lilith—Naamah—became the mother and queen of demons. When
God saw that Lilith had departed from Adam, God sent three angels after
her—Senoy, Sansenoy, and Semangelof—and charged them to bring her
back to the Garden of Eden. They went out seeking Lilith and found her
place in the desert by the Red Sea. They beheld her dark wrath churning
the waters of the Red Sea and the great and lesser demons to which
Naamah was giving birth. The angels gave God's message to Lilith and
pleaded with her to return, but she would have nothing of it. The angels
pleaded with her to cease from the generation of demons, because their
numbers were becoming a threat to creation, but she would not stop. The
angels then took their report back to God.

When God heard that Lilith refused to return to Adam and that she
had emanated Naamah and was breeding a great demonic horde, God
brought forth a second female emanation from within Adam, calling her

Eve. Eve was completely submissive, which eventually led to her submission to the serpent and the fall. God then sent the three angels back to Lilith to bind her power, lest the great darkness she was birthing should overwhelm all of creation.

When the three angels appeared to Lilith again, they told her what God had done and threatened to destroy her if she did not stop the generation of demons. Her fury was kindled even more upon hearing this, and from it emerged Iggaret, the hag of chaos. She appeared as an unspeakable horror—a great nothing filled with an unquenchable thirst and ravishing hunger seeking to devour the whole of creation. Even the three angels of God felt dread and terror when they beheld her.

Lilith spoke to the three angels, saying, "You, creatures of heaven, will destroy me? I am an emanation and I cannot be destroyed by you. Were you to destroy me, creation itself would not endure, for I am among the great powers in creation, without which creation would not be upheld. Creation exists for the human one, and I am part of the soul of the human one. The soul of the human one and the soul of creation cannot be divided. What will become of your precious human being and God's creation if you destroy me?" The angels responded, "We have misspoken, Lilith; we have not been given the power to destroy you, but to bind you. And bind you we shall if you do not cease from your rage against your creator and his creatures. Have you considered your own fate before Iggaret? If she devours the whole of creation, although an emanation, you also will return to the great unmanifest, and it will be to you as the second death of oblivion. And if you fill the whole of creation with demons, and all things are destroyed, will you not be condemned to exist forever and ever in the plains of desolation left in the wake of your rage?"

Upon hearing this, Lilith let out a great scream; she screeched and howled and wailed, and Iggaret returned into her. She spoke a magic name of God and said to the three angels, "My wrath is not kindled against the Lord God, but against Adam and the submissive woman, and against the weak children that shall be born of their union and the pitiful weakness in creation that shall be brought into being by this degenerate humankind. Therefore, hear the magic name of God I speak, and the spell of my vow. Every day, you and the company of heaven may cull the weak from among my children, and thus tend a balance between the light and the darkness; but so also shall I cull the weak from among the sons and daughters of Adam, and my children shall make sport of the children of Adam until the end of time. Where there are amulets, talismans, or seals placed bearing your names, I shall not enter, and when these are placed upon the children of Adam I will not seek to take the life of the child; but where knowledge and wisdom are lacking, there I will enter, and the unprotected child will fall to my domain. Those among the children of Adam that seek to fulfill the will of the Lord, I will leave unharmed, but those who stand against the will of the Lord, I shall go against and prevail. When the children of Adam abandon the covenant because of their weakness, when the house of the Lord lays in desolation and the Great Mother is in exile, then I shall dwell with the Lord in the place of the Mother and on earth it shall be called the end of days. Great darkness shall come upon the earth and I shall loose Iggaret in the world, and it shall be seen who are faithful and who are unfaithful, who are strong and who are weak, among the children of Adam. For this, I have come into being, and by the will of the Lord, it shall be done as I have spoken it." The angels affirmed the vow of Lilith and departed from her, having accomplished their mission.

This is the beginning of the story of Lilith—one variation among the many that are told in the oral tradition of Sophian Gnosticism. Her story could easily fill a large volume when coupled with the commentaries and teachings that have been generated from it. Previously, we have spoken of the integral role of evil in creation, which allows for the existence of free will and the resistance necessary for an actual evolution. Likewise, we have spoken of the ordeals of initiation and the challenge of power that an initiate must face in the process of self-realization. Essentially, Lilith is the personification of the Shekinah or the Bride's manifestation in these experiences—the dark nights of the soul that are critical to any actual enlightenment and liberation. It is the Holy Spirit that leads Yeshua out into the desert to be tempted by Satan, it is the Holy Spirit that causes the mystical death through which the resurrection is attained, and it is the Holy Spirit that manifests as the horror and beauty of the apocalypse— this is the black bride, Sophia Nigrans.

In Lilith's relationship with Eve, it is as though she personifies all aspects of the divine feminine and womanhood that are threatening and unacceptable to the patriarchal mind—the enigmatic and mysterious nature of the feminine. She is the female sensual-sexual dynamism; the irrational, unpredictable, and chaotic qualities of feminine creativity; the intensity of unbridled emotion and passion; true feminine intelligence and independence—the full power of womanhood. Eve and Lilith joined together, therefore, personify true womanhood or the complete woman. If manhood and womanhood fulfill and complete one another and if there is both a masculine and feminine aspect in men and women alike, then without Lilith, Adam and Eve are incomplete. It is for this reason that Sophian Gnosticism speaks of the redemption of Lilith as integral to the redemption of humanity—both men and women—and speaks of Eve and Lilith united in the person of the Holy Bride, St. Mary Magdalene.

In the story of St. Mary Magdalene, sexuality plays a significant role, from the event of her rape and her becoming a prostitute to her ultimate redemption as the consort and wife of Lord Yeshua and mother of his child. The Gnostic Gospel, which speaks of the union of the Holy Bride and Bridegroom, alludes to the healing and redemption of our sexuality as an integral part of our self-realization. This corresponds to another aspect of Lilith. In the story of Lilith, she is specifically associated with a class of she-demons and he-demons called *succubae* and *incubi*. These evil spirits are said to seek out lone men and women to lay with them and produce demonic children. Thus, Lilith personifies repressed sexual energy and the imbalance and perversions that result from repression. The redemption of Lilith, therefore, also relates to the healing of human sexuality, the importance of which becomes apparent when one considers the sexual misconduct and aberrations that occur in religious institutions where repression is the rule. As we have said, sexual energy is the most fundamental manifestation of the Shekinah-power in the human experience. Thus, denial and repression of our sexuality is a rejection of the Shekinah and prevents the sublimation of sexual energy that is crucial to the self-realization process. While some might think of sublimation as an abstinence from sexual relations, that is not the case in Gnostic Christianity and the Kabbalah. By sublimation is meant the ability to consciously direct sexual or desire energy and, through conscious control, to experience real satisfaction and happiness—hence to fulfill the more subtle and sublime desire within and behind the gross external form. When a sexual relationship is founded upon love, the sublimation of sexual energy is the natural result. This is equally true of any manifestation of desire energy. When manifest with love, it is inherently righteous.

The black bride—Lilith—will not be understood by way of a rational explanation nor will the importance that is placed upon her in the Sophian Tradition. As we have said above, the Bride does not teach and initiate us through philosophical arguments; rather, she imparts herself through life experience. To gain knowledge and understanding of the black bride, one must invoke her and embrace her completely, accepting the whole of oneself and one's life as it is and letting go to the divine passion wherever it leads. Through her, we are able to pass beyond our fears and discover the true delight of life and, perhaps more importantly, realize that there is no part of us that is not of God's presence. If one is so willing, she will lead one from the darkness into the light and bring about the deepest possible healing on all levels—a wholeness of being that is unimaginable.

The Doctrine of the Soul Mate

According to the Kabbalah, every human soul comes from Adam Kadmon, and every embodied human soul is within Adam Ha-Rishon. Adam Ha-Rishon is the supernal Adam at the level of Atzilut in which male and female were joined together in one holy image. When the supernal Adam was separated into man and woman—Adam and Eve—the holy souls (Neshamot) destined to become human beings were also divided into male and female. Thus, every person has a soul mate, a perfect spiritual counterpart, that he or she is destined to meet and unite with at some point in the transmigration of the soul.

The Kabbalah says that the patriarchs and matriarchs were soul mates and that all the holy couples in the living myth of the Scriptures represent soul mates. As we have seen, in Christian Gnosticism Lord Yeshua and Lady Mary are considered soul mates, the reincarnation of Jacob and Rachel. The association of soul mates with holy couples in the Scriptures indicates the dynamic circumstances, situations, and events that occur when soul mates are able to meet and unite with one another in the world, and reflects the conditions necessary for their meeting, for the soul-being of both partners must have a sufficient degree of evolution and have accomplished all necessary tikkune of the soul before they are ready to meet and restore their unity. Likewise, both must be incarnate at the same time in male and female form, corresponding to the aspect of the Neshamah they represent, both must attain and embody their supernal soul, and the conditions in their environment—place, time, and circumstance—must be just right. Only then do soul mates meet and unite with one another. Essentially, the soul-being must evolve to a higher grade and be near to the attainment of self-realization in order to meet its destined partner. The masters of the Tradition say that the union of soul mates is integral to the fulfillment of the ultimate mission of the Neshamah in creation and that the soul's mission cannot be completed apart from one's soul mate.

Soul mates may meet in an incarnation, but not be able to unite because the necessary conditions are not present. Likewise, souls destined for one another may meet and unite, but not accomplish the mission of the Neshamah and therefore not perfect their union. After all, a true mystical union must bear good fruit and the two who become one must fulfill and complete one another. In many lifetimes, one's soul mate may not even be incarnate or, if incarnate, may not be in synchronous movement for a meeting and union to take place. According to the Tradition, soul mates are able to meet and unite only through divine providence, which is to say, through divine grace. When soul mates meet and unite, however, it is a powerful and wonderful event and the blessing of their union extends light and life to others. Soul mates uplift humanity and the world. It is said to be a union of great beauty that facilitates the manifestation of the divine kingdom.

When speaking of soul mates, my teacher would always say, "You should not expect to meet your soul mate in this life, neither should you doubt that you will; but in all your relationships you should seek to create the conditions necessary for this holy union—for one never knows when it shall come to pass. You must have a good heart and clear conscience, and cultivate compassion and love. All our relations prepare us to meet our beloved, whom the Beloved has ordained for us at the outset of creation."

Previously, we spoke of our capacity to meet and recognize a holy tzaddik. According to the sages of wisdom, it is the same capacity necessary for us to meet and recognize our soul mate, for an authentic spiritual teacher is akin to a soul mate, and as the tzaddik is a face of the beloved, so also is our soul mate. As much as leading us to a conscious union with

God, the tzaddik also prepares us to meet our soul mate—hence to fulfill our true will or the mission of our Neshamah.

Apart from our soul mate, we may be able to draw upon something of our Yechidah and Hayyah, but only when we are in union with our soul mate are we able to embody them. Thus, the Kabbalah says that the fullness of the Shekinah—the upper and lower Shekinah—comes to rest only upon a man or woman when he or she is joined to his or her opposite: when a man and woman are completely united in true love.

The doctrine of the soul mate reveals the significance and holiness placed upon human relationships in Gnostic Christianity. It also serves to teach Gnostic initiates how to rightly approach intimate personal relationships. It teaches that one is to love one's partner as oneself and seek out a relationship in which the fulfillment of both partners is possible. Specifically, it teaches the Gnostic to seek out relationships that cultivate his or her humanity and that serve to facilitate conscious spiritual evolution. Whether one is with one's soul mate or in an exchange of sparks with another soul, the foundation of all intimate personal relationships is to be the same. This is reflected in the story of Jacob, who is married to both Leah and Rachel, and his equal respect and love for both partners, even though it was Rachel who was his soulmate.

The teaching on soul mates also reflects the Gnostic emphasis upon development of a coequality of men and women. While a great imbalance exists between men and women, the meeting and union of soul mates can only remain a relatively rare and exceptional phenomenon. True manhood cannot exist apart from true womanhood, and, in the Gnostic view, the second coming is dependent upon the meeting and union of a larger number of soul mates in the collective of humanity. Although a single man or woman may become a holy tzaddik, the perfect tzaddik is one who is joined with his or her soul mate in the great work and the two are able to act together as one holy person, as we see in the case of Lord Yeshua and Lady Mary. It is said that there is no greater manifestation of the Christ presence than that which comes into being through the union of soulmates.

The Community of the Elect—
The Gnostic Circle

Spiritual community is a manifestation of Malkut in the material world, closely associated with the angelic choir representing Malkut in Asiyah— the order of the Ashim, which means "souls of fire." Just as Malkut is the holy vessel receiving the influx of spiritual energy from all of the Sefirot, the spiritual community or Gnostic circle is a physical channel and vehicle of all divine powers in the material world.

This is reflected in Judaic Tradition. When prayer services are performed in a Jewish synagogue, there must be a minimum of ten people gathered together in worship; otherwise, the prayer service is considered null and void. According to Jewish Kabbalists, it is a great blessing to be among the first ten to arrive for prayer services, as the presence and power of a Sefirah naturally comes to rest upon each of the ten and from them the spiritual energy flows out to the entire congregation. While the number ten represents the Sefirot, it is also the number of the Hebrew letter Yod—the first holy letter of the Tetragrammaton. Thus, the spiritual community has the power to draw down a supernal blessing from the Sefirot of Atzilut. This is reflected when Lord Yeshua indicates that the Spirit of the Messiah is naturally present when "two or more are gathered" in the blessed name, Pentagrammaton—Yeshua.

The divine incarnation transpires through Lord Yeshua and Lady Mary, yet, as we have seen, it is the spiritual community that forms around the anointed one that creates the necessary conditions for the incarnation and the light transmission to occur. A matrix of souls is needed to form a holy vessel to receive the influx of the supernal light in the world and to impart the light-force to souls of various grades. The divine fullness of the Soul of the Messiah is, in fact, too great for a single individual, but requires a group of individuals to embody it. In the Gnostic view, the Soul of the Messiah entered into Lord Yeshua, Lady Mary, the Holy Mother, and all of the holy apostles, so that the sacred circle or spiritual community is, in truth, the mystical body of Christ—every initiate being a member of the mystical body through which the soul of the anointed is incarnate. Thus, the incarnation continues through the spiritual community that is founded upon the transmission of a living presence—the apostolic succession.

In Gnostic Tradition, this is something more than the poetic metaphor it has become in orthodox Christianity. Gnosticism is founded upon self-realization and understands that the Soul of the Messiah is embodied by initiates, more or less, depending upon their grade of attainment. Thus, there are elders and tau who embody something of the supernal or Messianic consciousness and there are circles of initiates that form around them and serve as a matrix of the light-presence. It is not merely the elder or tau who embodies something of the Soul of the Messiah, but the whole spiritual community. As a matter of fact, the degree to which a tzaddik is able to draw down the Soul of the Messiah is completely dependent upon the degree to which his or her spiritual community is able to receive and embody it. Regardless of how self-realized or enlightened an individual may be, it takes more than one single individual to embody and manifest the supernal light-presence in full—it takes a whole spiritual community.

As we pointed out when we explored the Gnostic circle or spiritual community as the third object of refuge of the outer sanctuary, the spiritual community in Gnostic Christianity is an esoteric order or Mystery school in which we receive a spiritual education. The nature of this education is a bringing forth of that which is within us and is based upon knowledge and experience—hence, initiation. More than any of the lessons we might receive in a Mystery school, it is the transmission of substantial and helpful spiritual energy that we need, which awakens the divine power of our soul of light and helps uplift us to a higher level of consciousness. In profane society, the individual always functions at a higher level than the group; however, in a spiritual community, the group functions at a higher level than any single individual and serves to activate the greater potential of the individual. This is the power of Malkut.

In speaking about spiritual community, it must be said that, in terms of Sophian Gnosticism, we are not referring to a communal setting. While there may be a center of the spiritual community, where meetings take place and initiates gather for prayer, meditation, and sacred ritual, members of the community live in their own homes, sometimes at great distances from the center. Diversity and individuality are prized in the Sophian Tradition. Thus, initiates come from all walks of life and are encouraged to live an independent lifestyle while also being an active member of the spiritual community to which they belong. The Gnostic ideal is a dynamic balance between the individual and the community in which both are mutually supported and fulfilled. This is the great lesson we must learn in the Aquarian Age on both a local and global level. In the Gnostic view it is critical for the continued survival and evolution of humanity on planet earth. It is a lesson of Malkut.

The Living Temple

As we have seen, the Kabbalah says that God's purpose in creation was the generation of the human one, who is the image and likeness of Yahweh Elohim. The purpose of the human one, as the image and likeness of Yahweh Elohim, is to recognize and realize the soul of light, which is the presence and power of God and Godhead in the human one—hence to consciously unite with God and embody something of God. When we speak of the divine incarnation of Christ in the person of Lord Yeshua, of the incarnation of Mother Sophia and Daughter Sophia in Mother Mary and St. Mary of Magdal, it is this state of self-realization and embodiment of the divine presence and power that we mean—the attainment of *enlightenment.*

As we have said, this attainment is not isolate to Yeshua, Mother Mary, or St. Mary of Magdal. It is the basis of a true apostolic succession from one generation to another, and represents our own divine destiny. Thus, it is also possible for us to attain various degrees of Christ consciousness and to experience conscious unification with God, just as Master Yeshua did, as well as others around him.

The Partzufim below, such as Lord Yeshua, Lady Mary, and Mother Mary, are akin to magical links to the spiritual and universal principles they represent. Thus, their names, images, and myths are vehicles through which we contact the light-presence and light transmission in our spiritual practice. There is divine power in their names, images, and myths. Yet, ultimately, it is within ourselves that we must recognize and realize the light-presence of Christ, and we, too, must seek to embody the Christos. This spiritual aim is the true heart of Christian Gnosticism, and through the study and practice of the Christian Kabbalah, we learn how to accomplish this aim.

Lord Yeshua makes it perfectly clear in the Gospels that the worship of God in spirit and truth is not dependent upon external temples or anything outside of ourselves. Rather, it is dependent upon the state of our minds, hearts, and lives, upon whether or not we live with the awareness of sacred unity or are deceived by the illusion of separation. Thus, the true temple in Sophian Gnosticism is first and foremost the human being—oneself and one's life, through which something of the divine presence and power is embodied—hence a living temple.

When we speak about individuals becoming Partzufim below, we are actually speaking of living temples of the holy Shekinah in the material plane. To the degree that we draw our mind, heart, and life into harmony with Christ and cleave with our soul to God, we also become living temples. In this sense, every Gnostic knows that he or she is a living temple and seeks to live as a vehicle of the light-presence.

In Gnostic Christianity, practitioners often set aside rooms in their homes as sanctuaries for prayer, meditation, and sacred ritual. Likewise, some Gnostic circles construct external temples as places for mystical and magical practices and the rites of initiation. Yet, in Gnosticism, spiritual practice, initiation, and self-realization are not dependent upon such things, however useful they might be in the process, but rather are dependent upon individuals making themselves the house of God. In the Christian Gnostic view, this is the purpose of the human being—to be living temples of God's presence and power in all planes of sentient existence, and thus to unite heaven and earth. One who does this, according to the masters of the Tradition, walks in beauty and holiness and manifests the divine kingdom. Hence, that person is a holy person, like unto Yeshua Messiah and Kallah Messiah. This is the true meaning of "Christian" to the Gnostic initiate.

The Power of Prayer—Simple Magic

Prayer is among the common spiritual practices of the Gnostic and Christian Kabbalist, which is a way of saying "holding a conversation with God." Many might think of prayer as somehow seeking to change the mind of God; however, quite the opposite is true. We pray to change our own mind and heart, to bring about a change in our own consciousness, so that it is aligned and in harmony with the divine will and divine kingdom—our own true will. The practice of prayer is quite amazing. Sometimes nothing at all is changed by our prayers, save our ability to accept what is happening—our ability to look and see reality as it is and to accept it as it is. Just as often, however, as we bring about a change in our own consciousness, a corresponding change happens outwardly in life, as though by magic! Some would say that the former are prayers unanswered, while the latter are prayers answered, but this reflects an immaturity in understanding prayer, or a misconception regarding prayer; for whether an inward change that brings us into harmony with what's happening or an inward change in consciousness that facilitates a corresponding outward change, our prayer has been answered.

We are all well acquainted with the constant and relentless internal dialogue in our heads that seems to never slow down. Thoughts continually flow, often quite fitfully and randomly, and all too often our thoughts become very negative and self-destructive. Aside from becoming a highly skilled meditator, it is extremely difficult to completely silence the mind, especially when we are under stress or plagued with negativity. Essentially, prayer is a method of directing our inner dialogue toward something positive and productive, using the inner dialogue as a way of turning to our inner and higher self and God for comfort and empowerment. The development of a daily prayer life is very interesting; at times we find that, when prayer is exhausted, we do experience a silence of mind and quieting of the vital—we come to meditation (a resting of the mind in its inmost nature).

According to the masters of the Tradition, a true adept abides in constant prayer; the instruction given to the neophyte in early initiation is to "enflame yourself in prayer, and invoke constantly." As a novice, I recall hearing this and thinking to myself, "I'll never be able to do that! How can anyone be in this world and pray constantly?" My beloved tzaddik, blessed be his memory, was quite aware of how I felt and he said to me, "Little one, you and everyone are praying all of the time. It is just that some prayers are not well spoken and perhaps would be best if not prayed. Every thought and feeling is a prayer, every action and gesture, every word spoken, every breath and beat of your heart—the whole of life is constant prayer. One need only be awake and alert and mindful in one's prayer. Whenever there is awareness, there is holy prayer."

While we often think of prayer in terms of something completely mental—an internal dialogue in thought or externalized in a spoken prayer—

there are also prayers of silence, prayers of the body, prayers of just breathing, prayers of good works, prayers of kindness, prayers of pure emotion and feeling, and so on. Anything can be a prayer if there is kavvanah. Sacred ritual is often called prayer, and in spiritual practice the boundaries between prayer and meditation become completely obscured. Prayer is not merely talking or thinking, but is any movement of being inward and upward—Godward. As much as with words, for example, one could pray by dancing. In other words, prayer is what you make it, and it is a completely creative adventure to the Gnostic!

In terms of what we might typically think of as prayer, we must say this: as much as talking to God, one must entertain silence and listen. After all, a real conversation is two-way, not one-way. In the Gospels, we hear of Yeshua's retreats at night to pray—a vigil he would hold all night. One thing is quite certain. He was not talking at God all night, but also abided in the silence to listen and hear what God might say. If people do not believe God talks to us, it may only be that they do not know how to listen and hear, and thus only that they have not heard God's voice. It is the "still small voice" of the Christ-self and the speaking silence in one's inmost heart. But life, itself, is also God speaking, for God continues to speak creation. This is reflected in the traditional vow of the magister templi: "I will listen and hear God speaking to my secret and undying soul in every circumstance, situation, and event of my life." As much as the aim of the master of the temple, it is a fine aim for the initiate of any grade, including the neophyte and zelator associated with Malkut.

There is a wonderful form of prayer, which also qualifies as a form of divine magic in the Tradition. Essentially, the initiate takes a candle, purifies it with prayer, and consecrates it with invocations, often anointing the candle with holy oil. White candles are good for any purpose, but a color may be chosen corresponding to the Sefirot best suited to one's prayer. The invocations can include the corresponding divine name, archangel and order of angels, or attributes of the corresponding Partzuf. Once purified and consecrated, the candle can be lit, along with some incense. This is the basis of candle magic and is also a form of prayer. Sometimes, initiates may even carve symbols in the candle or divine names or the names of angels. It is a wonderful and easy spiritual practice!

Prayer, in effect, makes oneself the vehicle or channel of the Life-power and of the divine powers. We have already established that the Spirit of Yahweh and the divine powers need vehicles or channels through which to enter and act upon the earth. Oftentimes, good things cannot happen because there is no vehicle or channel for the good that God intends. For example, a person may be in need of healing and it may be God's intention that the person be healed, but there must also be a desire to receive the healing power and a holy vessel willing to bring down and transmit that divine power. Thus, to pray and embody something of the divine presence and power or to not pray in order to create the necessary conditions and link for divine grace to act is a matter of our freedom of will. It is not only God who must will it; it is we who must also be willing. Through prayer, we become the holy vessel receiving the good the divine intends for ourselves, for others, and for this good earth—hence, the correspondence of prayer to Malkut.

Thanksgiving and the Blessing Upon Food

Praise and thanksgiving of all forms corresponds to Malkut, which is the act of uplifting consciousness and life to the divine and is an active expression of the awareness of God's presence in life and in oneself. It is common that Gnostics praise and give thanks for all things in life, but the center of thanksgiving is perhaps the thanksgiving and blessing upon the food we eat, which is most fundamental to life. In praise and thanksgiving, the initiate uplifts the holy sparks contained in everything in life, and this is especially true of the food we eat.

In the Gnostic view, the Holy Eucharist is not isolated to the wedding feast, but extends to all food. For when we eat and drink, we are eating and drinking the body of our earthly Mother and her children; every meal is the Eucharist of the Mother. In giving thanks and invoking a blessing upon the food we eat, we are mindful of the divine Mother who provides for all of our needs and of our heavenly Father who is the one life-power within and behind the whole of creation. According to the sages of wisdom, in blessing food, we serve to "enthrone the Bride in the Mother"—we uplift Malkut to Binah.

In the ceremony of the Holy Eucharist, the bread and wine are talismatic of the presence and essence of the Christos and represent Sophia and Logos, respectively. They become talismatic because of the consecration and spiritual energy with which they are imbued in the sacred ritual. On the most fundamental level, the bread and wine are pervaded with our positive thoughts and our joy in the celebration of the supreme mystery of the bridal chamber—our unity with the Christos. This imbuing substances and things with spiritual and psychic energy is not isolated to such ceremonies, however, but, in fact, is going on all of the time. We humans are constantly pervading the atmosphere around us and things in our environment with spiritual and psychic energies—vibrations. These vibrations serve to link things to spiritual forces of a corresponding frequency of vibration, whether it is positive, negative, or admixed. Thus, it becomes, in effect, talismatic.

Aside from whatever holy sparks of the life-power might be within something, it also bears the energy-intelligence with which it has been charged by human beings. All individuals involved in the process of cultivating our food are unlikely to be happy, and certainly many individuals involved with the cultivation, harvest, and preparation of our food are unlikely to be of a completely positive and loving state of mind. Thus, along with a need to uplift the holy sparks contained in our food, there is a need to transform any negative energy or vibration that might be in it and to imbue it with positive and loving energy. Some adepts and masters of the Tradition propose that failure to be mindful with our food and to bless it is a cause for many problems in health and happiness. For, in mindlessness with our food, we take in all manner of unwholesome energies or vibrations.

Thus, while preparing our food and before partaking of our meals, we give thanks and bless the food. We give thanks to the divine Mother and her children who give us life, and we invoke a blessing upon all who have served to provide us with our food. All the while, we are conscious of the many people and creatures involved, and seeking to uplift one and all alike through the awareness of sacred unity—God. Thus, the Gnostic initiate makes his or her meals talismans of positive spiritual forces and, in mindfully partaking of the meal, serves to uplift the sparks through service to the great work. Every form of thanksgiving and blessing has the same objective in mind, and in so doing, we link ourselves with Malkut—the divine kingdom.

The Great Ofan of the Faithful—The Shoe-Angel

At the level of Beriyah, Malkut manifests as the archangel Sandalfon, which literally means "the Ofan (wheel) of the Sandal" or the "shoe-angel." As we saw in our study of the Ofanim, they are angels of interfacing, and as the term shoe-angel suggests, Sandalfon is the interface of the divine kingdom with the earth in Beriyah. Essentially, Sandalfon is the archangel whose principal mission is to unite the heavens and the earth and, more specifically, the earth and the world of supernal light. This latter idea of a link between the supernal abode and the earth is reflected in the saying in the Christian Kabbalah that "Sandalfon is the twin sister of Metatron" or that "Sandalfon is the presence of the great prince below."

In the Book of Exodus, we are told that a pillar of cloud went before the children of Israel by day and a pillar of fire by night while they wandered in the wilderness. This is said to be Metatron and Sandalfon, the pillar of fire being constant lightning flashes within the pillar of cloud that stood out in the night. Metatron and Sandalfon are also said to be attributed to the two kerubim on the ark of the covenant, Sandalfon being the female kerub on the left. Metatron is called the great angel of Enoch and Sandalfon is called the great angel of Elijah. In Merkavah mysticism, they are said to be the great Ofan of the Chariot. Thus, while they are the archangelic manifestation of Keter and Malkut, they are also the archangels of the Pillar of Severity and Pillar of Mercy.

The masters of the Tradition have said that Metatron is the matrix of the supernal abode and that Sandalfon is the matrix of the universe. In the experience of supernal consciousness, the initiate discovers that the light above is everywhere below; hence Metatron is the supernal light beyond the heavens and Sandalfon is the supernal light at the center of every particle of matter. Indeed! These two are inwardly one great angel, their unity being called the great angel Hua, as previously discussed. Metatron-Sandalfon is, thus, the holy angel of the Shekinah, the angel of the presence of the Lord. In Christian Gnosticism, Metatron is the angel of Lord Yeshua and Sandalphon is the angel of Lady Mary—the angel Hua being their union: one Christ-presence.

Associated with the Holy Bride, Sandalfon is the archangel of this good earth, as though the body of the holy angel is planet earth; likewise,

Sandalfon is the holy angel of spiritual community, present wherever the faithful and elect gather for prayer, meditation, and sacred ritual. Accordingly, it is said that Sandalfon serves to uplift the prayers of the faithful and elect, bearing them up before the presence of the Lord in the supernal abode. Likewise, any time a person enters into a prophetic consciousness, the archangel Sandalfon is said to be present as the space of that holy awareness. It is also said that Sandalfon is present whenever one encounters a tzaddik, for the angel of the light-presence is the constant companion of the holy ones.

Sandalfon is commonly envisioned as a great pillar of fire, but also as a great angel whose entire body and wings are filled with eyes and who is radiant with rainbow glory. Holding either image of the great angel in mind, initiates invoke Sandalfon through the divine name of Adonai and the chant *So Da Yo Ma Sandalfon*.

Sandalfon is invoked in works of unification, mystical prayer, and prophetic meditation. She knows mysteries of creation and the ascension of the soul; mysteries of Arabot (the seventh heaven), merkavah and prophecy; magical evocation, extradimensional travel, works of manifestation, secrets of nature, certain forms of healing; mysteries of the incarnation of souls from among the elder races, among other things. Although she is such a lofty and great holy angel, Sandalfon is said to be easily invoked and quick to come, as she is already very near!

The Order of the Ashim—Souls of Fire

Malkut at the level of Yetzirah manifests as the order of the Ashim, which literally means "burning angels," "angels of fire," or "souls of fire." Some have written that the Ashim are angelic forces that serve to bind matter together, and this is certainly true. Some classes of the Ashim serve in this function. Among the Ashim are also angels that serve to facilitate evolution by generation of increasingly higher and more refined life-forms; likewise, the Ashim represent something of the fiery light of the supernal world within matter. Higher classes of the Ashim also serve as angels of fates and divine providence, and labor to facilitate the divine plan in creatures and creation. For example, Azrael, the angel of death who draws for souls from the body at the conclusion of life, is of a higher class of the order of Ashim. By the same token, so also is the angel said to put its finger on the lips of newborn babes, causing the soul to forget all previous incarnations, so as to be fully present in the new life. As we have seen previously in our discussion of the other holy choirs, the orders of angels are complex and multileveled, so that to speak of the full mystery and function of any order is humanly impossible. They are other than human and certainly not linear in any way.

In the Gospel of St. John we hear of the "angels of the seven churches," which are Ashim. According to the masters of the Tradition, there is an Ashim associated with every spiritual community—an angel involved in the mind and mission of every spiritual group. One can only wonder if there are Ashim associated with the writing of spiritual books and other such activities, as they are angels of manifesting the spiritual in the material.

There are also teachings in the Tradition of a very different nature concerning the Ashim, in which the Ashim are said to be "souls set on fire with the Holy Spirit"—hence, the translation of Ashim as "souls of fire." The soul of a holy tzaddik and, indeed, any person among the faithful and elect on fire with the Lord is Ashim. Likewise, the term is also used to denote an elect soul who has received the gift of the fiery intelligence. There is also a more esoteric use of this word to allude to the idea of souls that come from among the elder races and incarnate among us to serve as light-bearers on earth. While many might think of aliens coming in spaceships, and gawk up at the stars looking for UFOs, according to Gnostic masters, truly advanced races do not need space traveling machines to visit the earth, but rather can spontaneously generate bodies to appear in the world or transmit their consciousness into an incarnation here. Thus, Gnostic masters would suggest that "aliens" already live and move among us and have since the dawn of human history—bearing the gift of the fiery intelligence to humankind! As fantastic and fanciful as this might seem, it certainly proves an incredibly interesting contemplation and sparks the imagination. If one were to ever encounter a master of the magical art and be blessed to observe him or her in the continuum (a ceremony in which he or she fully engages his or her art), one would certainly be given to wonder about their human status! But then, by definition, the great work is the process of becoming more than human. The word

Ashim is often used to remind us of this in the Christian Kabbalah. This well represents the broad spectrum of teachings concerning the order of the Ashim in the mysteries of Malkut.

The Zealous One

These ideas concerning the Ashim naturally lead us to a brief comment of the Rosicrucian grade associated with Malkut, which is called the zelator. While the neophyte is also associated with Malkut, the grade of zelator is an entrance proper to the sphere of Malkut, whereas the Neophyte is one who as yet remains the outsider. Zelator implies the zealous one or a person filled with zeal and, we might add, filled with holy awe and wonder—hence, a sense of the mystery. It implies one who is being reborn of the spirit or who is experiencing a quickening of consciousness—an awakening of faith and holy remembrance of the soul and why the soul has come here. It also suggests the dawn of an awareness of God's presence within oneself and within creation, a growing sense of sacred unity. This is the zelator and it is the experience of being set on the path.

It implies something more, as well. For the path in Gnosticism, at least in the Sophian and Kabbalistic Tradition, is one of initiation and discipleship. As an individual who was a disciple of a sacred tau (tzaddik), I can definitely say that meeting and recognizing my teacher, and experiencing the light-presence that moved with, in, and through him, generated great zeal and spiritual hope in me. Meeting Tau Elijah led to my initiation and being set upon the path. Were it not for that day, I really could not say what I would be doing today, and without a doubt, I would not be experiencing the joy of writing this book on the mysteries of the Kabbalah. I might well have never become a Gnostic and Kabbalist! To this day, the zeal of meeting my spiritual friend fills me and inspires me. I have never left Malkut—the divine kingdom.

On a more esoteric level, the title zelator implies something else: the delightful awareness that the kingdom of heaven is spread out upon the earth—hence, that living life to its fullest can be the experience of the kingdom, as surely as any experience in the hereafter. Zeal is the natural result of experiencing Malkut in this life. In Gnostic Tradition, we experience the kingdom here, and ever beyond!

Spiritual Practice Associated with Malkut

Meditation of Kallah Messiah—St. Mary Magdalene

> Find the time to sit, breathe, and feel the life in your body, the sacredness of being and becoming. (This, in itself, is a meditation of the Holy Bride.) Once you are settled, shift the focus of your attention to the spiritual sun within behind your heart, envisioning it clearly and feeling it deeply. See it pervade your whole body-mind and let it completely consume you, banishing all negativity and darkness. Let there be peace and joy. From the sun in your heart, imagine a ruby ray of light shooting forth and that the image of the Holy Bride magically appears in the space before you. Her inner robe is brilliant white, her outer robe is crimson, her face shines like ten thousand stars, and there is rainbow glory all around her. She is the most beautiful woman imaginable.

> She does not stand still but dances like flames of fire, as you take up her most simple chant: *Kallah Messiah, Nukva Messiah.* As you chant, envision her blessing you, pouring out light and fire upon you, and that she merges to dance in your very body, as though a great fire of divine passion within and all around you. It is All-Joy! It may be that you cannot sit still but must get up and dance too. It's all good, whatever the Holy Bride inspires you to do! When all is said and done, ground the energy and abide a while in silence. When you go out into the world, see the Bride in everything and everyone, hear her voice in every sound, and whatever thoughts, emotions, and feelings arise, know them as the radiance of her wisdom. Some have attained Christ consciousness in this way!

The end of the book; the beginning of another

HEBREW TABLE

OF LETTERS

Names	Figures	Value		Meaning
(M) Aleph	א	1		Ox or Bull
(D) Bet	ב	2		House
(D) Gimel	ג	3		Camel
(D) Dalet	ד	4		Door
(S) Heh	ה	5		Window
(S) Vau	ו	6		Nail or Hook
(S) Zayin	ז	7		Sword
(S) Het	ח	8		Fence
(S) Tet	ט	9		Snake
(S) Yod	י	10		Hand
(D) Kaph	כ	20	500	Grasping hand
(S) Lamed	ל	30		Ox-goad
(M) Mem	מ	40	600	Water
(S) Nun	נ	50	700	Fish
(S) Samek	ס	60		Tent peg or prop
(S) Ayin	ע	70		Eye
(D) Peh	פ	80	800	Mouth
(S) Tzaddi	צ	90	900	Fishhook
(S) Qoph	ק	100		Back of the head
(D) Resh	ר	200		Face
(M) Shin	ש	300		Tooth or Fang
(D) Tau	ת	400		Mark or Cross

When a Hebrew letter is written in a larger form, the value of the letter is multiplied by one thousand its normal value. For example, an enlarged Aleph would equal 1000. This is true of all the letters.

Letters in Hebrew do not exist to signify vowels, but rather vowel points are used. The vowel points have not been included or discussed as they are not relevant to our study.

(M), (D), or (S) appearing in front of a letter name in the first column indicate Mother-letters, Double-letters, and Single-letters, respectively. Mother-letters refer to the force of the primordial elements—air, fire, and water. Double-letters represent the seven traditional planetary forces. The Single-letters represent the twelve zodiacal forces. The letter Tau often doubles as the symbol for the primordial earth. Shin is often used to represent the Holy Spirit. Aleph and Tau have a special association with the Christos—hence, Alpha and Omega. Nun, the fish, and Tet, the serpent, also have a special association with Christ. The study of the Netivot (paths) and holy letters will be the subject of a companion volume to be written as a continuation of this present book.

Much wisdom can be gleaned through contemplation and meditation on the holy letters themselves. In their contemplation and meditation on the holy letters, some initiates combine the major arcana of a proper tarot deck that has Kabbalistic value. The *Rider-Waite Tarot Deck* is adequate for this purpose; the tarot deck put out by the Builders of the Adytum (BOTA) is even better. Letters, numbers, words, and images prove an interesting divine play!

APPENDIX II

THE DIVINE

NAMES AND

VIBRATIONS

The art of vibration or intonation of the divine names plays a significant role in the methods of mystical prayer, meditation, and sacred ritual in Christian Gnosticism. As we have seen, the divine names are an expression of the holy Sefirot at the level of Atzilut-emanation. Thus, vibrating or intoning the divine name of a Sefirah (or Sefirot) brings into our prayer, meditation, or ritual the spiritual energy of the corresponding Sefirah (or Sefirot) and, likewise, brings our consciousness in ascent and joins it to the divine power. Essentially, using the divine names in this way, we are empowered by the divine powers and invoke the corresponding manifestation of the living presence. Their use strengthens the auric field or sphere of sensation, energizes the subtle body, and activates the hidden powers of our soul. Without a doubt, prayer is made extremely effective when the divine names are used; meditations are loftier and our rituals more potent.

There is great power in the divine names, for they have come by way of divine revelation, and the art of their pronunciation and vibration has been evolved by adepts and masters of the Kabbalah for literally thousands of years. While the divine name of Yahweh is not openly pronounced by Jewish practitioners of the Kabbalah, through the grace of the divine incarnation, the Gnostic Christian practitioner is empowered to do so, although, as with all of the divine names, the great name must be respected and used wisely. In this regard, the third commandment specifically relates to the esoteric or mystical use of the divine names: "You shall not make wrongful use of the name of the Lord your God . . ." Indeed! They are energy that needs to be mindfully directed and used wisely, with reverence and respect for the divine presence and power. According to the masters of the Tradition, the divine names should be used only in sacred moments and with full kavvanah (concentration and conscious intention) and devekut (proper attachment).

It is impossible to teach and initiate a person into the true art of vibrating the divine names through the medium of a book. The true art is something that is demonstrated and experienced between an initiate and an aspirant seeking to learn the art. It typically takes a few years to learn the art and to develop it through practice. There are many pronunciations, permutations, and intonements of all the divine names, and there are techniques of breath, gesture, and visualization that accompany the art. Nevertheless, we can put the aspirant on the trail of actual vibration of the divine names and give some clue as to how he or she might find a valid way to vibrate the names.

Some years ago, I watched the author of a popular book on the modern practice of magic give a demonstration of vibrating divine names, using a well-known Kabbalistic ceremony. I was quite surprised to hear him screaming the divine names in so-called vibration. This is an all too common mistake and the worst of all mistakes. It does not properly direct or radiate energy, but rather disturbs energy and tends to cause violent and chaotic movements in subtle body, aura, and environment. The other common mistake is singing the divine names, which, while beautiful, does not necessarily produce the effective vibration of the names. Vibration of the divine names is neither singing them nor screaming them, although it is certainly closer to song than to shouts.

When vibrating or intoning a divine name, what the practitioner is seeking to do, in general, is create an inward resonance of vibration that fills his or her body and sphere of sensation, and therefore also fills the atmosphere or environment around him or herself. More than how one might sound outwardly, one must first be concerned with this inward vibration, which tends to produce an electrical or energetic sensation in the body and quickens the vital and mental being. Indeed, it is a peculiar sound that, once experienced and heard, one will recognize any time it is encountered. As a matter of fact, this peculiar sound is one very easy way to discern initiates of the Tradition from noninitiates, along with pronunciation of the names in vibration: However, in practice, we find that vibration is more important than exact pronunciation. Finding the vibration, it is easy to refine pronunciations and pitch.

A good divine name for general practice seeking to discover vibration is Eheieh, pronounced: *Ah-Ha-Yah* (soft A's). First, it is a divine name of a wonderful affirmation, "I am" or "I shall be," which is always a good prayer and meditation in itself. Second, this pronunciation of Eheieh is very easy and is swiftly effective for recognizing what is meant by vibration. Let each syllable be drawn out and start with a quieter intoning, focusing on the vibration it produces. Then, gradually, increase the volume maintaining the sensation of vibration. In this way, one is very likely to stumble upon it. Then one can practice with other names. Obviously, in the beginning, lower intonations will more swiftly lend themselves to good results. Eventually, whether at a lower or higher pitch, given some practice, one should be able to find the vibration. Equally obvious, some individuals will have a natural talent at this, just as some people have a natural talent to sing, while for others, it will require some effort and it might never exactly become the strong point of their practice. However, as a general rule, everyone can learn to vibrate divine names.

The Names

Yah (E-Ah): The pronunciation is a long "E" and soft "A." This name has an expansive effect on consciousness and is intoned to invoke divine grace—pure energy that can be directed in almost any way. It is also used to increase life-force and prolong life.

Yahweh (E-AU-A): The pronunciation is a long "E," short "A" and "U," and long "A," and is one consistent flow of vowel sounds. This name invokes incredible force and has an elevating and energizing effect on consciousness. It is a name of Gnostic worship, which is to say a conscious unification with the divine. It is used to receive and transmit blessings.

Elohim (El-Oh-Heem): The pronunciation is a short "E," long "O," and long "E." This name has a sealing or enclosing effect on consciousness, a concentration of the consciousness. It reminds one of a womb—the mother. It is intoned to produce the effect of sanctuary, as a matrix of forces or creative potential.

El (El or Al): The pronunciation can be either with a short "E," short "A," or long "A," with the tip of the tongue curved up to the roof of the mouth while intoning it. This name is akin to Yah, although on a lower arc, and has a similar effect, although there is a focusing of the expansion—concentration and expansion at the same time. With an intention held in mind and the vibration of El, a corresponding blessing of abundance is invoked.

Elohim Givor (Gi-Voor): The pronunciation is forceful, Elohim as above and Givor with a short "I" or long "E," and Voor being pronounced as in "door." This has a radical focusing effect on consciousness and a fiery forceful energy—like lightning. It is intoned for protection, force, and fire; to dispel klippotic influence; to bring about radical change or transformation; and to invoke justice. It is often coupled with prayers for tikkune correction.

Yahweh Elohenu (El-Oh-Hey-New): Yahweh is pronounced as given above and Elohenu as it appears. The effect on consciousness is one of inward holiness and spirit-connectedness. It is vibrated to invoke awareness of Christ indwelling—the inner and higher self; for healing and for understanding of the word and empowerment to speak one's truth (the word).

Yahweh Tzavaot (Za-Vey-Ot): The pronunciation is a soft "A", long "A," and long "O." It has the effect on consciousness of connection with spiritual forces and sacred unity with creation. It is intoned to link with positive spiritual forces and to celebrate the sacred unity within and behind creation.

Elohim Tzavaot: The pronunciation is as given above. While Yahweh Tzavaot links, Elohim Tzavaot informs and specifies forms of the forces to manifest. It is intoned to manipulate the forms forces assume in a specific situation.

Yahweh Elohim Tzavaot: Combines the function of the two divine names.

Shaddai (Sha-Die): The pronunciation is a short "A" and long "I," and it has the effect on consciousness of stimulating desire-energy and directing it. This name is intoned for the sake of bliss and acceptance of life. It also tends to invoke good dreams and may bring visions (also the sight of auras).

Adonai (Ah-Doe-Nie): The pronunciation is a soft "A," long "O," and long "I." This name has a centering and grounding effect on consciousness. It is intoned for the purpose of grounding and manifesting things and for the awareness of the divine presence and power all around oneself—hence, God's presence pervading creation.

Yeshua Messiah (Yah-He-Shoe-Ah Me-See-Ah): The pronunciation is a short "A," short "E," short "U," soft "A," short "E," long "E," and short "A." This name has an illuminating effect on consciousness and is used to invoke the Christos and for an ascent toward Christos. Adonai Yeshua is similar, although more grounding—more a bringing down of the Christos rather than an ascent.

Kallah Messiah: The pronunciation of Kallah is with short "A's." This name has a nurturing effect on consciousness and also a healing effect. It is vibrated to invoke the presence and the Bride and to join the soul to her.

There are other pronunciations of these divine names and there are other names; however, these pronunciations are good for beginning practice of vibration and the names provided should be a sufficient selection. This should be enough to set one on track to discover the way of vibration for oneself.

APPENDIX III
CHANT
PRONUNCIATION

Kabbalistic Cross

Atoh: pronounced Ah-Toh (as in "dough" with a short "A")

Io Adonai: pronounced EE-Oh Ah-Doh-Nah-ee

Malkut: pronounced Mal-Koot (as in the "hoot" of an owl)

Ve-Gevurah: pronounced Vay-Gevurah (short vowels in Gevurah)

Ve-Gedulah: pronounced Vay-Ge-Dew-Lah

Le-Olam: pronounced Lay-Oh-Lawm

Mother's Practices

Aima-Aima: pronounced Ama-A-EE-Ma (short "A," long "I")

Aima Elohim: pronounced A-EE-Ma El-Oh-Heem

Ha Isha Ha Elyona, Aima Israel: pronounced with all short vowels, except for long "O" in Elyona and long "A" in Israel

Archangel's Chants

Yo Ma Tzafkiel: pronounced Yoh-Ma-Zah-f-Kee-El (Yo as in "dough," short "A")

Maggid Ha-El Elyon Tzadkiel: pronounced Mah-Gid Ha-El El-yon Zah-d-kee-El (Gid as in "kid," Yon as in "telephone," and short "A" throughout)

Ah Ya Ko Ma Kamael: pronounced Ah-Ya-Koh-Ma Ka-May-El (short "A" and Koh as in "dough")

Ar Iyah Raphael: pronounced Ar-EE-Yah Ra-Fay-El (Ar as in "you are" and Ra with short "A")

Ha Al Ha Na Haniel: pronounced Ha-Al-Ha-Na Ha-Nee-El (all short vowels)

Ya Mi Ha Michael: pronounced Ya-Mee-Ha Me-Kay-El (short "A")

Gya Ko Ho Ge Ba Gabriel: pronounced Gee-Yah Koe-Hoe Gee-Bah Gah-Bree-El

So Da Yo Ma Sandalfon: pronounced Soh-Da-Yoh-Ma San-Dal-Fon (Soh as in "to sow seed" and Fon as in "telephone")

As you work with these chants, let them speak to you and find your own way with them. In this way, you will find them very effective and empowering.

GLOSSARY

Ab: Father not having conceived a child; Partzuf of Hokmah; Hokmah before the emanation of Binah and the lower Sefirot; Father self-contained.

Abba: Father; Partzuf of Hokmah; Hokmah after emanating Binah and the lower Sefirot.

Abyss: A term for Da'at; the division between the supernals and the Sefirot of construction; the separation between Atzilut and the lower Olamot universes.

Adam: Human one, not necessarily the male gender.

Adam Ha-Rishon: First human being; supernal human being, male and female in one body; the ideal state of the human being; the androgynous one.

Adam Kadmon: Primordial human being; the first universe, which is inseparable from Ain Sof Or (the Endless Light); the universe of the Soul of Messiah.

Adept: A term for an experienced and highly skilled spiritual practitioner; an initiate who has a grade of self-realization to the level of cosmic consciousness; an elder or Gnostic teacher.

Aima: Mother; Partzuf of Binah; Binah having generated the seven Sefirot of construction.

Ain: No-thing or no-thingness; an aspect or quality of the Godhead; the inmost nature of the soul and God; the void or emptiness; the great unmanifest; the essence of divine potential.

Ain Sof: The infinite; the infinite and eternal; one-without-end; an aspect or quality of the Godhead indicating the exhaustless nature of the divine potential or unmanifest.

Ain Sof Or: Endless light or light of the infinite; an aspect or quality of the God-head; the radiant or creative quality of the divine potential or unmanifest; the divine fullness of the emptiness.

Ama: Mother before giving birth; Partzuf of Binah; Binah prior to the generation of the seven Sefirot of construction.

Apostle of apostles: A title of Lady Mary.

Arabot: The seventh and highest heaven.

Aralim: Thrones; Binah of Yetzirah; angelic order of Binah.

Arayot: Sexual mysteries; sexual mysticism and magic of the Kabbalah; secret teachings of the wonder-working or magical Kabbalah based upon the love-play between two lovers.

Archon: Ruler; cosmic forces under the dominion of the demiurgos or cosmic ignorance.

Arik Anpin: Big face or greater countenance; Partzuf of Keter.

Asiyah: Making or action; the universe emerging from Yetzirah; the material dimension of the universe; this world.

Assembly of the Elect: The inner circle of initiates of a Gnostic community; initiates of the adepti and realm of the sacred tau; the inner and secret order.

Assembly of the Faithful: The outer circle of initiates in a Gnostic community; the outer order.

Astral Earth: Astral dimension of the world.

Atarot: Crowns; a term signifying the supernal soul and transcendental aspects of the soul, specifically, Hayyah and Yechidah.

Atik Yomin: Ancient of days; Partzuf of Keter.

Atzilut: Emanation, nearness or archetypal; the universe emerging from Adam Kadmon; supernal universe; world of supernal light.

Aura: See sphere of sensation.

Azazel: Goat-demon; one of the fallen; one of the leaders of the fallen.

Azrael: The angel of death or brother death.

Beliel: Son of rebellion; archdemon of the northern quarter of the circle.

Ben: Son; title of the Partzuf of Tiferet or Zer Anpin.

Beni Elohim: Sons of God; Hod of Yetzirah; angelic order of Hod.

Bereshit: In the beginning; Genesis; creation; abode of house of the beginning or house of initiation.

Beriyah: Creation; the universe emerging from Atzilut; world of archangels and cosmic forces.

Binah: Understanding; third Sefirah.

Black Earth: Primordial earth or ancient earth.

Bridegroom: Partzuf of Tiferet; also a title of Lord Yeshua.

Chrism: Anointing.

Christed: Anointed.

Da'at: Knowledge; the abyss; Keter as Keter is known or appears.

Daimon: Spirit; term for the wrathful guardians encountered in the abyss; wrathful guardians associated with the night side of the tree or the tree of death.

Demiurgos: False god or false creator; misperception or misconception of God; cosmic ignorance; demon of the abyss.

Demon of the Abyss: Cosmic ignorance; demiurgos of forgetfulness; the appearance of cosmic evil; the egoistic-self that must ultimately be shed.

Devekut: Cleaving or attachment; rapturous union; divine passion.

Earth Sphere: See astral earth.

Earthly Mother: The higher intelligence of the earth; the divine presence and power (Shekinah) manifesting as the earth and nature.

Elder: A term for a recognized Gnostic teacher. See Adept.

Elder Races: Souls enlightened in other worlds beyond the earth; also angels.

Elect Adept: An initiate of the grade of Hesed; third degree of the adepti or elders of the Tradition and the apostolic succession.

Fire Snake: A term for the Holy Spirit power of what Eastern schools call kundalini; also called the serpent power.

First Apostle: A title of Lady Mary.

Gabriel: Strength of God; Yesod of Beriyah; archangel of Yesod; also the archangel associated with the western quarter of the circle.

Gedulah: Glory; an alternative title of Hesed.

Gematria: The science and art of numerology and esoteric mathematics in the Kabbalah.

Gevurah: Rigor, severity, or judgment; fifth Sefirah.

Gilgulim: The transmigration of souls; the wave-like motion of becoming.

Gnosis: Knowledge of direct spiritual or mystical experience; knowledge of becoming, spiritual insight or intuitioin

Gnostic: One who has acquired gnosis; one who is an initiate of Gnosticism.

Gnosticism: Path of direct knowing (gnosis); path of self-realization.

Great Beast: Force of violence or self-destructive tendency in the collective consciousness of humanity.

Great Seth: A gnostic title for the Christos; fiery or radiant cross.

Greater Adept: An initiate of the grade of Gevurah; second degree of the adepti or elders of the Tradition and the apostolic succession.

Guph: Legendary repository from which souls are drawn.

Haniel: Inspiration of God; Netzach of Beriyah; archangel of Netzach.

Hashmalim: Speaking-silences; Hesed of Yetzirah; angelic order of Hesed.

Hayyah: Life-force; an aspect of the soul; also an angel of the order of the Hayyot.

Hayyot: Holy living creatures; Keter of Yetzirah; angelic order of Keter.

Heavenly Father: Transcendental and hidden aspect of the divine.

Hesed: Mercy or loving-kindness; fourth Sefirah.

Hitbodedut: Meditation or self-isolation; spiritual retreat; the state of meditation proper; mystical attainment.

Hitbonenut: Contemplation; an entrance to devekut or an entrance to hitbodedut; a stage of meditation.

Hod: Splendor, submission, or surrender; eighth Sefirah.

Hokmah: Wisdom; second Sefirah.

Holy Spirit: The divine power in creatures and creation; also the Mother and Bride.

Holy Threefold Sanctuary: The sanctuary of discipleship-initiation, spiritual practice-realization, and mystical attainment-fruition.

Hua: The great angel of the Lord (Metatron-Sandalfon).

Ipsissimus: "One who is most truly him- or herself"; an initiate of the grade of Keter, highest degree of the sacred tau or masters of the Tradition; the grade of the Risen Christ.

Kali Kallah: Black or dark bride; Lilith; Sophia Nigrans, dark wisdom of God.

Kallah: Bride; Partzuf of Malkut; title of St. Mary Magdalene.

Kallah Messiah: Anointed Bride; Christ the Sophia; St. Mary Magdalene.

Kamael: Burner of God; Gevurah of Beriyah; archangel of Beriyah.

Kavvanah: Concentration or conscious intention; feeling and devotion; a form of contemplation or meditation.

Kavvanot: Specific forms of kavvanah (plural of kavvanah).

Kerubim: Strong ones; Yesod of Yetzirah; angelic order of Yesod.

Keter: Crown; first Sefirah; the Sefirah that is not.

Klippah: Singular of klippot. See Klippot.

Klippot: Husk or shells; husks of darkness; the night-side or other side of the tree; impure emanations; dominion of darkness; dominion of the Demiurgos.

Klippotic: Demonic; having the influence of klippot. See Klippot.

Lessor Adept: An initiate of the grade of Tiferet; first degree of the adepti or elders of the Tradition and the apostolic succession.

Leviathan: Destroyer or destruction; the arch demon of the western quarter of the circle.

Lilith: See Kali Kallah.

Logos: Word; the divine word; Christ the Son.

Lord of the Dance: A title of Lord Yeshua.

Lord of the Rainbow: A title of Lord Yeshua.

Lord of the Shabbat: A title of Lord Yeshua.

Lucifer: Light-bearer; the archdemon of the eastern quarter of the circle; also a gnostic title of the Christos negating death and darkness.

Maggid: Angel; a term used to designate any archangel or angel; also a term for an adept or master who is otherworldly in nature; sometimes used for disincarnate adepts and masters.

Maggidim: (Plural) See Maggid.

Magister Templi: An initiate of the grade of Binah; first degree of the sacred tau or masters of the Tradition.

Magus: An initiate of the grade of Hokmah; second degree of the sacred tau or masters of the Tradition.

Makifim: Envelopments; a term for the transcendental aspects of the soul—Neshamah, Hayyah, and Yechidah.

Makom: Place of meeting; sixth heaven.

Malachim: Angels or messengers; Tiferet of Yetzirah; angelic order of Tiferet.

Malkut: Kingdom; tenth and final Sefirah

Ma'on: Dwelling place; fifth heaven.

Master: A term for a realized or enlightened individual; an initiate who has attained one grade or another of supernal or Messianic consciousness; a sacred tau in Gnostic tradition.

Mekubal: A Kabbalist. See Mekubalim.

Mekubalim: Those who have been received or those who have received; those who have been disciples of a Kabbalist; Kabbalists.

Melchizedek: Priest-king (or priestess-queen) of righteousness; a figure that appears in Genesis to initiate Abraham and Sarah; the universal order of enlightenment or Messianic consciousness; an initiate of the divine order; the state of enlightenment or supernal or Messianic consciousness; the holy order of the elder races; the holy third order or secret order; the assembly of secret chiefs.

Messiah: Anointed; Christ.

Metatron: Prince of the countenance; Keter of Beriyah; archangel of Keter; also the archangel that stands above the circle.

Michael: Who-Is-Like-Unto-God; Hod of Beriyah; archangel of Hod; also the archangel associated with the southern quarter of the circle.

Midrashim: Myths, legends, and stories inspired by the Scriptures; creative adaptation of the myths, legends, and stories of the Scriptures; found in both Judaism and Gnosticism.

Mystical Death: The shift from a lower level of consciousness to a higher consciousness; also radical self-transformation; a stage of metanoia (authentic spiritual conversion); Sophia Nigrans; also a powerful healing experience.

Mystical Union: Union of the worshipper and worshipped; conscious unification with the divine or a divine power; term for Gnostic wedding ceremonies.

Navi: Seer or prophet.

Nechash: Serpent in the Garden of Eden, but also a title of the Messiah; good serpent.

Nefesh: Vital soul or earthly soul; an aspect of the soul

Nefesh Behamit: Bestial soul; nefesh unregenerated.

Nefesh Elokit: Godly soul; nefesh regenerated.

Nefeshim: (Plural) See Nefesh.

Neophyte: Novice of the Gnostic tradition; a probationer or aspirant in a Gnostic circle.

Neshamah: Holy soul; supernal soul; heavenly soul; divine nature; an aspect of the soul.

Netzach: Victory or dominion; seventh Sefirah.

Nukva: Daughter; Partzuf of Malkut; also a title of St. Mary Magdalene (Daughter of God).

Ofan or Ophan: Wheel-angel; an angel of the order of Ofanim.

Ofanim or Ophanim: Wheels; Hokmah of Yetzirah; angelic order of Hokmah.

Olam: Universe or dimension of the reality-truth continuum.

Olamot: Universes or dimensions of the reality-truth continuum.

Ordo Sanctus Gnosis (O.S.G.): An esoteric order or lineage of the Sophian Tradition; an outer order.

Pachad: Fear or holy awe; an alternative title for Gevurah.

Palace of Light: The Tree of Life; also a title of Binah-Elohim.

Paroket: Veil between the moral and action triad; causal plane of karmic matrix.

Penimi'im: Internalizations; aspects of the soul that can be embodied, specifically, Nefesh, Ruach, and Neshamah.

Pentagrammaton: A phrase for the blessed name of Messiah—Yeshua or Yeheshuah ("Jesus").

Perud: Separation; specifically, the reality of separation composed on Beriyah, Yetzirah, and Asiyah.

Philosophus: An initiate of the grade of Netzach; highest degree of initiation in the assembly of the faithful.

Practicus: An initiate of the grade of Hod; third degree of the assembly of the faithful.

Qeshet: Veil between Malkut and the upper Sefirot; the glow of the Astral Planes.

Qoph Nia: The Eye of the Void or the Eye of the Storm; also the force of atavistic resurgence.

Queen of the Shabbat: See Shekinah.

Rahamim: Compassion; an alternative title for Tiferet.

Rainbow Glory: A title of Lady Mary.

Rakiya: Firmament; the second heaven.

Raphael: Healing of God; Tiferet of Beriyah; archangel of Tiferet; also the archangel associated with the eastern quarter of the circle.

Ratziel: God's wisdom; Hokmah of Beriyah; archangel of Hokmah.

Ratzon: Will or desire; alternative title of Keter.

Reshit: Beginning or initiation; also an alternative title of Hokmah.

Rite of Ransom: Gnostic term for divine magic; also the mystery of the crucifixion.

Rite of the Bridal Chamber: Gnostic worship founded on the Arayot. See Arayot; also the Rite of Mystical Union. See mystical union.

Rosicrucian: Christian Gnostic; an initiate of the Rosicrucian order or belonging to the Rosicrucian order; the inner or second order; the order of the adepti.

Ruach: Spirit or intelligence; an aspect of the soul.

Ruach Ha-Elijah: Spirit of the prophets; an aspect of the Holy Spirit.

Ruach Ha-Enoch: Spirit of the initiates; an aspect of the Holy Spirit.

Ruach Ha-Kodesh: Spirit of holiness; Hebrew for the Holy Spirit.

Ruach Ha-Messiah: Spirit of the Messiah; an aspect of the Holy Spirit.

Ruhaniyot: Radiant holy breath; spirit or essence of the Sefirot.

Samael: Poison of God; Gevurah of Beriyah; another archangel of Gevurah; an arch demon associated with Gevurah; the adversary; consort of Lilith.

Sandalfon: Shoe-Ofan; Malkut of Beriyah; archangel of Malkut; also the archangel of the circle.

Satan: Enemy or adversary; demon of the abyss; the egoistic self; cosmic igno-rance; the shadow of God or dark face of God; also the archdemon of the southern quarter of the circle.

Sefirah: Emanation or sphere; a quality or attribute of God; a divine power.

Sefirot: Plural of Sefirah. See Sefirah.

Sefer Ha-Bahir: Book of Brilliance; a classical source-work of the Kabbalah pre-dating the Zohar and less refined than the Zohar.

Sefer Ha-Zohar: Book of Splendor; a classical source-work of the Holy Kabbal-ah that assumes the form of commentary on the Torah (first five books of the Old Testament).

Sefer Yetzirah: Book of Formation; a classical source-work of the Kabbalah focus-ing primarily upon Ma'aseh Bereshit and the meditative and magical Kabbalah.

Seraphim: Fiery serpents or burning ones; Gevurah of Yetzirah; angelic order of Gevurah.

Serpent Power: See Fire Snake.

Serpent's Skin: The mortal coil or physical body.

Serpent-Sun: Gnostic term for Christ or Gnostic title of Lord Yeshua.

Shamaim: Firmaments or heavens.

Shedim: Demons.

Shefa: Influx; Spiritual energy of the Sefirot.

Shehakim: Sky-like or clouds of grace; third heaven.

Shekinah: Divine presence and power; God the Mother and God the Bride.

Sophia: Wisdom; divine wisdom, created and uncreated; Christ the Daughter (primordial or uncreated wisdom = God the Mother).

Sophian Gnosticism: A tradition of Gnostic initiation that considers St. Mary Magdalene coequal and codivine with Yeshua Messiah (Jesus Christ).

Spell of Omega: Gnostic term for the Book of Revelation; also a certain aspect of the magical Kabbalah.

Sphere of Sensation: The aura surrounding the human body, which is the radi-ance of the subtle body.

Spiritual Sun: Messiah or Christos; a title of Lord Yeshua; also a term for the union of Lady Mary and Lord Yeshua as one Messiah or Christ, male and female.

Subtle Body: A body of subtle energy within and beyond the physical body; a body of consciousness; a body through which consciousness can exist independent of the physical body.

Tau: Master; title of a Gnostic master; a holy tzaddik; initiate of the order of Melchizedek; initiation of the grade of magister templi or higher Rosicrucian grades.

Temple of King Solomon: A specific configuration of the magical temple in the wonder-working Kabbalah as taught in the Christian Kabbalah; the ceremonial art of the wonder-working Kabbalah.

Tetragrammaton: A phrase for the great name of God—Yahweh.

Theoricus: An initiate of the grade of Yesod; second degree of the assembly of the faithful.

The Elohim: Gods and goddesses; dominions and principalities; Netzach of Yetzirah; angelic order of Netzach; the subject of a secret teaching of the Gnostics.

Threefold Body of Melchizedek: The resurrection body or body of light attained with the dawn of supernal or Messianic consciousness (body of enlightenment or Christhood).

Threefold Rite of Initiation: First Gnostic initiation on the path; baptism in living waters, chrism-anointing, and wedding feast (Holy Eucharist of the Bride and Bridegroom).

Tiferet: Beauty; sixth Sefirah.

Tikkune: Correction, repair, mending, or healing; restoration of the holy Sefirot to the ideal or original state; spiritual work on the soul.

Titanic: Admixed forces, neither good nor evil.

Transference of Consciousness: The practice of shifting the center of consciousness into the subtle body or beyond the physical body.

Tzaddik: Righteous one; an adept or master of the Tradition, incarnate or disincarnate; also tzaddik not capitalized is a term for any elect soul or initiate.

Tzaddikim: Righteous ones; a term for spiritual adepts and masters of the Tradition; also a term for all of the faithful and elect.

Tzadkiel: Righteousness of God; Hesed of Beriyah; archangel of Hesed.

Tzafkiel: Remembrance of God; Binah of Beriyah; archangel of Beriyah.

Tzimtzum: Constriction; the process of creation.

Uriel: Light of God; replaces Haniel as one of the seven archangels of the Messiah; also the archangel of the northern quarter of the circle.

Uzza: Dark demon; one of the Fallon; one of the leaders of the fallen.

Vilon: The veil; first heaven.

Yechidah: Holy spark; inmost secret aspect of the soul; spark of the Soul of Messiah.

Yeshua: Aramaic for Jesus.

Yesod: Foundation or reciprocity; ninth Sefirah.

Yetzirah: Formation; universe emerging from Beriyah; world of Angels; world of Spirits.

Yichud: Unity; specifically, the realm of unity composed of Adam Kadmon and Atzilut.

Zebul: Dwelling; fourth heaven.

Zelator: An initiate of the grade of Malkut; first degree of the assembly of the faithful.

Zer Anpin: Little face or lesser countenance; Partzuf of Tiferet.

BIBLIOGRAPHY

Berg, Yehuda. *The Power of Kabbalah*. Jodere Group, Inc., 2001.

Cohen, Martin Samuel, translator. *The Shi'ur Qomah: Texts and Recensions*. J. C. B. Mohr (Paul Siebeck), Tubingen, 1985.

Cooper, David A. *God is a Verb: Kabbalah and the Practice of Mystical Judaism*. Berkeley Publishing Group, A division of Penguin Putnam, Inc., 1997.

Davidson, Gustav. *A Dictionary of Angels: Including the Fallen Angels*. Free Press, A division of Macmillan Publishers Company, Inc., 1967.

Davis, Avram. *The Way of the Flame: A Guide to the Forgotten Mystical Tradition of Jewish Meditation*. HarperCollins Publishing Inc., 1996.

Douglas-Klotz, Neil. *The Hidden Gospel: Decoding the Spiritual Message of the Aramaic Jesus*. Theosophical Publishing House, 1999.

———. *Prayers of the Cosmos: Meditations on the Aramaic Words of Jesus*. HarperCollins, First paperback edition, 1994.

Filoramo, Giovanni. *A History of Gnosticism*. Blackwell Publishers, 1990.

Fox, Matthew. *The Coming of the Cosmic Christ*. Harper & Row Publishers, Inc., 1988.

Frankiel, Tamar. *The Gift of the Kabbalah: Discovering the Secrets of Heaven, Renewing Your Life on Earth*. Jewish Lights Publishing, 2001.

Freedman, H., and Maurice Simon, translators & editors. *Midrash Rabbah*, Vols. 1–10. The Soncino Press, Ltd., 1983.

Gikatilla. *Sha'are Orah—The Gates of Light: The First English Translation of a Classic Introduction to Jewish Mysticism*. Translation and introduction by Avi Weinstein. HarperCollins Publishing, Inc., 1994.

Ginzberg, Louis. *The Legends of the Jews.* Vols. 1–7, Translated by Henrietta Szold. The Jewish Publication Society of America, 1937.

Godwin, David. *Godwin's Cabalistic Encyclopedia: A Complete Guide to Cabalistic Magick.* Llewellyn Worldwide, 1979.

Gruenwald, Ithamar. *Apocalyptic and Merkavah Mysticism.* E. J. Brill, 1980.

Halevi, Z'ev ben Shimon. *Kabbalah and Exodus.* Shambhala, 1980.

Hanson, Kenneth. *Kabbalah: Three Thousand Years of Mystic Tradition.* Council Oak Books, 1998.

Hirsch, Samson Raphael. *Horeb: A Philosophy of Jewish Laws and Observances.* Translated by Dayan I. Grunfeld. The Soncino Press, Sixth Edition, 1997.

Horowitz, Isaiah. *The Generations of Adam.* Translated, edited, and with an introduction by Miles Krassen. Paulist Press, 1996.

Idel, Moshe. *Kabbalah: New Perspectives.* Yale University Press, New Haven & London, 1988.

Jonas, Hans. *The Gnostic Religion: The Message of the Alien God and the Beginnings of Christianity.* Beacon Press, 1958.

Kaplan, Aryeh. *The Bahir Illumination.* Samuel Weiser, 1979.

———. *Inner Space: Introduction to Kabbalah, Meditation and Prophecy.* Moznaim Publishing Corporation, 1990.

———. *Jewish Meditation: A Practical Guide.* Schocken Books, Inc., 1985.

———. *Meditation and the Bible.* Samuel Weiser, Inc. First paper edition, 1988.

———. *Meditation and Kabbalah.* Samuel Weiser, Inc. First paper edition, 1985.

———. *Sefer Yetzirah the Book of Creation: In Theory and Practice.* Samuel Weiser, 1990.

Kushner, Lawrence. *God Was In This Place & I, I Did Not Know It.* Jewish Lights Publishing, 1991.

———. *The River of Lights: Spirituality, Judaism, Consciousness.* Jewish Lights Publishing, Second paperback printing, enhanced reprint, 1990.

———. *Sefer Otiyot: The Book of Letters.* 15th Anniversary Second Edition. Jewish Lights Publishing, 1990.

Lea, Simcox, and Bligh Bond. *The Apostolic Gnosis: Part I & II,* Research into Lost Knowledge Organization, 1985.

———. *Gematria: A Preliminary Investigation of the Cabala.* Research into Lost Knowledge Organization Trust, 1977.

Matthews, Caitlin. *Sophia Goddess of Wisdom: The Divine Feminine from Black Goddess to World Soul.* Mandala, An imprint of Grafton Books, A division of Harper-Collins, 1991.

Munk, Elie. *The Call of the Torah: An Anthology of Commentary on the Five Books of Moses.* Vols. 1–5. ArtScroll Series, Translated from French by E. S. Mazer. Mesorah Publications, Ltd., 1995.

Munk, Rabbi Michael L. *The Wisdom of the Hebrew Alphabet: The Sacred Letters as a Guide to Jewish Deed and Thought.* ArtScroll Mesorah Series, General Editors. Rabbis Nosson Scherman/Meir Zlowitz, Mesorah Publications, Ltd., Second Edition, 1983.

Oberg, Hugo. *3 Enoch or The Hebrew Book of Enoch.* Cambridge University Press, London, 1928.

Pagels, Elaine. *The Gnostic Gospel.* Vintage Books, A Division of Random House, 1981.

―――. *The Origin of Satan.* Random House, 1995.

Patai, Raphael. *The Hebrew Goddess.* Third enlarged edition, originally published by KTAV Publishing House, Inc. and Avon Books, Wayne State University Press, 1990.

Patai, Raphael, and Robert Graves. *Hebrew Myths: The Book of Genesis.* Greenwich House, 1983.

Ravindra, Ravi. *The Yoga of Christ: In the Gospel According to St. John.* Element Books Limited, 1990.

Rudolph, Kurt. *Gnosis: The Nature and History of Gnosticism.* Harper & Row Publisher, 1983.

Schaya, Leo. *The Universal Meaning of the Kabbalah,* originally published in French as *L' Homme et l' Absolu selon la Kabbale* by Editions Buchet/Chstel, Correa, Paris, 1958. Translation by George Allen & Unwin Ltd., University Books, Inc., 1971.

Schneur, Zalman. *Likutei Amarim Tanya.* Bilingual Edition. "Kehot" Publication Society, 1984.

Shneur, Zalman of Liadi. *Siddur Tehillat Ha-Shem: Nusach Ha-Ari Zal.* Translated by Rabbi Nissen Mangel. Merkos L'inyonei Chinuch, Inc., 1978.

Simon, Maurice, and Harry Sperling, translators. *The Zohar,* Vols. 1–5. Soncino Press, Ltd., 1984.

Smith, Richard, and Marvin Meyer, editors. *Ancient Christian Magic: Coptic Texts of Ritual Power.* HarperCollins, 1994.

Tishby, Isaiah. *The Wisdom of the Zohar: An Anthology of Texts,.* Vols. 1–3. Translated from Hebrew by David Goldstein. Littman Library of Jewish Civilization, 1987.

Vital, Chayyim. *The Tree of Life: Palace of Adam Kadmon,* Vol. 1. Translated with introduction by Donald Wilder Menzi Zwe Padeh. Jason Aronson Inc., 1999.

Walker, Benjamin. *Gnosticism: Its History and Influence.* Aquarian Press, 1983.

Welburn, Andrew. *The Beginnings of Christianity: Essence Mystery, Gnostic Revelation and the Christian Vision.* Floris Books, 1991.

Williams, Jay. *Yeshua Buddha: An Interpretation of New Testament Theology as Meaningful Myth.* Theosophical Publishing House, 1978.

INDEX

Free Magazine

Read unique articles by Llewellyn authors, recommendations by experts, and information on new releases. To receive a **free** copy of Llewellyn's consumer magazine, *New Worlds of Mind & Spirit,* simply call 1-877-NEW-WRLD or visit our website at www.llewellyn.com and click on *New Worlds.*

🌙 LLEWELLYN ORDERING INFORMATION

Order Online:
Visit our website at www.llewellyn.com, select your books, and order them on our secure server.

Order by Phone:
- Call toll-free within the U.S. at 1-877-NEW-WRLD (1-877-639-9753). Call toll-free within Canada at 1-866-NEW-WRLD (1-866-639-9753)
- We accept VISA, MasterCard, and American Express

Order by Mail:
Send the full price of your order (MN residents add 7% sales tax) in U.S. funds, plus postage & handling to:
Llewellyn Worldwide
P.O. Box 64383, Dept. 0-7387-0591-8
St. Paul, MN 55164-0383, U.S.A.

Postage & Handling:

Standard (U.S., Mexico, & Canada). If your order is:
Up to $25.00, add $3.50
$25.01 - $48.99, add $4.00
$49.00 and over, FREE STANDARD SHIPPING
(Continental U.S. orders ship UPS. AK, HI, PR, & P.O. Boxes ship USPS 1st class. Mex. & Can. ship PMB.)

International Orders:
Surface Mail: For orders of $20.00 or less, add $5 plus $1 per item ordered. For orders of $20.01 and over, add $6 plus $1 per item ordered.

Air Mail:
Books: Postage & Handling is equal to the total retail price of all books in the order.
Non-book items: Add $5 for each item.

Orders are processed within 2 business days.
Please allow for normal shipping time. Postage and handling rates subject to change.

GODWIN'S CABALISTIC ENCYCLOPEDIA
Complete Guidance to Both Practical and Esoteric Applications

David Godwin

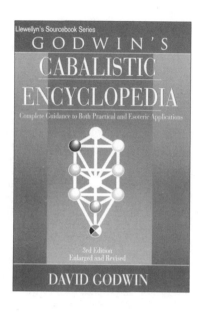

One of the most valuable books on the Cabala is back, with a new and more usable format. This book is a complete guide to cabalistic magick and gematria in which every demon, angel, power and name of God ... every Sephirah, Path, and Plane of the Tree of Life . . . and each attribute and association is fully described and cross-indexed by the Hebrew, English, and numerical forms.

All entries, which had been scattered throughout the appendices, are now incorporated into one comprehensive dictionary. There are hundreds of new entries and illustrations, making this book even more valuable for Cabalistic pathworking and meditation. It now has many new Hebrew words and names, as well as the terms of Freemasonry, the entities of the Cthulhu mythos, and the Aurum Solis spellings for the names of the demons of the Goetia. It contains authentic Hebrew spellings, and a new introduction that explains the uses of the book for meditation on God names.

The Cabalistic schema is native to the human psyche, and *Godwin's Cabalistic Encyclopedia* will be a valuable reference tool for all Cabalists, magicians, scholars, and scientists of all disciplines.

1–56718–324–7, 832 pp., 6 x 9 $29.95

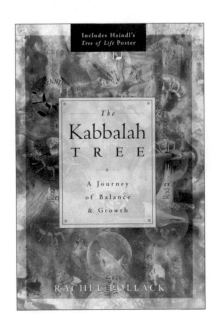

THE KABBALAH TREE
A Journey of Balance & Growth

Rachel Pollack

Haindl's Tree of Life is our gateway into this ancient mystical tradition.

Kabbalah's most famous symbol, the Tree of Life, has become the organizing principle behind our human efforts to understand the world. Using Hermann Haind"s lush depiction of the Tree of Life, Rachel Pollack examines the message behind this ancient symbol. She takes a non-denominational approach—drawing upon unusual sources such as tribal and shamanic traditions, modern science, contemporary Kabbalists, tarot interpreters, and a comic book writer—to explore the Tree's meaning. Along the way, we learn more about Kabbalah's history, texts, mystical concepts, and why this esoteric tradition has sprung up again in the twenty-first century.

0-7387-0507-1, 192 pp., 6 x 9, illus. $16.95
Includes poster of Haindl's Tree of Life Painting

KEYS TO THE KINGDOM
Jesus & the Mystic Kabbalah

Migene González-Wippler

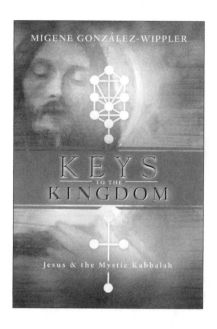

Was Jesus a master Kabbalist? Are Jesus' teachings based on Kabbalism? How do the Ten Commandments tie into the Tree of Life? Is the Lord's Prayer a Kabbalist invocation? Migene González-Wippler reveals secrets of the Bible and the life of Jesus in her intriguing introduction to the Christian Kabbalah.

Emphasizing Christian aspects, Keys to the Kingdom presents an easy-to-read overview of the Kabbalah, describing its major principles and historical elements. Drawing on the gospels and historical records, González-Wippler examines Jesus as a man and a teacher, providing convincing evidence—based on historical and traditional Jewish law—that Jesus was a master Kabbalist . . . as well as the Messiah.

0-7387-0593-4, 240 pp., 6 x 9, illus. $12.95

THE TREE OF LIFE
An Illustrated Study in Magic

Israel Regardie

Edited and annotated by
Chic Cicero and
Sandra Tabatha Cicero

In 1932, when magic was a "forbidden subject," Israel Regardie wrote The Tree of Life at the age of 24. He believed that magic was a precise scientific discipline as well as a highly spiritual way of life, and he took on the enormous task of making it accessible to a wide audience of eager spiritual seekers. The result was this book, which adroitly presents a massive amount of diverse material in a remarkably unified whole.

From the day it was first published, The Tree of Life has remained in high demand by ceremonial magicians for its skillful combination of ancient wisdom and modern magical experience. It was Regardie's primary desire to point out the principles of magic that cut across all boundaries of time, religion, and culture—those fundamental principles common to all magic, regardless of any specific tradition or spiritual path.

1-56718-132-5, 552 pp., 6 x 9, illus.,
includes full-color, 4-pp. insert $19.95

SIMPLIFIED QABALA MAGIC

Formerly titled *Simplified Magic*
Ted Andrews

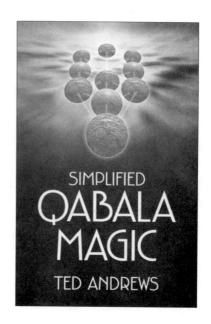

The mystical Qabala is one of the most esoteric yet practical systems for expanding your consciousness and unfolding your spiritual gifts. Within its Tree of Life lies a map to the wisdom of the ancients, the powers of the universe and to ourselves. As the earliest form of Jewish mysticism, it is especially suited to the rational Western mind.

The Qabala has traditionally been presented as mysterious and complex. Simplified Qabala Magic offers a basic understanding of what the Qabala is and how it operates. It provides techniques for utilizing the forces within the system to bring peace, healing, power, love, and magic into your life.

This book presents the basics of the Qabala from a nondenominational background. It provides sufficient working knowledge of the Tree of Life without intimidating, unnecessary detail, and includes easy-to-follow meditative techniques. It is the perfect introduction for those who wish to pursue the complex study of ceremonial magick

Qabalistic Cross and Middle Pillar exercises for strength and protection are introduced, along with the basics of Pathworking

0-7387-0394-X, 240 pp, 5³⁄₁₆ x 8. $9.95

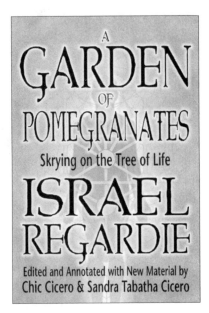

A GARDEN OF POMEGRANATES

Skrying on the Tree of Life

Israel Regardie

**Edited by Chic Cicero and
Sandra Tabatha Cicero**

(*Annotated with new material*)

When Israel Regardie wrote *A Garden of Pomegranates* in 1932, he designed it as a simple yet comprehensive guidebook outlining the complex system of the Qabalah and providing a key to its symbolism. Since then it has achieved the status of a classic among texts on the Hermetic Qabalah. It stands as the best single introductory guide for magicians on this complex system, with an emphasis on direct experience through meditation on the twenty-two paths.

Now, Chic Cicero and Sandra Tabatha Cicero—Golden Dawn adepts and personal friends of the late Regardie—have made the book even more useful for today's occult students with full annotations, critical commentary, and explanatory notes. They've added practical material in the form of pathworkings, suggested exercises, and daily affirmations—one for each Sephirah and each path. Brief rituals, meditations, and Qabalistic mantras complement Regardie's section on gematria and other forms of numerical Qabalah.

1-56718-141-4, 552 pp., 6 x 9 $17.95

To Write to the Author

Llewellyn Worldwide cannot guarantee that every letter written to the author can be answered, but all will be forwarded. Please write to:

Tau Malachi
℅ Llewellyn Worldwide
P.O. Box 64383, Dept. 0-7387-0591-8
St. Paul, MN 55164-0383, U.S.A.

Please enclose a self-addressed stamped envelope for reply,
or $1.00 to cover costs. If outside U.S.A., enclose
international postal reply coupon.

Many of Llewellyn's authors have websites with additional information and resources. For more information, please visit our website at http://www.llewellyn.com.